"RIGHTEOUSNESS" IN THE NEW TESTAMENT

"RIGHTEOUSNESS" IN THE NEW TESTAMENT

"Justification" in the United States
Lutheran—Roman Catholic Dialogue

by
John Reumann

with responses by
Joseph A. Fitzmyer
Jerome D. Quinn

1982
Fortress Press • Philadelphia
Paulist Press • New York/Ramsey

Library of Congress Cataloging in Publication Data

Reumann, John Henry Paul.
    Righteousness in the New Testament.

    Includes index.
    1. God—Righteousness—Biblical teaching—Addresses,
essays, lectures.   2. Justification—Biblical teaching—
Addresses, essays, lectures.   3. Bible. N.T.—Theology—
Addresses, essays, lectures. I. Fitzmyer, Joseph A.
II. Quinn, Jerome D. III. Title.
BS2398.R48   234′.7   81–43086
ISBN 0–8006–1616–2 (Fortress Press)   AACR2
ISBN 0–8091–2436–X (Paulist Press)

Published by

Fortress Press
Philadelphia, Pennsylvania

and

Paulist Press
New York/Ramsey

Printed and bound in the
United States of America

Contents

1

"Justification by Grace through Faith"
as Expression of the Gospel:
The Biblical Witness to
the Reformation Emphasis
John Reumann
1

2
The Biblical Basis of
Justification by Faith:
Comments on the Essay
of Professor Reumann
Joseph A. Fitzmyer, S.J.
193

3
The Pastoral Epistles
on Righteousness
Jerome D. Quinn
229

Abbreviations

The Dead Sea Scrolls:

1QH	Hôdāyôt (*Thanksgiving Hymns* from Qumran)
1QM	Milhāmāh (War Scroll)
1QS	Serek hayyahad (*Rule of the Community, Manual of Discipline*)
1QpHab	*Pesher on Habakkuk* from Qumran Cave 1

Monograph and commentary series and other abbreviations:

AB	Anchor Bible (Garden City, NY: Doubleday)
AnBib	Analecta biblica (Rome: Pontifical Biblical Institute)
Ap.	Apology of the Augsburg Confession, 1531 (Book of Concord)
ATANT	Abhandlungen zur Theologie des Alten und Neuen Testaments (Zürich: Zwingli)
BAGD	W. Bauer, *A Greek-English Lexicon of the New Testament,* trans. W. F. Arndt and F. W. Gingrich; 2d ed. rev. and augmented by F. W. Gingrich and F. W. Danker (Chicago: University of Chicago Press, 1979)
BEvT	Beiträge zur evangelischen Theologie (Munich: Chr. Kaiser)
BHT	Beiträge zur historischen Theologie (Tübingen: Mohr-Siebeck)
Bib	*Biblica*
BJRL	*Bulletin of the John Rylands University Library of Manchester*
Book of Concord	*The Book of Concord: The Confessions of the Evangelical Lutheran Church* (1580; cited from the "Tappert ed.")
BZNW	Beihefte zur *ZNW* (Berlin/New York: De Gruyter)
CA	Confessio Augustana, the Augsburg Confession, 1530 (Book of Concord)
CBQ	*Catholic Biblical Quarterly*
chap(s).	chapter(s)
CNT	Commentaire du Nouveau Testament (Neuchatel & Paris: Delachaux et Niestlé)
CTM	*Concordia Theological Monthly*
diss.	dissertation
DS	H. Denzinger and A. Schönmetzer, *Enchiridion Symbolorum* (Freiburg: Herder, 33rd ed. 1965)
EBib	Etudes Bibliques (Paris: Gabalda)
EKK(NT)	Evangelisch-katholischer Kommentar (zum Neuen Testament) (Zürich: Benziger Verlag, Neukirchen-Vluyn: Neukirchener Verlag)

esp.	especially
EvT	*Evangelische Theologie*
ExpTim	*Expository Times*
FBBS	Facet Books Biblical Series (Philadelphia: Fortress)
FRLANT	Forschungen zur Religion und Literatur des Alten und Neuen Testaments (Göttingen: Vandenhoeck & Ruprecht)
fs	Festschrift
Ges. Augs.	Gesammelte Aufsätze
Hermeneia	Hermeneia—A Critical and Historical Commentary on the Bible (Philadelphia: Fortress)
HNT	Handbuch zum Neuen Testament (Tübingen: Mohr-Siebeck)
HNTC	Harper's/Black's New Testament Commentaries (New York: Harper & Row; London: A. & C. Black)
HTKNT	Herders Theologischer Kommentar zum Neuen Testament (Freiburg: Herder)
HTR	*Harvard Theological Review*
ICC	International Critical Commentary (Edinburgh: T. & T. Clark)
IDB	G. A. Buttrick (ed.), *The Interpreter's Dictionary of the Bible* (New York & Nashville: Abingdon, 1962)
IDBSup	Supplementary volume to *IDB* (1976)
Int	*Interpretation*
JAAR	*Journal of the American Academy of Religion*
JB	*Jerusalem Bible,* ed. A. Jones (1966)
JBC	R. E. Brown et al. (eds.), *The Jerome Biblical Commentary* (Englewood Cliffs, NJ: Prentice-Hall, 1968; both vols. are cited by article and section, e.g., 59:19)
JBL	*Journal of Biblical Literature*
JTC	*Journal for Theology and the Church* (New York: Harper & Row)
JTS	*Journal of Theological Studies*
KD	*Kerygma und Dogma*
KJV	King James Version of the Bible, 1611
R. Knox	Ronald A. Knox, *The New Testament* (New York: Sheed & Ward, 1944)
L	Luke's "special source"
LCUSA	Lutheran Council in the United States of America
LW	*Luther's Works,* American ed. (St. Louis: Concordia; Philadelphia: Fortress)
LW	*Lutheran World*

LWF	Lutheran World Federation
LXX	Septuagint, Greek OT version
M	Matthew's "special source"
Malta Report	Lutheran/Roman Catholic international dialogue, 1967–71, final report (see Editor's Note, n. 3 and § 353, n. 1)
Metzger,	*Textual Commentary* Bruce M. Metzger, *A Textual Commentary on the Greek New Testament* (New York: United Bible Societies, 1971)
MeyerK	Kritisch-exegetischer Kommentar über das Neue Testament, begründet von H. A. W. Meyer (Göttingen: Vandenhoeck & Ruprecht)
MNTC	Moffatt New Testament Commentary (New York: Harper & Brothers)
MS(S)	manuscript(s)
MT	Masoretic Text (Hebrew)
n(n).	(foot)note(s)
NAB	*New American Bible,* 1970
NCB	New Century Bible (London: Oliphants; Greenwood, SC: Attic Press, subsequently Grand Rapids: Eerdmans)
NEB	*New English Bible,* NT 1961, OT and Apocrypha 1970
Nestle	*Novum Testamentum Graece* . . . curavit Eberhard Nestle . . . elaboraverunt Erwin Nestle et Kurt Aland . . . (Stuttgart: Deutsche Bibelanstalt, 25th ed. 1963, 26th ed. K. Aland et al. 1979)
NIDNTT	Colin Brown (ed.), *The New International Dictionary of New Testament Theology* (Grand Rapids, MI: Zondervan, 1975, 1976, 1978)
NovT	*Novum Testamentum*
NovTSup	Novum Testamentum, Supplements (Leiden: Brill)
NT	New Testament
NTD	Das Neue Testament Deutsch (Göttingen: Vandenhoeck & Ruprecht)
NTS	*New Testament Studies*
OT	Old Testament
par.	parallel(s)
PE	Pastoral Epistles
Phillips	J. B. Phillips, *The New Testament in Modern English* (New York: Macmillan, 1958)
PL	J. P. Migne, *Patrologiae cursus completus, series latina* (Paris, 1844–55)
Q	Material or source common to Matthew and Luke
RNT	Regensburger Neues Testament (Regensburg: Pustet)

RSV	Revised Standard Version of the Bible, NT 1946, OT 1952, Apocrypha 1957
SBLSBS	Society of Biblical Literature Sources for Biblical Study (Missoula, MT: Scholars Press)
SBS	Stuttgarter Bibelstudien (Stuttgart: Katholisches Bibelwerk)
SBT	Studies in Biblical Theology (London: SCM)
SD	Solid Declaration of the Formula of Concord, 1580 (Book of Concord, Tappert ed., pp. 501–636)
SNTSMS	Society for New Testament Studies Monograph Series (New York: Cambridge University Press)
Str-B	Hermann L. Strack, and Paul Billerbeck, *Kommentar zum Neuen Testament aus Talmud und Midrasch* (Munich: C. H. Beck, 4th ed. 1965)
t.	Tosefta
Tappert ed.	*The Book of Concord,* trans. and ed. T. G. Tappert et al. (Philadelphia: Muhlenberg [Fortress], 1959)
TDNT	G. Kittel and G. Friedrich (eds.), *Theological Dictionary of the New Testament* (Grand Rapids, MI: Eerdmans)
TEV	Today's English Version, NT 1966, OT 1976 (Good News Bible, New York: American Bible Society)
TEx	Theologische Existenz heute, N. F. (Munich: Chr. Kaiser)
THKNT	Theologischer Handkommentar zum Neuen Testament (Berlin: Evangelische Verlagsanstalt)
TR	Textus Receptus (Received Text of the Greek NT; Stephanus 1550, Elzevir 1633)
TS	*Theological Studies*
TTZ	*Trierer theologische Zeitschrift*
UBSGNT	*The Greek New Testament,* ed. Kurt Aland et al. (New York: United Bible Societies, 3d ed. 1975)
UNT	Untersuchungen zum Neuen Testament (Leipzig: Hinrichs)
v(v).	verse(s)
WA	Weimar Ausgabe, *D. Martin Luthers Werke* (Weimar: Hermann Böhlau, 1883–)
WMANT	Wissenschaftliche Monographien zum Alten und Neuen Testament (Neukirchen-Vluyn: Neukirchener Verlag)
ZNW	*Zeitschrift für die neutestamentliche Wissenschaft*
ZTK	*Zeitschrift für Theologie und Kirche*

Editor's Note

As explained by the dialogue cochairmen, our papers on righteousness/justification in Scripture are very much a part of an ongoing dialogue process involving U.S. Lutherans and Catholics, in the course of which six volumes have appeared to date,[1] plus two by task forces of New Testament scholars on Peter and Mary in early Christianity.[2] Against the background of the international Lutheran-Catholic report of 1971, with its brief treatment of justification,[3] we have presented our analyses of the biblical materials for our colleagues in 1980–1981 dialogue sessions in a way that reverses procedure in Round 6 on "teaching office and infallibility" when Father Fitzmyer made the chief presentation, with a Lutheran response, as the basis for discussion.[4]

1. Lutherans and Catholics in Dialogue: 1. *The Status of the Nicene Creed as Dogma of the Church* (1965); 2. *One Baptism for the Remission of Sins* (1966); 3. *The Eucharist as Sacrifice* (1967); 4. *Eucharist and Ministry* (1970); 5. *Papal Primacy and the Universal Church* (1974); 6. *Teaching Authority and Infallibility in the Church* (1980). Vols. 1–4 were originally published by the Bishops' Commission for Ecumenical and Interreligious Affairs, Washington, D.C., and the U.S. National Committee of the Lutheran World Federation, New York, NY. Vols. 1–3 have been reprinted in one volume by Augsburg Publishing House, Minneapolis, MN, the publisher of vols. 5 and 6.

2. *Peter in the New Testament: A Collaborative Assessment by Protestant and Roman Catholic Scholars,* ed. Raymond E. Brown, Karl P. Donfried, and John Reumann (Minneapolis: Augsburg, and New York: Paulist, 1973). *Mary in the New Testament: A Collaborative Assessment by Protestant and Roman Catholic Scholars,* ed. Raymond E. Brown, Karl P. Donfried, Joseph A. Fitzmyer, and John Reumann (Philadelphia: Fortress, and New York: Paulist, 1978). *Peter in the New Testament* has been translated into French (1974), Spanish, Dutch, and German (1976), and Japanese (1977), in addition to a British ed. (1974); details in *Mary,* p. 1, n. 1. *Mary in the New Testament* is being translated into German.

3. "The Gospel and the Church" (Malta Report of the Joint Lutheran/Roman Catholic Study Commission), sections 26–30 esp.; Eng. trans. in *LW* 19 (1972): 259–73, and in *Worship* 46 (1972): 326–51; for the German, see below § 353, n. 1.

4. Joseph A. Fitzmyer, "The Office of Teaching in the Christian Church according to the New Testament," and John Reumann, "Teaching Office in the New Testament? A Response to Professor Fitzmyer's Essay," in *Teaching Authority and Infallibility in the Church,* pp. 186–212 and 213–31.

The essays that follow are presented in print very much as they were originally circulated for each dialogue session. The authors have done a minimum of revision. A system of abbreviations such as is used in biblical journals and monographs today has been followed, and references to the secondary literature are frequently incorporated into the text in order to avoid additional footnotes. In all cases the concern was to convey accurately the essayists' judgments amid the plethora of scholarly and confessional views, with precise documentation as required, but without excessive footnotes. Since most members of the dialogue are not experts in exegesis, there was therefore a concern to communicate from the outset with nonspecialists, while at the same time presenting the intricacies of centuries of varying views. In many cases, however, we have been content simply to indicate our positions on, e.g., authorship and date of a document, without arguing the matter in detail. For general presuppositions in such matters, readers are referred to the more thorough statements in the earlier task-force volumes on Peter and Mary, in which Professors Reumann and Fitzmyer were participants.[5]

To facilitate cross-references and discussion, sections (usually a paragraph or two in length) have been numbered from 1 to 440 on the left in bold. The Table of Contents provides a detailed outline for the first essay, and when one notes that the initial paper usually discusses passages in righteousness/justification in the sequence of chapter and verse within each biblical book and that the second essay follows the order of the first one in its response, one can, without an index, locate by these devices most New Testament passages discussed.

We are grateful to the editors of Paulist Press and Fortress Press for their prompt willingness to spread quickly and more widely the dialogue papers on biblical foundations of justification/righteousness. A grant from the Aid Association for Lutherans, Appleton, Wisconsin, to Professor Reumann was helpful for his duties as editor. Thanks are also due to Sister Grace Boehling, Lutheran Deaconess Center, Gladwyne, Pennsylvania, who retyped portions of the manuscript, and to Peter Pettit, Philadelphia Seminary, who checked Hebrew transliterations and references. A section of the first essay, on 2 Peter, was read at the Society of Biblical Literature/ Hudson-Delaware Region, May 3, 1981.

This note for the volume is dated on the 451st anniversary of what for Lutherans is a minor festival, the Presentation of the Augsburg Confession, that irenic document of 1530 which sought Lutheran-Catholic unity through the gospel of God's righteousness and the teaching of justification by grace through faith.

Philadelphia   J.R.
June 25, 1981

---

5. *Peter in the New Testament,* pp. 7–22; *Mary in the New Testament,* pp. 7–31.

Preface

The essays that follow on "righteousness in the New Testament" are an integral part of the current Lutheran-Catholic dialogue in the United States on the topic of "justification."

Biblical studies from a modern, historical-critical perspective have played an important role in official dialogue sponsored since 1965 by Lutheran World Ministries (the U.S. National Committee of the Lutheran World Federation) and the Bishops' Commission for Ecumenical and Interreligious Affairs. Our volumes of findings have regularly included a treatment or treatments on biblical aspects of such topics as baptism, the Lord's Supper, and the ministry, and the discussions and Common Statements of the dialogue team regularly have found useful insights from contemporary exegetical science and biblical theology.

In particular, the national dialogue, in connection with its consideration of "papal primacy" and "teaching authority and infallibility in the church," delegated task forces of Lutherans, Catholics, and other Christians to deal in greater depth with Peter and then with Mary in the New Testament. The results of those studies not only have proven helpful to the U.S. national dialogue and other Christian ecumenical discussions, but have also been well received for study purposes in colleges and seminaries and by more general readers who wished to survey the biblical data on those persons and issues as assessed by contemporary scholarship. Indeed, these task-force volumes have received attention far beyond the English-speaking world. They have also served to indicate not merely that, but more precisely how, the historical-critical approach can be useful in transcending old impasses and in presenting new insights.

Since September 1978, the national dialogue has been directing its attention to the theme of justification. The first papers were discussed at the February 1979 meeting. There was initially some feeling—because of the extensive literature already existing on the subject in commentaries, monographs, and specialized articles, plus the fact that the International Joint

Lutheran/Roman Catholic Study Commission had treated, among other matters, "the problem of the doctrine of justification"—that no further analysis of biblical material would be needed. But because of the significance of these biblical materials—especially in the minds of our Lutheran constituency and the growing attention by Catholic scholars to the topic as part of a Bible study movement along critical, historical lines since 1943, so that some of the most significant work on righteousness/justification has been done in Catholic circles, particularly in Europe—it was deemed necessary that the dialogue assign papers in this area. Because of the integral nature of the work to the current dialogue topic, the presentations and discussion were to be within the national dialogue group and not in a separate task force.

Since a Catholic New Testament scholar had been asked to treat in Round 6 of our dialogue what has been termed a peculiarly Catholic concern, "teaching authority and infallibility," with a Lutheran respondent making the reply, so on this topic of justification, which has been especially identified with Reformation concerns, a Lutheran was asked to make the presentation, with Catholic response. The Rev. John Reumann, professor at the Lutheran Theological Seminary, Philadephia, a clergyman of the Lutheran Church in America, who has been involved in the national dialogue since 1965, presented his material dealing with every New Testament passage using "righteousness" or "justification" terms (from the Greek root *dikaio-*), along with Old Testament background and attention to broader theological, hermeneutical questions pertinent to the dialogue, in sections spread over three meetings of the dialogue, at Atlanta, Georgia (March 1980), Gettysburg, Pennsylvania (September 1980), and Cincinnati, Ohio (February 1981). The Rev. Joseph A. Fitzmyer, S.J., professor at the Catholic University of America, Washington, D.C., was the respondent at each of these meetings. Professor Fitzmyer was also a member of the international joint commission that had dealt with the topic from 1967 to 1971. Another Catholic member of the U.S. dialogue, the Rev. Msgr. Jerome D. Quinn, professor at the St. Paul Seminary, St. Paul, Minnesota, presented a briefer response in his area of specialization, the Pastoral Epistles, when he rejoined the dialogue at the Gettysburg meeting after a period of teaching in Rome.

Because of the importance of these presentations and the considerable areas of agreement, significant for our current round of dialogue yet too lengthy for inclusion for what is planned as Volume 7 of Lutherans and Catholics in Dialogue, the participants in the national discussions approved at the September 1980 meeting separate publication of the Lutheran presentation and the Catholic responses on the biblical material. At the conclusion of discussion of the New Testament papers during the March 1981 meeting, the essayists were able to report arrangements for publication of their papers in this volume, which thus serves both as a general biblical introduction to the topic and as a resource and background for the national dialogue report now being drafted on justification, a doctrine long considered divisive between our two traditions but on which, especially in light of contemporary biblical studies, there are growing signs of convergence.

It should be underscored that the essays that follow here are not "a collaborative assessment" but were originally presented within the context of a national dialogue that had examined and continued to discuss aspects of the topic in patristic interpretation, the Reformation debate, pre- and postreformation aspects, including the Lutheran confessional writings (especially those around 1530 and 1580) and the decrees of the Council of Trent (especially in 1546–1547), and modern discussion among systematic theologians, in the Second Vatican Council, and at the Helsinki meeting of the Lutheran World Federation in 1963 when justification was the major topic under the theme "Christ Today." Occasionally there are references in the essays in this volume to documents available and papers presented at the dialogue; some of these are already published and others may be expected to appear in Volume 7, Lutherans and Catholics in Dialogue, on justification.

We reiterate what Prefaces by the late Paul C. Empie and the Catholic cochairman of the national dialogue have said in the volumes on Peter and Mary, affirming the fundamental importance for our bilateral work of sound scriptural study, and we express the hope that these presentations on righteousness/justification may prove beneficial in broader ecumenical circles as well as among those interested in study of the theme in the Bible.

H. George Anderson
President, Lutheran Theological
Southern Seminary, Columbia, SC
May, 1981

✝ T. Austin Murphy
Auxiliary Bishop of Baltimore, MD
Bishops' Commission for Ecumenical and Interreligious Affairs

"Justification by Grace through Faith" as Expression of the Gospel: The Biblical Witness to the Reformation Emphasis

————————————————————1

John Reumann

Introduction

1   The insistence of the Lutheran Reformation in the sixteenth century was that the gospel stands as norm and rule over church, Ministry and
ministries, bishops, councils, pope, and all the life of God's people, and
that the gospel is expressed above all as "justification." Justification was
therefore "the main doctrine of Christianity" for the reformers (Ap. 4:2),
the article that, because it sets forth what God has done for us in Christ,
cannot "be given up or compromised," the article on which "rests all that
we teach and practice" (Smalcald Articles, Part II Art I:5).

2   Lutherans have also expressed this point by speaking of "the word
of God" as supreme over the church and, indeed, over the Bible. (That, of
course, carries with it an implication for the church of *semper reformanda*
and of a hermeneutic for the Scriptures.) By "the word" Lutherans have
meant above all the oral proclamation of the message from and about God,
the gospel; more specifically, Jesus Christ himself as the word; and, further, Scripture as the word of God.[1]

3   The word of God, it should be noted, speaks and functions as both
"law" and "gospel," as, respectively, e.g., the Mosaic decalogue and the
promises of God and Christ so as to present, on the one hand, God's demands in such a way as to convict us of our transgressions and, on the other, God's deeds and their further implications in such a way as to sustain
and comfort us. (Cf. Ap. 4:5–6.) By the former, law, "sin is recognized but
its guilt is not relieved" (Ambrose, as cited in Ap. 4:103); by the latter we

---

1. In scriptural usage, "word of God" as a message is the most frequent sense; cf. Phil
1:14 in the context of 1:12–18; 1 Thess 1:5–8; Luke 5:1; Acts 10:36–37; 1 John 1:1–5, among
dozens of NT passages, not to mention the 241 OT references to "the word of Yahweh."

Of Christ—John 1:1, 14, 17; 1 John 1:1; Col 1:27; Rev 19:13; cf. also 2 Cor 1:19, Heb
1:2–3 and 11:13.

Of Scripture—Matt 15:6; perhaps 2 Tim 2:15. Cf. J. Reumann, "The New Testament
Concept of the Word," *Consensus: A Canadian Lutheran Journal of Theology* 4 (1978): 15–
24; 5 (1979): 15–22.

receive promises of "forgiveness of sins, justification, and eternal life" for Christ's sake (Ap. 4:5). That "God is righteous and demands righteousness from us"—as the Lutheran reformers claimed, insisting on a "righteousness of reason" or "civil righteousness" as something that every human being is commanded to perform and that they claimed, "to some extent, reason can produce" (Ap. 4:22)—can be "bad news" or "good news" (*kakangelion* as well as *euangelion*). That God, who is righteous, demands a righteousness to which human reason and the human will cannot attain is "law." That he "is himself righteous and justifies him who has faith in Jesus" (Rom 3:26) is gospel.

4   Our topic here is not "the word of God" or "law and gospel," related to it as these are, but "justification as gospel": How has this Reformation emphasis functioned as good news in Scripture and specifically what is the notion of justification in the biblical witness? The aim is to present, against the background of the extensive and ever-growing literature on the theme, an account of the scriptural roots for what the reformers made so central. Inevitably we must look at certain points involved in light of historic Lutheran-Catholic controversy of the past.

The Reformation Claim Reviewed

5   At the outset it is important to be clear on those things to which Lutherans regard themselves pledged not to "give up or compromise" and what things they may have held dear over the years but to which they are not bound. (*Semper reformanda* can also apply to the restatement of doctrine in new situations or as deeper perceptions of biblical meanings come.)

6   At issue is nothing in the ecumenical creeds of the ancient church, for justification is not an item in the heavily christological Apostles', Nicene, and Athanasian creeds.

7   Rather, the authoritative statements for Lutherans are those in the Book of Concord and, of course, behind them statements to which the confessions point, in the Scriptures. This means that what Luther said in exegetical lectures or Melanchthon and the other reformers in their writings is of interest and may have helped shape the Lutheran understanding of justification over a considerable portion of its history, but their judgments are not on the same level authoritatively as the confessions or, of course, Scripture.

8   Obviously, what Lutherans have thought about justification has had a complex history, one that still continues. At many points it merges with the exegetical and theological analyses of other Christians or at least with those of some Christians. And at points details in the doctrine of justification are still debated among Lutherans themselves or have become adiaphoral.[2]

---

2. Cf., as illustrative, papers from the LWF Assembly at Helsinki in 1963, esp. "A Study Document, On Justification" (New York: National Lutheran Council, 1963); *Justification*

9   It is therefore all the more important to be clear on exactly what the confessions say regarding justification.[3] The Augsburg Confession is the obvious focal point, not only in its Article 4 on justification, but even in 1–3 as the traditional, preludial doctrines about God, Adamic humanity, and Christ, and also in many of the articles that follow 4 as consequences and clarification of justification. In the Apology about a third of the document directly concerns justification.

10   The Smalcald Articles deal specifically with justification at II.1, under the heading "Christ and Faith," and at III.13, "How Man Is Justified Before God, and His Good Works," but most all of the Smalcald Articles "are more clearly structured around the doctrine of justification than any other confessional documents."[4]

11   The Formula of Concord exemplifies inner-reformation discussions in Article III of the Solid Declaration, "The Righteousness of Faith before God."[5] In 1580 justification remained the "high and important article . . . on which [our] salvation depends" (SD III:67). It rests solely on "the entire Christ" in his obedience, not on our love or virtues; it means forgiveness of sins, and also repentance, with love and good works following (Formula, Epitome III:3–11; Tappert ed., pp. 473f.; cf. IV). For more detail one is referred by SD III:67 to Luther's exposition of Galatians.[6]

Today: Studies and Reports, Supplement to *LW* 12, No. 1 (1965); "Helsinki 1963 . . .," *LW* 11 (1964): 1–36, esp. 4–10, cf. also pp. 83–86. One might also mention the 1980–81 discussion within the Lutheran Church–Missouri Synod over "objective" and "subjective" justification. Cf. also the reactions to the Malta Report by a Lutheran participant, Georg Strecker, in his *Evangelium und Kirche nach katholischem und evangelischem Verständnis* (Sammlung gemeinverständlicher Vörtrage . . . 257–258; Tübingen: Mohr-Siebeck, 1972), pp. 20–22, who regards justification as a mere polemical doctrine against Paul's opponents not repeatable today. But he would hold on to what the doctrine intended, esp. in its critical functions against church institutions.

3. See the papers previously discussed in this dialogue, especially Eric W. Gritsch, "The Historial Origins of the Lutheran Teaching on Justification: A Summary," and Robert W. Jenson, "An Exegesis of the Apology of the Augsburg Confession, Article IV."

4. Ralph A. Bohlmann, *Principles of Biblical Interpretation in the Lutheran Confessions* (St. Louis: Concordia, 1968), p. 74.

5. At issue was whether "the righteousness of God" (or of faith) is Christ as "the true, natural, essential Son of God" or "only according to his human nature" (*The Book of Concord,* trans. and ed. T. G. Tappert et al. [Philadelphia: Muhlenberg, 1959], p. 539). The errors rejected are that (1) our love or good works are a meritorious basis or cause of our justification; (2) a person must by good works become worthy to have Christ's merit applied to himself or herself; (3) our real righteousness before God is our love or the renewal the Holy Spirit works within us; (4) righteousness by faith consists of, first, forgiveness, then renewal or sanctification; (5) righteousness is begun in us by faith but is incomplete without love or renewal; (6) believers are justified both through the reckoned righteousness of Christ and their inchoate new obedience; (7) the promise of grace is made our own through faith in the heart, confession in the mouth, and other virtues (pp. 547–48).

6. Luther lectured on Gal in 1516–17 (*WA* 57/2:i–xxvi, 5–108); published in commentary in 1519 (*WA* 2:436–618; LW, Vol. 27, pp. 151–410); and, after lectures in 1531, published another commentary in 1535 (*WA* 40/1–2; LW, Vols 26–27). The 1531 lectures thus come just after the CA, at the time Melanchthon was completing the Ap., and prior to the

12   Besides analyses of these documents, such as have been presented in this dialogue, one might gain an overview of what the Lutheran confessions are committed to with regard to justification simply by skimming the references in the index to the Book of Concord (some selected themes follow, all cited from Ap. 4)[7]:

Justification: (a) *concept and nature*—it means "to be *pronounced* or accounted righteous" *and* "to *make* persons righteous or regenerate them," for "Scripture speaks both ways" (Ap. 4:72).

It is *forensic* (4:252, 305, citing Rom 5:1).

It means *forgiveness of sins* (4:75), *and* becoming God's children, *and* receiving *eternal life* (4:196) and *reconciliation* (4:97; "justification is reconciliation for Christ's sake," 158).

"Justifying *faith*" is "no mere historical knowledge," but the wanting of and "firm acceptance of God's offer promising forgiveness of sins and justification" (48).

"Faith *alone*" is involved, not to the exclusion of word or sacraments but solely to exclude any claim of merit on our part. "Alone" may rightly be added to make Romans 3:28 clear ("allein durch den Glauben," as Luther phrased it) because there Paul says that justification is "apart from works of the law" and elsewhere he says it is given "freely" (Eph 1:6), "as a gift" (Rom 3:24, 5:15–16), "the gift of God, not because of works" (Eph 2:8–9)—all exclusive terms (4:73–74).

13   (b) The doctrine *excludes* all confidence in our *works and merits* as a basis for justification, but the believer who is "accounted righteous because of Christ" *is,* renewed by the Holy Spirit, *to "keep the law,"* love and obey God, practice love, and so forth. This "incipient keeping of the law pleases God," not because the works are a "worthy righteousness" that "earns eternal life without needing Christ," but "because of faith," whereby our failures are "not imputed to us" (cf. Rom 4:8). Christ is "the mediator *continually* and not just at the beginning of justification" (4:177, 293, 317).

14   (c) *The "conditions" of justification* (as the Tappert ed., index, p. 682, puts it) are therefore not our works but God's gift, Christ's righteousness, and faith. By *faith* is meant not "the mere act of confessing" (4:384), but acceptance in the heart of God's offer and promise (48); not "idle thought, but . . . a work of the Holy Spirit" that "brings forth a new life in our hearts, and . . . whenever it appears . . . good fruits" (64). Thus one can even speak of "good works" and "new works" as the goal of justification (348–49).

15   (d) The Apology plainly uses *regeneratio* (rebirth) and *vivificatio* (making alive) to "mean the same thing" as justification. The Formula of Concord, fifty years later, is more careful not to "mingle or insert that

---

Smalcald Articles of 1537. Cf. Robert Bertram's paper to this dialogue, " 'Faith Alone Justifies': Luther on *Justitia Fidei*."
   7. Tappert ed., pp. 681–82, 705–06.

which precedes faith or follows faith into the article on justification" (SD III:24), and so it distinguishes a series of steps: (1) repentance, contrition, or conversion; (2) justification in the strict sense of "absolve" or "pronounce free from sin" (Epitome III:5 [Tappert ed. 473.7] termed "the usage of Scripture," citing Prov 17:15, Rom 8:33); (3) regeneration (renewal), vivification, or sanctification, and "the good works that follow," above all love.[8]

The Formula here uses "justification" in a more limited sense, excluding these other items. One must ask, if only because the Solid Declaration itself refers one to Luther's exposition on Galatians concerning such matters, whether our exegetical probes today must not be alert to the possibility that biblical usage of justification terms may reflect both a "broader" and a "more narrow" sense, as in the Apology and the Formula respectively. Here, in any case, the question surfaces of whether justification is to be used as a broad "salvation" term or as one step in an *ordo salutis*. One must note above all what the Solid Declaration (III:25) lists as "the only essential and necessary elements of justification," namely, "the grace of God, the merit of Christ, and faith which accepts these in the promise of the Gospel, whereby the righteousness of Christ is reckoned to us and by which we obtain the forgiveness of sins, reconciliation with God, adoption, and the inheritance of eternal life" (note the almost unconscious expansion of synonyms, in spite of the "narrow" definition of justification).

16   "Righteousness" may similarly be traced as a theme. In the Apology it may refer to an "original righteousness" for *humanity*, "implanted in man" at creation but lost after the fall of Adam (2:9, 15–18), and further to *outward* (civil) righteousness of reason, which continues in all human beings. Contrasting to the human situation is *Christ's* righteousness, in his obedient, expiatory death, bestowed on us, not *ex opere operato* in, e.g., the Lord's Supper, but "communicated to us through faith" (24:12; 4:305). " 'Christ our wisdom, our righteousness and sanctification and redemption' (1 Cor 1:30)" is received by faith as God's promise (4:86). The "righteousness of Christ is given to us through faith, therefore faith is righteousness in us by imputation" (4:307, citing Rom 4:5); "by it we are made acceptable to God." Thus "in justification our business is with God" (4:224).

17   Although the (biblical) phrase "the righteousness *of God*" seems not to appear in the Apology, it does come to the fore in the Formula and the debates reflected there. There is an effort in the Formula to distinguish "the righteousness of faith" (Rom 1:17, 3:5, 22, 25; 2 Cor 5:21), by which persons are justified, and "the eternal and essential righteousness" of God

---

8. Epitome III: 5, 8 (Tappert ed., pp. 473–74, 7–8, 11); SD III:17–28; A. C. Piepkorn, in the *Book of Concord* (Tappert ed.), p. 542, notes that the statement "justification is regeneration" does not occur in the Apology, though the (Melanchthonian) idea is implied (Ap. 4:72, 78, 117). On *iustificatio* as *vivificatio*, cf. Ap. 4:250; 7:31. For a brief account of inner-Lutheran discussion on issues in connection with justification, 1530–80, cf. Eric W. Gritsch and Robert W. Jenson, *Lutheranism* (Philadelphia: Fortress, 1976), pp. 45–64.

the Father, Son, and Holy Spirit. Using such categories, a distinction is then made between the former (involved in "justification in the narrow sense" and focused on Christ's obedience) and the latter, which is connected with the indwelling of God in the believer, which follows on justification so conceived (SD III:54–58). The "righteousness of God" is also spoken of as what "God manifests toward the impenitent and despisers of his Word," like Pharaoh (SD XI:86).[9] Here in connection with the article on election the Formula employs God's righteousness in the sense of "law" and judgment.

18   The Book of Concord thus exhibits both the centrality of the doctrine of justification for Lutherans and a history of development, debate, and openness on certain matters. Not all is fixed and settled, precisely because the scriptural evidence may admit of varied interpretations. "To justify" may mean both "to pronounce righteous" and "to make righteous." Justification is used in a broader and in a more narrow sense. There are differing nuances for Luther, Melanchthon, and each confessional document in its historical situation. Yet through it all runs a constant emphasis on God's work, not ours; Christ; grace; and faith as receptivity of what God in Christ has done (Ap. 4:48, 112), firm trust or confidence (4:79), and true knowledge of Christ, as mediator and propitiator; "this faith is the true knowledge of Christ, it uses his blessings, it regenerates our hearts, it precedes our keeping of the law" (4:46). "To know Christ is to know his benefits" (Melanchthon).

19   If there is such development and fluidity on the doctrine in the Book of Concord as a whole, there is also a certain lack of fixity in the Augsburg Confession and related documents around 1530 when Lutherans first proposed the theme and experience of justification as central. All would agree that CA Article 4 is the premier assertion of the claim:

> It is also taught among us that we cannot obtain forgiveness of sin and righteousness before God by our own merits, works, or satisfactions, but that we receive forgiveness of sin and become righteous before God by grace, for Christ's sake, through faith, when we believe that Christ suffered for us and that for his sake our sin is forgiven and righteousness and eternal life are given to us. For God will regard and reckon this faith as righteousness, as Paul says in Romans 3:21–26 and 4:5. (German version, Tappert ed., p. 30)

---

9. Cf. Rom 9, especially vv. 17, 22–23, 28, 30, where there is "righteousness" terminology. At 9:28, where *RSV* has "The Lord will execute his sentence upon earth with rigor and dispatch," the TR added the words italicized below in the citation from Isa 10:22–23, "He will accomplish his word and cut it short in *righteousness, because* God will make *a word* (or *account*) *cut short* in all the world." Did the authors of the Formula take the Greek addition *en dikaiosynē̦ hoti logon syntetmēmenon* as a reference to "the righteousness of God" and "the word which has been cut short"? Cf. the Luther Bible, and below, n. 89.

20 Elsewhere it has been argued that study of the development of this article, like its later expansion and expounding, shows a surprising amount of "inchoateness and fluidity," for it is "a doctrine *in process of development.*"[10] What Melanchthon articulated here, especially from Luther's writings and earlier drafts, is a combination of emphases, including stress on the Spirit and living in righteousness, and employs a host of other biblical themes, like reconciliation, forgiveness, and eternal life in expounding "the chief teaching of the Church" (CA 20). It has been pointed out also that the Lutheran doctrine reflects especially Paul's letters to Galatia and Rome and Luther's own struggle to come to faith in a gracious God.

21 If there is thus fluidity around 1530 and also in subsequent discussion of the doctrine in the confessions, the same thing is likewise true of subsequent theological and exegetical treatment among Lutherans and the whole Christian world. We leave to others the details of that history,[11] a history that includes further interpretation under Orthodoxy, Pietism, the nineteenth century (especially Liberalism), Neoorthodoxy, the Helsinki Assembly of LWF, and the work of the Bultmann-Käsemann School of NT exegesis.

22 Illustrative of this ongoing development is the discussion among Lutherans as to how Article 4 of the Augsburg Confession shall be understood in relation to the rest of the CA: Is it the one central theme and doctrine in light of which all else is to be understood (cf. Gritsch-Jenson, *Lutheranism*)? Or one doctrine among many? Or part of a constellation of articles and doctrines, such as 3 and 4 (Christology and justification) or 3-4-5 (the Holy Spirit), or 4-5-6 (faith), among other possibilities?[12]

---

10. Cf. J. Reumann, "The Augsburg Confession in Light of Biblical Interpretation," in *Confessio Augustana 1530–1580: Commemoration and Self-Examination,* ed. Vilmos Vajta, *LWF Report* 9 (Geneva, 1980): 13–17.

11. Ibid., pp. 17–21. See the **research reports** by Christian Müller, *Gottes Gerechtigkeit und Gottes Volk: Eine Untersuchung zu Römer 9–11* (FRLANT 86; 1964), pp. 5–27, on *dikaiosynē theou* from F. C. Baur to Bultmann; Peter Stuhlmacher, *Gerechtigkeit Gottes bei Paulus* (FRLANT 87; 1965), pp. 11–73, interpretation of the phrase from the second century till 1963; J. A. Ziesler, *The Meaning of Righteousness in Paul: A Linguistic and Theological Enquiry* (SNTSMS 20; 1972), pp. 1–16, on noun and verb from the Council of Trent till the present; Manfred T. Brauch, "Perspectives on 'God's Righteousness,' " in E. P. Sanders (cited below, n. 129), pp. 523–42; Ulrich Wilckens, *Der Brief an die Römer, 1. Teilband, Röm. 1–5* (EKKNT VI/1; 1978), pp. 223–33; Colin Brown, "Contemporary Interpretations of Righteousness," in *NIDNTT,* 3 (1978), pp. 371–77; and P. J. Achtemeier, "Righteousness in the NT," *IDB,* 4, pp. 91–99. For the OT, cf. also Reventlow (cited below, n. 28), pp. 16–36. Not available to me when these pages were being drawn up for the dialogue were the articles on *"dikaios, dikaiōs"* (G. Schneider) and on *"dikaiosynē, dikaioō, dikaiōma"* (K. Kertelge), in *Exegetisches Wörterbuch zum Neuen Testament,* ed. H. Balz and G. Schneider (Stuttgart: Kohlhammer), Vol. 1 (1980), cols. 781–810. For discussion of Rechtfertigung in the context of the CA, see Peter Stuhlmacher, "Schriftauslegung in der Confessio Augustana: Überlegungen zu einem erst noch zu führenden Gespräch," *KD* 26 (1980): 188–212, esp. 196–202.

12. At the international consultation "Confessio Augustana 1530–1980: Commemoration and Self-Examination," sponsored by the Institute for Ecumenical Research, Strasbourg, 22–27 October, 1979, the report of Discussion Group 2, "The Interpretation of the CA—in

23   It is to be expected that the doctrine of justification, like any great and vital article of faith, has had a history of developing interpretation, which is still going on. The point of this introduction has been to show how comprehensive and varied the Lutheran interpretations have been, what is normative and binding, what is under discussion. The task is now to examine the biblical foundations in light of contemporary scholarship.

A Note on Methodology and Biblical Terminology

24   In the historical-critical approach to Scripture, the "word-study method" is basic for ascertaining what the biblical writers meant by justification/righteousness. Aware of the strictures about that method, especially by James Barr, we may, nonetheless, use it with proper cautions.[13] For our purposes, however, it will not be necessary to trace all words from the Hebrew root *ṣdq* and the Greek word group derived from *dikē*, or all steps such as, e.g., etymology or the total history-of-religions background. It will be necessary to supplement word study with the fuller range of historical-critical techniques. Crucial segments and passages in the NT literature for our purposes will receive greatest attention. Generally blocks of material like the Pauline corpus or Matthew's gospel will be taken up in their chronological order of appearance and, within a corpus, by emerging chronological stages, e.g., prepauline, Paul himself, and deuteropauline documents.

25   The history of research on the topic makes one especially aware of how the starting point chosen or delimitation of the evidence may slant results.[14] We must deal therefore not only with, e.g., "the righteousness of

---

Past and Present," listed among the hermeneutics for reading the CA the following: propositional truths in light of the entire Book of Concord; justification as center; the theology of the young Luther (or of Melanchthon) as interpretative principle; use in the service of Christian reunion; the primacy of biblical exegesis over confessional formulations of the CA; or use of modern world views to reinterpret or replace the CA. Group 2 preferred a "constellation of articles" approach.

   13. J. Barr, *The Semantics of Biblical Language* (New York: Oxford Univ. Press, 1961). David Hill, *Greek Words and Hebrew Meanings: Studies in the Semantics of Soteriological Terms* (SNTSMS 5; 1968), attempts to meet such objections in treating "righteousness" among other terms, pp. 82–162. Cf. Barr's response, "Common Sense and Biblical Theology," *Bib* 49 (1968): 377–87.

   14. Cf. "The Augsburg Confession in Light of Biblical Interpretation," p. 17. In the literature cited there (and in n. 11 above), Chr. Müller and P. Stuhlmacher may be criticized for concentrating on "God's righteousness" at the expense of "righteousness" in general (though they believe the former to be a technical term). J. Ziesler criticizes previous efforts for stressing only either the noun *dikaiosynē* or the verb *dikaioō*, and for how some investigators have been prone to transfer their findings on the one to the other without further checking. The Latin Fathers took all too many passages from the Bible to have the Greek sense of "distributive justice." H. Cremer in the nineteenth century rightly redirected attention to OT backgrounds, Käsemann's pupils (more debatedly) to specific apocalyptic roots. Rom 3:5 provides the starting point for the approach of some like A. Schlatter and Käsemann; Phil 3:9, for many other scholars. One must, paralleling Günther Bornkamm's observations on the history

God" but "righteousness" generally. While effort will be made to pull the meanings of a term together for a book or author, we shall try to avoid the pitfall of any possible "stacking of the evidence" by employing in our presentation the passages generally in the order of the book as we have it today.

26   A final problem, in English terminology, stems from the usage of words from both Latin and Anglo-Saxon roots to render the same Hebrew and Greek roots:

Adjective	Noun	Verb
just	justice	to justify
righteous	righteousness	to rightwise (n)

The problem of an English verb formed from the adjective "righteous" as a rendering of the Greek *dikaioō* is well known: Shall it be "declare righteous" or "make righteous," a double possibility already noted in Ap. 4:72. We shall resort in some instances therefore to the Middle English form, which Kendrick Grobel used in translating Bultmann's New Testament theology, to "rightwise."[15]

---

of interpreting the Sermon on the Mount (*Jesus of Nazareth* [New York: Harper's 1960], pp. 224–25), be wary of any view that claims that justification/righteousness is "always this" or "only that."

15. Rudolf Bultmann, *Theology of the New Testament* (New York: Scribner's, 1951, 1955), Vol. 1, p. 253.

I. The Biblical Background:
Old Testament and Jesus

A. The Old Testament

27 "There is absolutely no concept in the Old Testament with so central a significance for all the relationships of human life as that of *ṣdqh*. It is the standard not only for man's relationship to God, but also for his relationships to his fellows, reaching right down to . . . the animals and to his natural environment . . . for it embraces the whole of Israelite life."[16] The scholarly literature on "righteousness," even just in terms of recent treatments, is appropriately huge in volume.[17]

28 The verb root involved in Hebrew, *ṣdq*, occurs 41 times in the Kittel OT text, meaning "to be righteous," or (hiphil) "declare to be in the right." The adjective *ṣaddîq*, "righteous," "just," 208 times; the nouns *ṣe-*

---

16. Gerhard von Rad, *Old Testament Theology* (New York: Harper & Row, 1962, 1965), Vol. 1, pp. 370, 373.

17. G. Quell, G. Schrenk, "*dikē, diakios, dikaiosynē,* etc.," in *TDNT,* Vol. 2 (1964), pp. 174–225, especially 174–78, 185–87, 195–98, 212–14 (German, published 1935). Elizabeth R. Achtemeier, "Righteousness in the OT," *IDB,* 4, pp. 80–85; A. Cronbach, "Righteousness in Jewish Literature," 4, 85–91; E. C. Blackman, "Justification, Justify," 2, pp. 1027–28. Günther Klein, "Righteousness in the NT," *IDBSup,* pp. 750–52, is relevant for the OT also.

Further, J. A. Ziesler, *Righteousness* (cited above, n. 11), pp. 17–127. H. Seebass and Colin Brown, "Righteousness, Justification," *NIDNTT,* 3, pp. 352–77. Klaus Koch, "*ṣdq* gemeinschaftstreu/heilvoll sein," *Theologisches Handwörterbuch zum Alten Testament* (Munich: Chr. Kaiser, 1976), Vol. 2, cols. 507–30. It is in light of the OT background that D. H. van Daalen suggests that the interpretations by Augustine and Luther still "find a certain relative justification"; cf. "The Revelation of God's Righteousness in Romans 1:17," in *Studia Biblica 1978: Papers on Paul and Other New Testament Authors, Sixth International Congress on Biblical Studies,* ed. by E. A. Livingstone (JSNT Supplement Series, 3; Sheffield, 1980).

deq and *sĕdāqâ,* "righteousness," "justice," 115 and 158 times respectively. Of these more than 500 cases, about 90 per cent are rendered in Greek by a form from *dikaios* (statistics from Ziesler, pp. 18–36; Koch, col. 511, differs but slightly). Statistically, therefore, the term is a major one in the OT.

29 The root occurs most frequently in Psalms, Proverbs, Isaiah, and Ezekiel. Indeed, two-thirds of the examples are in those four books, where Jerusalem traditions and the wisdom theme are strong (Koch, col. 511). Ziesler (pp. 18, 21) finds present both forensic and ethical senses, dealing respectively with juridical processes and with behavior in life generally and in liturgy.

30 Research over the past century has often sought some master concept that would explain all *sdq*-passages. Ziesler (pp. 36–43) describes how Kautzsch championed "conformity to a norm" (so also Norman Snaith); Wheeler Robinson, the forensic sense ("acquittal at the bar of God"); Ludwig Koehler, "innocence" (being "not guilty"). Cremer stressed *sdq* as a "relationship" term (cf. the quotation from von Rad above; E. Achtemeier in *IDB*), and others have more specifically emphasized the covenant context of relationships (so Schrenk in *TDNT;* D. Hill): "When Israel thought of relationship (our term) she thought of covenant (her term)," so "covenant-behaviour" and "-loyalty" are involved (Ziesler, pp. 38–39).

An account of the development of the theme in Israel's history runs, in light of current views, along the following lines.

31 1. In the ancient Near Eastern context *sdq* related to the loyalty a king or priest owed as servant to his god or suzerain. It may indeed have actually been the name of a deity, "Sedeq"; cf. Gen 14:18, the theophorous name of a king, Melchizedek, *Malkî-sedeq,* perhaps "(the god) Sedeq is my king"; and Josh 10:1; "Adonizedek king of Jerusalem." In Egyptian religion Maat, daughter of Re, was a goddess of justice and righteousness but was also connected with world order; the Pharaoh ruled with Maat (Ps 89:15 could reflect this background—"righteousness and justice are the foundation" of Yahweh's throne; the king's throne "is established by righteousness," Prov 16:12).

32 H. H. Schmid[18] has insisted that *sdq* in Hebrew thought can be appreciated only against a background like this, a background of cosmic order. Under this heading the ancients would have brought together such basic ideas as kingdom, wisdom, law, nature and its fruitfulness, war and victory, and cult and sacrifice; all these things depend on "righteousness/ justice," in a unified view of the world (cf. Koch, col. 516). To "rule" and to "judge" are to acknowledge such a world order and to work for it or to restore it. God, king, and subjects participate, each in his way, in all that

---

18. Hans Heinrich Schmid, *Gerechtigkeit als Weltordnung* (BHT 40; 1968). See also his later article, "Rechtfertigung als Schöpfungsgeschehen: Notizen zur alttestamentlichen Vorgeschichte eines neutestamentlichen Themas," in *Rechtfertigung: Festschrift für Ernst Käsemann zum 70. Geburtstag,* ed. J. Friedrich, W. Pöhlmann, and P. Stuhlmacher (Tübingen: Mohr-Siebeck, and Göttingen: Vandenhoeck & Ruprecht, 1976), pp. 403–14.

"righteousness" thus means (something about as comprehensive as *šālôm*).
33   The *ṣdq*-concept thus has a cosmic orientation of great breadth, from the world in which Israel lived and from which she took, though not uncritically, such terms. Righteousness is a key part of Yahweh's "fixed order" for the universe (cf. Jer 31:35–36).
34   2. To scan the range of OT references produces the following broad sets of meanings:

  a. *ṣdq* as the activity or behavior *of human beings* (cf. Ziesler, pp. 23–32):
   • legal activity—judging, establishing (social) justice in the community (e.g., Isa 5:7, parallel to *mišpāt,* "justice)
   • governing, ruling activity—as when a (Davidic) king rules with "justice and righteousness" (Jer 23:5)
   • ethical uprightness—of Noah (Gen 6:9), the term is parallel with "blameless . . . walking with God"; "doing what is lawful and right" (Ezek 18:5, 9:23) means "life"; a righteous God, in Israel's cult life, calls for righteous behavior (Pss 7:9, 15:1–2, 97:11–12)
   • covenant-loyalty among Yahweh's people—the "righteous" are those poor, humble, faithful folk who abide by their relationship to God and trust in vindication from him against their oppressors (e.g., Ps 37:12; Isa 26:2–3; Jer 20:12)
   • obedience to torah—because the covenant at Sinai calls for obedience to God's will there expressed, keeping torah became the hallmark of doing what is *ṣdq* (Isa 51:7; Ezek 18:19, 21)
   • loving good, speaking truth—sometimes these aspects of *sdq* are especially highlighted (cf. Ps 52:5; Prov 8:8). A particularly striking example combining many illustrations of what righteous human activity among God's people involves in a period after the fall of Jerusalem in 586 B.C., when it was no longer possible to speak simply of "the nation" but one had to spell out righteousness for the individual, is Ezek 18:5–9 and indeed the whole chapter: The prophet seems to have adopted an old priestly, liturgical formula (vv. 5, 10, 14; 9*b,* 13*b,* 17*b*) and used it to produce a declaratory verdict of righteousness and life (vv. 9, 17, 23) for despondent exiles who questioned whether Yahweh was just[19]
   • forensic, relational righteousness—a number of *sdq* passages are in the setting of a tribunal, human or divine (Isa 5:23; Deut 24:13; Job 35:2; Prov 17:15)

---

19. In addition to commentaries on the passage and the literature in n. 17, cf. Ronald M. Hals, "Methods of Interpretation: Old Testament Texts," in *Studies in Lutheran Hermeneutics,* ed. J. Reumann (Philadelphia: Fortress, 1979), pp. 271–82.

- finally, gracious activity, reflecting God's own—Isa 58:8, cf. 6–7 (the "righteousness" that "goes before" the remnant involves feeding the hungry, clothing the poor, etc., as a reflection of Israel's relation with Yahweh)

35 b. *ṣdq* as the activity *of God:*
- legal activity—judging, giving torah and legal decisions that make for justice in the community (Pss 9:5, 119:7; Isa 42:21, 58:2)
- acting reliably, trustworthily, faithfully—Jer 9:24, "I am the Lord who practices steadfast love, justice, and righteousness in the earth"; cf. Dan 9:7; Deut 32:4; Yahweh is "the Righteous One" (Isa 24:16)
- He speaks truth, what is right—Isa 45:19
- He is therefore "right" or "in the right"—so Pharaoh confesses (Exod 9:27; Jer 12:1); this is really a forensic application to Yahweh himself
- vindication, giving victory or prosperity—Yahweh acts or will act to vindicate his people (remnant) in "the triumphs (*sidqôt*) of the Lord" (Judg 5:11); Isa 62:1–2 (*RSV* "vindication" is in Hebrew *ṣedeq*); Isa 41:2 (*RSV* "victory") (the old "Holy War theme," that "Yahweh does it all," probably lies behind this usage)
- gracious, saving activity—here we find the most amazing of all the OT uses, where especially in Deutero-Isaiah (53 cases, Ziesler, p. 29), *ṣdq* terms come to mean virtually "salvation" (as *RSV* often renders it), with an emphasis on God's gracious nature as the reason he thus works salvation; note the parallel terms:

> I bring near my deliverance (*ṣidqātî*) . . . ,
> and my *salvation* will not tarry (Isa 46:13; cf. 51:5, 6, 8; 61:10).

Sometimes this is related as the "indicative" supporting an "imperative" to do *ṣdq* therefore: "Thus says the Lord, 'Keep justice (*mišpāṭ*) and do *righteousness* (*ṣĕdāqâ*), for soon my *salvation* will come, and my deliverance (*ṣidqātî*) be revealed' " (Isa 56:1). To confess "The Lord is our righteousness" (Jer 23:6) or to hear him say, "I have called you in righteousness" (Isa 42:6) is nothing else but gospel (good news) against the background of this dynamic idea of what Yahweh's *ṣdq* means for his people.

This lengthy survey of but a part of the OT evidence makes it clear that "righteousness/justice/justification" terminology in the Hebrew scriptures is "action-oriented," not just "status" or "being" language, and binds together forensic, ethical and other aspects in such a way that some sort of more unified ancient Near Eastern view can readily be presupposed. **36** If it is asked, "Are God's activity and man's activity as *ṣdq* linked?" the answer is, "Of course," not only in the thinking of the day but also in some passages. It is thus within the covenant(s) that Yahweh has made with Israel that *ṣdq* is considered to be possible for human beings (Ziesler, p. 42). Hence "righteousness language" appears especially in covenant-making situations, e.g. Gen 15:6, Abram "believed the Lord and he reckoned it to him as righteousness" is in the chapter that describes Yahweh making a covenant with him; likewise Gen 18:19, "I have chosen him . . . to keep the way of the Lord by doing righteousness and justice." The covenant relationship is assumed in liturgical formulas when they emphasize righteous behavior for those who will be admitted to the worshiping congregation (Ps 15; Ezek 18). Use of the verb *ṣdq* in the hiphil (Ziesler, pp. 18–19) often suggests "declare to be not guilty" and so "restored to proper position within the covenant community" (1 Kgs 8:32; Ps 82:3; Isa 50:8). The king, as Yahweh's anointed in the covenant relationship, is especially expected to rule with righteousness and justice received from God (Ps 72:1–4). Israel's future hope, particularly after 586 B.C., takes the form of *ṣĕdāqâ* as God's vindicating action, yet king and people must practice what is also God's gift (cf. Isa 32:16–17; Jer 23:5–6, 33:15–16); thus *ṣdq,* which is *šālôm,* is God's righteousness, vindicating and saving, but with implications for how the vindicated live and indeed for the land and for nature itself.

37 3. Against this background of the ancient Near East and Israel's varied but related usages of *ṣdq*-terms, we may now note the usages in terms of the following literary-historical categories.

a. The *prophets* (cf. Koch, cols. 526–27) used such terms less than we might suppose, certainly less than a Liberal view of them as "preachers of social justice" would suggest. But in Amos *ṣdq* does function in social and cultic critique (5:6–7, 21–24). Jeremiah, trusting in a God of righteousness (9:20), called for a return to uprightness (4:1–2). After 586 B.C. he used God's righteousness as a hope (23:5), as did the Second and Third Isaiahs (Isa 51:5; 54:14–17, where "their vindication" in v. 17 is literally *ṣidqātām;* 59:16–17). At times the notion of a courtroom setting and a lawsuit between Yahweh and Israel is apparent (Isa 1:2–9; Mic 6:1–8; Jer 2:4–13).[20]

---

20. More attention should be paid to the "*rîb*-pattern" or "covenant 'complaint' " or "prophetic lawsuit" than Ziesler, e.g., pp. 37–38, suggests. In such a passage Yahweh or the prophet summons the offending party (often Israel) to judgment, recites the acts of past beneficence and the current accusations, and then calls on the witnesses to the covenant in both earth and heaven. Cf. Hos 4:1–20 and Ps 50 as further examples. Rom 1:18–3:20 is read in such terms by Markus Barth, *Justification: Pauline Texts Interpreted in the Light of the Old and New Testaments* (Grand Rapids: Eerdmans, 1971), pp. 18–19, 25–34. Originally in M. Barth et al., *Foi et salut selon S. Paul* (AnBib 42; 1970). See also Chr. Müller, *Gottes Gerechtigkeit* (cited above, n. 11), pp. 57–72.

38   b. The *Psalms,* through notoriously difficult to date, reflect widespread use of *ṣdq*-terminology in cult settings. The language is used when God's actions are praised; Ps 40:9–10 is typical of such doxology:

> I have told the good news (*bśr,* Greek 39:10 *euēngelisamēn*) of deliverance (*ṣedeq,* Greek *dikaiosynē*) in the great congregation; . . .
> I have not hid thy saving help (*ṣidqātĕkā,* Greek *tēn dikaiosynēn sou*) within my heart,
> I have spoken of . . . thy salvation. (Hebrew 40:10–11)

It was common to extol the *ṣdq* at Yahweh's throne (89:14, 16) and to sing of righteousness coming down to earth (85:10–13) to be received as a blessing by the worshiper (24:5, *RSV* "vindication"). God on his throne gives righteous judgment that, in vindicating the oppressed (Israel), is cosmic, rebuking their enemies (9:4–6). Whether these allusions are simply poetic or at times reflect a fall festival on Mt. Zion where a deity (*Ṣedeq?*) was thought to come down and renew nature, king, and people remains disputed (cf. Koch, cols. 519–20). In any case, Israel's God was "*Yhwh-ṣedeq*" (cf. 4:1, 17:1), there was a "way (or paths) of righteousness" (23:3; 37:5–7), and the "poor" cried out for righteousness from Yahweh and from their human oppressors (Ps 7, esp. vv. 8–11). The king in Jerusalem played a special role, as "mediator" of righteousness (Pss 45:4–7; 72).

39   c. The *wisdom literature,* often international in its contents and in its outlook, constantly stressed *ṣdq* for king and all who seek to be "wise" (Prov 25.5, 8:15, 9:9, 1:3). Only occasionally is God directly mentioned (3:33; 10:3, 6). Job and Ecclesiastes belong here, as both explore traditional views. In the former Job insists on his righteousness (27:5–6, 29:14), but his "comforters" assert that in that case he cannot be righteous, afflicted as he is, if God judges righteously (36:5–9; 35:6–8; 22:2–3). Eventually the question is one of theodicy (the justification of God, 40:8) and how a person can be just before him who speaks from the whirlwind (9:2; chaps. 40–42). The Preacher (*Qoheleth*) openly questions the old axioms about righteousness, for he has too often seen "the righteous man perish in his righteousness" (7:15; 8:14), so that it is not to be believed that one is "in the hand of God" (9:1–2); if there is thus one fate for all, "do not be righteous overmuch" (7:16).

40   d. This pessimistic attitude was exacerbated in *apocalyptic* as times grew worse: The only solution is for God himself to intervene and "bring in everlasting righteousness" (Dan 9:24). One longed for a world, in the age to come, where "righteousness has increased and truth has appeared" (2 Esdr 7:114). Where human righteousness is lacking, only the "righteousness of God" will do. Righteousness had always been a characteristic of the anointed king's rule; increasingly in the intertestamental period it became a mark of the messianic age to come.[21]

---

21. Cf. Schrenk on the messiah as the "righteous one," *TDNT* 2, pp. 186–87. On devel-

Especially debated is whether "the righteousness of God" became a fixed formula in apocalyptic literature whence it provides the significant background for Pauline use (so Käsemann, Stuhlmacher). The attempt has been to trace the phrase *ṣidqat Yhwh* starting from Deut 33:21 (*RSV,* "with Israel he executed the commands and *just decrees* of the Lord"; Greek, *dikaiosynēn kyrios epioēsen*), through apocalyptic (Isa 24–27, Daniel, and Qumran), with the result that the technical term "righteousness of God" relates Yahweh's *ṣĕdāqôt* (righteous deeds)—his fidelity to the covenant and to creation, a rightful, creative power that will in the future establish justice anew.

41   e. More perhaps should be said about *intertestamental developments.* Words in Greek derived from *dikaios* may have carried a more limited connotation in Greek use and have tended to distort the sense of *ṣdq* in the direction of *iustitia distributiva* (so Descamps). C. H. Dodd found the LXX polarized the richness of *ṣdq* along two different lines, sometimes as "justice" (*dikaiosynē*), sometimes as mercy (*eleēmosynē*).[22] Ziesler (p. 51) thinks the Greek terms "successfully communicated to an ordinary non-Jewish Christian," but that that depended on the "accompanying ideas of God and of man's relation to him," not "the words themselves." In Sir and other Greek books in the Apocrypha and Pseudepigrapha Ziesler finds verb usage (*dikaioō*) to be heavily forensic, but noun and adjective "almost wholly ethical," a key contention for his analysis of Paul, but for the Hebrew writings of the period (Sir, Qumran) forensic use is said to drop away.

42   Analysis of the Dead Sea scrolls has led to awareness of a particular emphasis on righteousness at Qumran and suggestion that "justification by faith" appeared there prior to its appearance in Paul.[23] At Qumran, under its remarkable "teacher of righteousness" a theological outlook developed that stressed human sinfulness in a manner akin to Paul, and God's righteousness as both judgment and forgiveness in a manner characteristic of the OT; if anything, God's absolute righteousness is heightened alongside

---

opments from 597 B.C. till the time of Daniel, cf. Walther Zimmerli, "Alttestamentliche Prophetie und Apokalyptik auf dem Wege zur 'Rechfertigung des Gottlosen,' " in *Rechtfertigung* (Käsemann fs, cited above, n. 18), pp. 575–92. On the "righteousness of God" in apocalyptic, see P. Stuhlmacher, *Gerechtigkeit* (cited above, n. 11), pp. 145–75.

22. A. Descamps, "La Justice de Dieu dans la Bible grecque," *Studia Hellenistica 5* (Louvain, 1948): 69–92, esp. 75ff., 88–91. C. H. Dodd, *The Bible and the Greeks* (London: Hodder & Stoughton, 1935), pp. 42ff., especially p. 53.

23. Helmer Ringgren, *The Faith of Qumran: Theology of the Dead Sea Scrolls* (Philadelphia: Fortress, 1963), pp. 63–67. W. Grundmann, "The Teacher of Righteousness of Qumran and the Question of Justification by Faith in the Theology of the Apostle Paul," in *Paul and Qumran,* ed. Jerome Murphy-O'Connor (London: Geoffrey Chapman, 1968), pp. 85–114 (originally in *Revue de Qumran* 2 [1959–60]: 237–59). S. Schulz, "Zur Rechtfertigung aus Gnaden in Qumran und bei Paulus," *ZTK* 56 (1959): 155–85, sees both resemblances and differences; Paul is deemed to have known and used the theology of Qumran.

human depravity (Ringgren, pp. 64–65). Two passages have attracted special attention. The Manual of Discipline concludes, in column XI,

2   As for me, my justification (*mišpāṭî*) is with God . . .

3   He will wipe out my transgression through his righteousness (*ṣidqôṭāw*). . . .

5   From the source of his righteousness (*ṣidqāṭô*) is my justification (*mišpāṭî*). . . .

6   My eyes have gazed on . . . a foundation of righteousness (*ṣĕdāqâ*). . . .

12 As for me, if I stumble, the mercies of God (*ḥasdê 'ēl*) shall be my eternal salvation.
 If I stagger because of the sin of flesh,
   my justification (*mišpāṭî*) shall be
   by the righteousness of God (*ṣidqat 'ēl*) which endures forever.

13 . . . He will draw me near by His grace

14 and by His mercy will He bring my justification (*mišpaṭî*).
 He will judge me in the righteousness (*ṣidqat*) of His truth
   and in the greatness of His goodness
   He will pardon all my sins.
 Through his righteousness (*ṣidqāṭô*) He will cleanse me

15 of the uncleanness of man
 and of the sins of the children of men,
 that I may confess to God His righteousness (*ṣidqô*)
 and his majesty to the Most High. (1QS 11, Vermes trans.)

Commentators claim that here God's righteousness effects both forensic salvation and moral renewal (e.g., Ziesler, p. 102).

43   The Habakkuk Commentary from Qumran remarks on Hab 2:4*b*, the famous verse that Paul cites, "The righteous shall live by his faith":

Interpreted, this concerns all those who observe the Law in the House of Judah, whom God will deliver from the House of Judgement because of their suffering and because of their faith in the Teacher of Righteousness (*'ĕmūnāṭām bĕmôrēh haṣṣedeq*, 1QpHab 8:1–3, Vermes).

But does *'ĕmūnāṭām* mean "their faith in" or "fidelity to" the group's teacher? personally or as an interpreter of torah? Presumably he was not an object of faith or one who worked redemption. Others have taken the phrase to mean simply "faithfully following the torah as interpreted by the Teacher of Righteousness" (Jeremias, p. 69). The sect's commentary does parallel the debated phrase with "observing the law" and with "their suffering."

All would agree such passages approach the Pauline emphasis as no other documents of their day do. We are on the threshold of the NT usage. But there are differences, not least of which is the torah-orientation of Qumran, in contrast to the atonement-theme in Paul about Jesus' cross.[24]

44   4. In light of what the OT and related documents say about *ṣdq*, it is now time to summarize some emphases not always noted in discussions about our topic, emphases to which our examination above should have pointed.

The Hebrew concept of righteousness has a *cosmic* background. It often relates to *creation* and to the *covenant(s)*.[25] Therefore it is involved in *cult* and *worship*. There are links to *wisdom* and to *eschatology*. It is by no means an individualistic concept but strongly *communal,* though in the period after 586 B.C. the expression (as so much in Israel's life) is less national and more individual. The concept is *dynamic,* dealing with actions of God and of persons. If Schmid is correct, the ancient Near Eastern background made a *unity* of what to us are often separated, unrelated elements.

45   One could begin analysis of the OT concept at various points, as specific scholars have attempted—Deut 33:21 (see 3.d, above); or Ps 143 ("no man living is righteous before thee, . . . Lord, answer me in thy righteousness"); Judg 5:11 (the "saving acts of God," in the Song of Deborah); Gen 38:26, Judah's acknowledgment about Tamar, his daughter-in-law who has played the harlot, "She is more righteous than I" (i.e., she has done what the relationship justly demanded)[26]—covenant, the lawcourt, apocalyptic, ethical behavior, all are included, but the interrelatedness ought to be kept in mind.

---

24. Translations from G. Vermes, *The Dead Sea Scrolls in English* (Penguin, 1962), pp. 92–94 and 237. J. Jeremias, "Justification by Faith," *The Central Message of the New Testament* (London: SCM, 1965; reprinted Philadelphia: Fortress, 1981) pp. 51–70. Ziesler, pp. 102–3; Koch, col. 530; Stuhlmacher, pp. 148–66, treat the matter. Further, Otto Betz, "Rechtfertigung in Qumran," in *Rechtfertigung* (Käsemann fs cited above, n. 18), pp. 17–36. Betz emphasizes that the Qumran texts do *not* speak of justification (Rechtfertigung) of persons by God, nor do they use *ṣdq* in the hiphil ("gerecht sprechen"); like the OT, they do speak of Gerechtigkeit (justice). According to Qumran, there is to be an eschatological revealing of God's Gerechtigkeit. Paul shares many emphases with Qumran, but there is no "justification of sinners *contra legem* at Qumran." So Betz.

Additional literature between 1959 articles (see n. 23, above) and the Betz treatment is discussed in Herbert Braun, *Qumran und das Neue Testament* (Tübingen: Mohr-Siebeck, 1966), Vol. 22, pp. 167–72, with the judgment offered that Paul and Qumran differ not only over Christology but above all on the role ascribed to torah. Ernst Käsemann, *Commentary on Romans* (Grand Rapids: Eerdmans 1980), pp. 28–29 regards 1QS 10:25 along with 11:12 and 1QM 4:6 as most significant.

25. A Lutheran discussion in Walter R. Roehrs, "Covenant and Justification in the Old Testament," *CTM* 35 (1964); 583–602.

26. K. Stendahl, "Biblical Theology," *IDB* 1, p. 425: "A descriptive study of, e.g., Paul's concept of justification would find roots in the Song of Deborah, perhaps the oldest piece of tradition in the whole Bible (Judg. 5:11; *sidqōt* = 'saving acts of God')." On Gen 38:26, cf. Ziesler, p. 43. Cf. also Isa 63:1, Yahweh comes from Edom, "announcing vindication" (*bisĕdāqâ*).

46   What might be perceived as a mere OT "background section" in this presentation may seem to some overly long (yet in reality it is often too brief to do justice to many questions). But it is an area that is "biblical theology" in its own right and has come to the fore prominently in recent years. It is also one the Lutheran-Catholic discussions on the topic of justification have seldom, if ever before, considered. The Malta Report (sections 26–30) and the papers and discussions of the Joint Lutheran/Roman Catholic Study Commission on "The Gospel and the Church" seem to have dealt primarily with the Pauline doctrine of justification as an expression of the gospel.[27] Indeed, it is an approach that Lutherans too seem to have overlooked and yet one that, it has been suggested by Henning Graf Reventlow, might be the answer to the "riddle of Helsinki," which resulted when the LWF tackled justification in 1963.[28]

47   For perhaps the most significant example of this newer, broader approach to the problem is Reventlow's book, which began as a presentation to the Theological Committee of the United Evangelical Lutheran Church in Germany (VELKD) in 1969, on "justification in the horizon of the OT." Eschewing individualistic, introspective notions of justification, and critical of overemphasis on the "covenant" theme, he builds on Schmid's view of "righteousness as world order," whereby *sdq* means the proper, salutary ordering of the world willed by Yahweh, *sdqh* the proper, salutary relations in accord with it ("*sdq* bezeichnet die richtige, jahwe-gewollte, heilvolle Ordnung der Welt, *sdqh* das ihr gemässe, richtige heilvolle Verhalten," Schmid, p. 179) For Reventlow, justification is a cosmic activity of God, a *creatio continua; "sdq* ist von Jahwe gewirkte Ordnung, *sdqh* das heilvolle Handeln Jahwes, das sie in Kraft setzt. Aber den Frevler, der sich ausserhalb dieser Ordnung stellt, ereilt Jahwes strafende *sdqh*" (p. 36; *sdq* is the ordering worked by Yahweh, *sdqh* the salutary acts of Yahweh which set it in force; but Yahweh's punishing *sdqh* overtakes the transgressor who places himself outside this order). Thus we deal with God's salvatory world order, his saving actions to bring it about, his punitive actions against the impious. All of God's acts may thus be seen in the OT as Rechtfertigungsgeschehen ("justification events," p. 41):

    I. With regard to the people of God:
        A. In OT reflection on history, e.g.,
            1. in the theology of the Yahwist, as a history of how God graciously elects persons (Gen 12:2–3)

---

27. Cf. Malta Report, (26)–(30), in *LW* 19 (1972): 263–64; prior sessions, summarized in interim reports, *LW* 16 (1969): 363–79, especially 371–72; *LW* 18 (1971): 161–87.

28. Henning Graf Reventlow, *Rechtfertigung im Horizont des Alten Testaments* (BEvT 58; 1971), p. 10. He notes (p. 14), on the one hand, that there was a new awareness in some of the papers at Helsinki that justification is an action of God (and the very sequence of CA 4 after CA 1–3 indicates the reformers were aware of this) and so a cosmic action, and thus individualization and spiritualization are misunderstandings; but, on the other, that in this event the individual always is intended, that it happens in Christus *pro me,* and in word and sacraments must relate to every individual.

2. in the Deuteronomist's history—the kerygma here is that of repentance: if "Israel with all her heart will listen to the voice of her God alone and expect from him alone all that is good, then she will be God's peculiar possession in the world of the nations"

3. Hosea—a God who is both a jealous God and one of great mercy acts so that "justification means the judgment of the sinner, judgment over his previous ways, *and* acquittal and a new beginning" (Hos 2:15; p. 48)

B. In the basic structure of God's actions with his people—Israel's history is one of Rechtfertigungsgeschenen (p. 66)

II. With regard to individuals:

A. In the "psalms of the individual," the ordering of the world by righteousness forms the background for the person who prays

B. And determines the self-understanding of the person before God (e.g., Pss 17:1–5; 18:22–24; 33)

C. The delivery of the person who prays in the psalms reflects thanksgiving (*tôdâ*) for God's mighty deeds, that is, "righteousness" (*ṣdq*), God's "justification" (77:16–18; 40:9–10)

Then Reventlow goes on to suggest the significance of this OT idea of justification for Christian theology, especially by showing its importance for interpreting the cross of Jesus (see below, Section II).
48   The book can be criticized for attempting to subsume too much under justification/righteousness, for speaking too broadly in biblical theology and spreading the nets too widely in equating one theme with another, and for assuming, in Israel's case, a basis in the doctrine of creation, rather than in that of redemption, for "Gerechtigkeit als Weltordnung."[29] But unless we are to be blind to the NT itself, the roots for early Christian understanding of justification/righteousness are in the OT, and too often that broad horizon has been ignored in concentrating on Paul alone.

B. Jesus

49   While the OT background is especially relevant for the ministry and teachings of Jesus, his employment of righteousness/justification as a theme can be treated very briefly, for he seems not to have employed this

---

29. Cf. the review by Norman Habel, then at Concordia Seminary, St. Louis, in *JBL* 91 (1972): 544–46. On creation and redemption, see for further bibliography and my own views, *Creation and New Creation: The Past, Present, and Future of God's Creative Activity* (Minneapolis: Augsburg, 1973), pp. 57–82, 102–04. For a more recent "Lutheran" reading of themes usually associated with Paul, in their locus in the Hebrew Scriptures, cf. Ronald M. Hals, *Grace and Faith in the Old Testament* (Minneapolis: Augsburg, 1980).

language very much. Only by looking at the content of ideas and actions, rather than at vocabulary, can any significant links be suggested.

1. Statistically, *dikaiosynē*, the noun, occurs chiefly in Matthew among the gospels (once at Luke 1:75; twice at John 16:8, 10); the seven Matthean occurrences may all be redaction. See below in § IV. A.3.c, 229–37, 239–40, 242.

The verb *dikaioō* carries a juridical sense of "be justified (or condemned, *katadikaioō*) by your words" at Matthew 12:37 and of "justify oneself, represent oneself as righteous" at Luke 10:29 and 16:15. Luke 7:29, in narrative, reports that the tax collectors justified or vindicated God by accepting baptism, i.e., they acknowledged God's justice instead of rejecting his purpose (7:30). In the Q-statement, "Wisdom is justified by (all) her works/children" (Matt 11:19 par. Luke 7:35), the sense is presumably "vindicated." Only Luke 18:4 (on which, see below § IV.B.1, 247) can be accounted significant for our topic in the seven verb examples.

The adjective *dikaios* (17× in Matt, 2× in Mark, 11× in Luke, 3× in John) is used of Jesus by Pilate's wife (Matt 27:19, cf. 27:4) and by the centurion at the cross in Luke (23:47) in the sense of "innocent." It is used of other persons frequently in the OT sense of "just" or "righteous," keeping God's laws (Matt 1:19, 13:17, 23:29, 35; cf. Luke 1:6, 2:25), and, in a pejorative sense, of hypocritically appearing to be righteous (Matt 23:38, cf. Luke 20:9). Mark 2:17 and parallels (". . . not to call the 'righteous' but 'sinners' ") probably belongs here, used ironically of those who thought themselves respectable before God.

None of these passages can claim to be significant for establishing a view on Jesus' part about God's righteousness or justification. He reflects OT senses of the term without making it a major theme.[30]

50 2. Jesus' central message was "the kingdom of God," i.e., Yahweh as king. If that is related to the view of *ṣdq* as cosmic order, which includes the reign of the Lord throughout the world (cf. Pss 93, 97, 99), Jesus is then proclaiming something related to God's righteousness (see above, § 32, Schmid's view), but Synoptic passages do not make this connection overt, unless Matthew 6:33 be counted as authentic rather than its Lucan parallel: "Seek first the kingdom and his righteousness" (Luke 12:31, "Seek his kingdom").

Perhaps more significant is the closing verse in the parable of the Pharisee and the tax collector (Luke 18:14, L), that the latter "went down to his house justified (*dedikaiōmenos*) rather than the other." Because the term has good Jewish background in the sense of "find justice, be vindicat-

---

30. Statistics above from Robert Morgenthaler, *Statistik des neutestamentlichen Wortschatzes* (Zürich/Frankfurt: Gotthelf-Verlag, 1958); cf. *TDNT* and the BAGD under each term. J. Arthur Baird, *The Justice of God in the Teaching of Jesus* (Philadelphia: Westminster, 1963) has little on *ṣdq* (cf. pp. 44–45), focusing rather on "judgment" in biblical theology.

ed, find favor, be treated as just," Pauline influence here is usually excluded (see below, §§ 247, 253). For Jesus' listeners a judicial verdict was involved "in which God attests the integrity of the righteous man."[31] In this case the tax collector did not presume to point to his own righteous deeds and attitudes but threw himself on God's mercy. From the passage, Jeremias suggests that "the Pauline doctrine of justification has its roots in the teaching of Jesus."[32]

Still more telling is the way Jesus shared fellowship at meals, contrary to all kosher regulations, eating and drinking with outcasts. People protested, "This man receives sinners and eats with them" (Luke 15:2; cf. Mark 2:15–17 and par.). The "new quest of the historical Jesus" has widely endorsed this trait as bedrock historicity, and there has often been seen here an implicit expression of the acceptance of sinners, which becomes explicit in the later doctrine of the *justificatio impii.*

51 3. The most direct attempt, hermeneutically, to link the historical Jesus and Paul comes in a book by Eberhard Jüngel in 1962, based on his dissertation, "Das Verhältnis der paulinischen Rechtfertigungslehre zur Verkündigung Jesu."[33] Jüngel (pp. 17–70) takes the doctrine of justification to be the center of Paul's theology and "as the theological design, a theology of hope." In Rom 1–3 "wrath" and "righteousness" function as "law and gospel" respectively, and the reading of Paul is reflective of Reformation theology.

Jüngel finds Jesus' message centered in the kingdom of God. This kingdom is to be seen not merely in the parables, as a topic of them, but present "as parable," so that the parables are themselves the coming of the kingdom, spoken "onto" the hearer (*ansagen,* p. 172; see 173–74 and 196–97 for his summaries on Jesus' message). If Jesus' teaching about the kingdom represents the nearness of God coming to expression, his sayings about the Son of man (eight of which are accepted as genuine) represent the distance of God. The kingdom thus makes us think of God's grace; the Son of man, of God's judgment.

52 The relationship between Jesus' proclamation and the Pauline doc-

---

31. Eta Linnemann, *Jesus of the Parables: Interpretation and Exposition* (New York: Harper & Row, 1967), p. 63.

32. Joachim Jeremias, *The Parables of Jesus,* rev. ed. (New York: Scribner's, 1963), p. 141. Jeremias observes later (p. 155, n. 13), in connection with Luke 18:8 (God will vindicate his elect, but "when the Son of man comes, will he find faith on earth?"), that the emphasis on "faith" there "can hardly be attributed to Pauline influence." Schrenk, *TDNT,* 2, p. 215, speaks at Luke 18:14 of "saving righteousness," comparing Paul, and notes the fact that it is a present righteousness here in Luke (Greek, "having been rightwised and therefore in a righteous relationship") without any reference "to the saving act of the cross." But the latter point is perfectly understandable against an OT background and as a feature of Lucan theology (see §§ 247, 249, 252–53).

33. Diss. under Ernst Fuchs, Berlin Kirchliche Hochschule. Published as *Paulus und Jesus: Eine Untersuchung zur Präzisierung der Frage nach dem Ursprung der Christologie* (Hermeneutische Untersuchungen zur Theologie 2; Tübingen: Mohr-Siebeck, 1962; 2nd ed. 1964 cited below).

trine of justification then lies, first, in the eschatological character of each (pp. 263–68): In the terms *basileia tou theou* (for Jesus) and *dikaiosynē theou* (for Paul) an eschatological phenomenon is being expressed. Jüngel argues for another link in the way the old word of the law comes to new expression in both Jesus and Paul, particularly in their view of the love-command as the basic content of the law (Mark 12:28–31, par.; Rom 13:8–10). This position involves Jüngel in seeing a positive sense for Paul in his reference to "the law of Christ" (Gal 6:2).

The difference between Jesus and Paul, according to Jüngel, is the fact that "Jesus looks to the future, to the *coming* kingdom of God—which is coming or dawning *now*. But Paul looks back . . . to an event which enables him to maintain that in Jesus the eschaton has occurred."[34] There is also a seeming difference in the way they look at faith. For Paul, it is *pistis Iēsou Christou* (objective genitive), "faith in Jesus Christ," and justification is "a theological interpretation of the faith-event": "In believing on Jesus the Christ, one participates in the *dikaiosynē theou,* where God proclaims a person justified by faith" (p. 275). In Jesus' proclamation, faith scarcely has a role. But in the healing miracles we do find faith stressed ("be it unto you according to your faith") as "participation in God's power"; indeed, these stories "are exemplary stories for the power of faith which is awakened through Jesus."[35] One can go further and say that precisely in the words of Jesus "Only believe!" (*monon pisteue,* Mark 5:36) one has in essence Paul's phrase, "faith alone"![36]

53   Thus, even though there is a terminological difference, historically, between Jesus and Paul, there is an identity eschatologically of eschaton and history: "Paul looks back to the eschaton in that he brings it to expression as the revelation of God's righteousness in Jesus' death and resurrection, while Jesus looks to the future, since he brought the eschaton to expression as the kingdom of God".[37] Paul's gospel thus becomes Jesus' kingdom message, restated, in light of his death and resurrection.

---

34. Ibid., p. 272, quoting Rudolf Bultmann, "The Significance of the Historical Jesus for the Theology of Paul," original German essay in *Theologische Blätter* 8 (1929), later in *Glauben und Verstehen I* (Tübingen: Mohr-Siebeck, 1933), p. 195; trans. in *Faith and Understanding I,* ed. R. Funk (New York: Harper & Row, 1969), p. 233.

35. Willi Marxsen, *The Beginnings of Christology* (FBBS 22; 1969), p. 55; 2d ed. (1979), p. 66.

36. Gerhard Ebeling, "Jesus and Faith," an essay originally in *ZTK* 55 (1958): 64–110, which supplements a serious deficiency in Bultmann's *TDNT* article on *pisteuō, pistis;* trans. in Ebeling's *Word and Faith* (Philadelphia: Fortress, 1963), pp. 201–45, especially 230, n. 2, and 245.

37. Jüngel, *Paulus und Jesus,* p. 282: "Das *eschatologische Identität* von Eschaton und Geschichte zeitigt sich als *sprachliche Differenz* innerhalb der Geschichte. So erklärt es sich aber auch, dass Paulus auf des Eschaton zurückblickt, indem er es als Offenbarung der *dikaiosynē theou* im Tod und in der Auferstehung Jesu zur Sprache bringt, während Jesus in die Zukunft blickte, wenn er das Eschaton als *basileia tou theou* zur Sprache brachte." The importance of the book for existential heremeneutics and the new quest was indicated in reviews by James M. Robinson, *Int* 18 (1964): 346–59, and by E. Käsemann, *Theologische Li-*

Without attention to the OT, in spite of the paucity of *dikaio-* vocabulary, using an existentialist hermeneutic, Jüngel has forged a claim for continuity between Jesus and justification in Paul in terms of content of their central messages. The two relate in terms of the *sachlich,* not in vocabulary.

More than one commentator has been struck with Jesus' message and actions as "grace" and with "faith" as the response the kingdom calls for—as Mark's summary of the kerygma puts it, "The kingdom of God is at hand, repent and believe in the gospel." Paul will speak of justification (only occasionally of the kingdom of God) as coming "by grace . . . through faith."[38]

54   4. Whether or not one gives credence to such links between Jesus and justification in Paul, the fact is that righteousness/justification as a theme, in express terms, will be applied by early Christianity only after Easter. It is part of the apostolic message, connected above all with the atonement, not a theme in Jesus' own preaching. In that way, it lies at the heart of the basic Christian proclamation, about the meaning of Christ's death.

---

teraturzeitung 90 (1965): 184–87, who differs over whether Paul has a "positive" view of the law such as Jüngel assumes.

38. Reventlow, *Rechtfertigung,* pp. 114–15, points out that what Jüngel suggested about the *basileia tou theou* and *dikaiosynē theou* as "gospel" in different situations "shows once again the unity of Herrschaft and Recht, as they are included in the OT concept of *sdq/sdqh,* as foundation for the NT thought-world."

II. In Earliest Apostolic Christianity: Kerygma, Christology, and Atonement, ca. A.D. 30–50

55 By whatever name we choose to designate the emerging "Jesus-movement" after Easter, the earliest Christian community (Urgemeinde), in a matrix of apocalyptic expectation now that God had raised Jesus from the dead, developed from Palestinian to Jewish-Hellenistic to more specifically Hellenistic Christianity. It is customary in contemporary biblical scholarship to trace Christian origins and development from Jerusalem and Galilee through such steps of advance on the basis of materials in Acts and traditions recovered from the epistles and from the gospels, before examining the work of Paul himself and other specific author-theologians.

56 1. The *kerygma* or apostolic preaching has, even before the analysis by C. H. Dodd in 1936, been a standard starting point for treating this period. But neither Dodd's analysis of the "Jerusalem kerygma" based on sermons in Acts nor even his summary of the "Pauline kerygma" yields any reference to justification or righteousness as part of the basic contents. The same result obtains from the treatments by Harnack or more recently by Bo Reicke. That is not surprising since the basic Easter gospel concerned the assertion that God had raised the crucified One and now offers salvation through him, that is, forgiveness of sins, the gift of the Spirit, and life in the kingdom, to those who repent and believe. Cf. especially Acts 3:19, 5:31, 10:43, and 13:38 on "forgiveness of sins" as a key theme in the *ordo salutis* of these sermons, even though no direct connection is made with the death of Jesus. Forgiveness and faith were thus part of the offer and response, but other aspects, including christological titles and a "doctrine of the atonement," were not yet developed to any considerable degree.[39]

57   We may mention just one relevant epithet for Jesus: He is sometimes referred to as "the Righteous One" (*ho dikaios*). Where used in Acts (3:14, 7:52, 22:14), this possible messianic designation (see n. 21) may refer to nothing more than Jesus' piety and obedience in conforming to God's will, as in the OT "righteous ones," but 22:14 uses the title for the Just One who, risen, spoke to Paul on Damascus Road, and 1 Pet 3:18 and 1 John 2:1 more definitely relate the term to Jesus' work of atonement and of intercession (cf. also 1 John 2:29, 3:7).[40] It has been urged that "the title was used for a time in the primitive community at Jerusalem," in light of Isa 53:11 (". . . the righteous one, my servant, shall make many to be accounted righteous").[41]

58   2. An alternative approach for this period is to see as basic not so propositional a kerygmatic summary as in Dodd but rather brief confessional slogans such as "Christ died for our sins" or "God raised Jesus from the dead." These are the "building blocks" with which Paul and others then do theology, and they take us back to the earliest accessible period of Christian theology after Easter. Such oral formulations from early Christianity took many forms, including the elaborate hymns of Phil 2:6–11 and Col 1:15–20, which are about the work and person of the Redeemer but which do not mention justification or, for that matter, "covenant" or the cross (assuming Phil 2:8*c* is Paul's own addition).

59   Hans Conzelmann has, following others, especially in the Bultmann School, stressed these creeds about the work of Jesus and "homologiae" about his person.[42] It is in these early formulations that we find the signifi-

---

39. C. H. Dodd, *The Apostolic Preaching and Its Developments* (London: Hodder & Stoughton, 1936). Cf. Adolf Harnack's *History of Dogma,* trans. N. Buchanan, 1900 (New York: Dover Publications, 1961), p. 78. Bo Reicke in *The Root of the Vine* (London: Dacre Press, 1953), pp. 128–60. Further analysis and bibliography in J. Reumann, "The Kerygma and the Preacher," *Dialog* 3 (1964): 29–31. On the Lucan sequence of ideas, cf. Ulrich Wilckens, *Die Missionsreden der Apostelgeschichte* (WMANT 5; 3d ed. 1974), pp. 178–86.

40. Schrenk, *TDNT* 2, pp. 188–89. Ziesler, *Righteousness in Paul,* pp. 136–38.

41. Vincent Taylor, *The Names of Jesus* (London: Macmillan, 1954), pp. 82–83. Space does not permit treatment of the possibility that in some NT passages Jesus is identified as the "righteous, vindicated sufferer" of OT piety, as in Hartmut Gese's proposal that the Lord's Supper of the early church arose out of the "*tôdâ*-ceremony" of ancient Israel (*ZTK* 65 [1968]: 1–22; more recently, in his *Zur biblischen Theologie* [Munich: Kaiser, 1977], pp. 107–27; discussion in J. Reumann, "Psalm 22 at the Cross," *Int* 28 [1974]: 43–48, 54–55), or "der leidende Gerechte" of Isa 53, the Pss, and other OT and intertestamental literature, as developed in the two-volume Würzburg dissertation *Passio iusti* (published 1972–73) by Lothar Ruppert, summarized in his *Jesus als der leidende Gerechte?* (SBS 59; 1972).

42. *An Outline of the Theology of the New Testament* (New York: Harper & Row, 1969) pp. 62–71, 87–88. His classical passage is Rom 10: 9, ". . . if you confess (*homologēsēs*) . . . that 'Jesus is Lord' and believe . . . that 'God raised him from the dead,' you will be saved." The first slogan he designates as a homologia or acclamation, the latter a creed. The importance of the prepauline materials on justification, especially in connection with baptism, was noted by E. Lohse, among others, in LWF theological discussions for Helsinki as early as 1959; see *Justification Today* (cited above, n. 2), p. 21.

cant beginnings for Christian use of righteousness/justification terminology, especially in presenting the meaning of the cross (and of the resurrection). Dating such materials with any precision is impossible, but it is widely acknowledged that such passages as we now examine are older, often far older, than the documents in which they appear.

60 a. **1 Peter 3:18** is a good example of such a creedal summary using righteousness terminology: "Christ suffered [or, variant reading, "died"] for sins once for all, the Righteous One for those who are unrighteous (*Christos hapax peri hamartiōn epathen* [*or apethanen*], *dikaios hyper adikōn*), in order that he might bring us to God."

The epistle and its milieu are well acquainted with the OT sense of *dikaios* for a "righteous person." Cf. 3:12 (= Ps 34:16); 4:18 (= Prov 11:31 LXX). One verse speaks of God as "Him who judges justly" (*dikaiōs*, 2:23). There is specific citation of Isa 53 in describing Christ who suffered for us (2:21) at 2:22 (= Isa 53:9, "[sin] he did not commit, guile was not found in his mouth") and at 2:24–25 ("he himself bore our sins," ". . . by his wounds you were healed," ". . . like sheep straying"; cf. Isa 53:4, 12, 5, 6). The possibility is mentioned that Christians may have to suffer "for righteousness' sake" (3:14, cf. Matt 5:10).

A number of scholars, beginning at least with Hans Windisch in 1930, have seen behind such references an early Christian hymn, now to be found in 3:18a or 18–19, or running through the whole epistle, perhaps also in a fragment at 1:20, and behind 2:21–24. Others add more or all of 3:18–22 to this hymnic creed. E. G. Selwyn (pp. 17–18) thought 3:18, 19, 22 rested "on the credal hymn quoted in 1 Tim iii. 16." Others see the line of influence running from 1 Pet or a form behind it to 1 Tim 3:16. The subject in 3:18 is, in any case, the righteous, suffering One (E. Schweizer) and his death, which may be seen as a "sin offering" for the impious (*peri hamartiōn* can be in the LXX a sacrificial term, cf. Lev 6:23, 14:19; cf. further Heb 10:6, 8). The verb *dikaioō* does not occur in 1 Peter.[43]

---

43. H. Windisch, *Die katholische Briefe* (HNT 15; 3d ed., 1951), pp. 70, 154. E. G. Selwyn, *The First Epistle of Peter* (London: Macmillan, 1952), pp. 17–18, 273–77 (a hymn stressing "belief" behind 2:4–8); 195, 325–26 (possible doctrinal adaptation at 3:18–4:6 of an earlier hymn). R. Bultmann, "Bekenntnis- und Liedfragmente im ersten Petrusbrief," *Coniectanea Neotestamentica 11* (Lund, 1974): 1–14, reprinted in Bultmann's *Exegetica*, ed. E. Dinkler (Tübingen: Mohr-Siebeck, 1967), pp. 285–97 (includes 1:20, but ignores 1 Tim 3:16 as a parallel). Eduard Schweizer, *Lordship and Discipleship* (SBT 28; 1960), pp. 59, 67. Jack T. Sanders, *The New Testament Christological Hymns: Their Historical Religious Background* (SNTSMS 15; 1971), pp. 17–18, 95–96. K. H. Schelkle, *Die Petrusbriefe* (HTKNT 13/2; 1964), pp. 110–12, treats material from 1:18–21, 2:21–25, and 3:18–22 as "Christologische Formeln" (kerygma, hymnic material). Kazuhito Shimada, "The Christological Credal Formula in I Peter 3, 18–22—Reconsidered," *Annual of the Japanese Biblical Institute* 5 (1979): 154–76, is very thorough on method and bibliography; he finds a creedal formula in vv. 18ac, 19a, 22, but views *dikaios hyper adikōn* as a "traditional fragmentary formula" added to this formula "to reiterate the vicarious significance of the death of Christ." C.-H. Hunzinger, "Zur Struktur der Christus-Hymnen in Phil 2 und 1. Petr 3," in *Der Ruf Jesu und die Antwort der Gemeinde* (Jeremias fs; Göttingen: Vandenhoeck & Ruprecht, 1970), pp. 142–56, reconstructs a three-stanza hymn from 3:18–19a, 22b(a)c, akin to that at Phil 2:6–11.

61   b. **1 Timothy 3:16** is even more readily singled out as a hymn that is earlier than its present context, perhaps stemming from Hellenistic-Jewish Christianity. It is about Christ,

> Who was manifested in the flesh,
> vindicated (*edikaiōthē*) in the spirit,
>   seen by angels,
> preached among the nations,
> believed on (*episteuthē*) in the world,
>   taken up in glory.

Six verbs, all in the aorist passive, plus a noun in the dative case with each, five of these nouns with the same preposition in Greek, clearly suggest a rhythmic structure. There seems a careful alternating between the earthly and heavenly spheres, *ab, ba, ab* in sequence. But there is no reference to the cross or to Jesus' death. What does the second line mean?

Jeremias saw here an "enthronement hymn," as in the Psalms and the ancient Near East: exaltation, presentation, and enthronement, over heavenly and earthly worlds. Others have seen the stages of Jesus' career presented in terms of epiphanies at his birth (line 1), baptism, etc.; line 2 then reflects the baptismal account we know in Matthew (the angelic voice from heaven, and "to fulfill all righteousness," Matt 3:15; cf. A. Descamps, *Les Justes;* Holtz).

Analogues have been suggested from later, often Gnostic materials (cf. Dibelius-Conzelmann, Hermeneia, pp. 62–63), but the most likely explanation is that we have reflected here the "justification" of Jesus in the OT sense of "vindication," in a forensic setting: He who was manifested in the flesh is exalted to the heavenly realms and thereby shown to be "in the right." This means eschatological victory in the "lawsuit" of God and Christ against the world (cf. Rom 3:4 = Ps 51:4, an OT sense about the vindication of God that is not Paul's normal usage).[44] Such is part of "the mystery of our religion" (3:16*a*).

---

44. **Literature on 1 Tim 3:16** (cf. n. 43 for full titles): E. Schweizer, *Lordship,* pp. 64–66, and his article "Two Early Christian Creeds Compared, I Corinthians 15. 3–5 and I Timothy 3.16," in *Current Issues in New Testament Interpretation* (Otto Piper fs; ed. W. Klassen and G. F. Snyder; New York: Harper & Row, 1962), pp. 166–77. J. T. Sanders, *Hymns,* pp. 15–17, 94–95.

J. Jeremias, *Die Briefe an Timotheus und Titus* (NTD 9; 4th ed., 1947), pp. 23–25 ("gerechtfertigt im Geist" means here Gerechtsprechung: "God shows before all the world that the one who was condemned on the cross as a law-breaker is den Gerechten"). Albert Descamps, *Les Justes et la justice dans les évangiles et le christianisme primitif* (Louvain: Gembloux, 1950), p. 87. Gottfried Holtz, *Die Pastoralbriefe* (THKNT 13; 1965), p. 91, who treats 3:16 in a eucharistic setting as a "Präfationshymnus," refers to the possible sequence of incarnation, Jesus' baptism, proclamation of the gospel, ascension, and exaltation, but prefers the sense "er wurde zum Sieg geführt." See also the penetrating analysis in R. Bultmann, *The Gospel of John* (Philadelphia: Westminster, 1971), pp. 564–65, especially nn. 2 and 3. Ziesler,

62   c. Jesus, in such early Christian creedal formulas, is the Righteous One who died for the unrighteous and who has been vindicated by God against this world; he who is to be believed on is thus *dikaios* in the double sense of "obedient to God's will," especially at the cross, and "declared righteous, vindicated by God" at the resurrection. It is but a short step, therefore, to speak of him as "our righteousness . . . from God." Some interpreters see this application at **1 Cor 1:30** as a prepauline coinage. The verse reads, literally,

> From him [God] you are (exist, have a real being, in contrast to *ta mē onta,* "the things which do not exist," v. 28) in Christ Jesus, who became wisdom for us from God, both righteousness and sanctification and redemption . . . (*hos egenēthē sophia hēmin apo theou, dikaiosynē te kai hagiasmos kai apolytrōsis . . .*).[45]

J. B. Lightfoot, in the last century, pointed out that here "righteousness and sanctification" go closely together and suggested that they are in apposition to "wisdom." All would agree that the four terms applied to Christ are alien to human nature, for they are "from God" in Christ "for us." In the history of interpretation Theodor Zahn and Ernst Gaugler have viewed the verse as central for understanding Paul's doctrine of justification and as exemplifying the close identity of Christology and justification. In more recent years the tendency has been to see here a prepauline formula quoted and adapted to meet the situation Paul is addressing in Corinth, i.e., those who stress a "wisdom-Christology" of their own that

---

Righteousness, pp. 154–55. Martin Dibelius-Hans Conzelmann, *The Pastoral Epistles* (Hermeneia; 1972), pp. 61–63: "vindicated" in the sense of "enter into the divine realm" of righteousness.

Strong on the OT backgrounds is W. Stenger, "Der Christushymnus in I Tim 3,16. Aufbau—Christologie—Sitz im Leben," *TTZ* 78 (1969): 33–48 (originally a hymn praising the exalted Lord, in Jewish-Christian liturgy; line 2, *edikaiōthē* reflects the idea of God's mighty acts, *sidqôt YHWH;* the angels and nations are part of the cosmic lawsuit setting).

45. **Literature on 1 Cor 1:30:** J. B. Lightfoot, *Notes on the Epistles of St. Paul* (London: Macmillan, 1895), p. 167; Th. Zahn, *Römer* (Kommentar zum Neuen Testament 6; 1925, ad loc.) and E. Gaugler, *Die Römerbrief* (Prophezie; Zürich: Zwingli-Verlag, 1945–52), as cited in Stuhlmacher, *Gerechtigkeit,* pp. 41 and 65, cf. 185–86. Karl Kertelge, *'Rechtfertigung' bei Paulus: Studien zur Struktur und zum Bedeutungsgehalt des paulinischen Rechtfertigungsbegriffs* (Neutestamentliche Abhandlungen, N.F.3; Münster: Aschendorff, 1967), pp. 52, 302, 304. E. Käsemann, "Some Thoughts on the Theme, 'The Doctrine of Reconciliation in the New Testament,' " in *The Future of Our Religious Past,* ed. James M. Robinson (New York: Harper & Row, 1971), p. 53 (originally in *Zeit und Geschichte, Dankesgabe an Rudolf Bultmann* [1964], p. 50). C. K. Barrett, *1 Corinthians* (HNTC, 1968), pp. 60–61. Jean Héring, *1 Corinthians* (London: Epworth, 1962), p. 13. H. Conzelmann, *1 Corinthians* (Hermeneia; 1975), p. 52. Wilhelm Thüsing, "Rechtfertigungsgedanke und Christologie in den Korintherbriefen," in *Neues Testament und Kirche* (Schnackenburg fs, ed. J. Gnilka; Freiburg: Herder, 1974), pp. 301–24. Ronald Y.-K. Fung, "Justification by Faith in 1 & 2 Corinthians," in *Pauline Studies* (F. F. Bruce fs; ed. D. A. Hagner and M. J. Harris, Grand Rapids: Eerdmans, 1980), pp. 246–61, deals solely with the present expression of the theme in 1 and 2 Cor.

threatens to isolate "the Lord of glory" from "Christ crucified" (on the formula, cf., e.g., Käsemann, Stuhlmacher, Kertelge). The early, likely Jewish-Christian formula ran thus:

> who became righteousness-and-sanctification and redemption
>   for us from God.

Paul would be employing it as an agreed formulation to expound "wisdom" before going into the *sophia* question in chap. 2, much the way he cites the tradition they all accept at 1 Cor 15:3–5 before discussing the resurrection in chap. 15.

63   What does *dikaiosynē* here mean? Of the commentators, Barrett (like Fung, p. 248) sees it as forensic, "a direct product of Christ's self-offering for men, the work of redemption"; Héring, as "justification." Stuhlmacher views Christ in 1:30 as "the founder and thereby the embodiment of our *dikaiosynē,* our *hagiasmos* and the *apolytrōsis* which befalls us . . ., the pardoning demonstration of God's fidelity to his covenant." Kertelge speaks of Christ in the verse thus: he "uns von Gott her zur Gerechtigkeit geworden ist" (pp. 302, 304). F. Hahn (in *Rechtfertigung,* Käsemann fs, pp. 95–124) suggests a christological correspondence (in reverse order) to the baptismal formula at 6:11. While Conzelmann doubts that the three "soteriological concepts" are "systematically arranged," he stresses here the alien character of *dikaiosynē* in the reference (*apo theou*). Thüsing (p. 304) suggests that *dikaiosynē apo theou* is in Paul's "redaction" a synonym for *dikaiosynē theou*. The likelihood that we have here a prepauline formula about Christ as God's righteousness (mighty deed? *sidqôt*) who brings us justification/sanctification/redemption is made more persuasive only when we look at two other possibly prepauline passages, 1 Cor 6:11 and 2 Cor 5:21.

64   d. **1 Corinthians 6:11** is widely conceded to be a prepauline formulation about baptism (so Lohse, Kertelge, Stuhlmacher, among others):[46]

> You were washed (*apelousasthe*), you were sanctified (*hēgiasthēte*), you were justified (*edikaiōthēte*) in the name of the Lord Jesus Christ and in the Spirit of our God.

---

46. **1 Cor 6:11:** In addition to the commentaries in n. 45, see Eduard Lohse, "Taufe und Rechtfertigung bei Paulus," *KD* 11 (1965): 308–24, esp. 321–22. Kertelge, pp. 242–45, 277, 297–98. Stuhlmacher, pp. 219, 221, 223. Ferdinand Hahn, "Taufe und Rechtfertigung: Ein Beitrag zur paulinischen Theologie in ihrer Vor- und Nachgeschichte," in *Rechtfertigung* (Käsemann fs, cited above, n. 18), esp. 104–08; one may remain doubtful, however, on Hahn's theory that Paul is correcting an earlier view found in these prepauline formulas of "justification through baptism." Ziesler, pp. 156–58 (three aspects of the Spirit's action in our redemption; "justified" is forensic and also implies moral renewal; but Ziesler is discussing only the passage as it stands, not distinguishing a prepauline formula).

On the present context, E. Dinkler, "Zum Problem der Ethik bei Paulus: Rechtsnahme und Rechtsverzicht (I Kor. 6, 1–11)" is helpful, in *ZTK* 49 (1952): 167–200, esp. 188–89;

Clues: three verbs in the passive voice (or the first one middle for passive), the parallelism, the liturgical-sounding phrases at the end; the use of *apolouō* (otherwise Paul uses *baptizō*), and perhaps the sense of *dikaioō*.

Commentators, particularly those under the influence of the *ordo salutis* espoused in Lutheran Orthodoxy (cf. the Formula of Concord) have often been troubled by the sequence "sanctified," then "justified." The phrases are not describing a sequential process except in the "formerly/now" contrast between what the Corinthians once were (6:9–11a) and what they are now "in Christ." Paul has a different starting point at 6:11 (baptism) than at 1:30, and so perhaps the difference in order from "righteousness/sanctification" there. It is likely that the terms were originally synonymous.

65   What does *dikaioō* mean here in the formula? If a distinction is to be made from "sanctified," then in the formula quoted it means simply the "forgiveness of sins" (so Bultmann, *Theology,* 1, p. 136; Lohse). While Conzelmann finds in 6:11 "the full sense of the Pauline concept of justification" (p. 107), Kertelge, who notes the verse was long "the *locus classicus* for the Catholic doctrine of justification," follows Lohse in seeing in the formula the sense of "forgiveness of sins on the ground of Christ's atoning death" (p. 245), as at Rom 3:25 (where Paul, however, will also give his own further meaning to a traditional formulation).

66   e. **2 Corinthians 5:21** is described by Conzelmann (*1 Corinthians,* p. 52) as "the commentary" on 1 Cor 1:30. Käsemann has suggested "a pre-Pauline hymnic fragment" here running through vv. 19–21, on the basis of solemn style, use of participles, and affinity in content with Rom 3:25, among other reasons.[47]

Response has been reserved. Stuhlmacher's counterthesis (pp. 77–78, n. 2) allows in 5:18–21 at best reflection of traditionally stamped, liturgical formulations, and for v. 21 that, though it rests on Jewish-Christian tradition (like Rom 3:24ff.), its formulation and thought (cf. Rom 7:7) corresponds to Paul's own theology and the verse is styled by Paul himself. Thüsing (pp. 310–11) reacts similarly. Kertelge notes, however, that the verse does not connect directly either in grammar or in expression with the previous verses on reconciliation (19–20).

---

reprinted in his *Signum Crucis* (Tübingen: Mohr-Siebeck, 1967), pp. 204–40, especially 226–27.

47. **Literature referred to on 2 Cor 5:21:** Käsemann, "Reconciliation" (see n. 45), pp. 52–55. Stuhlmacher, pp. 74–78. Kertelge, pp. 99–107. On structure, cf. J. Jeremias, "Chiasmus in den Paulusbriefen," *ZNW* 49 (1958): 146 (= *Abba,* Ges. Aufs., p. 278); Barrett, *2 Corinthians* (HNTC, 1973), p. 179. A. Plummer (ICC, 1915). Ziesler, pp. 159–61 ("we . . . share the covenant loyalty which hitherto has been God's alone"). R. Bultmann's commentary in the MeyerK series (1976), pp. 167–68, holds to his consistent view that here *dikaiosynē theou* means "die von Gott geschenkte Gerechtigkeit"; he does not explore Käsemann's proposal of prepauline material. O. Hofius, "Erwägungen zur Gestalt und Herkunft des paulinischen Versöhnungsgedankens," *ZTK* 77 (1980): 186–99, argues that Paul himself wrote 5:18–21, based on Isa 52:13–53:12 and 52:6–10.

While I think a case can be made for more of vv. 19–21 as prepauline, as it can for 5:14, "One died for all," we shall confine ourselves to 5:21 as a possible earlier formula, running, literally,

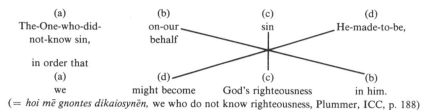

(a)	(b)	(c)	(d)
The-One-who-did-	on-our	sin	He-made-to-be,
not-know sin,	behalf		

in order that

(a)	(d)	(c)	(b)
we	might become	God's righteousness	in him.

(= *hoi mē gnontes dikaiosynēn,* we who do not know righteousness, Plummer, ICC, p. 188)

Barrett objects that the chiasmus (*b-d, d-b*) "is imperfect," but there are minor patterns like

ton mē gnonta ———————— *hamartia . . .*
hamartian ———————— *epoiēsen.*

In many chronological reconstructions of the sequence for Paul's letters, 2 Cor 5:21 marks the first time an extant letter employs *dikaiosynē theou.*
67   What is meant in this possible formula? First, the content is clearly christological. Some number of commentators even see "God's righteousness" as a title that refers to the presence of salvation in Christ; indeed, he is identical with *dikaiosynē theou* (Nygren, *Romans* [1975], p. 76; cf. Jer 23:5–6; further references in Kertelge, p. 104). The "sinless One" is said to have "become sin." Since at least Augustine this has been referred to the "sin offering" of ancient Israelite cult (cf. Rom 8:3), and that remains a possible interpretation (so Ziesler, p. 160, n. 1), though Barrett (p. 180) denies it.
Kertelge sees here "identification with our sins" (p. 103), and in the sense that *hamartia* designates "die Macht der Sünde," he points toward the Stuhlmacher line of interpretation where, in parallel to what God made Jesus subject to, namely *hamartia, dikaiosynē theou* means not just a gift of God but "eine Macht" (p. 75); as Stuhlmacher puts it, in the full context of the passage, "die im Wort des Paulus erscheinende, in Dienst nehmende, das Gericht und die Neuschöpfung in sich beschliessende kosmische Macht und Erscheinungsweise des Schöpfergottes" (p. 77). But that assumes the OT, cosmic apocalyptic sense of the phrase "God's righteousness" and a fuller context in chap. 5, either from Paul or a prepauline formula. The same thing is true when Ziesler allows the note of "new creation" (v. 17) as well as the forensic side (pp. 160–61). Barrett (pp. 180–81), too, hovers between the forensic sense and that of Stuhlmacher (p. 208), when the latter calls Christ "the embodiment" of the faithfulness of the Creator to his creation.
68   We do well for the prepauline formula to confine its meaning to a saving act by God through the deed of Christ for us, whereby we in Christ

become "God's righteousness." Interpreters have seen the heart of the verse in the idea of "substitution" (*hyper hymōn,* so Luther, Lietzmann, Strachan) *or* of "justification" (K. Prümm, H. D. Wendland), *or* in "our life or being 'in Christ,' " i.e., new creation (Kertelge, pp. 105–06, where references for the other views mentioned are given). But the last-mentioned emphasis depends on going beyond the putative formula.

Like other such eschatological formulas at which we have looked in early Christianity, the emphasis is, in any case, on the atonement and its meaning, but there is no explanation of (a) how Christ's suffering/dying/vindication effects the forgiveness implied, or (b) what the ethical implications are beyond "sanctification."

We may note in these last three passages a communal side (as in 2 Cor 5:21, "for us, we"), a baptismal connection (1 Cor 6:11), and a link to the Spirit (6:11). The next passage is the major one reflecting prepauline thinking about Jesus' death in terms of God's righteousness. Here, more so than in previous verses, "the death of Jesus is now no longer merely a transitional stage on the victorious road to exaltation. It is conceived of soteriologically" (Käsemann, "Reconciliation," p. 56).

69   3. *The formulas in Romans.* It is in Paul's letter to Rome that the most extensive work, debate, and probably agreement has occurred with regard to prepauline formulas using *dikaiosynē*-terminology. There is no question but that Rom 10:9–10 employs the slogans "Jesus is Lord" and "God raised him from the dead" in connection with confession of what is believed, faith, and justification, but the composition there is surely Paul's own. A case has been made for seeing a chain of phrases known in the church to which Paul is writing, which runs from chap. 4 (at the end) through chap. 8, reconstructed as follows (by Ernst Fuchs):

> [We believe in] Jesus our Lord,
>   who was put to death for our trespasses
>   and was raised again for our justification,
>   who is at the right hand of God,
>   and intercedes for us,
>   through whom we have access to God (4:24–25; 8:34*cd;* 5:1–2).[48]

Most of these ideas are ones with which we have already met in putative early Christian formulas or are classified as prepauline by C. H. Dodd in his analysis of the kerygma (notably 8:34), but because this concatenation has received less discussion in the critical literature, we here put little emphasis on it as a whole, familiar as the association of justification with the atoning death and resurrection is from slogans already noted. (For 4:24–25, §§ 73–75 below.)

70   a. Pride of place among these formulas belongs to that centered in

---

48. Ernst Fuchs, *Die Freiheit des Glaubens: Römer 5–8 ausgelegt* (BEvT 14; 1949), pp. 115–18.

Rom 3:25 and embracing, in most analyses, material before and just after that verse. The literature on it since 1950 is immense, especially by continental Lutheran (Evangelical) and (Roman) Catholic scholars.[49] There are, of course, some who attribute composition of the entire passage to Paul himself (e.g., Kuss; Lyonnet; Cranfield, p. 200, n. 1; Ziesler, pp. 209–10, cf. 192–94, regards the formula as "not implausible" though he seeks to make sense of the verses as they stand). But the trend has clearly been in the direction of recognizing a prepauline fragment here. A very few scholars have gone in the opposite direction and suggest a *post*pauline gloss, at least in v. 25*b* (Talbert, Fitzer), a notion that has attracted little sympathy in the scholarly literature. The chief decision is between a prepauline citation that included only vv. 25–26*a* (in *RSV,* just v. 25; in Greek, include *en tē anochē tou theou* of v. 26) (so Stuhlmacher 1975; Wilckens, p. 183) and one that includes v. 24 as well as 25–26*a* (Bultmann, Käsemann, and others cited in Wilckens, p 183, n. 490). My own judgment (1966), with which Kertelge's careful analysis agrees with only a word or so difference (cf. also Stuhlmacher 1965, p. 88) is that the formulation Paul quotes ran originally like this:

> [24]Being declared righteous as a gift (*dōrean*) through the redemption (*apolytrōseōs*) which is in Messiah Jesus, [25]whom God put forward as a *hilastērion* in his blood, for showing God's righteousness, because of the passing over (*or:* with a view to remission) of former sins, [26a]in the forebearance of God.

---

49. **Earlier literature on Rom 3:24–26** cited in J. Reumann, "The Gospel of the Righteousness of God: Pauline Reinterpretation in Romans 3:21–31," *Int* 20 (1966): 432–52, esp. n. 2; and in Reumann and W. Lazareth, *Righteousness and Society: Ecumenical Dialogue in a Revolutionary Age* (Philadelphia: Fortress, 1967), pp. 26–28. A prepauline quotation here was suggested as early as 1936 by Bultmann; Käsemann developed the suggestion further. A. M. Hunter, *Paul and His Predecessors* (London: SCM, 1940; rev. ed. 1961), pp. 120–22 (rev. ed.), seems first to have advanced the idea in the English literature. Some later literature is summarized in Peter Stuhlmacher, "Zur neueren Exegese von Röm 3, 24–26," in *Jesus und Paulus: Festschrift für Werner Georg Kümmel* (Göttingen: Vandenhoeck & Ruprecht, 1975), pp. 315–33.

Further: Alfons Pluta, *Gottesbundestreue. Ein Schlüsselbegriff in Röm 3: 25a* (SBS 34; 1964). Stuhlmacher, *Gerechtigkeit,* pp. 86–91. Kertelge, pp. 48–62. U. Wilckens, *Römer* (EKKNT) pp. 182–84 and *passim.* C. E. B. Cranfield, *Romans* (ICC) Vol. 1 (1975), pp. 199–218. G. Strecker, "Befreiung und Rechtfertigung: Zur Stellung der Rechtfertigungslehre in der Theologie des Paulis," in *Rechtfertigung* (Käsemann fs), pp. 501–02. For the views of Sam K. Williams, see below, n. 80. Seyoon Kim, *The Origin of Paul's Gospel* (diss. F. F. Bruce; Wissenschaftliche Untersuchungen zum Neuen Testament 2/4; Tübingen: Mohr-Siebeck, 1981), p. 278 finds it "impossible to reach a definite conclusion" on Käsemann's position, which favors a prepauline tradition in contrast to Cranfield's reservations on the point, but then Kim seeks to derive Paul's doctrine of justification (and most of his theology) from his "Damascus experience."

Kertelge (p. 53) would omit "as a gift" and believes Paul himself added both *dōrean* and "by his grace," as well as "through faith." Because Paul never uses *dōrean* in quite the same sense elsewhere (cf. 2 Cor 11:7; Gal 2:21; 2 Thess 3:8) and it is a term drawn from the OT (cf. Rev 21:6, 22:7, based on Isa 55:1), it was likely, I suggest, part of the Hellenistic-Jewish Christian formula that began *dikaioumenoi dōrean*. . . . I am a bit less certain than Kertelge that *en Christō Iēsou* (rendered above, "in Messiah Jesus") was in the original phrasing.

71   What did this Jewish-Christian formulation emphasize? Obviously, Jesus' death ("his blood"—*haima* is regularly employed to refer to it in material that Paul quotes) and the meaning of that death. One key term is *apolytrōsis*, which could, especially in the Greek world, mean "ransom" (of a slave); more likely it means here "redemption" or "liberation" (Büchsel, *TDNT*, 4, p. 355; Kertelge, pp. 53–55). A second significant term is *hilastērion*, where one must choose between two possibilities. (a) Most exegetes give it a cultic background from the OT, relating it to the "mercy seat" of the ark of the covenant in the tabernacle (Exod 25:17–22; 31:7; 35:12; 37:7–9), involved in the ritual for forgiveness of sins on the Day of Atonement (Lev 17); in Hebrew, *kappōret;* Luther, Gnadenstuhl; *RSV,* expiation (*not* "propitiation," as traditionally; it is an expiation for sin, not a propitiation of God; God in the Bible never is or can be propitiated by human beings; at 3:25 it is God who sets forth the expiatory Christ[50]). "Means of expiation" will do as a translation, probably with reference to the Day of Atonement and its ritual imagery, perhaps even in the sense of "place of expiation." (b) The alternative is to take the word to mean "expiatory *sacrifice*" (so Lohse, citing 4 Macc 17:21–22 and even assuming the word *thyma* once stood in the Greek formula).[51] With Kertelge, we may continue to opt for the traditional rendering of "expiation."

72   The formula is specifically about "justification" (*dikaioumenoi*, v. 24), being declared righteous in and through the death of Jesus, which is also a making known of God's righteousness (v. 25): He remains true to his covenant (rigorously argued by Pluta), remitting sins, with forebearance. Those who have broken covenant are "justified" (cf. Kertelge, pp. 59–61). The relationship is renewed by a sacrifice whom God himself puts forth.

Surely the description of what Jesus' death means is being presented

---

50. Cf. C. H. Dodd, *Romans* (MNTC), pp. 54–55, and "Hilaskethai, Its Cognates, Derivatives, and Synonyms, in the Septuagint," *JTS* 32 (1931): 352–60, and more fully in *The Bible and the Greeks* (London: Hodder & Stoughton, 1935), pp. 82–95. Summary and discussion of conservative Protestant literature in favor of "propitiation," by C. Brown, in *NIDNTT,* Vol. 3 (1978), pp. 151–60.

51. Eduard Lohse, *Märtyrer und Gottesknecht: Untersuchungen zur urchristlichen Verkündigung vom Sühntod Jesu Christi* (FRLANT 46; 2d ed. 1963), p. 152. In 4 Macc 17:21, which is roughly contemporaneous with the rise of early Christianity, Eleazer and the other Maccabean martyrs are said to have "as it were become a ransom for our nation's sin."

in terms derived from the OT and Judaism. It must therefore have arisen in Jewish Christianity, which was Greek-speaking, perhaps, we may guess, at Antioch. Its Sitz im Leben der Gemeinde may have been at the Lord's Supper (so Käsemann, Kertelge, because of the reference to Jesus' blood) or, possibly, in connection with baptism (Strecker, p. 504). There is some possibility that the text could once have been connected with a Christian occasion of "covenant-renewal," perhaps even an annual Christian "Good Friday"/Day of Atonement service.

73   b. **Romans 4:25,** it is highly likely, also reflects a prepauline formula about belief in "Him who raised Jesus our Lord from the dead,

> who was put to death for our trespasses (*dia ta paraptōmata hēmōn*),
> and was raised for our justification (*dia tēn dikaiōsin hēmōn*).

Even Cranfield, who is not prone to find prepauline slogans, allows here that v. 25 "looks like a quotation of a traditional formula" (ICC *Romans,* p. 251). The skepticism of Otto Kuss, or the denial of its prepauline nature by W. Kramer, seems unwarranted, compared with the evidence cited by those who find a formula here (Bultmann, Michel, Althaus, Barrett, Bruce, Best, Käsemann, Strecker).[52] The evidence: use of the relative pronoun *hos* at the start of v. 25; the participial construction at the end of v. 24; the syntactical parallelism; two verbs aorist passive, each with a phrase introduced by *dia;* the noun *dikaiōsis* (in the entire NT, only here and Rom 5:18, where it may be a reflection of this passage), and the connection of "put to death" (literally "was handed over," *paradidōmi,* as at the formula in 1 Cor 11:23; contrast Rom 8:32) and the resurrection associated with remission of sins and *dikaiōsis.*

---

52. Kuss and the first six names mentioned who support a formula at Rom 4:25, as cited in Käsemann, *Romans,* p. 128. Werner Kramer, *Christ, Lord, Son of God* (SBT 50; 1966), sections 5e, 26d; Kramer sees here reflections of *two* formulas, one about the "giving" of the Son of God and the other what he calls the "*pistis* formula," likely constructed by Paul. W. Popkes, *Christus traditus* (ATANT 49; 1967), p. 261, would trace the verse back to Mark 9:31 (passion prediction by Jesus). Strecker, "Befreiung" (see n. 49 above), pp. 502–04. Ziesler speaks, pp. 195–96, of a possible prepauline formula here (so already A. M. Hunter) but is interested primarily in what Paul means by *dikaiōsis* (cf. his general comment on such matters, p. 148, n. 1). *Righteousness and Society,* p. 25. U. Wilckens, *Römer* (EKKNT), pp. 278–80, speaks of a "Glaubensformel" but does not regard the prepauline nature of the whole verse as assured; v. 25a may be traditional, but the less usual soteriological nature of the resurrection, he objects, could point to an effort on Paul's part to link the resurrection reference in 4:17 with the assertion about justification in 3:25. But this argument misses the point that Jesus' resurrection seems already to have been associated with justification/vindication in prepauline formulas (cf. above, on 1 Tim 3:16). Martin Hengel, *The Atonement: The Origins of the Doctrine in the New Testament* (Philadelphia: Fortress, 1981), pp. 35–36, underscores how such formulas about "atoning sacrifice" were "not essentially strange" to the Greco-Roman world.

74   The passage obviously reflects Isa 53; cf. 53:5, 6, 12 as background for "(God) giving him over for our sins or lawlessness" in v. 25*a*. Isa 53:11 LXX (*dikaiōsai*), about the Servant's "justifying many," could also lie behind v. 25*b* (cf. Cranfield; Ziesler takes *dikaiōsis* to mean more especially "juridical vindication and justification," p. 196). Many commentators see a difference in sense in the two uses of *dia:* "for our trespasses" uses it causally; "for our justification," in a final sense (Cranfield, Ziesler, Käsemann, Wilckens), though Strecker suggests that, while the distinction fits Paul's own thought, an "analogous meaning of both lines is more likely" for the prepauline level: "(Christus) wurde um unsere Übertretungen willen dahingegeben und um unsrer Gerechtmachung willen auferweckt" (cf. Rom 8:10) (p. 503).

75   There has also been an attempt to distinguish what is worked by the death of Jesus and what is effected by his resurrection, especially in light of Rom 5:10 ("we were reconciled to God by the death of his Son, . . . we shall be saved by his life"), so that "righteousness and life, justification and resurrection are therefore synonymous."[53] It is better to take the parallelism as saying simply,

> He died and rose for the sake of our trespasses
>   i.e., in order that we should be justified (Ziesler, p. 196).

Unlike some of Paul's own statements (cf. Rom 8:10–11, 5:21, cf. 6:23), the formula looks not to the future but to the past Christ event, as at Rom 3:25; forgiveness of (past) sins is grounded in Jesus' death and resurrection. "The forgiveness of transgressions is the making righteous (Gerechtmachung) of sinners" (Strecker, p. 503). This (past) forgiveness, Strecker adds, does not basically stand in opposition to a positive evaluation of the law with reference to the future, at least for Jewish Christianity. Paul's own contribution will be along the lines of extending the significance of justification in that direction, so that it is always "apart from law."

The formula at 4:25 may be placed in Jewish-Hellenistic Christianity, probably in connection with baptism (Strecker, Käsemann).

76   4. *Summary:* Justification/righteousness terminology first appears in primitive Christianity not in the original work of some one theologian like Paul but as part of the common apostolic faith, in Jewish and more

---

53. Markus Barth, *Justification* (cited above, n. 20), p. 25; cf. also M. Barth and Verne H. Fletcher *Acquittal by Resurrection* (New York: Holt, Rinehart & Winston, 1964), pp. 37–38; more cautiously, C. F. D. Moule, *An Idiom Book of New Testament Greek* (New York: Cambridge Univ. Press, 1953), pp. 194–95. For the opposing view preferred above, cf. C. K. Barrett, *Romans* (HNTC, 1957), p. 100, cf. 108; U. Wilckens, *Römer* (EKKNT), pp. 278–79 (a logical but not an actual difference, not a distinction between objective and subjective justification); Käsemann, *Romans,* p. 129 (a single event, the contrast results from the rhetoric of the antithetical parallelism; the christological tradition is being interpreted from the standpoint of the doctrine of justification).

particularly Jewish-Hellensitic communities. It does not appear in the simple kerygmatic announcements that "Jesus died for our sins" and "God raised him up," but rather in reflection on the meaning of that death and of Jesus' resurrection. It therefore has to do with the atonement and the significance of Christology. In this sense, justification can be called "proper Christology." It has to do not only with the passion, death, blood, and expiation but also the resurrection and exaltation as vindication of the Righteous One and of God.

Justification/righteousness is thus, at this stage, remission of (past) sins or transgressions (1 Pet 3:18; Rom 3:25, 4:25), liberation from them (1 Cor 1:30; Rom 3:24) for the unrighteous (1 Pet 3:18) from God, as he keeps loyal to his covenant promises. It implies access to God (1 Pet 3:18), sanctification (1 Cor 1:30, 6:11), the Spirit (1 Cor 6:11), righteousness for us. It is connected with baptism (1 Cor 6:11; 1 Pet 3:18), perhaps with the Lord's Supper (Rom 3:24–26a).

The formulas use OT-Jewish imagery from cult (2 Cor 5:21; Rom 3:25), the righteous sufferer motif, and Isa 53 (suffering servant). Many of the themes related to sdq in Hebrew are present, including vindication, God's righteousness, and the justification of human beings. All this should not surprise us, for what would be more natural, indeed inevitable, than that Jewish Christians should turn to so prominent a theme in the Hebrew scriptures to explicate the heart of their Easter gospel?

III. The Pauline School

A. Paul Himself

77   We shall distinguish, insofar as possible, as in much of contemporary NT studies, what Paul himself in his generally acknowledged letters does with this primitive Christian theme of righteousness/justification and the subsequent handling of the theme in the deuteropauline literature (Colossians, Ephesians, the Pastorals).

For those who do not accept such distinctions in authorship between the Apostle and his pupils in the Pauline School, the items treated in section B below may simply be thought of as Paul's work later in his career. One caveat: If traditional views are followed and the imprisonment epistles are taken as deriving from one place, traditionally Rome, then Philippians (a document of obvious importance for our topic) stems from the same period as Colossians and Ephesians and, indeed, apart from the Pastorals, may be the last extant letter from Paul.

In a sense, all of Pauline theology could be elaborated around our topic, and some scholars have tried just that. We shall, while noting all passages using *dikaio*-vocabulary, stress items important in this Lutheran-Catholic dialogue.

78   1. *Statistics and Spread.* Even including what were claimed as prepauline passages above, *dikaiosynē* terminology appears in Paul's letters primarily in Galatians and Romans. The figures (following Morgenthaler, cited n. 30) are in the accompanying table.

By no means are all these occurrences significant. For our topic, the important passages may be said to occur in Gal 2–3, Rom 3, 4, 6, 9–10 especially, and Phil 3 (the examples are proportionally high for so short an epistle).

From this evidence, the conclusion has often been drawn that Paul came to use this vocabulary and to make justification prominent only when he encountered "the Judaizers" in Galatia (and elsewhere), a situa-

Word in Greek	Rom	1 Cor	2 Cor	Gal	Eph	Phil	1 Tim	2 Tim	Titus
dikaiosynē	33	1	7	4	3	4	1	3	1
dikaioō (verb)	15	2		8			1		1
dikaiōma	5								
dikaiōs (adv.)		1							1
dikaiōsis	2								
dikaiokrisia	1								
dikaios (adj.)	7			1	1	2	1	1	1
TOTALS:	63	4	7	13	4	6	3	4	4

(Also: *dikaios* 2× in 2 Thess, 1× in Col; *dikaiōs* (adv.) 1× in 1 Thess)

tion reflected in the often similar statements of Romans and in the angry words of Phil 3:2 ("look out for the dogs!"). On this view, justification cannot be his chief theme, but merely one forced on him for but a brief period of his ministry, in a polemical situation. It is an aberration of the Lutheran Reformation, on this view, to have perpetuated the importance of what for Paul, to use Albert Schweitzer's figure, was but "a subsidiary crater."

79   a. *Prepauline background.* Against this view stands our contention (above) that righteousness/justification was not just a theme into which Paul was forced for a time by opponents but a common, prepauline one to which he appeals at times, when he must make certain points. True, the opponents in Galatia may have forced him to clarify and extend the apostolic, Jewish-Christian emphasis, but he has not invented it for the occasion, or totally ignored it elsewhere. With the prepauline evidence also evaporates the charge that Paul lifted the theme from his opponents.[54]

Absence of references in other letters does not prove that either Paul or his audience was unaware of justification/righteousness as a way of expressing the gospel at that time, any more than absence of, say, "reconciliation" language outside of 2 Corinthians and Romans among the acknowledged letters demonstrates that it was unknown to him in Thessalonica or in his relations with Philippi. The line of argument we here oppose might in another case imply that early Christians celebrated the Lord's Supper only in Corinth, because only for that congregation do we have specific Pauline reference to it; such a conclusion would surely be erroneous.

80   For Galatians, note particularly the comments of Hans Dieter Betz, in the Hermeneia series *Galatians* (1979), pp. 114–15, 119, among other references: "Justification by faith is part of a Jewish-Christian theol-

---

54. So Heitmüller, Wrede; more recently, C. H. Buck, Jr., "The Date of Galatians, *JBL* 70 (1950): 121–22. Cf. also Buck and Greer Taylor, *Saint Paul: A Study in the Development of His Thought* (New York: Scribner's, 1969), and the reply to it by Victor Paul Furnish in *JAAR* 38 (1970): 289–303.

ogy"; "Paul's claim that he shares this doctrine with Jewish Christianity should be taken seriously"; at 2:17, "the disagreement [between Paul and his opponents] does not pertain to the doctrine of justification by faith for Jewish Christians, but to the implications of that doctrine for Gentile Christians."

81   In Romans, the centrality Paul gives to justification is even more impressive: in this "generalized summary of Paul's gospel" he is writing to a church he had not founded or visited as yet,[55] in order to seek aid and support for a pioneering missionary endeavor in Spain, and he may have sent copies of the same letter (or most of it—the mystery of chap. 16 and the various endings in the manuscripts of Romans!) to his churches in the east (Ephesus, Corinth, to say the least; there are even those who see Jerusalem as the "secret addressee"—E. Fuchs). If ever there was an epistle to the "church catholic" in the A.D. 50s, it is Romans. And so just as Paul employs a Jewish-Christian formula from Christology at 1:3*b*–4 to establish his orthodox credentials and gain a hearing from the Roman audience at the outset, so he likely chose a main theme (1:17, 3:24–26, etc.) with which they would be familiar from common apostolic, specifically Jewish, Christianity, namely *dikaiosynē theou.*

82   b. *Paul's earlier letters.* Against this all too prevalent notion that righteousness/justification was Paul's way of expressing the gospel only for a brief spell, against opponents, are also to be noted what *dikaios*-terms do occur in his earlier letters.

(1) We illustrate the general situation from what is reputed to be Paul's earliest extant letter, *1 Thessalonians.* In terms of word study, the only relevant verse, **2:10,** "our behavior was holy, righteous (*dikaiōs*), and blameless," simply means "we lived in conformity to right standards of behavior," but as a recent commentator points out, the fact that in 1 Thessalonians "there is no reference to the righteousness of God or justification by faith . . . does not imply he did not teach it to them," for "the death of Jesus receives little attention" either (chiefly, 5:10), "in Christ" only rarely appears, and "reconciliation" not at all; the form Paul's theology took in a given letter and its emphases are determined to a considerable degree by the situation which he faced, and "the problem in Thessalonica is eschatology"—hence the kergymatic summary cited at 1:9–10.[56] To have cited what we know as Rom 3:24–26*a* would not have helped either to forge links or to correct the situation in Thessalonica.

83   But, Ernest Best goes on (pp. 220–21), 1 Thess 4:13–5:11 "approaches most closely the type of theological discussion we find in . . . notably Rom., Gal.," and we have an indirect suggestion Paul already knows of God's righteousness at this point but omits it because he needs to score

---

55. Robert W. Funk, in the John Knox fs, *Christian Interpretation and History* (New York: Cambridge Univ. Press, 1967), pp. 267–68.

56. Ernest Best, *The First and Second Epistles to the Thessalonians* (HNTC, 1972), p. 221.

other points for the Thessalonians. At 5:8 he clearly reflects the well-known verse of Isa 59:17,

> God put on righteousness as a breastplate
> and a helmet of salvation on his head.

(God's "mighty and victorious action" is the sense Ziesler gives to *sĕdāqâ* there, p. 30). Unlike Eph 6:14, which applies the verse as it stood to the Christian, Paul at 5:8 inserts into the Isa quote (italicized) a familiar triad:

> ... *put on the breastplate* of faith and love,
> *and for a helmet* the hope *of salvation.*

Why? This same triad he has already employed at the outset of the letter:

> remembering before our God and Father your work of faith (*ergon tēs pisteōs*), and labor of love (*kopos tēs agapēs*), and steadfastness of hope (*hypomonē tēs elpidos*) in our Lord Jesus Christ.

Probably each genitive here is a subjective one, "achievement arising out of faith, toil which arises from agape, patient endurance which comes from hope," unless one sees a genitivus qualitatis, *pisteōs* being parallel to *ergon Kyriou* or *Christou,* i.e., work done by God, in contrast to *ergon nomou* (cf. 2 Thess 1:11).[57] In the Thessalonian situation, Paul wants to establish at the opening and ending of his letter what is important in their new lives as converts, above all for practical issues that he must discuss in 4:13–5:11, the steadfast endurance that springs from hope. "Righteousness/justification" is not at issue in this first experiment (at least the first one extant) in Christian epistolography.

In any case, "work" here "is the fruit of faith, ... a unitary character is thus given to Christian action evoked by God and proceeding from faith" (G. Bertram, *TDNT,* 2, p. 649). There is no opposition between "work" and "faith"; the former arises out of the latter.

84 (2) *2 Thessalonians,* which we shall treat here though some regard it as not by Paul himself, seems insignificant for our topic, for there are only two uses of the adjective *dikaios.* Both occur at **1:5–6** as the opening thanksgiving moves into the topic of eschatology and the coming judgment:

> [1:5]This [apparently Paul's boast of the faith and endurance of the Thessalonians as they face persecutions and tribulations] is evi-

---

57. Cf. ibid. for the first view; for the second, see Hermann Binder, *Der Glaube bei Paulus* (Berlin: Evangelische Verlagsanstalt, 1968), pp. 54–55, cf. 43, 85 (against Bultmann's view of 1:3 as *Gläubigkeit,* "the attitude of having faith," in his *Theology* [above, n. 15], 1, p. 90), and 103.

dence of the righteous judgment (*dikaias kriseōs*) of God, that you will be deemed worthy of the kingdom of God, for which you are suffering—⁶since indeed it is right (*dikaios*) in God's sight to repay affliction to those who afflict you and rest to you who are being afflicted along with us, at the revelation of the Lord Jesus from heaven.

This "judgment theophany" (Dibelius)—or, better, Christophany—which serves to introduce the more detailed apocalyptic picture in 2 Thess 2, has a pastoral intent of helping the Thessalonians to persevere amid afflictions. The OT content is obvious: The "judgment will be righteous because God is righteous."[58] The *lex talionis* is at work, as shown in a chiasm:

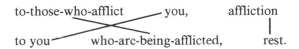

But it is really a matter of promise that depends upon God that is involved, not a matter of reward. Plainly the picture is forensic. "This is God's judicial righteousness in action. . . . Both punitive and saving elements are present, directed towards different groups." (So Ziesler, p. 152, claiming Descamps in support.) Hence Best's comment: "Because God is righteous . . . he justifies, redeems and saves the unrighteous who respond to him in faith. Those to whom he writes are indeed those who are being justified through their faith called forth by God's grace in Christ" (p. 256).

Read against the OT background and the prepauline background, 2 Thessalonians can thus be seen to reflect at this one point at least the theme of justification, in the reference to the "justice of God's judgment. It will prove you worthy of the kingdom of God" (*NEB*).

85   c. Possible *chronological and theological development* during Paul's "mature years."

All of the evidence we have considered thus far we have regarded as prepauline or as stemming from what we term in Acts "the Second Missionary Journey" (Acts 15:36–18:22), a ministry especially in Greece, centered in Corinth, whence he wrote to Thessalonica. There are no letters from the period of the "First Missionary Journey" (Acts 13–14). Therefore all of Paul's other extant letters, in our view, come from the period of the so-called Third Missionary Journey (Acts 18:23–21:16), which is actually a long period of ministry and evangelism centered in Ephesus, ending with the trip to Jerusalem (Acts 21), bearing the collection for "the saints" there from Paul's primarily Gentile churches.

---

58. Best (see n. 56), p. 255. Cf. also M. Dibelius, *An die Thessalonischer I–II* . . . (HNT, 2d ed. 1923), ad loc.

(1) A crux for our discussion is the *dating of Galatians*. If the recipients were in the *province* of Galatia in the south, then Paul could have visited there on his "first journey" (Acts 13:13–14:26) and the letter could have been written any time thereafter, in the mid or late forties. In that case his emphasis on justification would be established from that relatively earlier point in his missionary career. On the other hand, if "Galatia" refers to the *territory* in central Asia Minor, then Paul visited there on the second and/or third journeys (Acts 16:6, 18:23), and the latter stems from a later period. We find the latter (or North Galatian) theory more convincing (so *JBC* 49:4; Betz, *Gal.,* p. 5).

At the other extreme, some would date Galatians very late in this period, from Ephesus or Corinth, just before Paul writes Romans, with which Galatians has obvious affinities. Galatians, which thus could be dated as late as A.D. 57, would then, with its polemic against the "Judaizers" on justification, come only after he had said other things on the theme in earlier letters. But "developments of thought can be shown to have taken place between Galatians and Romans" (Betz, p. 11, citing Udo Borse; cf. *JBC* 49:8).

Betz suggests A.D. 50–55 as "a reasonable guess" for the writing of Galatians (p. 12). About 54 can be more specifically suggested, neither an early or late extreme dating.

86   (2) In the *working sequence* suggested below, it is assumed that Paul's correspondence with Philippi comes during an imprisonment in Ephesus, not Caesarea or (traditionally) Rome (so recent commentaries by, e.g., Gnilka, HTKNT, 1968; J. F. Collange, CNT, 1973). Further, it is assumed that Philemon was written during an imprisonment in Asia Minor, and that 2 Cor 6:14–7:1 is out of place in its canonical location and may be an interpolation with Qumran affinities (*JBC* 52:24) or even an *anti*-Pauline fragment reflecting a torah-covenant theology akin to that of the opponents he faces in Galatia (cf. H. D. Betz, *Galatians,* pp. 9, 329–30, and *passim; JBL* 92 [1973]:88–108). We personally prefer to regard 2 Corinthians and Philippians as combinations of several letters by Paul to those churches. Perhaps precision in the sequence of fragments is unnecessary for the problems we address, but it is of some aid in asking about possible development in Paul's thought on justification.

Sequence of Paul's Letters

A.D.

50–51   in *Corinth,* writes 1 (and 2) THESSALONIANS

53–56   in *Ephesus* and Asia, as missionary base

54   1 CORINTHIANS (a "previous letter" mentioned at 5:9 is probably lost)

GALATIANS

Letter A to PHILIPPI (4:10–20, a note of thanks for aid)

55   Letter B to PHILIPPI (at least 1:3–2:31, from prison)
            Extant Letter B to CORINTH (2 Cor 2:14–6:13, 7:2–4)
            Letter C to PHILIPPI (at least 3:1b–21, a polemic against "the
            dogs")
            "Painful Visit" to Corinth (not in Acts; cf. 2 Cor 12:14, 13:1,
            7:12, 2:4, 9)
            Letter C to CORINTH ("letter of tears," cf. 2 Cor 2:4) (chaps.
            10–13)
56   Asian imprisonment (?) (cf. 2 Cor 1:8ff.) PHILEMON (?)
            Travel to Macedonia (cf. Acts 20:1; 2 Cor 2:12)
            Letter D to CORINTH (2 Cor 1:3–2:13, 7:5–16) + chaps. 8, 9
56–57   Winter in *Corinth*—ROMANS
57   Through Macedonia (Acts 20:3ff.), to Asia and Jerusalem and, af-
            ter arrest and imprisonment in Caesarea, to Rome (A.D. 60?)

87   (3) Such matters are not just academic niceties. As much precision as possible in determining this sequence is important for two reasons:
(a) the question of the opponents or false teachers whom Paul faces, and
(b) possibility of development in his thought. Understanding Paul on justification hinges, at least in some reconstructions, on decisions made about
each matter.

(a) It has already been noted (and denied) that, in the judgment of a
few scholars, Paul got his emphasis on justification from *opponents* in Galatia (see above §79, n. 54). We have insisted he shared it with common,
apostolic, especially Jewish Christianity. How each side interpreted it was
what mattered.

It has often further been alleged that Paul was battling a single group
of opponents in Galatia, Philippi, and in Rome (or at least a reflection of
their views as he writes Romans). That group is said to be what brought
justification into prominence. Some scholars have also long been prone to
see a single type of opponent in all the Pauline literature, from F. C. Baur's
"Judaizers" (Jewish Christians) to W. Schmithals "Gnostics." The opponents in a document like Philippians have been variously defined as Jews,
Jewish Christians, "Judaizers," Gnostics, libertines, pneumatics, and all
sorts of combinations of these terms. The matter is still hotly debated. We
shall assume that Paul faced a variety of Christian, semi-Christian, Jewish,
and pagan groups, and that no one profile will do. The opposition in Galatians is not precisely the same as that in Philippians, nor the group in 2
Corinthians 10–13 the same as what Paul faced in 1 Corinthians.[59]

---

59. So Helmut Koester, "Häretiker im Urchristentum," *Die Religion in Geschichte und
Gegenwart* (Tübingen: Mohr-Siebeck) 3d ed., Vol. 3 (1959), cols. 17–21; "The Purpose of the
Polemic of a Pauline Fragment," *NTS* 8 (1961–62): 317–32. John J. Gunther, *St. Paul's Op-
ponents and Their Background: A Study of Apocalyptic and Jewish Sectarian Teachings*
(NovTSup 35; 1973).

88   (b) It may also be noted that a number of scholars have proposed schemes of "development" whereby Paul's final and "mature" positions are to be found in a particular epistle (usually with the implication that his "earlier" views are thereby to be minimalized). These attempts have often been based on supposed progression in his eschatology, supposedly from a red-hot apocalypticist early in his career and still so in 1 Thessalonians to a more serene theologian who avoids emphasis on the future parousia and stresses realized eschatology.[60] Or the approach has attempted to trace out changes in Paul's attitude toward the law,[61] or a supposed development from "charismatic" to "institutional" structures.[62]

Such approaches often depend on particular decisions about sources. The view that makes Paul, at the last, a "realized eschatologist" depends on assigning to him Colossians and Ephesians, denying to him the Pastoral Epistles, and indeed on separating Philippians (cf. 3:20–21) from the other imprisonment epistles.

In our judgment, such theories of "progression" in Paul's thought are arbitrary and unproven, and he remained remarkably consistent in his theological thinking during the period of eight years or so that one can most fully document (ca. 50–57). His eschatology emphasizes the decisive thing that God has done in Christ (which Paul can variously describe with regard to the cross and resurrection), and it regularly looks forward to a consummation to come, in the fullness of which Christians do not yet participate. It is in this consistent theological stance of his, shaped in emphasis as it is by the situation addressed, that righteousness/justification plays such a major role.

d. *The Corinthian correspondence.*

89   (1) The initial extant letter, *1 Corinthians,* apparently prior to Galatians, and thus an "early" letter in terms of demonstrable references to righteousness/justification, uses *dikaiosynē* of Christ at 1:30 and *edikaiōthēte* of Christians at 6:11 in what are, we have argued, prepauline formulas (see above, §§62–65). Paul cites (or says, if one does not accept them as earlier tradition) these things because they undergird points he wants to make about such topics as "Christ and wisdom" (1:17ff.) and the nature of Christian existence and conduct. We would assume Paul can allude to the phrases effectively precisely because he and the Corinthians were familiar with them from his prior teaching (for 6:11, the formula at 6:9, "Do you not know . . .?" especially suggests this).

If commentators differ over the exact nuance of the justification terminology here (cf. above, §§63, 65), it may be a reflection of the fact that

---

60. Cf. C. H. Dodd, esp. "The Mind of Paul," *BJRL* (1933–34), reprinted in *New Testament Studies* (Manchester Univ. Press, 1953), pp. 67–128; critique by John Lowe, "An Examination of Some Attempts to Detect Developments in St. Paul's Theology," *JTS* 42 (1941): 129–42. Or John C. Hurd, Jr., *The Origin of 1 Corinthians* (London: SPCK, 1965).

61. Cf. Buck and Taylor (n. 54, above).

62. Cf. Robert Jewett, "The Redaction of 1 Corinthians and the Trajectory of the Pauline School," *JAAR* 44 (1978), Supplement B, pp. 389–444.

the words of the formulas take on a fuller meaning when read in light of Paul's "doctrine of justification," which is known to us from other, later letters. Thus, one could interpret:

Formula	Paul
1:30 Christ = righteousness, he "embodies the divine *justice*, i.e., God's faithfulness to his promises of salvation" (*JBC* 51:17) (cf. the relation to *covenant*, Stuhlmacher, §63 above).	= righteousness "for us" (*hēmin*), he will emphasize more the meaning *pro nobis;* "You are God's 'in him.' " (1:30*a*)
6:11 "You were justified" = remission of sins (Bultmann, Lohse).	= the full Pauline sense of justification by faith (Conzelmann, p. 107; Kertelge, p. 245).

In any case, Paul uses these significant phrases here apart from any debate with Jews or Jewish Christians over the law (Kertelge, p. 296).

90   Other references in 1 Corinthians: **4:4,** "I am not aware of anything against myself, but I am not thereby acquitted (*ouk . . . dedikaiōmai*). It is the Lord who judges me." Plainly forensic. One stands at the bar of God. Neither Paul's conscience (which does *not* accuse him) nor human opinion (v. 3) either condemns or saves him; only God does. Some commentators (H. D. Wendland, NTD; Barrett; Conzelmann) see behind this paragraph (4:1–5) on "the servants of Christ" Paul's concept of the Christian facing the judgment of God as "justified in Christ by grace." The difficult verses at 3:14–15 (cf. Ap. 4:194 and 366) are also "to be understood in the wider context of the doctrine of justification" (Conzelmann, p. 77). **15:34,** "Be sober, *dikaiōs*" means merely "sober up as you ought" (BAGD), or "properly" (Barrett, cf. Enoch 106:18). But **1:8,** while not employing any *dikaios*-word, when it says that Christians will be sustained "to the end guiltless (*anenklētous*) in the Day of our Lord Jesus Christ," suggests to Barrett (p. 39) that "Paul is stating the doctrine of justification by faith without the use of the technical terms he employs elsewhere."

91   At least some commentators have thus been struck by the fact that Paul's doctrine of justification stands, unarticulated, behind what he writes in 1 Corinthians (cf. also Barrett, p. 60; Conzelmann, pp. 11, 40–41). If so, why is it not voiced more fully? The answer lies in the situation at Corinth, where an "overrealized" eschatology has given rise to a variety of questions and problems. The cross of Jesus is at issue, not so much for its atoning value (cf. 15:3) but because the Corinthians stress the fact they are not only forgiven but also sanctified and *teleioi* (perfect), filled, rich, already reigning in the kingdom (4:8), with no stress on a further fulfillment to come. Against their theology of glory, Paul stresses "the word of the cross" (1:18ff.), "Christ crucified," and the cruciform life-style for apostles and all believers. But the message of the cross does not differ from that of justification in, e.g., Romans. Both present "the ideas of *sola gratia, sola fide,* of the destruction of human *kauchēsis* [boasting, pride], and of the transportation [Überführung] into the freedom of faith" (Conzelmann, p.

11, cf. pp. 40–41). Indeed, it is characteristic of Lutheran thought to express its gospel of justification also in terms of *theologia crucis.*

92   (2) In *2 Corinthians,* where only the noun *dikaiosynē* occurs (yet 7×), we shall examine the references first in their present order in the letter, and then inquire whether consideration of them in the order of the fragments supposed above sheds any light on emerging Pauline use. It is to be remembered that **5:21** (and others say some preceding verses) is or reflects prepauline material (see above, §§66–68), and is the earliest passage in Paul using "righteousness *of God.*"

In the new covenant passage of 2 Cor 3, Paul compares the old (v. 14) *diathēkē* of Moses with the new *diathēkē* of Christ:

in terms of death (v. 7)	and Spirit (v. 8),
condemnation (*katakrisis,* v. 9)	and righteousness (v. 9),
and that which faded (v. 11).	and what remains as permanent (v. 11).

In each comparison, if the splendor (*doxa*) of the former was great, the latter is greater. What is meant in the second comparison, "If the ministry (*diakonia,* RSV "dispensation") of condemnation was glory, much more will the ministry of righteousness (*diakonia tēs dikaiosynēs*) abound in glory" (**3:9**)? It is surely not a ministry that has righteousness or justice as the object of a quest, but rather a ministry that proceeds from righteousness and the Spirit and life given by the Spirit (v. 6). The contrast to condemnation and death implies the judgment, so it is forensic. Thus Bultmann: "the acquittal itself, i.e., the Gerechtigkeit spoken by God, Rom 1:17" (MeyerK, *2 Kor* [1976], p. 86). Further, Ziesler (p. 159): "Righteousness refers to God's whole intervention in Jesus"; he compares the OT background of "forensic salvation" and "God's own saving righteousness" (as in 2 Isa).

A correspondence of *diakonia tēs dikaiosynēs* with the "*diakonia* of the Spirit" (3:8) and also with "the ministry of reconciliation" (*diakonia tēs katallagēs,* 5:18) was pointed out some years ago by Wendland (NTD 7 [1946], p. 156). In Käsemann's ground-breaking new approach to the righteousness of God in Paul, further amplification was offered, affecting the meaning of 3:9.

93   It is now time to look at the proposal of the Käsemann School.[63] Briefly put, it involves these claims:

(1) *dikaiosynē theou* is a technical term in Judaism and Qumran, deriving ultimately from Deut 33:21 (see above, §40);

(2) it is not only a gift from God (as Bultmann held) but also the power of God;

---

63. See especially Käsemann's "God's Righteousness in Paul" (1961), trans. in *The Bultmann School of Biblical Interpretation: New Directions?* (*JTC* 1; 1965), pp. 100–10; Stuhlmacher, *Gerechtigkeit;* and the literature and history of interpretation noted in my background paper (cited above, n. 10) in *LWF Report,* pp. 19–20.

(3) *dikaiosynē theou,* which meant in prepauline formulas God's faithfulness to his covenant (Rom 3:24–25, cf. above, §72), is for Paul "the divine loyalty to the community . . . but with regard to the entire creation" (Käsemann, *JTC* 1, p. 107);

(4) "Characteristic of the fidelity of God to creation is the fact that it compels those whom it addresses to enter into its service. Hence Paul speaks of a Dienstbarkeit der Gerechtigkeit" (Stuhlmacher, p. 70); cf. Rom 6:1ff., especially 6:13, 16, 18–19, and Rom 12–14, as well as our verse currently under discussion.

(5) Thus, with "God's righteousness" is indicated the theme of Paul's whole proclamation and theology (Stuhlmacher, pp. 69–70, cf. 76).

94   The fourth item concerns us here. It deserves consideration even if one is not convinced of all the prior points. Stuhlmacher (pp. 224, 248, and *passim*) goes on to point out the almost "military" aspect of "the service of righteousness" at 3:9—"den Kampf um Gottes Recht im neuen Dienst der Gerechtigkeit" (cf. Rom 6:16–23, and Paul's picture of the apostolic ministry, 2 Cor 4 and 10:3–6). However, Stuhlmacher's appeal to backgrounds in the Qumran literature is another matter;[64] Barrett (*2 Cor.* [HNTC, 1973], p. 117) finds it does not do full justice to Paul's sense of *diakonia.*

We may see in 2 Cor 3:9 an expression of God's Spirit, righteousness, and new covenant in Christ, which mean for believers "life," "hope" (v. 12) and confidence, freedom, and a ministry that stems from God's action. Stuhlmacher (p. 76), with 2 Cor 5:17–21 in view, comments, "The forensic situation is the way by which this new world and creation, characterized by freedom, is reached." Barrett specifically sees in view the result of this action as "justification and the status of righteousness thereby conferred on man" (p. 117). The Lutheran confessors at Augsburg viewed this experience of justification, it may be remembered, as including eternal life, reconciliation, and the Spirit.

95   The formula at 2 Cor **5:21,** when taken in its present context, clearly suggests that God's action in Christ means that we become in Christ "new creatures" (v. 17),[65] reconciled to God, having a *diakonia* of reconciliation (v. 18), forgiven ("trespasses" not counted, v. 19), ourselves "the righteousness of God," recipients of grace (6:1) and servants of God whose lives are characterized by the host of paradoxes that mark Christian existence (6:4–10). In the context Ziesler takes the words "so that in Christ

---

64. Stuhlmacher, p. 158, cf. 224, refers especially to 1QS 4:9, *ba'ăbôdat sedeq* (negligence of the hands "in the service of righteousness"), a phrase that reoccurs at 1QH 6:19. H. Braun, *Qumran und das Neue Testament,* 1, pp. 198–99, refers to differences as well as similarities here between Qumran and Paul—including the fact that Paul uses *dikaiosynē* in 3:9 the way "*mišpāṭ* is applied at 1QS 11:5, 12, while the general Pauline usage of *dikaiosynē* corresponds to that of *sĕdāqâ* in 1QS"—and the opinion of W. D. Davies that 2 Cor 3:4–9 is directed *against* "Qumran influences" at Corinth.

65. For the translation of 5:17 as "if any is in Christ, he (or she) is a new creature," rather than "there is a new creation," cf. J. Reumann, *Creation and New Creation,* pp. 89–99, especially 94–97.

we might become *dikaiosynē theou*" to mean "participation in, not possession of, God's righteousness," including the forensic note of "being accepted," but sees obviously more than that to be involved, for it includes *kainē
ktisis,* new creaturehood. But this result is corporate, not individualistic
(contrary to implications of v. 17; note the plurals in vv. 18–21). Kertelge
remarks that it is not a matter of our attaining to God's righteousness or
becoming just but of our succeeding to the realm that is designated by
"God's righteousness" (p. 107, n. 228). This means "being in Christ," for
the two could not be more closely bound together—*dikaiosynē theou en
autōi.*[66] And this is "new creation," the "signature of which" is the "righteousness of God." Paul came to his sense of *dikaiosynē theou,* he thinks,
from OT, Jewish backgrounds; it is a concept, "eschatologically stamped,"
referring to "the human situation 'in Christ' as a situation of salvation
which is offered by God to all now in the midst of the elapsing 'old aeon',
as the new decisive possibility" (p. 107).

96　　At **6:7** "the weapons of righteousness (*hoplōn tēs dikaiosynēs*) for
the right hand and for the left" that God's servants use fit well with the
"military" sense Stuhlmacher suggested in connection with 3:9 (see
above). The genitive may be subjective ("weapons which righteousness
provides") or explicative ("weapons which consist of righteousness") or
qualitative ("weapons suitable to, corresponding to righteousness"), Bultmann thought, but scarcely an objective genitive, "weapons for (the defense of) righteousness" (MeyerK, *2 Kor.,* p. 174). Barrett (p. 188)
surmises there might be a reference to the gospel in the phrase "the word
of truth" in v. 7; a link to the sort of definition Paul gives for the gospel in
Romans 1:16–17, as "the power of God," is suggested by the other phrase
in v. 7, *dynamis theou* (cf. Stuhlmacher, on *dikaiosynē theou* as "the power
of God"). Ziesler allows both a moral sense and a reference to God: "fair
means, not foul," and God's "vindicating righteousness" aiding his servants. The parallelism with the immediately preceding phrase (*en dynamei
theou*) argues for taking *dia tōn hoplōn tēs dikaiosynēs* as "the weapons
which righteousness provides."

6:14, "What do righteousness and lawlessness have in common?" employs *dikaiosynē* in an ethical sense, just as at Qumran and widely in Judaism.

9:9–10 shows Paul, in an appeal to "sow abundantly" in giving to the
collection for the saints (9:1), citing a verse from Ps 112:9,

"He scattered abroad, he gave to the poor,
His righteousness (*dikaiosynē*) abides for ever" (v. 9).

---

66. Note *en Christōi* in 5:17 (and 19, "In [= by?] Christ, God was reconciling . . ."). It is
possible that *en autōi* in the formula meant "become the righteousness of God by (means of)
him," but for Paul takes on fuller overtones of his *en Christōi* theme.

Then he goes on (v. 10), God "will increase 'the harvest of your righteousness.' " The wording here draws on Hos 10:12 (and Isa 55:10). "Mercy, charitableness, benevolence" is meant. The sense is similar to that of *dikaiosynē* as "almsgiving" at Matt 6:1, viewed against rabbinic background.

Finally, at **11:15** the false apostles who are really "servants of Satan" are said to disguise themselves as "servants of righteousness" (*diakonoi dikaiosynēs*). There is an ethical sense here but possibly also the notion of "a power to be served" (Ziesler, p. 161). Dieter Georgi[67] has argued that this was a proud title that these opponents of Paul used for themselves. By "righteousness" they meant, presumably, the sort that comes by obedience to the law (Barrett, p. 287). Bultmann finds a link to 3:9 attractive. Since *diakonoi* can be equivalent to *apostoloi,* these "deceitful workers" (11:13) who claim to be "Christ's apostles" must have been missionaries who stressed righteousness in a sense different from Paul's.

97 If we put these references in the sequence of the putative letter fragments now in 2 Cor, Paul's letter B to Corinth (2:4–6:13) used the inherited formula about Christians as "God's righteousness in Christ," having life, the Spirit, and all that eschatological salvation suggests (5:21). Hence theirs is a ministry created by God's righteousness, a service of righteousness that is almost militant, with "weapons" of righteousness involved (6:7). In letter C Paul was confronting opponents who claimed to be ministers too "of righteousness," but of another kind of *dikaiosynē.* But in a later letter Paul himself can use the word *dikaiosynē* to refer, in OT style, to "benevolence" in giving, for God's righteousness leads to that sort of response (9:9–10). (Omit 6:14.)

We now turn to what are the Hauptbriefe for any study of justification/righteousness in Paul.

2. Galatians.[68]

98 a. *The situation.* It is important in reading Galatians—where *dikaiosynē* vocabulary bursts into such prominence (noun 4×, verb 8×, ad-

---

67. Dieter Georgi, *Die Gegner des Paulus im 2 Korintherbrief* (WMANT 11; 1964).
68. **Commentaries on Gal:** J. B. Lightfoot, *St. Paul's Epistle to the Galatians* (London: Macmillan, 1865; rev. ed. 1910). Ernest de Witt Burton (ICC, 1920). Heinrich Schlier (MeyerK, 14th ed. 1971, written before his conversion to Roman Catholicism but still printed in the Meyer series; cf. Siegfried Schulz, "Katholisierende Tendenzen in Schliers Galater-Kommentar," *KD* 5 [1959]: 23–41; cf. H. D. Betz, Hermeneia *Galatians,* pp. xiii–xiv, 66, 87 n. 282, 93, 99 n. 399, 107 n. 453, 109 n. 468, 111 n. 485, 123 nn. 86 and 88, 124 n. 92, 125 n. 101, 131 n. 34, 186 n. 39, esp. 187–89 [on Schlier's strongly "objective" view of baptism "which interprets a combination of Rom, Eph, Col in terms of Roman Catholic sacramental dogma," a view that has been "widely accepted" in "a strange case of ecumenical consensus"], 212 n. 97, 248 n. 98, 271 n. 4, 274 n. 24, and 289 n. 172, among other references less pertinent to modern dialogue). Ragnar Bring, *Commentary on Galatians* (Eng. trans., Philadelphia: Muhlenberg, 1961; Swedish Lutheran Lundensian School). John Bligh, *Galatians* (Householder Commentaries, London: St. Paul Publications, 1969, heavy on chiastic structure). Hans Dieter Betz (Hermeneia, 1979). On the issue of objective vs. subjective genitive, cf. A. J. Hultgren, "The *Pistis Christou* Formulation in Paul," *NovT* 22 (1980): 248–63.

jective 1×), chiefly in chaps. 2 and 3 (five occurrences and six respectively in these two chapters)—to recall that Paul is here defending his gospel and his apostleship against interlopers (1:7, 9; 2:12; 3:1; 5:7, 9, 12) who have appeared in Galatia, though the exact contours of their positions can no longer be reconstructed. The following groups seem to be reflected (from left to right theologically) within the Christian movement:

"Gnostics" (?)	Gentiles		Jewish Christians		Jews
(so Schmithals,	(addressed in		1:22, 2:13, etc.		
cf. chaps. 5–6)	letter)	Barnabas			
		Cephas	James, 1:19	John	
	Paul 1:18, 2:9, 11f.		2:9	2:9	
Titus		"those of repute" 2:(2), 6			"false brethren" 2:4

It remains debated whether one or two "fronts" are involved in Paul's defense of the gospel. Indeed, the fronts may at times have shifted; e.g., Cephas (Peter) is charged with behaving differently at Antioch (2:11ff.) from previously, when measured by Paul's standard, "the truth of the gospel" (2:14, cf. 2:5).

It must also be observed where "righteousness/justification" vocabulary begins to appear in Galatians. It is not in the brief references to the gospel Paul preached, which has been defined only as "preaching Christ" (1:16) or "preaching the faith" (1:23, the Faith? or *pistis* as its characteristic emphasis?)—the gospel Paul preaches to the Gentiles (2:2). Justification-language appears when Paul fleshes out what this gospel, which is "the truth" and a revelation from God (1:16), is all about. It is, of course, one that concerns God's Son, who "gave himself for us" (1:4; 2:20), but what does the atonement mean? Paul begins to speak of *dikaiosynē* and human beings being rightwised when he must make specific this gospel, and he does so in the context of the dispute with Cephas at Antioch (or of his reflection on that incident).

99   b. *2:15–21* as "Paul's Résumé of his Gospel" (*JBC* 49:18). Like the passage at John 3:1–21, especially vv. 16–18, where it is so difficult to tell how much of the discourse Jesus spoke to Nicodemus and how much is subsequent reflection, Gal 2 poses the problem of whether only 2:14 is a quotation of what Paul has said publicly to Cephas at Antioch (so *RSV*) or part or all of 2:15–21 also stems from that occasion (Phillips: "and then I went on to explain . . .," v. 15). In any case, it is Paul speaking, and Betz, who analyzes Galatians, as Luther did, with emphasis on reflection there of ancient rhetorical practices, calls these verses the *propositio* or summing up of Paul's contention in light of the previous narrative, before going on to "proofs" for it (*probatio*). In other words, it is the heart of Galatians and is packed with "dogmatic abbreviations, i.e., very short formulaic summaries of doctrines" (*Gal.*, Hermenia, p. 114; cf. 113, n. 6, for literature on the ancient problem of how far the quotation extends). For our purposes we need not try here to unpack every last detail (cf. Betz, pp. 26–28, for a list of such traditional and formulaic materials used by Paul).

The key statement lies in what Paul says (as if) to Cephas:

> [15]We, Jews by birth and not "sinners from among the Gentiles" [i.e., Gentile = sinner, because without the law, a Jewish phrase], [16]because we know that a person is not rightwised (*dikaioutai*) on the basis of works of law but only through faith in Christ Jesus, we too have come to believe on Christ Jesus, in order that we might be rightwised on the basis of faith in Christ and not on the basis of works of the law.

The sense is plain: justification not *ex ergōn nomou* but *ek pisteōs Christou*. In spite of occasional efforts, currently revived, to take *Christou* as a subjective genitive after *pistis* the two times the phrase occurs in this passage, the traditional interpretation of "faith in Christ" (objective genitive) is to be followed (*JBC* 49:18; Betz, p. 117).

100   More debated is the sense of the verb *dikaioo*. There is agreement that it is first of all juridical (as in the LXX), "pronounced just/righteous/upright"; there is dispute whether it here also implies "*made* upright," and even implies reshaping "man anew internally, supplying him with a new principle of activity on the ontological level of his very being," with a resulting "symbiosis" (*JBC* 49:18–19). Ziesler concludes for "the usual declaratory force" of the verb here (p. 172), though I am very doubtful of his general thesis that the verb concerns "justification" (forensically) and the noun "righteousness" (ethically); his own discussion of specific passages, including 2:21, raises questions on such a sharp distinction. With Betz (p. 116) we opt for "being justified," in a declarative sense. This is particularly likely if, as he argues, we are dealing with a Jewish (Pharisaic) doctrine of salvation, which has already been interpreted afresh in a Jewish-Christian atonement formula:

> *Jewish position:* One needs to be declared righteous at the final judgment by God, and this justification can be obtained by successfully doing the requirements of the law (*ex ergōn nomou*).

> *Jewish-Christian atonement formula:* one needs that, yes, but justification can be obtained now through the expiatory death of Jesus on the cross, whom God raised up as lord. (Unclear is whether Christians at this stage thought of the blood of Jesus as covering only past sins or as effective on into the future, and what the role of the law was for believers.) The "Judaizing" *opponents* in Gal insisted on circumcision and acceptance of the Mosaic torah as necessary for salvation (*ex ergōn nomou*).

> *Paul:* Justification is only by faith in Jesus and his cross, not by the works of the law, for all persons, Gentiles as well as Jews;

circumcision avails nothing, doing the works of the law contributes nothing to the rightwised believer as regards salvation. Everyone who accepts torah must "abide by all things written in the book of the law, and do them"—which no one can (3:10–11). To that the alternative is to be "justified . . . through faith in Jesus Christ," 2:16, 3:11–13.

Paul's contribution in this situation, vis-à-vis Gentile converts, is to develop the Jewish-Christian atonement formulation to exclude works of the law henceforth, as well as initially.

101 Gal 2:17–20 goes on into further questions about this stance. All that need be said for our study is that v. 17 uses *dikaiothēnai* in the same way as above: "If we, while seeking to be rightwised *en Christō$_i$*, be found, even we ourselves to be 'sinners' [in the Jewish sense of v. 15, i.e., not seeking salvation by means of law-observance], is Christ then a 'minister of sin'?" The last phrase is a slogan, no doubt, from opponents directed against Paul's doctrine, which he goes on to deny in what becomes a further argument: to seek salvation by law would be for us Jewish Christians, to say nothing of Gentile Christians, to return to (or in the latter case, ironically now, to succumb to) what we have rejected; besides, we have "died to the law," v. 19). The phrase *en Christō$_t$* (v. 17) may be nothing more than instrumental ("by means of Christ's blood"), but Betz argues that it also means "participation in the blood of Christ," which can mean both his body that was given for us on the cross and his body, the community of believers. The whole answer is couched in first person plurals (vv. 15–17, even though 18–21*a* shifts into Paul's personal statements of faith), and so a communal side of justification is suggested.

Gal 2:21 rounds out the argument: By this stance of "justification and life on the grounds of faith" (v. 20), "I do not nullify the grace of God; for Christ has then died in vain if justification (*dikaiosynē*) comes 'through law.'" But it does not; it is by grace—not grace in the sense of a torah covenant with its stipulations, by adherence to which one can remain in a proper relationship to God, but grace in the sense of a promise (cf. 3:15–18) that depends entirely on God. *Pace* Ziesler (p. 174) who suggests that *dikaiosynē* here means "real righteousness" and is "ethical in that it is essentially something one does"—though he cannot avoid saying that "the main drift of the argument is indeed forensic" and those who see it as "chiefly forensic" (e.g., *RSV;* Burton ICC *Galatians,* p. 140) are not "entirely mistaken"—*dikaiosynē* "describes what the act of justification (*dikaiousthai*) is expected to produce: the status of righteousness before God" (H. D. Betz, p. 126).

102 c. Among the "proofs" Paul cites in *chap. 3* for the fact that the new status and situation the Galatians enjoy came about "by faith, not by works" (3:2, "hearing with faith," *ex akoēs pisteōs,* a missionary term for the proclamation that features faith, calls for it, and by its power creates faith, cf. Betz, p. 133, n. 50) are the gift of the Spirit to them (3:1–5), an argument from scripture (3:6–14), an analogy *kata anthrōpon* about a covenant as a "last will and testament" (*diathēkē* in both cases, 3:15ff.), and use of common Christian (baptismal) tradition (vv. 26ff., especially 27–28). Our terms occur when Paul is arguing scripturally. (On the outline above for the chapter, cf. Betz, pp. 19–20 and *JBC* 49:20.)

The biblical argument Paul employs revolves around the case of *Abraham* (3:6ff.) It was by promise solely on God's part, without any strings attached, that Abraham, by faith, found *dikaiosynē* (3:6). Scripture "foresaw" that God would rightwise (the verb *dikaioi*) the pagans too "on the basis of faith" (3:8). Scripture makes manifest that it is "the-person-who-is-righteous (*dikaios*) on-the-basis-of-faith who will 'live' " (v. 11). No law has ever been given (by God) that can make people really "live"; righteousness is not by law, it depends on Christ and faith (v. 21). We are rightwised by faith (v. 24). That is, in essence, the message Paul asserts throughout the chapter. Graphically put, it assumes:

Abraham	promise, by grace,	fulfilled in Christ
430 years	Moses, law "slips in" "works of the law" as a basis for salvation	now canceled

Thesis (v. 7): It is "persons of faith" (those rightwised on the basis of faith) who are the children of Abraham, not those who seek instead of, or on top of, this, to be rightwised by deeds demanded in the law.

103 Paul's argument is built around *two OT quotations:*

V. 6 (= *Gen 15:6*), Abraham "believed God, and this was credited to him as righteousness." The Genesis verse already had a long exegetical history prior to its use here. Judaism stressed Abraham's faithfulness and trust in God, or applied it to some deed of Abraham, such as being circumcised or offering his son Isaac as a sacrifice (cf. Jas 2:21). Paul's argument, which was "probably developed by him (or others?) in missionary work among Gentiles and Gentile Christians under the pressure of Jewish opposition" (*JBC* 49:21), takes it as the *dikaiosynē* that comes from hearing-and-receiving-in-faith the proclamation about Christ. Even Ziesler must admit that here "the reckoning of faith as righteousness is apparently the same as justification by grace," and his passing attempt to read in being ethically "righteous" is lame (p. 175).

V. 11 (= *Hab 2:4*) is again a verse with a history of interpretation. While the Hebrew MT may mean "The person who is *ṣaddîq* will live by his (own) fidelity (or Yahweh's faithfulness to the relationship?)," the LXX word order (*ho de dikaios ek pisteōs mou zēsetai*) implies, "the person who is *dikaios* on the basis of My faithfulness (or on the basis of faith in Me) shall live." Paul's citation of it here and at Rom 1:17, without *mou,* opens up the possibility for him to take it to mean, "The person-who-is-*dikaios*-on-the-basis-of-faith shall live (or have life)." It is again forensic (Ziesler, who nonetheless wants to drag "the ethical" in here too), and (with Feuillet, *NTS* 6 [1959–60]: 52–80; Tobac; Nygren) he holds that the point is "not to establish how the righteous live, but to decide what kind of righteousness is necessary in order to live" (p. 177, n. 1). The answer is, "By faith, not by works of the law."

The other verses that use *dikaio*-terminology (esp. 3:8, 21, 24) reiterate Paul's basic position on the theme of *dikaiosynē ek pisteōs*. Gal 4 adds further arguments to support the freedom Christians enjoy on the basis of God's promise and justification by faith.[69]

104   d. Finally, in *chap. 5*, where Paul, as always but perhaps especially significantly for the Galatians situation, gets into the *paraenesis* that is part of the gospel (and therefore of justification/righteousness when the gospel is put into those terms), we have two uses of our terms. The context is a warning (5:1), exhorting the Galatians to stand firm in the liberty for which Christ has liberated them from the "yoke of slavery" (the law and other forms of tyranny, including "the elements of the world"—involving not only pagan forms of legalism but also astral powers and "fate"). He reiterates, "You who are trying to get rightwised (*dikaiousthe*) by means of law have become severed from Christ, you have fallen from grace" (v. 4). Then he goes on,

> ⁵For through the Spirit, on the basis of faith (*ek pisteōs*) we are awaiting something hoped for, namely *dikaiosynē* (epexegetical genitive, i.e. in apposition).

If *dikaiosynē* is taken as "uprightness," this verse clearly makes it a future hope. Ziesler, in order to avoid the notion that it refers to "the hope of acceptance at the Judgment," opts "more probably" for the meaning to be "the full realisation of the new character now in Christ begun" (p. 179), but that is to say this ethical "uprightness" for the Christian is a not-yet attainment. Ziesler also allows that the phrase could be "the hope which springs from justification," so that righteousness is an *arrabōn* (cf. 2 Cor 1:22, 5:5; Eph 1:14 for the term)—a word *not* involved here or elsewhere in connection with *dikaiosynē*.

Why not simply say that justification (in a broad sense, not just as an initial juridical act) has a future side as part of its eschatological character? It *is* hope—but a sure hope because based on God's promise and not on our doing the works of the law. The judgment-to-come is within the hori-

---

69. Bligh views Paul's speech at Antioch when he confronted Peter (2:14ff.) as extending (minus some insertions by Paul for the Galatian situation, like 4:11–20) as far as 5:13*a*, with its climax in the allegory about Sarah and Hagar (4:21–31)! Much more persuasive is the position of C. K. Barrett, "The Allegory of Abraham, Sarah, and Hagar in the Argument of Galatians," *Rechtfertigung* (Käsemann fs), pp. 1–16, that, like other OT quotations in chaps. 3 and 4, the "*locus classicus* for the doctrine of the *iustificatio impiorum*," Paul in 4:21–31 is reworking scriptural emphases of his opponents to favor his own gospel of justification by faith; in this case it is by use of Isa 54:1 (Gal 4:27) to interpret the Sarah-Hagar story via the rabbinic device of *gĕzērâ šāwâ*.

zon of justification (cf. 5:10, 6:7–10). This does not mean, however, a "double justification" (first at baptism and then at the Last Judgment again), as Jeremias has argued (*ExpTim* 66 [1954–55]: 369), but simply that justification runs through the whole life of the believer and beyond.

105   A further particular example of the implications of justification is given in *5:6,* a verse traditionally divisive for Lutherans and Catholics:

> For in Christ Jesus
> neither circumcision avails anything nor uncircumcision,
> but faith (*pistis*) through love *energoumenē*.

The participle at the end is middle voice (*JBC* 49:29, among other references), therefore, "working itself out in *agape.*" *RSV* note: "made effective in love"; *NEB:* "active in love"; *JB* "faith that makes its power felt through love." Ziesler comments, rather surprisingly, on how the forensic underlies this verse; "the letter's main concern is forensic, . . . the ethical is rather our preoccupation . . . subordinate in our thinking in this debate" (p. 180). In Paul's abbreviations, "faith" means "faith in Jesus Christ"; new is the definition of it as "power" (*energein,* the verb), though not if "the righteousness of God" is itself a power that empowers; from here on, *agape* predominates the paraenetic section. Freedom itself means to be slaves/servants to one another (5:13); that way, as fruit of the Spirit, the intent of the whole law is fulfilled, but not as works to gain satisfaction (5:14, 22–23).

In the interpretation above, "love" has been taken, as commonly (cf. Betz, pp. 262–63), to refer to the response-in-love of those in Christ and thus actions of loving service by Christians. It is part of "faith as obedience" (Rom 1:5, 16:26). An alternative is to refer *agape* to *God's* love, which stands behind the salvation event of Christ, in which we believe; apart from 1 Cor 13 (which shows enough uncharacteristic usages of Pauline terms to be considered by some a passage that he quotes, not one of his own authorship), *agape* in the Pauline corpus usually means the love of God for human beings (cf. 2 Cor 13:14; Gal 2:20; and Furnish, *Theology and Ethics of Paul,* pp. 202–03).

106   We need not, in interpreting Paul, pause over all the later theologizing based on the Latin rendering *fides caritate formata,* which took *energoumenē* as a passive participle, "faith formed or activated by love," and then regarded *caritate* as human deeds of love (believers empowered by the Spirit).[70] Rather we may underscore Betz's observation that 5:6 is a sum-

---

70. Gal 5:6 has often been regarded as a prototype of 1 Cor 13:13, "Now abides faith, hope, love, these three; but the greatest of these is love"; cf. Conzelmann, *1 Corinthians,* p. 229, esp. n. 114. When coupled with 1 Cor 13 and verses like 1 Thess 1:3 ("the work of faith and the labor of love") and Phil 2:12 ("work out your own salvation"), the Latin rendering of 5:6 could give rise to an interpretation of Paul that viewed faith as arising out of deeds of love.

mary of Paul's doctrine of the church, in light of his summary on justification at 5:5. On the background of *agape* for v. 6 in 2:20, the love shown in Christ's cross, compare specifically Betz, pp. 263–64.

Luther, to bring the matter even more closely into connection with our dialogue concerns, spoke vigorously in his 1535 commentary on Galatians (n. 6 above) about the danger of a new "works-righteousness" arising from this passage when Christian acts of love are combined with faith as the basis for an idea of justification by faith *and* by works of love. Lutherans have continued to fear all that might thus undercut the sole sufficiency of God's deed in Christ as the basis for human salvation.

For Galatians we may let Paul have the last word in the postscript, which he wrote with his own hand (6:11–18). It is a reiteration of the gospel that he had been defending in the Galatian situation, this time without justification/righteousness terms. Opposing law and circumcision as in chaps. 2 and 3, it centers in "the cross of our Lord Jesus Christ" and the principle (*kanōn*), "neither circumcision, nor uncircumcision, but *kainē ktisis,* new creaturehood" (cf. 2 Cor 5:21; above, §95; *JBC* 49:32, "creature," not "creation"); "upon those who walk thus (note the plural, corporate sense), be peace." What Lutherans seek to defend by the gospel of justification by grace through faith is here articulated in other terms.

3. Philippians.[71]

107   Although we have already noted above a preference for viewing Philippians as a redacted combination of three letters by Paul about A.D. 54–55 from Ephesus and environs (§86), we shall here first examine the references to righteousness/justification in their canonical sequence. Even so, it is necessary to recall that Paul wrote with joy, though imprisoned (specific references in 1:7, 13; cf. 2:19, 23), in spite of "rival preachers" where he is (1:12–18, rivalry not over doctrinal matters but differing opinions about Paul and his imprisonment and perhaps whether, in order to avoid martyrdom, he should have invoked his Roman citizenship—so Collange); pagan opponents (1:28); and, pertinent to our interests, "the dogs" and "evil workers" of 3:2ff., cf. esp. 3:18–21. We assume for chap. 3 one group of interlopers, akin to the Hellenistic–Jewish Christian missionaries in 2 Cor 10–13, who were seeking to convert Paul's converts to a type of Christianity that insisted on circumcision (3:2f.) and Hebrew prerogatives; on "knowing Christ" in the sense of "the power of his resurrection" (but not, apparently, sharing his sufferings, 3:10); a libertine or legalistic ethics (3:19), not centered in a theology and life-style of the cross (3:18); and with a realized rather than any future eschatology (hence Paul concludes the section with 3:20–21, on the transformation to take place only when Christ shall come).

---

71. **Commentaries on Phil:** Lohmeyer (MeyerK, 11th ed., 1956); F. W. Beare (HNTC, 1959); J. Gnilka (HTKNT 10/3, 1968, 3d ed. 1980); J.-F. Collange (CNT Xa, 1973), cited from trans by A. W. Heathcote, *The Epistle of Saint Paul to the Philippians* (London: Epworth Press, 1979); R. P. Martin (NCB, 1976).

108   a. *Chap. 1.* The most significant references to *dikaiosynē* in Philippians (the verb is never used, nor is the phrase "righteousness *of God*," the adjective *dikaios* occurs only twice) are in chap. 3. The phrase at **1:7**, "it is right (*dikaion*) for me to feel thus about you all," is a routine reference to Paul's warmth for the Philippians and their "partnership in the gospel" ever since the founding mission there (cf. 4:15–16).

More enigmatic is the conclusion of Paul's prayer for them (**1:11**) that "for the Day of Jesus Christ" you may be

> filled with the fruits of righteousness which come through Jesus Christ (*RSV; karpon dikaiosynēs ton dia Iēsou Christou*).

Clearly the phrase deals with something begun by God (1:6) and to be completed only at the final judgment, and dependent on Jesus Christ. The phrase should be read in light of 3:9 and of Paul's general doctrine of justification. The genitive here, "of righteousness," could be epexegetical, i.e., "fruit consisting in righteousness" (cf. 4:8), but Ziesler (p. 151, rightly, I think) prefers "a genitive of origin"—"the fruit [sing.] which comes through Jesus Christ from (God's) righteousness that depends on faith [3:9]," something that is not ours but his, yet allows us to stand "pure and blameless at the Day of Christ." The setting is forensic; there is stress on relational and ethical results from justification.

109   b. In *chap. 3* Paul responds to the heretical interlopers by citing (vv. 4*b*–6) his personal example as one who had once sought security in precisely those human, fleshly features that were emphasized by these teachers ("workers" as they may have called themselves, 3:2; cf. 2 Cor 11:13). He had learned, in the "great reversal of values" in his life, to count what he had once treasured as so much *skybala* (v. 8, *KJV* "dung" or *TEV* "garbage") compared now with "knowing" and "gaining" Christ and being "found in him." The great reversal Paul describes in terms of *dikaiosynē* (3:6, 9). The rest of the chapter makes clear that, in contrast to the opponents, he does not yet understand himself to have arrived "at the goal," perfection; that, for him and for all Christians, can come only at the parousia (3:12–16). Paul is *in via,* and in that way eschatologically he serves, rather than the interlopers, as a model or example for the Philippians (3:17–21).

Some commentators see in the structure of the chapter a parallel to other Pauline passages:

antithetical statements—	Phil	cf. Rom	
(1) Saul, seeking security in	3:4–6	1:18—	7:7–25
the human and fleshly		3:20 (sin)	(law)
vs. (2) Paul and his great reversal		3:21—	8:1–17
via justification by faith	3:7–11	4:25	(Spirit)
leading to			
(3) what is true for every	3:12–16	chap. 5	8:18–39
Christian—		("no longer . . . but not yet"; justified . . . life in hope and the Spirit).	

110   More to the point of this passage is the double, contrasting, chiastic structure of **3:9–11** on the *two kinds of righteousness* (cf. also Rom 10:5–17). Note that a concern in each case is to be "blameless" (3:6; Paul insisted that, as Judaism maintained was possible, he, Saul, had been "as to the righteousness under the law, blameless [*amemptos*]"; cf. 1:10, with reference to the Day of Christ, *aproskopoi;* 2:15, *amemptoi*). Now comes the contrast, after the reversal of old values: "I count all [previous] things as refuse (v. 8) . . . in order that I may be found 'in Christ,' not having

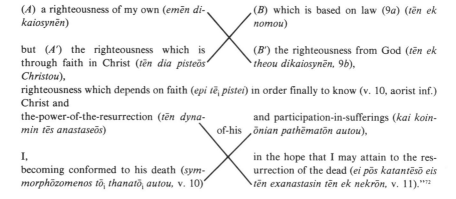

(*A*) a righteousness of my own (*emēn dikaiosynēn*)

(*B*) which is based on law (9a) (*tēn ek nomou*)

but (*A'*) the righteousness which is through faith in Christ (*tēn dia pisteōs Christou*),

(*B'*) the righteousness from God (*tēn ek theou dikaiosynēn, 9b*),

righteousness which depends on faith (*epi tē₁ pistei*) in order finally to know (v. 10, aorist inf.) Christ and

the-power-of-the-resurrection (*tēn dynamin tēs anastaseōs*)

and participation-in-sufferings (*kai koinōnian pathēmatōn autou*),

of-his

I,

becoming conformed to his death (*symmorphōzomenos tō₁ thanatō₁ autou,* v. 10)

in the hope that I may attain to the resurrection of the dead (*ei pōs katantēsō eis tēn exanastasin tēn ek nekrōn,* v. 11)."[72]

111   The verses are directed against the position of the interlopers who stress Christ as resurrection power (Paul ties together with this, through a single article *tēn,* "the . . . participation in Christ's sufferings" also, and then in 10*b*–11 presents the proper sequence, first conformity with Christ's death, then resurrection; cf. Rom 6:5) and against their eschatology (v. 11, with its *ei pōs* clause, amply makes clear that the general resurrection of the dead, unlike that of Christ, is something that has not happened as yet; cf. also 3:12–21).

Further, the verses are directed against the view the opponents have on justification (cf. above, §100). Both groups insist on righteousness/justification. In contrast to what the opponents hold, Paul states his view:

---

72. Grammatical details on the rendering above of Phil 3:9–11:

In v. 9, *Christou* is an obj. gen. (cf. above, § 99).

In v. 9 *dia pisteōs* and *epi tē₁ pistei* are not tautologous (cf. *NAB,* righteousness "which comes through faith in Christ" and "is based on faith"), nor do they give first the cause and then the basis on which the result rests (cf. Gnilka), nor does *dia* refer to Christ's faithful obedience to the Father (R. P. Martin); rather, omit the punctuation after v. 9 (*RSV* semicolon) and take, as Collange does: la justice que donne Dieu et (qui s'obtient) par la foi en Christ, cette foi qui est connaissance de Christ . . ." (inf. of purpose, or epexegetical inf.), "the righteousness which God gives which is (obtained) by faith in Christ, the faith which is a knowledge of Christ" (p. 127).

At the end of v. 11, the "if possible" clause (*ei pōs*) suggests not doubt or uncertainty but expectation with humility ("hope," *TEV, NAB*).

(1) In contrast to that which comes on the basis of obedience to law, Paul stresses the sort of *dikaiosynē* that comes from God and so is alien to human beings.

(2) This "God-kind of righteousness" (A. T. Robertson) comes through faith in Christ, faith to know him, *both* the power of his resurrection *and* participation in his sufferings. It is related to Christ's death (atonement, 3:10).

(3) Righteousness/justification possesses both the aspects of gift and of power (vindication from God; cf. Isa 54:17, R. P. Martin).

(4) The individual, personal side is here emphatic because Paul is speaking in personal, individual terms; it is "justification of the ungodly" (Saul of Tarsus, who persecuted believers). To rest on Phil 3, alone, however, is to miss the communal, cosmic aspect to be seen in Romans and elsewhere.

(5) Even so there is present in Phil 3 a close link to the "in Christ" theme (3:9, *euretho en autō,*), participation in his spiritual body (Stuhlmacher, p. 99), and also to ethical results (see above on 1:11).

This participation in God's righteousness through Christ is termed by Ziesler forensic, relational, ethical, though he hesitates to find here "imputation" (which some claim by recourse to the rabbinic doctrine of "merits," imputed for forensic purposes, pp. 150–51). What the Phil 3 passage lacks are the present side of justification (because the opponents in Philippi were stressing that), the cosmic (because Paul here writes so personally), and use of the term "grace" (but cf. *ek theou,* v. 9, "from God"). What emerges as prominent, as in Galatians, is the Pauline note of faith, something not *ek nomou* (3:6, 9).

112 c. The paraenetic advice in **4:8,** "Finally, Christians, whatever things are true, honorable, just (*dikaia*), pure, etc., think on these things," sounds like reflection of typically Greek virtues. V. 9 gives them a theological and Christian setting ("the God of peace" and "what you have learned, received, heard, and seen in me"). Furnish senses here, however, "a distillation of . . . the Hellenistic secular ethic," broadening rather than restricting Christian responsibility, with an admonition to action (*prassete,* "keep doing").[73] The ethic is, of course, undergirded by eschatology (4:5, "The Lord is near," refers to the parousia, not incarnation theology) and rests, as imperatives, on the indicative—of justification (cf. Kertelge, pp. 251–62).

113 d. *A reconstructed sequence.* If Philippians is interpreted in the supposed *order of* its (3) *fragments,* then Paul, in his normal correspondence with the congregation, makes passing reference to his hope that they may stand at the parousia, filled with the fruit that comes through Jesus Christ from God's righteousness (1:11). This prayer reflects his normal teaching on the topic. Later, when missionaries come teaching a different

---

73. Victor Paul Furnish, *Theology and Ethics in Paul* (Nashville: Abingdon, 1968), pp. 88–89.

kind of *dikaiosynē,* he responds by stressing its God-given, Christ- and cross-centered nature, and above all its appropriation by faith, not via works of the law. It is, in Phil 3, the focal point of the gospel, but not in isolation, for righteousness/justification relates intimately to Christology, ethics, and especially eschatology.

4. Romans.[74]

114 a. The *importance* of Romans has already been indicated, both as climactic among the unquestioned letters of Paul (§§81, 86 above) and for the prevalence in it of prepauline formulas about righteousness/justification (above, §§ 69–75; 3:24–26a, 4:25 esp.). The significance of *dikaiosynē* (*tou theou*) as the theme in Romans is impressive whether Paul wrote the letter solely to Rome (and hence had to present his form of common apostolic Christianity to a community he had not founded and did not personally know) or regarded Jerusalem as "secret addressee" (and therefore found it absolutely necessary to deal with this particularly OT, Jewish-Christian way of speaking about God's actions and of the cross of Jesus) or, reflecting battles he had been through in Galatia and elsewhere, was addressing a definitive farewell account of his gospel to Greece and Asia Minor, especially Ephesus.[75] Justification as a theme for Paul was therefore both considered and catholic (as over against the often ad hoc and local in other letters).

115 That the gospel as "the righteousness of God revealed through faith for faith" (1:16–17) is the theme of Romans is widely affirmed, certainly for the doctrinal section of the letter. Obviously it is central in the compressed verses at 3:21–31. Abraham (chap. 4) becomes the scriptural example to illustrate justification by faith, not by works. Käsemann terms 3:21–4:25 "the thesis," with polemical development and scriptural proof, for the document. Cranfield, like Nygren, takes the citation at 1:17 from Hab 2:4 and regards Rom 1:18–4:25 as expounding the words "he who through faith is righteous" and 5:1–8:39 as Paul's treatment of the rest of the OT verse, that such a person "shall live" (but cf. Kertelge, p. 41, n. 139). Better and more common is treatment of chaps. 5–8 as "the results of justification" or the fuller meaning of salvation for the justified, or "the righteousness of faith as a reality of eschatological freedom" (Käsemann). The work of Munck and Chr. Müller and others has called attention to chaps. 9–11 as not an intrusion but an integral part of the argument and indeed a further exposition of the righteousness of God (cf. especially

---

74. **Commentaries on Rom** (in addition to those already cited in nn. 48–50, 52–53 above): Otto Kuss, *Der Römerbrief* (Regensburg: Pustet, 1957, 1959, 1978); Ernst Käsemann, HNT (1973), cited from the Eng. trans., *Romans* (above, n. 24); C. E. B. Cranfield, *Romans* (ICC, Vol. 1, 1975; Vol. 2, chaps. 9–16, plus essays, 1979); Roy A. Harrisville, *Romans* (Augsburg Commentary on the New Testament; Minneapolis: Augsburg, 1980).

75. On possible destinations for Rom or drafts of Rom, cf., in addition to § 81 above, *JBC* 53:3, 8–11; W. G. Kümmel, *Introduction to the New Testament* (rev. ed.; Nashville: Abingdon, 1975), pp. 311–20; and *The Romans Debate,* ed. K. P. Donfried (Minneapolis: Augsburg, 1977).

10:5ff.) re Israel (cf. Cranfield, pp. 445–47, 824). Finally, the paraenetic section (12:1ff.) may be called "the righteousness of God in daily Christian life" (Käsemann) or "the obedience to which those who are righteous by faith are called" (Cranfield). In the last forty years or so, since Adolf Schlatter wrote on Romans as *Gottes Gerechtigkeit,* this massive unity of the epistle has been increasingly and widely seen.

116 Rather than attempt an analysis of all of Romans along such lines, we shall follow our procedure of discussing the passages that employ any of the six *dikaio*-words, of which there are sixty-three instances in Romans. Because of the neuralgic nature of some sections in disputes since the Reformation, we shall have to enter into considerable detail at some points. Because of new insights from recent exegetical analysis of *dikaiosynē theou* we shall also be discussing some passages that have not necessarily been prominent in interconfessional discussion.

117 b. *The theme (1:16–17; on 1:18, see c, below)*

> [16]For I am not ashamed of the gospel (*euangelion*): it is the power of God for salvation (*dynamis gar theou estin eis sōtērian*) to every one who has faith (*pisteuonti*), to the Jew first and also to the Greek. [17]For in it the righteousness of God (*dikaiosynē tou theou*) is revealed through faith for faith (*ek pisteōs eis pistin*); as it is written, "He who through faith is righteous (*dikaios*) shall live" (Hab 2:4).
>
> Note: OR The righteous shall live by faith.   (*RSV*)

After the salutation (1:1–17) and prayer (1:8–15), Paul announces the gospel that he proclaims and is eager to preach at Rome also, in terms of God's power and God's righteousness, to be received through faith. (Note *pistis,* 3×; participle 1×; the particular emphasis on faith that Paul himself had developed over against "works," as we have seen.)

118 That the gospel is power, anthropologically directed, and universally at that, by revelation (*apokalyptetai*), is clear. The phrase "to the Jew first but also to the Greek" not only suggests the subdivision for the following chapters (1:18–32 is commonly taken as treating God's wrath against pagan-Gentiles and 2:1–3:8 against the Jew) but also shows Paul's universalism (to be expressed in 3:21ff. by "all" and "every"; cf. 1:16 "every one who has faith"). The gospel of God's righteousness will have to do not just with his loyalty to his covenant or covenant people but with his whole creation and all peoples. Implied in 1:16–17 (and stated elsewhere) are the points that this gospel concerns Jesus Christ, God's Son (cf. the prepauline formula at 1:3–4) and is now eschatologically at work (present tenses in vv. 16–17; 3:21 *nyni de*). It is *justitia efficax ad salutem,* "God's effective power active in the world of men [and nature, cf. 8:18–23] to bring about deliverance from His wrath in the final judgment and reinstatement in that glory of God which was lost through sin" (Cranfield, p. 89; cf. Kertelge, p. 87).

119   The *gar* clause of v. 17 ("for") declares God's *dikaiosynē* to be the particular content of the gospel, according to Paul in Romans. The genitive "of God" has been the topic of much discussion. The options:

- *objective genitive*—"the righteousness which is valid before God" (Luther, "die Gerechtigkeit die vor Gott gilt"; cf. Kertelge, pp. 6–8);
- *subjective genitive*—"righteousness as an attribute or quality of God" (Schlatter, Lyonnet, Kuss; cf. Kertelge, pp. 12–14; Käsemann School; cf. "power *of God*" and "wrath *of God*");
- *genitive of authorship*—"righteousness which goes forth from God" (cf. Phil 3:9; Nygren, Bultmann; cf. Kertelge, pp. 9–12); or *genitive of origin* (Cranfield, pp. 97–98, "man's righteous status [which he concludes is the sense of *dikaiosynē*] which is the result of God's action of justifying").[76]

"The Reformation view" has often been taken to be that righteousness is a gift from God that allows the believer to be treated as righteous at the judgment. "The Catholic view" has often been presented so that *dikaiosynē* is something imparted to persons so that God's uprightness makes them upright. Ziesler (pp. 188–89) understands himself to be mediating between these two views when he claims that both the forensic (in the verb) and the ethical (in the noun) are involved: "God's saving righteousness . . . for men . . . restores their relationship with God, and . . . makes them new (ethical, righteous) beings." Käsemann comments, "There is virtual consensus today in speaking of a genitive of author, yet everyone conceals his own opinion behind this grammatical cipher"; Greek grammar can help somewhat, "but grammatical distinctions merely label and abridge what is perceived to be a material problem . . ." (pp. 28, 26). We must add that in our opinion not every use of *tou theou* need be uniform after *dikaiosynē;* each passage must be judged for itself in context.

At 1:17 Paul leaves the exact sense in "righteousness *of God*" still to be defined. If one is convinced that an apocalyptic formula from Judaism lies behind it (see above, § 40), then the sense already here is that of "God's covenant faithfulness" (Käsemann, p. 30). But in Paul's hands what he regards as a quality of God (Rom 3:5) will be seen also as a dynamic power from God effecting, through Christ's cross, forgiveness, justification, life in Christ, and all that "redemption" implies (3:21–31).

120   The emphasis on faith at 1:16–17 is not to be taken here as "growth in faith" (going from faith to faith; Lagrange, Huby; though 2 Cor 10:15 can suggest such a notion was not impossible for Paul), or merely so that *eis pistin* underscores *ek pisteōs*, "having much the same effect as the 'sola' of 'sola fide,' " i.e., man gains "a righteous status which is altogether by faith" (Cranfield, p. 100). The *RSV*'s "through faith" (for *ek pis-*

---

76. See "The Augsburg Confession" (cited above, n. 10), pp. 17–19.

teōs; cf. 3:22 *dia pisteōs*) obviously reflects the same Greek phrase as in the Habakkuk quotation; *eis pistin* certainly does not denote "a faith multiplied through human cooperation, but also not only the goal, which has been reached in faith, of the revealed righteousness of God [though I do find attractive Schlatter's idea of *ek* as causal and *eis* as teleological], but much more its continuing activity to which the person is to respond with continuing faith" (Kertelge, p. 89). Thus, faith, like God's righteousness, has an ongoing role all through the Christian life, not just at the outset as initial response; "the revelation of God's righteousness, because it is bound to the gospel, takes place always only in the sphere of faith" (Käsemann, p. 31).

121   Last of all, there is the Habakkuk citation itself in v. 17, with which we previously have met in a polemical situation at Gal 3:11 (see above, § 103). The citation is not uniquely Paul's usage but that of common primitive Christianity from its reflection on the Hebrew scriptures (Käsemann, p. 31; Kertelge, p. 91). From the use of Hab 2, vv. 3 and 4 at Heb 10:37–38, Strobel has endeavored to read into Rom 1:17 the eschatologically imminent note that "the coming one shall come and not tarry," Hab 2:3 = Heb 10:37), but that is dubious (Stuhlmacher, p. 83, n. 3; Kertelge, pp. 92–93). The theme of God's righteousness *is* eschatological, pointing to the "new age," but apocalyptic imminence is not Paul's point here. "Righteousness/justification *by faith*" is the point that he will develop from the Habakkuk verse (*RSV* text, therefore, rather than note; *NEB;* Kuss, Cranfield, among others). His doctrine of justification will thereby express "the specifically Pauline understanding of christology" (Käsemann, p. 24).

122   c. *Romans 1:18–3:20* is a negative development of the 1:16–17 theme: "Without the gospel God's wrath is manifested against all men" (*JBC* 53:22), or, taking the section as an exposition of "by faith (alone)" in the theme verses, 1:18–3:20 show that "in the light of the gospel there is no question of men's being righteous before God otherwise than by faith" (Cranfield, p. 104). Three aspects are of particular concern in our investigation.

123   (1) Does *1:18* belong with 1:16–17 as part of the revelation? The parallelism has often been noted:

> 1:17 *dikaiosynē gar tou theou en autō₁* [the gospel] *apokalyptetai . . .*
>
> 1:18 *apokalyptetai gar orgē theou ap' ouranou . . .*

"The wrath of God" that "is being revealed from heaven" is not to be taken as an affect of God in the sense of capricious emotion or as simply an effect of nemesis or "an inevitable process of cause and effect in a moral universe" (so C. H. Dodd and A. T. Hanson in the English literature) but as God doing his work of judgment against those who "suppress the truth by their unrighteousness (*adikia*)" (1:18; cf. in 1:24, 26, 28, the OT way of speaking, "*God* gave them over to . . ."). But does this wrath of God happen outside God's righteousness (Dodd, Hanson), along with it but as an irrational element (R. Otto), under it (J. T. Beck), prior to it (Lietzmann, Nygren), or in it (K. Barth; all references in Herold, pp. 2–6)?[77]

Put grammatically, does the *gar* in v. 18 (the same connective as in vv. 16 and 17) suggest that Paul is appealing to the "observable situation" in the world as proof that God's righteousness and wrath are being revealed (cf. Barrett)? Cranfield speaks of 1:17 and 1:18 as revealing "two aspects of the same process," so that "*orgē theou* also is being revealed *in the gospel*" and "the reality of the wrath of God is only truly known . . . in Gethsemane and on Golgotha" (pp. 109–110). Herold, on the basis of OT oracles of salvation in the midst of passages of judgment like Isa 42:14–17, with the schema "Salvation, because of judgment" (Heil weil Gericht), argues that in the wrath-exhibited-in-judgment Paul sees revealed God's fidelity to his promise; the parallelism and contemporaneousness of both revelations are for him grounded in the gospel, above all in the cross (pp. 329–30). But this carries the connection too far. "From heaven" (v. 18) is not the same as "in it" (v. 17, = in the gospel, v. 16).

One may better say, with Käsemann (pp. 35–38), that, while only with the gospel does one come to know what bondage to sin really is, "wrath" as Paul presents it in Rom 1 and 2, though "of God," is not the content of the gospel, nor condemnation part of "the righteousness from God" that Paul is going to expound. God's "power" is a better clue: He exercises his dominion over all creation by meeting, as he always has, "the disobedient with retribution" before and apart from Christ, but he also exercises his dominion by a "power for salvation" revealed in his saving righteousness to all who have faith in Christ—for them, no condemnation (8:1).

Lutherans have especially wrestled with the questions posed here, and they have often done it with concepts like "the proper work of God and God's strange work" or "law and gospel." Their concern has been to give proper place to God's wrath and judgment over sin that is part of revelation, but to make sovereign the good news of justification.

124   (2) The universal indictment in *Rom 1:19ff.* of "all persons, both Jews and Greeks," as "under the power of Sin," shown in light of what God has revealed, not only in Scripture (3:10–18) but also from what can be perceived in the Gentile and Jewish worlds (as missionary preaching even in behalf of Judaism must have developed it), so that before the bar of God "every mouth is stopped" and "the whole world stands guilty (*hypo-*

---

77. Gerhart Herold, *Zorn und Gerechtigkeit Gottes bei Paulus: Eine Untersuchung zu Röm. 1:16–18* (Europäische Hochschulschriften, Reihe XXIII, Bd. 14; Bern: Herbert Lang, Frankfurt: Peter Lang, 1973), diss. Munich (L. Goppelt). Against the view of Dodd and A. T. Hanson, cf. Cranfield, *Romans,* pp. 108–110. For Dodd see his Romans commentary (MNTC), and for Hanson, *The Wrath of the Lamb* (London: SPCK, 1957).

dikos) before God" (3:20), occasionally employs words from the *dikaio*-family.

At **1:32** the relatively rare word *dikaiōma* is used in the sense of "decree, ordinance" (Ziesler, p. 189, cf. 209): Those who do such things as Paul has listed in a catalogue of vices, "though they know the righteous decree of God (*to dikaiōma tou theou*), deserve to die." In discussing God's judgment on the Jews, Paul uses the same word at **2:26** to refer to "the precepts of the law" (*RSV*): if a non-Jew (lit., "the uncircumcision") keeps "the righteous requirements of the law (*ta dikaiōmata tou nomou*), will not his uncircumcision be reckoned as circumcision?"

At **2:5** Paul uses (for the only time in the NT) a rare Hellenistic word that combines the root for "judgment" and that for "righteousness" when he refers to the "day of wrath and revelation of the righteous judgment (*dikaiokrisia*) of God." Presupposed are the linking of "judgment on the guilty and the established right of God" (Käsemann, p. 56). Perhaps Paul in using this uncommon term desired to distinguish God's (saving) righteousness and his "just judgment."

At **2:13**, as part of Paul's excoriation of those who possess torah but do not obey it, a traditionally rabbinic Jewish contrast (cf. also Jas 1:22) is cited with regard to God's future judgment: "It is not the hearers of the law who are righteous before God (*dikaioi para tō₁ theō₁*), but the doers of the law who will be justified (*dikaiothēsontai*)" (*RSV*). The sense is clearly forensic (Ziesler, p. 189), the meaning of the verb "will be pronounced righteous" (Cranfield, pp. 136, 154; Kertelge, pp. 143–44), the basis Jewish (by doing the law), the point to underscore v. 12*b*, "all who have sinned under the law will be judged by the law."

125   This section, especially 2:6–11, where Paul declares that God "will render to everyone *according to his works*" and where he seems to allow that "He will give eternal life . . . glory, honor, and peace" to "everyone who *does good*" (2:7, 10, cf. 14), has long (at least since Origen and Augustine) been a source of dispute, Roman Catholic dogmatics emphasizing it, Protestantism seeking to find some solution to avoid any suggestion of "justification by works." Cranfield sketches ten possible interpretations before opting for the probability that Paul is referring to Christians in vv. 7 and 10 and by their "well-doing" (*ergon agathon*) means "their conduct as the expression of their faith" (pp. 151–52).

Käsemann (pp. 56–59), who with K. Grobel senses here a "chiastic retribution formula" of hymnic or rhetorical style in vv. 7–10, rejects all explanations where Paul is said to be speaking hypothetically (so Lietzmann) or lapsing back into Jewish views (Bultmann), or that attempt a "both/and" answer, via "double justification" (Jeremias, at baptism and last judgment) or via the claim that "faith justifies but works contribute to sanctification." Nor is he willing to let it stand as a necessary contradiction. Rather, "the doctrine of judgment according to works" that Paul retains from the OT (cf. Ps 62:12) is to be understood now "in light of" his

doctrine of justification, the two linked inseparably. "A doctrine of justification which avoids the concept of judgment loses its character as proclamation of the lordship of God. . . . A concept of judgment which does not
receive its meaning from the doctrine of justification leaves no more room
for assurance of salvation" (pp. 56–57). When the Judge comes, believers
stand under the judgment of the same Lord along with Jew and Gentile.
What holds for them is the gift and power of God's righteousness, received
by faith. Justification and faith matter from the outset in the preaching of
"righteousness unto salvation" and its appropriation until the Day when
God judges. Käsemann's (p. 58) "here 'by works alone' in fact coincides
with 'by faith alone' (Althaus)," comes close to the view that the *ergon
agathon* in the passage equals "the 'good work' of faith"—a view Cranfield
rejected primarily because *ergon* as a reference to faith occurs only in John
6:29, not in Paul; cf., however, 1 Thess 1:3, *to ergon tēs pisteōs* (see above, §
83), and 2 Thess 1:11.

126   If Christians are meant here, Stuhlmacher (pp. 228–36) finds the
key in their tension between being still in the flesh but also in the Spirit:
With the gift of the Spirit, God's creative, justifying power works in the
life of the baptized in the contest between *dikaiosynē* and Sin. Justifica-
tion/righteousness reaches from baptism till that final epiphany. Fuchs
speaks of justification not "through works but *in* the work of obedience"
(ibid., p. 231). Herbert Braun in a 1930 study viewed Paul's references to
the judgment as having a legitimate though not consistent place in his theology, as "the background for the preaching of grace"; Kertelge (p. 256)
speaks similarly when he terms them a "Voraussetzung der Rechtferti-
gungbotschaft." Lieselotte Mattern[78] stresses the reflection in 2:5ff. of
"two-ways" material from virtue and vices catalogs (on which see also the
essay by E. Schweizer cited in n. 103 below) and agrees that Christians are
to be under the final judgment as pagans and Jews also are. But Rom 3:20
makes clear that "no human being will be justified in God's sight by works
of the law." Similarly the virtue/vices catalog concludes that those who do
the works of the flesh will not inherit the kingdom of God, but the Christians who walk in the Spirit thus fulfill the law of Christ (Gal 5:22–23, 25);
if they did the vices rather than the virtues, they would be no Christians.
Seeing the Pauline pattern of indicative and imperative behind 2:5ff., Mattern concludes that the Christian stands under God's *dikaiosynē* only so
long as he or she in obedience does the "(good) work" of God; if the

---

78. Lieselotte Mattern, *Das Verständnis des Gerichtes bei Paulus* (ATANT 47; 1966);
diss. Zürich (E. Schweizer). Involved also (pp. 141–51) is the distinction already noted by
Herbert Braun, *Gerichtsgedanke und Rechtfertigungslehre bei Paulus* (UNT 19; 1930), 51ff.,
between the plural "works" (of the law), always negatively used, never of Christians, never in
connection with justification except as the opposite to "faith" and the singular "work" (*ergon*), regularly positively, for the work of Christians (possible exception, Rom 2:5–16).
     Further, Ernst Synofzik, *Die Gerichts- und Vergeltungsaussagen bei Paulus: Eine tradi-
tionsgeschichtliche Untersuchung* (Göttinger Theologische Arbeiten 8; Göttingen: Vandenhoeck & Ruprecht, 1977), esp. pp. 80–81.

"Christian" no longer walks in the Spirit, he or she is no more "justified." No one is justified by works (3:20); only faith justifies (3:21, 28), but faith is "to walk in the Spirit," obediently. Therefore "justification by faith alone does not exclude justification by works alone but includes it" (p. 137). The judgment in Rom 2 is then for Christians a testing of faith, whether their faith is really faith and not pious illusion (so Mattern, p. 138). Synofzik (see n. 78) is doubtful, however, about this connection with virtue and vice lists. He sees Paul's real interest in vv. 7–10 to be on the negative aspect, i.e., retribution; the "positive" statements in vv. 7, 10 (and 14 and 26–27) are but "a foil for his accusation against the Jew" of 2:1ff. The preferential position of the Jew is turned by Paul into a "preference" in punishment, "the Jew first . . ." (2:9), in light of God's impartiality (2:11).

127   The structure of the passage may make clearer what we assume is Paul's intent. Those who, ostensibly the Jews, judge others while themselves presuming on God's mercy, without being aware of his righteous judgment, stand guilty too (2:1–5). The scriptural principle holds, that

God "will render to everyone according to his works" (2:6 = Ps 62:12),

i.e., to those (*tois men,* v. 7) who by patience in well doing (*ergou agathou*) seek for glory, honor, and immortality, God will give eternal life;	but to those (v. 8, *tois de*) who are factious and do not obey the truth but obey wickedness, there will be wrath and fury (*orgē, thymos*).
There will be (v. 9) tribulation and distress for every human being who does evil (*katergazomenou to kakon*)	but (v. 10) glory, honor, peace for everyone who does good (*ergazomenō, to agathon*)
—"the Jew first and also the Greek"	—"the Jew first and also the Greek,"

(v. 10). For "God shows no partiality" (v. 11).

128   It can be agreed that Paul uses the phrase "Jew first, also the Greek" in an ironic way, and that the overall aim is to underscore the guilt at the judgment of those described in 2:1–5. God's impartial consistency with all persons in exacting retribution is the point.[79] The whole section is part of an emphasis on God's universal reign, as judge and now as savior revealed in Christ (3:21ff.). The questions are how seriously Paul intended the allowances seemingly made in vv. 7 and 10 about those who do good (better "the good," for "works" good or bad are conceived of in a unified way), and whether these persons are Christians or not. My judgment would be that, if Christians, their status "in Christ" (as justified, walking

---

79. Jouette McCurdy Bassler, *The Impartiality of God: Paul's Use of a Theological Axiom* (diss. Yale, Nils Dahl, 1979); published as *Divine Impartiality: Paul and a Theological Axiom* (Society of Biblical Literature Dissertation Series; Chico, CA: Scholars Press, 1982).

in the Spirit, etc.) is what counts; 3:20ff. supersedes any impression given
here of salvation by faith *and* "well doing." If non-Christians are meant,
they are left to the fairness of a God who judges impartially; but 1:18–3:20
leaves grave doubt as to whether there are any not under God's wrath. It
should be observed that all Paul says here reflects the OT principle (Deut
10:17; 2 Chr 19:7; cf. Job 34:19, etc.) that "God shows no partiality"
(2:10), either in his judgment or his offer of salvation. Bassler emphasizes
how Paul uses this point to strike the note of universality with the judgment but also with justification: God's saving righteousness is for all.

129   Obviously, Protestant exegesis has gone far in recognizing that
(and how) Paul speaks of a judgment based on works. Catholic exegetes
now insist that the principle of Rom 2:6, repayment according to deeds,
"does not contradict Paul's ideas of justification by faith" (*JBC* 53:29). Total consistency in Pauline thought eludes most commentators. But the role
of God's judgment in the service of justification *by God* is now more widely
recognized.

130   (3) This section of Romans, on humanity under Sin, is rounded
out by three *dikaio*-terms in chap. 3:1–20. At **3:4** Paul strikes the contrast
between God as true and every human as false,

> that Thou mightest be justified (*dikaiōthēs*) in thy works,
> and prevail when thou art judged (*krinesthai*) (Ps 51:4, LXX 50:6).

3:5 goes on, "But if our wickedness (*adikia,* unrighteousness) serves to
show the justice of God (*theou dikaiosynēn*), what shall we say? That God
is unjust (*adikos*) to inflict wrath on us?" (*RSV*). Ziesler (p. 190), following
Kertelge and Stuhlmacher, catches the forensic setting, in a covenant lawsuit, where God, not man, wins the case. Both "covenant loyalty" and "divine justice" are involved.

3:10, at the start of a catena of OT passages about human sinfulness,
is also from a Psalm passage, "No one is righteous (*dikaios*), no, not one"
(Ps 14:3; cf. Eccl 7:20). This lack of righteousness is understood *coram deo*
(3:18). The conclusion of the section is that no human will be justified (*di-
kaiothēsetai*) before God (Ps 143:2, LXX 142:2) on the basis of works of
the law. The law serves only to bring knowledge of sin (3:20). Such is the
dilemma of the Jew (and all the pious) and of every human being on the
face of the whole earth. "The cosmos is represented in exemplary fashion
by the Jew" (Käsemann, *Romans,* p. 87).

131   **3:1–20** has not always been integrated very well by commentators
into the argument of Romans concerning righteousness/justification. It is
a statement on the human condition, Jew included, from the standpoint of
revelation and the gospel. It assumes a saving righteousness of God revealed in Christ that also draws the Jews "into the fellowship of the ungodly," those who need the God-kind-of-righteousness of which 3:21ff.
will speak (thus, to an extent, the "problem of Israel' and Rom 9–11 already loom).

What Paul says, especially in 3:1–8, becomes clearer when we realize (1) the connection (but not identification) between justification and judgment noted in 1:18ff.; (2) the covenant lawsuit background presupposed (3:5 is the best example of *theou dikaiosynē* as a subjective genitive, "righteousness" as an attribute of God; (3) the no doubt actual objections here reflected to Paul's teaching on justification, as to whether (v. 1) it cancels "the precedence of the Jews in salvation history" (cf. 2:12–29) and makes of God an unjust judge (vv. 3ff.) and ushers Christians into libertinism (3:7ff., cf. 6:1ff.). (Käsemann, pp. 77–85, is the best guide here.)

132   Briefly Paul answers that the advantage of the Jew is that the Jew was entrusted with (*episteuthēsan*) "the oracles of God," i.e., in Scripture (emphasized by Paul as witness to Christ and as promise, 1:2, 3:21, chap. 4, as well as for its testimony on the human condition). The theme of faith (*pisteuō*) in v. 2 is picked up in a series of antitheses (cf. human beings as false, God as true, v. 4):

> *apistia* (the faithlessness of [some] Jews) versus
> *ten pistin tou theou* (the faithfulness of God, v. 3, the juxtaposi-
>   tion in the Greek is striking);
> *hē adikia hēmōn* (our unrighteousness, *RSV* wickedness) versus
> *theou dikaiosynēn* (God's justice, rightness, righteousness, v. 5).

The parallelism of *pistis* and *dikaiosynē theou* suggests that his righteousness as fidelity to the covenant is meant. God remains "in the right" and faithful to his promise, no matter what Israel or all humanity does. But Paul's understanding has expanded God's *pistis/dikaiosynē* from fidelity to a covenant with Israel to fidelity with his whole creation. (Here note the shift from *Israel's* faithlessness *to "our"* unrighteousness"; the attention throughout 1:18–3:20 to "all peoples, Jew and Gentile alike"; Paul's general theological preference for comparison of Christ with Adam, while Moses and the Sinai covenant are otiose.) "Redemption" will be in Christ the power of God's *dikaiosynē* exerted not as renewal of a covenant with Israel but as a new covenant for all of God's creation (*kainē ktisis/kainē diathēkē*).

133   Hence, the result of God's *dikaiosynē* is not simply an assertion of an attribute of his or even his being justified in a court battle (though a theodicy is involved), but "declaration of the power of God working itself out forensically in the sphere of the covenant" for all humankind (Käsemann, p. 79). It is God's victory over a rebel world (11:32) through his justification of the ungodly (4:5). All of that is involved in understanding righteousness/justification (and it may be said that past Lutheran-Catholic polemics did not sense this fulness of meaning, nor did most exegetes on either side). Käsemann thus calls 3:3ff. "a key passage for the whole of Paul's doctrine of justification" (p. 81). To the list of features already noted (above, § 93), we must therefore add a sixth:

    (6) Righteousness/justification in Paul has a cosmic side, relating God's faithfulness and saving righteousness to all creation, within a new

covenant setting. This emphasis is utterly necessary alongside the individualistic emphasis (so dear to much later interpretation) that can be seen in, e.g., Phil 3:9, cf. above, § 111.

134   As to the charge of libertinism or moral laxity against Paul's gospel—here phrased, if our unrighteousness is necessary to make God's righteousness abound, "why not do evil that good may come?" (v. 8)—Paul denies it with what amounts to a curse on them (Kuss); "on persons who claim that, the judgment rightly falls (*endikon estin*)." So he repudiates such a misunderstanding of justification (cf. above, on 2:6–11, and cf. 6:1ff. below about "walking in newness of life"; Käsemann, pp. 88–90).

135   d. *3:21–31, the heart of Paul's gospel in Romans.* Difficulties in understanding Paul here stem especially from his use of traditional Jewish-Christian materials, only recently marked out with some clarity by scholarship, and from his brevity of expression. Might the topic have been more familiar to his audience, in Greece and Asia Minor, Jerusalem, and Rome, than we have often supposed? That is, righteousness/justification was a more prominent way of expressing the gospel in Christianity in the fifties than it often was subsequently (see section B below).

136   As the positive development of Paul's theme (1:16–17), 3:21–31 builds on, and in contrast to, 1:18–3:20 and anticipates further exposition and implications in 4:1ff. The Jewish-Christian formula in 3:24–26a (see above, §§ 70–72) is the core around which Paul constructs the passage. We paraphrase, with an emphasis on the pertinent *dikaio*-vocabulary.

²¹But now (*nyni de;* the phrase is eschatological, not just logical) apart from law (i.e., not *ex ergōn nomou,* 3:20 and Gal), God's righteousness (*dikaiosynē theou*) has been and is being made manifest (in the Christ event and the subsequent proclamation of the gospel). Though apart from law, it is testified to by "the law and the prophets" (Scripture, cf. 1:2, 3:10–18, 4:3, 7–8, etc.).

> ²²It is God's righteousness (*dikaiosynē de theou*) available through faith (*pisteōs*) in Jesus Christ for all persons who believe (*pisteuontas*). There is no distinction (cf. 2:11):
> ²³for all sinned and keep falling short of the glory of God,
> ²⁴(all now) "being declared righteous (*dikaioumenoi*) as a gift"— by his grace—"through the redemption which is in Christ Jesus,
> ²⁵whom God put forward as a means (or place) of expiation in his blood"—to be received through faith—
> "for showing God's righteousness (*tēs dikaiosynēs autou*) with a view to remission of former sins ²⁶in the forebearance of God,"
> for demonstrating his righteousness (*tēs dikaiosynēs autou*) in the present decisive time (the *nyn kairos;* cf. 3:21, 2 Cor 6:2),
> in order that He might be righteous (*dikaion*) even while justifying (*dikaiounta*) the person who lives on the basis of faith (*ek pisteōs*) in Jesus.

Paul goes on to argue (3:27–31) that any possibility of boasting (*kau-kēsis*) on the part of a person thus rightwised is excluded, not, of course, by the "law of works" but by the "law (or principle) of faith." A person is "justified without works of the law, by faith (alone)" (*dikaiousthai pistei,* 3:28). The One God is God of Jews and of Gentiles alike by justification: He "will justify (*dikaiōsei*) those who are circumcised on the grounds of faith (*ek pisteōs*) and will justify those who are not circumcised through faith (*dia tēs pisteōs*" (3:30). In announcing such a gospel, we do not abolish the law (the torah as at 3:21 and the will of God set forth in Scripture); rather, we establish it, as our use of passages from Scripture and the case of Abraham (chap. 4) will show.[80]

137   In these eleven verses we thus have four times each the noun *dikaiosynē* (3:21, 22, 25, 26) and the verb *dikaioō* (24, 26, 28, 30), plus the adjective once (v. 26). Reference to faith or believing occurs 9 times (3:22,

---

80. Cranfield, *Romans,* pp. 202, 212, especially emphasizes the ongoing preaching of the gospel involved in the paraphrase of 3:21 above.

In v. 26 it is attractive to take *kai* as "even" instead of as coordinating "just *and* justifying" (cf. *RSV*); Cranfield, p. 213; Käsemann, p. 101, "The Giver himself makes himself known in the gift."

In v. 27 *dia nomou pisteōs* is used ironically, paradoxically, *nomos* in the Hellenistic sense of norm, principle, as at Gal 6:2, "the 'law' of Christ."

V. 28, "faith *alone*"; the *allein* (Luther) is called for by the content of Paul's argument, as exegetes since Origen have seen; the translation is no longer divisive for Lutherans and Catholics (cf. *Righteousness and Society,* p. 43).

In v. 29, the OT credo, the *shema* of Deut 6:4, is reflected, *heis ho theos;* Paul uses it in the service of his universal gospel of God's righteousness.

In v. 30, I agree with those who find no difference discernible between *ek pisteōs* and *dia tēs pisteōs* (Ziesler, p. 195; Cranfield, p. 222, lists patristic and modern endeavors to make a distinction; Augustine rightly saw the two as rhetorical variations).

On *dikaiosynē theou* in this passage as the key to Romans, see Sam K. Williams, "The 'Righteousness of God' in Romans," *JBL* 99 (1980): 241–90. Williams had earlier published an analysis of 3:24–26 as a prepauline formula in *Jesus' Death as Saving Event: The Background and Origin of a Concept* (Harvard Dissertations in Religion 2; Missoula: Scholars Press, 1975). While we agree on the existence of a formula here and its general extent, I am unconvinced at the suggestion by Williams that the closing words of v. 26 ("God *is* righteous in that he *sets man right with him,*" *JBL,* pp. 277–78) stem from the formula, or that *dia pisteōs* (v. 25) was part of the prior formula and referred to "the faith *of Jesus,*" an interpretation Williams consistently presses. Methodologically, Williams's analysis is limited for *Paul* by the facts that he examines only *Romans* (though Gal 3 is treated) and limits himself to *dikaiosynē theou* not taking up all the *dikaioō*-terms (but cf. *JBL,* pp. 259–60). In light of an OT background, Williams takes "the righteousness of God" to mean "Yahweh's salvation," above all (3:1–7 esp.) his "faithfulness in keeping his promise to Abraham" (p. 265; *ta logia,* 3:2, as "promises," is emphasized). Rom 15:8–12 is then used, a passage we have not considered here, to weld together "the truth of God" (what 3:7 had mentioned along with God's faithfulness and righteousness) and "the fulfillment of the promises to the fathers" with "the idea of the eschatological inclusion of the nations/Gentiles into the people of God" (p. 289). The result of this exegesis is more effectively to make *dikaiosynē theou* the theme in all of Romans, stretching from God's dealings with Abraham to the current missionary advance among the *ethnē,* especially through Paul's preaching.

25, 26, 27, 28, 30, 31). The former emphasis, together with Jesus' death as expiation, leading to forgiveness of sins, already existed in the formula; "by faith" (in Jesus Christ), as over against "by works," is Paul's emphasis (cf. Synofzik, pp. 89–90, among others).

The universal note is to be seen notably in the inclusive language about "all" persons (22, 23) and in the Jew-and-Gentile reference (3:29), but also in Paul's invoking of a phrase at v. 23 about "the glory of God." As at Rom 1:23, "the glory of the immortal God," Paul has in mind the radiance God intended at creation, to which humans have never attained, but which apocalyptic (cf. Cranfield, p. 204, n. 4) promised the justified in heaven. Of this cosmic note, Käsemann (p. 95) writes, "the *doxa tou theou* is *dikaiosyne* within the horizon of the restoration of paradisaical perfection, while conversely *dikaiosyne* is the divine *doxa* within the horizon of controversy with the world, thus of temptation (Anfechtung)."

As for the *dikaiosyne* references, we have already argued that 3:24–26*a* was a formula interpreting Jesus' sacrificial death as a making known of God's continued covenant fidelity with those who have broken covenant; so they are declared righteous, and God remains *dikaios,* though sins are remitted. Paul extends the meaning of this act of expiation to all the world, the fidelity of the Creator to all peoples, via faith not works. His interpretation is especially clear in what he adds at 26*bc:* God's demonstration of forgiveness through Christ's cross extends (through the preaching of justification) into the "now-time," the eschaton which is paradoxically present (though the present is not the eschaton, Käsemann, p. 93); God remains just, precisely while justifying all who live by faith, because of the death of Christ.

138 How shall God's *dikaiosyne* be interpreted here? Ziesler (pp. 191–94), with his mediating view, must first grant the forensic sense, but "because man's dilemma is both forensic and ethical," he concluded that, even though "a purely imputative righteousness is not the likely meaning here," God's righteousness "becomes man's, both ethically and forensically," and so the passage has "justification restoring the relationship in which man may be righteous." Paul sees God "making man righteous, really and ethically, but only in faith and only in Christ." Such a view reflects Ziesler's characteristic analysis, already amply observed. Kertelge's analysis (pp. 71–85) begins with 3:21 as a subjective genitive and follows the Pauline exposition of the early Christian formula much as above in our paraphrase. Cranfield, hesitant about a formula (p. 200, n. 1), tends to view *dikaiosyne de theou* in v. 22 in terms of Phil 3:9 (p. 203) and takes vv. 25ff. as "referring to God's own righteousness" (p. 211), and a "righteous status" given by God (p. 98, cf. 825). With regard to the old debate about "declare righteous" versus "make righteous," Käsemann (p. 96) holds that the forensic declaration also means, because the power of God is involved, "to be made righteous" (*dikaiousthai* = hiphil of *ṣdq*), but this "righteousness of God" is, in the time before the judgment, "the righteousness of faith," which, as obedience, has a "no longer . . . not yet" character. It is, like the divine glory and image, not a *habitus* but "a right relation of the creature to the Creator," and "means eschatologically transformed existence" (pp. 92, 95, 96)—living in faith.

139 e. *The example of Abraham (chap. 4): justified by faith, not by works.* It was necessary for Paul to take up the case of the forefather of the Jews not only because of the desirability of establishing his contention scripturally but also, as in Galatians, because of the use made in Judaism (and Jewish-Christianity at times) of Abraham as one reckoned righteous (Gen 15:6) on the basis of his works (1 Macc 2:52, he was "faithful in testing"—e.g., at the sacrifice of Isaac, Gen 22); cf. for this theme Jas 2:21, "Was not Abraham our father justified by works, when he offered his son Isaac upon the altar?"

As is well known, Paul argues, using rabbinical exegetical methods, that Abraham was reckoned righteous, but on the basis of faith, not by works (4:1–18); this happened prior to, and so was not because of, his circumcision (4:9–12). Further, his rightwising was prior to the Mosaic law and was instead by promise from God (4:13–17*a*). As a result, he is "father of us all" whose faith is reckoned as righteousness, Jew and Gentile alike (4:17*b*–25). Thus the example supports Paul's universal outlook and introduces, as in Gal 3, the key category of promise (*epangelia*), which Reformation theology emphasized along with justification.

140 In the course of this argument from Scripture Paul uses *dikaiosynē* eight times and the cognate verb twice. In listing these instances we can follow much of the argument of the section. He concludes with an earlier Christian formula employing *dikaiōsis.*

"If Abraham were justified by works (*ex ergon edikaiōthē*), he would have something to boast about" (cf. 3:27 with these words of 4:2; Paul's argument would be exploded by such a case; we assume the condition is ultimately to be taken as contrary to fact). But, he goes on, turning to Scripture, this hypothesis does not hold up "before God." For in the words of Gen 15:6, "Abraham believed God, and it was reckoned to him as righteousness" (*eis dikaiosynēn,* 4:3). There is no mention of "works" here or indeed prior to this in the Abraham story in Genesis; so Paul emphasizes that it is believing or faith that matters:

4:4 to one who does works, wages are reckoned as a due;
4:5 to the person who does not do works but who has faith in "Him who justifies the ungodly" (*ton dikaiounta ton asebē*), his faith is reckoned for righteousness (*eis dikaiosynēn*).

Thus faith, not works. Paul interprets Gen 15:6 via the rabbinic device of *gᵉzērāh šāwāh,* appeal to another verse (Ps 32:1–2) where "reckon" is also used: there, for God not to "reckon sin" is parallel to "cover sin," and God's blessing is on such a person whose faith is reckoned as righteousness and whose sins are not reckoned (but are forgiven)—"*dikaiosynē* without works" (v. 6).

In the section on circumcision (4:9–12), Gen 15:6 (*pistis eis dikaio-synēn*) is quoted again (v. 9) to show that circumcision in Gen 17 as "a sign or seal of the righteousness which he had by faith while he was still uncircumcised (*sphragida tēs dikaiosynēs tēs pisteōs tēs en tē, akrobustia,* v. 11)" came *after* the event at Gen 15:6. This also makes of Abraham the father of the Gentiles "who believe without being circumcised and who thus have righteousness reckoned to them" (v. 11, *eis to logisthēnai autois [tēn] dikaiosynēn,* language of 15:6 again).

The section on "by promise, not by law" is summed up in v. 13, "The promise to Abraham and his descendants, that they should inherit the world [*kosmos,* not just *gē,* the land of Israel; universalism again] did not come through the law but through the righteousness of faith (*dia dikaio-synēs pisteōs*)." This last, compressed phrase relates *dikaiosynē* and faith as closely as possible, as at 4:11, cf. 5:1 and elsewhere; righteousness that comes through faith. In Käsemann's terminology (p. 119, following Barrett): "the sphere of power in which promise becomes possible."

141 At 4:25 the prepauline formula (above §§ 73–75) about Jesus "raised for our justification" (*dikaiōsis*) provides a fitting climax to the chapter. Belief in the lord who was put to death "for our trespasses" is what is reckoned to us for righteousness. While cross and resurrection are viewed as a single event, the inclusion of the latter emphasis is significant not merely as a continuation of the line of thought in 4:17 ("the God who gives life to the dead") but to make clear that "the event of justification . . . constantly wins new ground in encounter with the risen Lord" (Käsemann, p. 129). Ziesler, who sees Rom 4 as primarily forensic in nature, notes also how "past and future jostle each other" in Paul's references. Put otherwise, justification/righteousness as the realm where God's power and promise are at work looks ahead and stretches into the new life of the Christian till the day of judgment itself; cf. 5:1.

f. *Romans 5–8: Justification as freedom from death, Sin, and law, and as life in the Spirit.*

142 (1) It is a common enough misunderstanding of Paul—among Lutherans, already in the Formula of Concord—to separate "justification" (in a narrow sense) from "sanctification," and thus to see Rom 5–8 as a further stage or stages beyond the first step of justification in 3:21–4:25. In part, Paul is himself to blame because 5:1, "Having been justified by faith (*dikaiōthentes ek pisteōs*), we do have peace with God, access to grace, and hope . . .," suggests rightwising is but a past action. But the very nature of the Pauline concept, as we have already seen, overarching the entire Christian life till the judgment day, argues against that. So do the host of references to *dikaio*-terms, some twenty of them in chaps. 5–8 (compared with a similar number in 3:21–4:25, chap. 7 being the one with only a single reference). The concentration is particularly thick in Rom 5.[81]

---

81. The references in Cranfield, p. 253, are instructive, as is his discussion of whether 3:21ff. as a section should be extended through 5:11 or all of chap. 5. Part of the problem is

That Rom 5 resumes the discussion of justification is shown not only by 5:1 but also by 5:9, "Since, therefore, we are now justified (*dikaiōthentes*) by his blood, much more shall we be saved by him from the wrath of God." The same thing is then said in one of the two passages in Paul about reconciliation: We were reconciled to God by the death of his son while we were enemies, much more shall we be saved by his life (5:10). As at 4:25, it is doubtful that one should claim that part of reconciliation was effected by Jesus' *death,* part of it by his *"life"*; the two go together as basis for "our reconciliation," past, (present), and future. Likewise with justification; as we have seen, God's righteousness in Christ, received by us through faith, is what will deliver us from the future judgment. (The reference in 5:7, about the unlikelihood of someone dying for "a righteous man [*dikaiou*]," is simply part of the argument accenting how "Christ died for the ungodly.") Ziesler (p. 197) sees this link between past and future when he writes, "Justification guarantees salvation at the Judgment (*apo tēs orgēs*)" (v. 9).

143   In the contrast between Adam and the One who was to come (5:12–21), note the following verses:[82]

Adam	*Christ*
The judgment following one trespass (brought) condemnation;	the free gift following many trespasses (brings) justification (*dikaiōma*) (5:16).
Because of one man's trespass, death reigned through Adam;	much more those who receive the abundance of grace and the free gift of righteousness (*tēs dōreas tēs dikaiosynēs*) will reign in life through Christ (5:17).
As one man's trespass led to condemnation for all men,	so one man's act of righteousness (*dikaiōma*) leads for all men to acquittal and life (*RSV; eis dikaiōsin zōēs*) (5:18).
As by one man's disobedience, many were made sinners,	so by one man's disobedience many will be made righteous (*RSV; dikaioi katastēsontai*) (5:19).
Then the conclusion: law increased the trespass, sin increased;	grace abounded, to reign through righteousness to eternal life (*dia dikaiosynēs eis zōēn aiōnion*) through Jesus Christ our Lord (5:21).

---

the false assumption on the part of many interpreters that *diakiosynē* (*tou theou*) as Paul's theme has come to an end with chap. 4. Cf. Käsemann, p. 159: in Rom 5, Paul sets forth the universal (Adam-Christ) realization of what justification implies; in Rom 6–8, he seeks to make it intelligible for the everyday life of the believing individual and community. Cf. also Michael Wolter, *Rechtfertigung und zukünftiges Heil: Untersuchungen zu Röm 5, 1–11* (BZNW 43; 1978): "reconciliation," "peace," and hope in God's future glory are "the eschatological dimension of justification by faith." More recently, Brendan Byrne, "Living out the Righteousness of God: The Contribution of Rom 6:1–8:13 to an Understanding of Paul's Ethical Presuppositions," *CBQ* 43 (1981):557–81.

82. The precise rendering of the *dikaio*-terms in Rom 5:16–21 is often disputed. Besides the *RSV* wordings cited above, the following nuances are possible:

Absolutely clear is the association of justification/righteousness with Christ, by grace, as a free gift, for acquittal from trespasses, with eternal life as the result. Since we are dealing with corporate figures or two solidarities or humanities, the more-than-individual aspect of *dikaiosynē* is obvious, as is the connection with creation and indeed eschatology (the one who was to come has come!). The route of God's righteousness for the Adamic dilemma is through Christ's cross as justification and life, a gift, to those who believe.

144 (2) *Romans 6* goes on to present the meaning of justification as *freedom from the power of Sin*. By baptism into Christ's death one becomes dead to the dominion of Sin and, alive to God, under the lordship of Christ, free to obey a new Master. Ziesler (pp. 200–203) sees in this chapter the transition in Romans from the basic forensic sense of *dikaio*-terms to an ethical meaning, through the indicative-imperative connection. The precise sense of each reference must be examined, however. Even so, Ziesler is alert to the common error, especially found in Liberal Protestantism (cf. Furnish, 244ff., esp. 245, 262–65, cf. 153–55), of separating justification as "the first step in the Christian life" and then treating sanctification as a "moral process" of growth; for, as he remarks, "righteousness for Paul is ethical" too (p. 203).

In order to support the point of v. 6—that, the Christian's "old self" having been crucified with Christ, we can "no longer continue to be enslaved to Sin" (cf. 6:1, 3:8, the question about the justified doing evil things in order that good things may come, like grace and forgiveness)—Paul writes (**6:7**), "For he who has died is freed (*dedikaiōtai*) from sin" (*RSV*). The reference in the subject of the sentence is not to Christ (so Kearns, versus Scroggs, with references in Käsemann) but to the believer. The view that Paul means "he who has died has lost the very means of sinning, his 'body of sin' " (Lyonnet; *JBC* 53:65) is unconvincing. Commentators are hesitant about the applicability here of a rabbinic maxim that "death pays

---

5:16, *dikaiōma*, acquittal (in contrast to "condemnation," so Ziesler);

5:17, the gift of justification (Käsemann);

5:18, *dikaiōma*, Jesus' "act of justification" (Käsemann) is better than the rendering "righteous conduct" (Cranfield); the reference is to Jesus' obedient sacrifice on the cross;

5:18, "acquittal and life"—Ziesler suggests "justification leading to life" (similarly Cranfield); Käsemann, "life in justification" (*zōēs* as a gen. of quality, not direction, p. 156).

5:19, the verb *katastēsontai* is taken by others (e.g., Barrett) to mean "constituted" in future generations as "justified men" (relational, to God, not ethical character). Käsemann: "will be presented as righteous" (cf. Gal 5:5, righteousness awaited as a gift at the consummation).

5:21, does the phrase suggest that "eternal life" is a goal beyond righteousness/justification (cf. Ziesler, p. 200)? So perhaps 5:17; 6:22. But on the other hand, cf. 6:4, 23; 8:6, 10. It becomes misleading to limit such terms to past, present, or future exclusively. "Grace, righteousness, and eternal life can no longer be separated chronologically or causally" (Käsemann, p. 158).

all debts" and hence a meaning merely that the person who has died "has his quittance from sin." So the forensic sense is most likely (cf. *RSV*), with *dikaioō* meaning "is acquitted from," "freed from." Ziesler (pp. 200–01) and Cranfield specifically make it "has been justified from sin . . .," in a theological, not a general, sense.

145   The point just observed must be kept in mind as we move on into the antithetical section that follows on "the two masters" (6:12–23) that Paul thinks of Sin (almost personified) as a power, just as he thinks of God (and Righteousness) as a greater power:

Sin, wickedness, death	vs.	God, righteousness, life (vv. 12–13)
law	vs.	grace (vv. 14–15)
Sin, death	vs.	obedience, righteousness (16, 18, 20)
wages, death	vs.	free gift, eternal life (23).

Within this context must be examined these references:

6:13 Do not yield your members to Sin as instruments of wickedness (*hopla adikias*),

but yield yourselves to God as persons who have been brought from death to life, and your members to God, as instruments of righteousness (*hopla dikaiosynēs*);

6:16 If you yield yourselves to anyone as obedient slaves, you are slaves to the one you obey, either of Sin, which leads to death or of obedience, which leads to righteousness (*hypakoē eis dikaiosynēn*);

6:(17–)18 But thanks be to God that, (though) you were slaves of Sin, . . . having been set free from Sin, you have become slaves of righteousness (*edoulōthēte tē$_{i}$ dikaiosyne$_{i}$*).

6:19 . . . just as you once yielded your members slaves to impurity and lawlessness for (a life of) lawlessness (*tē$_{i}$ anonia$_{i}$ eis tēn anomian*),[83] so now yield your members to righteousness for (a life of) sanctification (*tē$_{i}$ dikaiosynē$_{i}$ eis hagiasmon*).

6:20 As slaves of sin, you were free with regard to righteousness (*eleutheroi . . . tē$_{i}$ dikaiosynē$_{i}$*).

Clearly the references are to living as justified believers, in everyday life (how you use your "members"), free from the lordship of Sin, now under God's righteousness in Christ.

146   At **6:13** "instruments of righteousness" might simply be taken as "weapons in behalf of righteousness" or "weapons which are upright," but one ought to recall 2 Cor 6:7 (see above, § 96). We prefer to understand the military phrase here as "weapons from (as well as for) God's righteous-

---

83. Reading *eis tēn anomian* (omitted in a few sources as merely repeating *tē$_{i}$ anomia$_{i}$*). *RSV*'s "to greater and greater iniquity" is, to say the least, a phrase that is "unlikely" (Cranfield, p. 327, n. 1); the parallel, if it were followed, would call for "greater and greater justification-sanctification."

ness" ("which has come on the scene in Christ and with justification,"
Käsemann, p. 177, "and which sets us in its service"). "The new Christian
condition can be called *dikaioysnē* ... not associated with the law" but
"the effect of God's benevolent favor" (*JBC* 53:66). **V. 18** indicates the
change in relationship very clearly: Believers are now slaves to God's righteousness (contrast v. 20). (*Pace* Cranfield, p. 325, the sense here is not just
"moral"; the exhortation to serve righteousness will come in the next
verse, so Ziesler, p. 202.) In 6:13, 18, cf. 19, 20, 22, as Kertelge says (p.
156), the *dikaiosynē* that has been given by God has the character of
" 'power,' which takes those who have been declared righteous (Gerecht-
gesprochenen) into service for God."
147   But do not 6:16 and 19 point to a process of development that goes
through several stages, of which righteousness/justification is only one
part? Romans 6 has been taken as a classical example of such a view:

Obedience leads to righteousness/justification (6:16),
   righteousness/justification leads to sanctification (6:19),
      and indeed sanctification leads to "its end, eternal life"
                                                            (6:22).

An illustration of such a reading of Paul, one of the most recent, is that by
an American Lutheran, K. P. Donfried, who summarizes his "Pauline pattern" in the following way:
   "1) justification—a past event, which has present implications
through sanctification;
   "2) sanctification—a present event, dependent upon a past event, justification, which has future implications, viz., salvation;
   "3) salvation—a future event, already anticipated, and partially experienced in justification and sanctification and clearly dependent upon
them."[84]
   Such a schema is demonstrably wrong (cf. Synofzik, pp. 152–54), as is
shown not only by the compromises Donfried has introduced in his description but above all by the Pauline texts themselves. "Salvation" (*sōtēria, sōzō*) is not simply future in Paul ("already anticipated and partially
experienced" compromise the three-stage pattern but say too little about
use of the verb and noun with prior-to-future references); cf. merely Rom
8:24 ("in this hope we were saved") and 1 Cor 15:2, cf. 1:18, about "being

---

84. "Justification and Last Judgement in Paul," *ZNW* 67 (1976): 90–110. A briefer version appears in *Int* 30 (1976): 140–52. The article is important for its thorough bibliography,
its summation of recent work, and its ecumenical concern. Ironically, the article endorses a
view of justification that conforms to the limited sense of it in the Formula of Concord. In
relating justification and last judgment, it concentrates more on the judgment of the work of
Christian *missionaries* and of *disobedient* Christians than on the results of a universal judgment (Rom 2:6–11 is not discussed); treatment of the judgment of obedient Christians seems
open to a synergistic emphasis on the third use of the law in a way that Käsemann's stress on
the obedience of faith is not. Cf. Byrne (above, n. 81), pp. 577–78.

saved" in the present through the gospel. Salvation thus embraces past, present, and future. Likewise with "sanctification": *hagiazō* can refer to past event (1 Cor 6:11, 1:2) or to the future (1 Thess 5:23). We have already stated our contention that righteousness/justification overarches past, present, and future (cf. Ziesler, pp. 208–09, and see below, n. 97).

148   **Rom 6:16,** which has shifted from the military metaphor to one of slavery, so as to emphasize service by believers in daily existence (*JBC* 53:67), does not speak of "increasing righteousness" for believers "in observable reality," as Ziesler claims (p. 202; he is more on target earlier in saying, "Probably, rather than speaking of development in righteousness, we ought to talk of submission to lordship . . ."). "Obedient slaves" (*doulous eis hypakoēn*) is the key phrase, slaves either of Sin *eis thanaton* or of obedience (*hypakoēs*) *eis dikaiosynēn*. Cranfield is probably right to take both *eis* clauses as result, "leading to death" and "leading to 'final justification' " (p. 322). The coupling of obedience (*hypakoē*) as a contrast to sin is surprising, however; the parallels in vv. 18, 19, and 20 would have led us to expect *dikaiosynē* as the contrast to *hamartia,* "righteousness/Sin." Instead, Paul contrasts *dikaiosynē* with death (as if "righteousness" is, as I think it sometimes is for Paul, synonymous with "[eternal] life"). Cranfield thinks that Paul, instead of writing in the second phrase "slaves *of God*" (in contrast to "slaves of Sin"), wanted to emphasize obedience—which after all is the point he is making against those who want to disobey by sinning so that grace may abound. So instead of "slaves of God (or Righteousness) *eis zōēn* (in contrast to death)," he underscores obedience (which is a Pauline definition of "faith," 1:5), thus stressing that in the Christian life "faith-obedience" must be its characteristic mark until the work of God's justifying righteousness is complete, at the final judgment.

149   At **6:19** *dikaiosynē eis hagiasmon* does not therefore refer to two "steps" or "stages" in an *ordo salutis,* "justification followed by sanctification," but to consecration to God in Christ Jesus as part of rightwising. One must be struck by the option presented for human life: either "slaves to . . . lawlessness for (a life of) lawlessness or slaves to Righteousness for (a life of) consecration" and, dare we add, a consecration that amounts to really living up to what the law intended. (With regard to the phrases, there is, contra Ziesler, a parallelism; but with Ziesler one may wish to speak of righteousness here as "power," including—but not just—the ethical, and describe what is involved as "the concrete actualization of righteousness," pp. 202–03). "Sanctification" thus is "the daily task of the living out of justification," as " 'ever repeated' service of God" through the neighbor (Käsemann, p. 183; cf. Furnish, p. 157).

150   Käsemann (pp. 172–76) attributes the long history of dispute over this chapter in Romans and the issues that appear in it to a separation of sanctification from justification (already, in the Lutheran tradition in the Formula of Concord); to separation of Paul's "ethics" from its theological basis in the gospel about what God has done for us (in his view, righteousness/justification); to sundering of both justification (and sanctification) and ethics from Paul's eschatology and the sacraments (in Rom 6, baptism); and even to treatment of "indicative and imperative" so that the latter is not integrated into the former. Above all, in his frequent phrase "the gift was separated from the Giver," i.e., justification was made into a doctrine or decree or first step, instead of transferral into the domain of a new Master, Christ, and life there; anthropology became the (sole) horizon, and one lost the sense of God's power at work in *dikaiosynē*. "The gift *is* the Giver himself" (p. 175, italics added), and Rom 8 will make clear that this is a matter of not only being "in Christ" and knowing that "God is there for us" (p. 180) but also of receiving the Spirit. The call is "not: 'Become what you already are in fact by baptism,' but: 'Become what you now can become' " (p. 173; cf. Furnish, pp. 224–27).

151   (3) *Romans 7,* on the Christian's freedom from the law, uses our terms only in a passing reference to the commandment of God as "holy, just (*dikaia*), and good." We may agree with Ziesler that the chapter shows that "not the Law, but man, is wrong" (p. 204). But what man?

The debate still rages over whether or not the verses in chap. 7 are autobiographical, and, if they are, of Paul "before or after his conversion." It is to be noted that the view of Augustine, Aquinas, Luther (and Barth), that Paul speaks of his experience as a Christian since his conversion (and thus of life in Christ as *simul justus et peccator*), still finds endorsement in recent treatments like those of Ziesler ("the believer who is righteous in Christ ... still must be exhorted (Ch. 6), because he still must struggle [Ch. 7]," p. 203) and Cranfield (autobiographical, of the experience of Paul as a Christian—and of other Christians, pp. 344–46). That it is not autobiographical and not about the Christian's present experience, has been widely accepted among many scholars, at least since Kümmel's 1929 monograph;[85] hence it is said that there is depicted in Rom 7 "pre-Christian being from a Christian standpoint" (Käsemann, p. 192). Even among those who take chap. 7 in a traditional way, 7:25 is not, however, necessarily used to support the view of *simul justus et peccator* (e.g., Cranfield, p. 370), and we may be dubious of Ziesler's distinction between 7:25 as "ethical deliverance" and 8:1 as "forensic."

152   (4) *Chap. 8* follows up the sections on "deliverance from . . ." in 5–7 by treating the life and destiny of those justified in Christ, especially in terms of the freedom brought to them in the Spirit. Reference to the "principle (*nomos*) of life-in-Christ-Jesus which has been given via the Spirit and which frees us" (8:2) is interrupted before Paul goes on to discuss the Spirit's work by a christological reference: "With regard to what the law could not do . . .,

---

85. W. G. Kümmel, *Römer 7 und die Bekehrung des Paulus* (UNT 17; 1929); cf. his "Die Bekehrung des Paulus als religionsgeschichtlichen Problem," *ZTK* 56 (1959): 273–93. Summary in Kümmel's *Man in the New Testament* (Philadelphia: Westminster,1963), pp. 50–61.

God, by sending his own Son in the likeness of sinful flesh and as a sin-offering (*peri hamartias*) condemned Sin in the flesh, in order that the just requirement of the law (*to dikaiōma tou nomou*) might be fulfilled in us, who walk not according to the flesh but according to the Spirit (8:3–4).

The flesh/Spirit contrast is what Paul goes on to discuss (8:5ff.) Most commentators agree that *dikaiōma* means the torah's requirement or ordinance (that God's people be righteous) (Ziesler, p. 204; Cranfield, p. 384; cf. 2:26 and 1:32, above). The exact sense of "in us" is disputed, whether "by us" (as agent) or "in us" (location, of both individual Christians and the community, so Stalder, p. 406).[86]

153   Rom 8:4 can even be rendered "the claim of the law should thus be fulfilled by us who . . . walk . . . according to the Spirit" (cf. Käsemann, p. 214)—anything but antinomianism! But would Paul have said that after he has written 7:1–6 ("dead to the law, we serve not under the old written code but in the new life of the Spirit")? Käsemann argues that Paul is here reflecting an early Christian formula about God "sending" Christ (cf. Gal 4:4–5, cf. 2 Cor 5:21) and that the language is therefore not his own. The danger in the formula is that the gospel will be made into a means to fulfill the law; or, the perpetual Lutheran fear, faith will be understood as deeds done out of love that fulfill the demands of the law and thus merit the verdict of "righteous." Yet Paul uses this wording (against the slanderers of 3:8 and 6:1, I suspect, and) to bring Christology (and the cross, expiation) to the fore as he discusses the Holy Spirit. For the Spirit is not simply "the law correctly understood" but the "power of grace," which, in evoking the new obedience, "points us back to the cross of Christ" and "continually actualizes justification" (pp. 218–19).

The next reference, **8:10**, fits into such a picture of Christology and the work of the Spirit: "If Christ (is) in you, although your bodies are dead because of sin, your spirits are alive because of righteousness (*dia dikaiosynēn*)." This possible *RSV* rendering is anthropologically oriented (*to pneuma* is taken as the new human self; so also Ziesler). It may, however, mean that God's Holy Spirit is life for us, on account of "justification" (*NEB*), or "righteousness being exercised" (Lagrange), or even (Käsemann, p. 224) "walking by the Spirit in bodily service in a way which is pleasing to God." In these past two cases, *dikaiosynē* is obviously far more than a first step toward salvation; it includes the Spirit, (eternal) life, and ethical "walk" or service.

---

86. Kurt Stalder, *Das Werk des Geistes in der Heilung bei Paulus* (Zürich: EVZ-Verlag, 1962), p. 406. We omit here the debate over 8:2, whether, in contrast to Käsemann, *Romans*, p. 215, "the law as such is restored by the Spirit," as suggested by E. Lohse, in *Neues Testament und christliche Existenz* (H. Braun fs; Tübingen: Mohr-Siebeck, 1973), pp. 279–87, or by Hans Hübner, *Das Gesetz bei Paulus* (FRLANT 119; 1978), pp. 125, 129.

154   Such a "broad" sense for *dikaio*-terms in Paul is suggested also by the final two examples in the chapter. **8:30** has the verb as part of a series of "links" in the work of God for salvation:

> those whom he (a) foreknew
> he also (b) predestined to be conformed to the image of his Son,
> in order that he might be the firstborn among many brethren.

8:30   And those whom he predestined (c) he also called;
> and those whom he called (d) he also justified (*edikaiōsen*);
> and those whom he justified (e) he also glorified.

The sense is forensic (Ziesler); "we" are the accused, God is both the judge and the advocate "for us" (cf. 8:31, 33; Kertelge, p. 124). There are charges against us. The outcome is either acquittal or condemnation (8:33). The accusers are the powers of Sin, law, flesh, and death; from them God, in sending his son, liberates us. Käsemann (pp. 245–46) suspects here a baptismal tradition (note the use of *eikōn*, "image," restored through the Son). Surprising is the use of *dikaioō* to cover everything (including "sanctification"!) from "call" to "glory" (normally in Paul, future; in Hellenistic Christianity, part of what is already given in the sacrament). Paul employs this traditional material as part of the climactic conclusion toward which he is moving about God's victory.

God, in v. 33, is referred to in the most characteristic way possible, given the theological patterns we have observed in Romans, as *theos ho dikaiōn* (cf. Isa 50:8, but Paul is not paraphrasing the Servant Song there): "God who justifies" (rather than condemns, cf. 8:1). This final use of the verb in Romans describes God in terms of the letter's central theme, rightwising.[87]

155   g. *Romans 9–11,* on Israel's unbelief and God's righteousness, fidelity, and promises, has often been either detached from Romans as an excursus or made the center of the epistle, either on the basis of interest in Heilsgeschichte or modern Christian-Jewish concerns. All too seldom have these chapters been related to righteousness/justification (cf. Käsemann, pp. 253–56). Some recent studies, however, have focused on how "God's people" and "God's righteousness" relate, particularly when *dikaiosynē theou* is viewed as cosmic, affecting more than the individual, and in light of an awareness that already in Gal 3 and Rom 4–5 Paul's treatment of

---

87. The point stands, whether we take "God who justifies" as an assertion (*RSV*) or itself a rhetorical question. More delicate is whether one is to accent *ho katakrinōn*, "Who is 'the-one-to-condemn'?" as a present or future participle (cf. Cranfield). Possibly the latter (future judgment). But *dikaioō,* to rightwise, as God's action (v. 33) encompasses all the links of "salvation" mentioned in v. 30, so that even *doxa* (v. 30, final verb, "he also glorified") and being conformed to the Son's image are part of justification/righteousness (cf. Kertelge, pp. 124–26).

justification in connection with Abraham and Adam takes on a salvation-history dimension[88] (cf. the charts above, § 102 and § 143).

Amid Paul's wrestlings with election and predestination (in Protestant and Catholic theology long the chief interest in these chapters), God's power and justice (there is no *adikia* in God, 9:14), and Israel's guilt and destiny, the Apostle, as at Phil 3:9, focuses on *two kinds of righteousness*.[89] He writes: "Gentiles who did not pursue righteousness (*dikaiosynē*) have attained it, that is, righteousness through faith (*dikaiosynēn de tēn ek pisteōs*)," but "Israel who pursued the righteousness which is based on law did not succeed in fulfilling that law (*nomon dikaiosynēs eis nomon ouk ephthasen*)" (9:30-31). The distinction between *dikaiosynē ek pisteōs* and that involving *nomos* is familiar from previous discussion (§§ 110–111, above). That some Gentiles have attained to the former type, by faith, relates not to some putative situation like Rom 2:14–16 involving pagans, but to what has been happening through preaching of the gospel: Gentiles are becoming believers and thus attain to justification/righteousness.

156   What is odd at **9:31** is the phrase about Israel "pursuing *nomon dikaiosynēs*." One would have expected *dikaiosynēn tēn ek nomou* or *tēn en nomō* (Phil 3:9, 6). At 9:31 *nomon* could mean "though pursuing a 'principle' of righteousness" (concessive participle); it is attractive, with *RSV* and *JB,* to think of "a righteousness derived from law," but some feel that strains the grammar too much (Cranfield, p. 507, n. 4). Cranfield, following Käsemann (p. 277), suggests "the law which requires righteousness" but opts finally for "the law which promises righteousness." To that Israel did not attain. But Paul uses *nomon* as object of the verb "attain," not *dikaiosynēn,* though he may have in mind the phrase just used, ". . . did not attain to the law which promises righteousness." That, in turn, could mean that Israel's failing was in not reaching what the law required, and Cranfield thinks Paul has used the term *nomos* here "to bring out the truth that Israel had been given the law to aid it in its quest for righteousness before God" (p. 508). But ultimately Cranfield, like Käsemann, Ziesler, and others, holds that the error lay in the way Israel sought for righteousness, i.e., *ouk ex pisteōs all' hōs ex ergōn* (9:32), Israel "did not pursue the righteousness which the law promised (cf. 3:21) on the basis of faith but as if it were based on works." It was never attainable by works, Paul has consistently held (Gal 3–4); it comes only as a gift from God by faith in Christ, who turns out to be the "stone of stumbling" (9:33).

---

88. Cf. especially Chr. Müller, *Gottes Gerechtigkeit.* On Heilsgeschichte, Johannes Munck, *Christ and Israel: An Interpretation of Romans 9–11* (1956; Philadelphia: Fortress, 1967). Käsemann, pp. 256–57 and 106, 114, and Cranfield, p. 225, n. 1, cite more of the extensive literature.

89. At 9:28 the TR added *en dikaiosynē, hoti logon syntetmēnenon* from the LXX version of the obscure text of Isa 10:23. It must have meant in the LXX that God's judgment would be executed "with justice." We omit it from discussion of 9:28 on textual grounds (UBSGNT, {A} level of certainty). Cf. above, n. 9.

157   That Paul's real contrast—at the heart of "the dilemma of Israel"—is not simply between two kinds of righteousness, that given by God
and that based on doing the deeds of the law, but between faith and works,
is shown by the concentrated use of our terms in 10:1ff. Paul says of the
Jews,

> 10:3   Since they did not know the righteousness of God (*tēn tou
> theou dikaiosynēn*) and sought to establish their own sort of righ-
> teousness,[90] they did not submit to the righteousness of God (*tē͵
> dikaiosyne͵ tou theou*). ⁴For Christ is the end of the law, that ev-
> ery one who has faith may be justified (*telos gar nomou Christos
> eis dikaiosynēn panti tō͵ pisteuonti*).

In **10:3** and **4** *dikaiosynē* has the sense(s) we found at 1:17, 3:21ff.,
chap. 6, and elsewhere: God's saving activity, the gift inseparable from the
Giver, a power of dominion to which one submits, forensic, i.e., received
not achieved (so Ziesler, p. 206). The knives of some exegetes carve up v. 3
even more precisely, however: In 3a *theou* may be taken as a genitive of
authorship and in 3b as subjective genitive (respectively, "the righteousness which comes from God and is appropriated to people" and "the righteousness which is God's property as expression of his saving will and
activity"); or 3a and b as (cf. Phil 3:9) "righteousness imputed to people
from God" or as a property of God. Kertelge (pp. 95–99), who gives references for all the views just cited, notes the use of the article with *dikaiosynē*
(otherwise, chiefly in prepauline tradition about "the righteousness of
God," e.g., 3:25); therefore, he suggests, 10:3b = the (well-known) righteousness of God that we have spoken of at 10:3a and earlier; 10:3a, in
contrast to "the righteousness of their own." But Kertelge's real contribution is to show the relation of 10:3 and what follows to the *Lehrsatz* at
10:4.

158   In spite of Cranfield's recent revival of the view that *telos* in 10:4
means Christ is the *goal,* "real meaning," or intention of the law, Pauline
thought generally and the context of this passage in Romans specifically
demand the sense *"end* of the law," i.e., the one who puts an end to the law
as a way of salvation by works; as 10:4b and 5ff. make clear, it is by faith
that one—anyone and everyone, universally—attains to righteousness (*eis
dikaiosynēn* to be taken with *Christos* [Kertelge, p. 97, n. 172] and/or with
pisteuonti [Käsemann, p. 283; cf. 6:16]; on the whole verse, Kertelge, pp.
97–98; Käsemann, pp. 282–83).

The significance of 10:4 is that it defines (note use of *gar*) "the righteousness of God" at 10:3 *christologically* (cf. discussion above of 1:17 and
1:3b–4, and of 3:21ff.). Christ "appears here as the personified righteousness of God" (Kertelge, p. 98), in whom God's saving power has drawn

---

90. Some MSS (P⁴⁶, B, the Koine tradition) insert *dikaiosynēn* here (cf. the Nestle appa-
ratus; Ziesler, p. 205; UBSGNT omits); in sense it is plainly to be added.

near (10:8); this power continues as "the preaching of Christ" (10:17) or "word of truth" (10:8). That the entire section and argument stand under the christological emphasis on Christ as the "bearer and representative" of the righteousness of God is suggested by the point that he is "lord" (10:9)—of all, Jew and Greek (10:12), offering "salvation" (10:13 = Joel 2:32, Hebrews 3:5) to everyone, i.e., rightwising by faith.

159   Additional references in 10:5ff. simply spell out the "faith versus works" theology of Paul, about the two ways to righteousness, in sharp antipathy:

10:5 "Moses writes that the man who practices the righteousness based on law (*tēn dikaiosynēn tēn ek nomou*) shall live by it" (Lev 18:5)

10:6 But the righteousness based on faith (*hē de ek pisteōs dikaiosynē*) says (Paul uses a *pesher*-style interpretation of Deut 30:11–14, originally about the "commandment," to show that you do not need to pursue Christ in heaven or in the world of the dead, for) "The word is near you" (this Paul takes not as the law's command but "the word of faith which we preach"), "on your *lips* and in your *heart*," because

10:9   if you confess (*homologēsēs*) with your *lips*
            that "Jesus is Lord"
            and believe (*pisteusēs*) in your *heart* that
            "God raised him from the dead,"
                you will be saved.
10:10 For a person believes with the *heart* and so is justified (*pisteuetai eis dikaiosynēn*)
            and confesses with the *lips* and so is saved (*homologeitai eis sōtērian*).
10:11 Scripture says, "No one who believes in him will be put to shame."
10:12 There is no distinction (cf. 2:11). . . . He is lord of all and bestows his riches (righteousness, life, etc.) on everyone who "calls on the name of the Lord" Jesus.

We prefer not to try to make a distinction (in English) between "justification" and "righteousness" or to make each but part of "being saved" (as Ziesler, pp. 207–08, does). *JBC* 53:106 rightly remarks about not over-stressing "the distinction between justification and salvation, or between faith and profession" in vv. 9–10. *Sōzō* and *dikaioō* intertwine, as at 5:9–10 and 1:16–17. The positioning of "confess" and "believe" in v. 9 is determined by the sequence of "lips" and "heart" in the Deuteronomy quote in v. 8; v. 10 provides what to us is a more normal sequence, though Käsemann suggests that for Paul even in v. 9 *pisteuein* denotes continuing adherence to the confession of the gospel (p. 291).

160 Thus, as 9:30–10:21 shows, the "problem of Israel" centers in the historical revelation of the righteousness of God in Jesus Christ and in the two ways to righteousness, by works of the law (which proves no way at all to it) or by faith in Jesus. In this sense, Christian Müller is correct in concluding that Paul interprets the problem of Israel at 9:30–10:21 through the doctrine of justification (p. 37, cf. 107–08). God's fidelity to covenant and people is involved, but his right as Creator and faithfulness to all creation are what come to the fore in the revelation of the righteousness of God in Christ. Kertelge (p. 99, e.g.), among others, is dubious whether the creation emphasis (seen by Müller, for example in 9:19–21) has been established (though Paul's concern certainly is universal, 10:12–13, 11:32, 36), and suggests the dialectic could just as well be grounded in eschatology.

161 h. *Ethical paraenesis, 12:1ff.* Though *dikaio*-terms are rare in these chapters, it must be remembered that all Paul says in exhortation rests òn the good news of God's saving righteousness previously set forth in the epistle. The concern is now "the righteousness of God in daily life" (Käsemann, pp. 323–31) or "the obedience of (those righteous by) faith" (cf. Cranfield, pp. 592–94, 824). If Ziesler is at all correct, the moral, ethical side of *dikaiosynē* has already been present in previous chapters of Romans. And, as we have sought to show, if justification is not unrelated to final judgment, then there is a seriousness and purposefulness in the Christian's living in the world that no one, reading Romans, could avoid.

Käsemann makes a case for justification as "the grasping of our lives by Christ's lordship" being relevant for "ethics" as well as for "dogmatics." Thus it lies behind 12:1–15:13 in the same way "the obedience of the liberated" ran through chaps. 6–8. This is true both of the general exhortations (12–13) and the specific teaching about "the strong and the weak" (14:1–15:13), addressed to Rome, though in light of experiences in Corinth and elsewhere.

162 It is in the latter section, at **14:17,** that we have the sole use of a *dikaios*-word in these chapters: "For the kingdom of God does not mean food and drink but righteousness (*dikaiosynē*) and peace and joy in the Holy Spirit." In context (14:15–16), Paul is making the point that the Christian believer is free in the Lord Jesus to eat and drink whatever he or she wishes, without scruple for *kosher* regulations, though with concern for the (weaker, Jewish-Christian?) brother or sister. God's kingdom does not consist of such rules about food and drink but rather of. . . . The three nouns may (so Käsemann) or may not (Cranfield) each be taken with "in the Holy Spirit." Just because of the kingdom-reference, we may have here traditional early Christian material, but likely reworked by Paul.

Exegetes continue to be split (cf. *Righteousness and Society,* pp. 63–64) over whether *dikaiosyne* in v. 17 means the believer's "righteous action" (Barrett), because it occurs in an ethical section, or God's righteous power that justifies, brings peace, and results in joy, all in the Spirit (Kertelge, p. 298). Cranfield opts for the latter, "the status of righteousness before God which is God's gift," as does Käsemann (p. 377, "divine power"). If there is traditional material here, the original sense probably was of a relating of the *basileia tou theou* with the *dikaiosyne tou theou* (cf. E. Jüngel), and the tradition as well as Paul understood righteousness in a broad sense. But the use here in context suggests an ethical side also: "The person who in this (way, *en toutō,* referring to the three nouns there, or to the whole sentence, = thus) is enslaved to Christ is pleasing to God—and approved by human beings" (v. 18).

Rom 14:17 is a reminder that Paul in his ethical section has not forgotten his gospel of righteousness/justification. Indeed the verse can be termed the "theological center" of chaps. 12–15 (Jüngel, quoted by Kertelge, p. 298). The righteousness of God, a power given as a gift, unfolds in practical, day-by-day experiences in the life of the community. That Paul uses many other terms in expounding this point reflects the difference between a Rechtfertigungs*begriff* and his Rechtfertigungs*botschaft*. The proclamation of what is involved in rightwising is what matters (Kertelge, p. 299).

B. Deuteropauline Epistles

163   In the later writings in the Pauline corpus—in our judgment by members of the Pauline school—the theme of *dikaiosyne* continues, though less frequently than in many of the genuine letters, and sometimes as a formal "doctrine" rather than as *the* expression of the gospel.

164   1. What little evidence exists in the tract about the judgment and apocalyptic expectations that we call *2 Thessalonians* has already been dealt with above (§ 84): *Dikaios* occurs twice, in a forensic setting, about God's righteousness, punitive and saving, at the judgment.

165   2. In *Colossians* the only vocabulary link is the neuter adjective *dikaion* used as an adverb in an admonition in a Haustafeln section (table of household duties and relationships), "Masters, treat your slaves *justly* and fairly" (4:1). The sense is ethical, the background Greek, from popular philosophy about "fairness" and "distributive justice." Responsibility to the *kyrios* in heaven, Jesus, undergirds the admonition, however (4:1*b,* "because you masters know that you have a Master in heaven"), and to that extent Paul's idea of the Christian life as a transfer of masters is reflected, as well as probably the motif of the future judgment.

Otherwise, Colossians shows no reflection of Paul's characteristic ideas such as Sin, law, promise, righteousness, or believing (*pisteuein;* the noun does occur at 1:4, 23; 2:5, 7, 12). The community is one bound to confessions of faith (1:15–20, parts of 2:12–15, and 3:1b reflect creedal slogans or hymns), whence its Christology and closely related ecclesiology are developed. But because (future) eschatology has receded, baptism reflects a notion of resurrection to new life *now* (3:1), more akin in Hellenistic Christianity than to Paul's emphasis on future fulfillment. Partly the situation addressed, more likely involving gnosticizing tendencies than Jewish emphasis on works of the law, is a factor in what Colossians says and how it says it. The cross of Christ (1:20, 22, 2:14–15), bringing forgiveness of sins (1:14, 2:13) and reconciliation with God (1:20–22), remains, along with Christ's resurrection, a central expression of the Pauline gospel.[91]

166   3. *Ephesians*[92] is the highwater mark among the deuteropaulines for *dikaio*-terminology. Statistically "the verb does not occur. The adjective is found once," in a Haustafeln section, and since the three examples of the noun are all in ethical sections, Ziesler (pp. 153–54) sees the references as basically ethical. But he is himself ambiguous at points and fails to discuss the most significant passage, 2:5, 8–10, because it uses other vocabulary than *dikaio*-words.

167   a. Clearly **4:24** is ethical: "put on the new nature (so *RSV; ton kainon anthrōpon;* M. Barth argues for "the New Man," or Person, in the sense of the church; cf. p. 309; 2:15; Gal 3:28), created after the likeness of God in true righteousness and holiness (*ton kata theon ktisthenta en dikaiosynē, kai hosiotēti tēs alētheias*)." Ziesler compares Phil 3:9 for thought and, while calling the righteousness here "surely ethical," points out that the language of "putting on" and the notion of a "new person which has been created after God['s image—which *RSV* is correct in inferring; cf. Col 3:10, M. Barth, pp. 509–10]" indicates "baptismal catechesis" (more firmly, *JBC* 56:32). Finally, Ziesler sees a link to Eph 2:8ff. M. Barth (pp. 510–11) and Stuhlmacher (p. 216) are content with an ethical sense for 4:24 ("gegenüber Paulus erneut ethisiert"). We have, moreover, already observed such an ethical sense for *dikaiosynē* in Paul's unquestioned letters (see above on, e.g., 2 Cor 9:11; Phil 1:7, 11, 4:8; Rom 6:19–20, 14:17).

The statement at **5:9**, "for the fruit of light is found in all that is good and right and true (*ho gar karpos tou phōtos en pasē, agathōsynē, kai dikaiosynē, kai alētheia*)" offers the same picture, with "righteousness" as "die Rechtschaffenheit des Verhaltens" (Stuhlmacher, p. 216). That sense is especially pertinent if one renders in a way that M. Barth (p. 568) suggests, "The offspring of light consists of all men who are good, righteous, and

---

91. On the theology of Col, cf. Eduard Lohse, *Colossians and Philemon* (Hermeneia; 1971), pp. 177–83.

92. **Commentaries and other literature cited on Eph:** T. A. Abbott (ICC; 1909); Heinrich Schlier, *Christus und die Kirche im Epheserbrief* (BHT 6; 1930) and *Der Brief an die Epheser* (2d ed.; Düsseldorf: Patmos Verlag, 1958); C. Leslie Mitton, *The Epistle to the Ephesians* (Oxford: Clarendon Press, 1951); J. Gnilka (HTKNT 10/2, 1971); Markus Barth (AB 34, 34A; 1974).

true," though in the last analysis Barth leans more toward a Hebraic sense of covenant-behavior here than a Greek meaning. It is Ziesler this time who demurs: "Something like the 'righteousness-in-Christ-by-faith' sense" is called for, because these believers are "light *en kyriō̦*," (5:8), i.e., by their being in Christ Jesus.

168 The reference to righteousness at **6:14** as part of "the whole armor of God" (6:11, 14) is the passage—ostensibly ethical—that gives the greatest pause. When the verse says, "Stand therefore,

> having *girded your loins with truth,*
> and having *put on the breastplate of righteousness* (*ton thōraka tēs dikaiosynēs*),
> and having shod your *feet with the equipment of the gospel of peace* . . .,*

is Paul speaking of "actual righteousness of character wrought by Christ" (T. K. Abbott, ICC, 1909) or something more or something else? Commentators observe that the words underlined above in English reflect Isa 11:5, 59:17, and 52:7 respectively (cf. also Wis 5:17–20) and that in these earlier scriptural passages the armor belongs to God. The "breastplate of righteousness" is thus loaned to the Christian believer for his struggle against the "principalities and powers" (6:12). Ziesler then concludes simply, "It is thus ethical, from God, according well with 'righteousness-in-Christ' " (p. 154).

169 Markus Barth makes a case for going further in terms of biblical theology with such phrases as "clad with righteousness as a cuirass" (his rendering of 6:14) and "the helmet of salvation" (Isa 59:17) and "the sword of the Spirit, which is the word of God" (cf. Isa 49:2). This imagery, which runs through Eph 6:13–17, Barth would take as "God's [splendid] armor" (for *panoplia*), reflecting the OT "Holy War" theme. It is *God's* armor, given to humans for the struggle not only on cosmic battlefields "but also in courtrooms," for judgment and cosmic-lawsuit imagery is mixed in, here and elsewhere in Ephesians (cf. pp. 238–42, 769, on Ephesians' use of the church in God's cosmic lawsuit as "proof" to the "powers" for God's grace, 2:7, 3:10). "Righteousness," then, like truth (6:14) and faith (6:16), "may mean something other than 'virtues,' " for "peace," "salvation," "Spirit," and "word of God" in the armaments list are gifts from God, not ethical virtues even of believers (Barth, pp. 795–97).

170 Barth specifically ties up *dikaiosynē* at 6:14 with a covenant background and the messianic promises of Isa 11:1–9. As in Paul's thought elsewhere, then, righteousness, peace, salvation, is each a gift from God. "The 'righteousness of God' is meant through which man is justified by grace alone (Rom 3:21–31)" (p. 796; n. 209 cites Oepke in *TDNT* for support in this "harmony between Eph 6:14 and Romans or Galatians" but also quotes Schlier's "obscure" observation in *Christus und die Kirche* [1930]—not forensic righteousness, but Glaubensgerechtigkeit, "acted out in life," i.e., "one of the four later so-called cardinal virtues"—that is surely to have it both ways!). Barth concludes that 6:14 means "being 'clothed with righteousness' " and hence the "great honor and heavy duty" entrusted to each saint, as part of "the obedience of faith." But much of this depends on how we understand a pillar passage in Eph 2.

171 b. *Ephesians 2,* on salvation through Christ for Gentiles as well as for "the circumcision," twice uses slogans reminiscent of Paul's gospel of righteousness/justification, but this time without *dikaioō:* 2:4, "by grace you have been saved (*chariti este sesōsmenoi*)," and 2:8, "by grace you have been saved through faith (*tē, chariti este sesōsmenoi dia pisteōs*)."

The study by Gottfried Schille in 1965 on early Christian hymns[93] brought into the arena of Ephesians study the possibility of an early Christian (even "prepauline") hymn used at baptismal initiation, incorporated at 2:4–10. Opinion varies even among those who allow for it over the extent (perhaps only vv. 4–7) and structure of this "Taufliturgie" (Stuhlmacher, pp. 216–17). Ulrich Luz, resting on Lindemann's counterarguments that so much of even 2:4–7 is part of the preferred vocabulary of Ephesians, regards the whole section as the work of the author of Ephesians.[94] Luz prefers as influences Col 2:13 ("You, who were dead in trespasses and the uncircumcision of your flesh, God made alive with Christ . . .") and other Colossian phrases and Titus 3:3–7 (pp. 369–70). Markus Barth, who holds that Paul wrote Ephesians himself, sees verses 4–10 as poetic, a "church theology which Paul feels free to quote," while also adding certain correctives (p. 218). (To take 5c and 8a as comments, either by Paul himself or the author of Ephesians, is certainly more likely than Barth's other supposition that the lines are "liturgical responses of the celebrating priest to the singing of the congregation," or an antiphon, pp. 217 and 221). In any case, 5c and 8a do stand out in the rhythmic context because they are cast in second person plural, in the midst of lines that are about "us" (vv. 4–5a, 6–7, 10; italicized below for contrast).

2:4   God who is rich in mercy,
        on account of his great love with which he loved *us,*
2:5   even while *we* were dead through *our* trespasses,
        made *us* alive together with the Christ.
2:5c   By grace *you* are saved!
2:6   He both raised up and enthroned (*us*)
        in the heavenly realms in Christ Jesus,

---

93. *Frühchristliche Hymnen* (Berlin: Evangelische Verlagsanstalt, 1965), pp. 53ff. Cf. Jack T. Sanders, "Hymnic Elements in Eph. 1–3," *ZNW* 56 (1965): 214–32, and his SNTSMS *Hymns* (cited above, n. 43), pp. 14–15, 88–92 on 2:14–16.

94. Ulrich Luz, "Rechtfertigung bei den Paulusschülern," in *Rechtfertigung* (Käsemann fs), pp. 369–75; cf. Andreas Lindemann, *Die Aufhebung der Zeit: Geschichtsverständnis und Eschatologie im Epheserbrief* (Studien zum Neuen Testament 12; Gütersloh: Mohn, 1975), pp. 116–17.

2:7   in order that he might prove in the ages to come
        the immeasurable riches of his grace
        through his goodness to *us* in Christ Jesus.
2:8*a*   By (this) grace *you* are saved through faith!
        And this (is) not *your* own doing (*ex hymōn*), God's (is) the
        gift—
2:9   not on the basis of works (*ex ergōn*), lest anyone boast.
2:10   For his creation (*poiēma*) are *we*,
        having been created (*ktisthentes*) in Christ Jesus
        for good works which God prepared beforehand,
        in order that *we* might walk in them.

172   Obviously the emphasis is on God and his action (mercy, love,
grace, goodness). The human situation is one of sins and death. The
"Christ event" is described in such a way as not to mention the cross (but
cf. 2:13, 16), but it does emphasize resurrection (cf. Col 3:1) and enthronement not only of Christ but also for believers. Faith is the means for being
saved,[95] faith in distinction to "works" (not merely just "works based on
the Jewish torah," but any works). Genuinely Pauline is the emphasis on
the gift-character of salvation and the exclusion thereby of boasting and of
"yourselves" as source of salvation. Even the notion that all this means
"(new) creation" in a Pauline sense follows from ample evidence in Paul's
previous letters.

173   What is different about the slogans in 2:5c and 8a and the entire
section, in comparison with material in Paul at which we have previously
looked, is (1) the use of *sōzō*, "save," instead of *dikaioō*. In this connection
attention is to be given also to the verb tense, "you have been (and are)
saved," the Greek perfect tense in vv. 5 and 8. Also, the resurrection and
enthronement of believers is presented in a past (aorist) tense (vv. 5, 6).[96]
This brings us to a second difference between Paul's other (genuine) letters
and Ephesians: (2) in eschatology, Paul viewed justification/salvation as
involving aspects in the past, the present, and the future; in Ephesians, we
have no emphasis on a future side, let alone any final judgment to come (at
best, cf. 4:30, 5:6, 6:13); the eschatology is, as by and large in the Fourth
Gospel, "realized" (*JBC* 56:20). M. Barth makes the interesting comment
that on this score "the two interspersed responses of 2:5, 8 are *less* in line
with Paul's habitual diction than the rest of the hymn" but, he explains,

---

95. M. Barth, *Ephesians,* pp. 224–25, argues that "faith" here means (a) God's faithfulness, and (b) Christ's fidelity, and (c) the faith of the saints, with emphasis on (c). We take it,
as in previous cases, as the trusting, obedient response of those who believe in Christ.

96. As to when in the believer's life this resurrection-enthronement took place, M. Barth
(pp. 233–38) suggests "conversion" or "enlightenment" as possibilities alongside baptism. As
to "enthronement," "the heavenlies" may be "the places elected by God for the manifestation
of his presence, glory, and power"; the event relates to being "sealed with the Spirit" (1:13)
when the Messiah wakens people from their dead condition in trespasses (2:1; 5:14).

Paul was not duty bound always to speak about justification. As he spoke on distinct occasions of *perfected, past, ongoing, and future justification and sanctification,* so he was also free to speak of completed "salvation," not just of its present progress or future attainment.[97]

But the difference in eschatology is so marked that many other commentators opt for deuteropauline status for Ephesians on that ground alone.

174 (c) *"Work(s)" in Ephesians.* We note a final difference in Ephesians from Paul: complex as use of *ergon* was in Paul (see above, especially on Rom 2), Ephesians seems to use the term differently again. Barth's extended note (pp. 242–51) suggests a useful outline:

(1) The "work" of God as salvation is suggested at 2:10, "We are his workmanship" (*RSV, poiēma*). This is passable Pauline vocabulary (cf. Phil 1:6, God "who has begun among us (a) good work [*ergon agathon,* salvation and/or the work of missionary advance] will complete it till the Day of Jesus Christ"), and with *ktisthentes* at 2:10*b* suggests salvation as "(new) creation."[98]

(2) "Not on the basis of works" (*ex ergōn,* 2:9) surely reflects Paul's use of *ex ergōn nomou* (Gal 2:16, 3:2, 5; Rom 3:20, etc.), "works based on the law," except that now in the Ephesians situation the phrase has become pro forma and the (Jewish) law was probably no more a lively issue.

(3) The "good works" (*ergois agathois*) that "God prepared previously" that "we (believers) have been created to do" (2:10) present a new idea. The rabbis could talk of certain things as "preexistent," but "good works" were not among them. Paul could refer to "vessels of mercy which God has prepared beforehand" (same verb as here, Rom 9:23, of those persons for whom he would "make known the riches of his glory"). But good works prepared beforehand by God, "in which believers walk," is seemingly unparalleled. The Ephesians passage simultaneously attributes to good works a higher value than rabbinical teachings do, but at the same time removes them from the sphere of law (by omitting any reference to it), avoiding boasting, and claiming that here too "all is of God—in advance"! The strange wording has translated Paul's "obedience of faith" connected with "justification" into "salvation" through faith by grace, with a "way of life" that includes good works previously prepared by God. This is the thought of Col 1:10 about "bearing fruit in every good work," safeguarded by the election and predestination emphases of Ephesians (1:4, 5, 11, etc.), to show it is "God's gift, not us or our works," all the way.

175 d. *Evaluation.* Has the author of Ephesians succeeded in preserving, as Luz asks (pp. 373–75), a theology of righteousness/justification,

---

97. M. Barth, *Ephesians,* p. 221, italics added. On justification (as well as sanctification and reconciliation) as past, present, and future in Paul, cf., p. 221, nn. 65 and 71 for references. On *sōzō* as past, present, and future in Paul, see n. 66. Cf. above, § 147.

98. M. Barth, *Ephesians,* p. 243. Cf. J. Reumann, *Creation and New Creation,* pp. 73–79, 89–99, 102–05.

severed from its apocalyptic world view and Paul's emphasis on future expectation? (1) As to the Pauline emphasis that righteousness/justification is not a private, individual matter but holds for the entire world, Ephesians preserves this aspect, though not without other dangers, through its emphasis on the church and its cosmic role. (2) The apocalyptic dimension to *dikaiosynē* as the power of God for believers is paralleled in Ephesians by the protological (rather than eschatological) emphasis on the predestined aspect of God's action as "prepared beforehand" (2:10). (3) Parallel to the way in which, for Paul, the tension between proleptic delivery (Vorausgabe) of the righteousness of God and its eschatological manifestation opens the room for human activity, in Ephesians the paraenesis of chaps. 4 to 6 is meant to be the crown of the theology in the opening chapters. Eph 2:10 shows that ethics is no option for those saved by faith, according to this epistle, but a necessity.

176   If Ephesians can be said to present counterparts to Paul on these points, nonetheless there is also the fact that, as the critical function receded into the past that righteousness/justification had for Paul against the Jewish law as providing grounds for boasting by observance of that law, so the polemical functioning of the doctrine against every form of human self-aggrandizement also recedes. And when justification is viewed as baptismal salvation and not in light of Paul's theology of the cross, with a future judgment, this plus the concept in Ephesians of the church as the "one new man" and as the "body of Christ" (1:23, 2:16, 4:16)—the possibility is lost of employing righteousness/justification as a critical yardstick in measuring the church in light of God's will; God's righteousness then becomes but a partial aspect of the dominant ecclesiology (so Luz).

177   For all these proposed "cons" in the theology of Ephesians, it must be observed that the Lutheran Confessions gladly quote Eph 2 in support of their understanding of justification (so already in Ap. 4:73 and 93, and especially in the Formula, SD III:20, Tappert ed. pp. 117, 120, and 542 respectively), and on "faith and good works" (CA 20:11; cf. Formula, Epitome IV: 7; SD II:26, 39; IV:7, VI:12). There is no difficulty for the Confessions over using "save" instead of "justify"; the language of Eph 2:10, about "good works which God prepared that we should walk in them," is accepted too. It is when Paul's reservations are dropped about the future side of salvation/justification, so that it becomes something already fully completed for the believer and the notion of a final judgment is lost, that Lutherans think one treads on dangerous ground. For they regard the "not yet" aspect of Christian life as absolutely clear from Scripture, and indispensable theologically.

178   4. *The Pastoral Epistles*[99] we may treat as a subsection of the Pau-

---

99. **On the Pastoral Epistles,** commentaries consulted include: W. Lock (ICC; 1924); C. Spicq (EBib; 1947); J. Jeremias (NTD, 6th ed.; 1953); Dibelius-Conzelmann (HNT, rev. 1955; Eng. trans. Hermeneia, 1972); J. N. D. Kelly (HNTC; 1963); C. K. Barrett (New Clarendon Bible, Oxford, 1963). "J. Quinn" refers not to his forthcoming AB commentary (non

line corpus, coming from after Paul's lifetime, even though they may contain materials from Paul himself and even from pre- or nonpauline, most likely Hellenistic, Christianity. The sequence among the three of Titus, then 1 and 2 Tim (J. Quinn) is attractive, but little of significance seems to result for our study by tracing development within the three documents.

Those treating *dikaio*-terms (11 examples) in the Pastorals usually call at least the noun (5×) and adjective-adverb (4×) uses "ethical"; only the 2 verb instances are defined otherwise by Ziesler (pp. 154–56; cf. *Righteousness and Society,* p. 65, for examples; U. Luz, p. 376). As with Ephesians, however, a (pre-)Pastorals passage or two that do not use *dikaioō* merit attention, and this broader context reopens the possibility that some of the "ethical" passages are more than that.

179   a. *Exegetical.* We may agree that **1 Tim 1:9** is a conventional enough example, discussing the author's point that "the Law in its penal aspect . . . was instituted for the unjust, not for the just" (*JBC* 57:15): "The law is good, if any one uses it lawfully, understanding this, that the law is not laid down for the just (*dikaiō;*) but for the lawless and disobedient, for the ungodly (*asebesi,* as at Rom 4:5) and sinners."

1 Tim 3:16, with its line, Christ "was vindicated (*edikaiōthē*) in the Spirit," we have previously examined as part of a Hellenistic-Jewish Christian hymn (§ 61, above); it reflects God's eschatological victory through Christ in his cosmic lawsuit against the world.

180   There are other passages in the Pastorals that, also claimed by some as quotations from such earlier Christian tradition, likewise set forth the salvation event in Christ. Particularly pertinent is **Titus 3:3–7.** After a brief description (v. 3) of the disobedient condition of humanity, the change wrought by "the goodness and loving kindness of God our Savior" (v. 4) is presented:

> 3:5   he saved us (cf. Eph 2:4–10)
> not because of deeds done by us in righteousness (*ouk ex ergōn tōn en dikaiosynē, ha epoiēsamen hēmeis*),
> but in virtue of his own mercy,
> by the washing of regeneration and renewal in the Holy Spirit,
>
> 3:6   which he poured upon us richly through Jesus Christ our Savior,
>
> 3:7   that, having been justified by his grace (*dikaiōthentes tē; ekeinou chariti*),
> we might become heirs in hope of eternal life.

---

vidi) but to this paper in the Lutheran-Catholic dialogue, "Notes on the Terminology for Faith, Truth, Teaching, and the Spirit in the Pastoral Epistles," and his summary thereof in *Teaching Authority and Infallibility in the Church* (cited above, Preface, n. 1), pp. 232–37.

3:8*a* (same paragraph in *RSV*) designates the section as a "sure saying" (*pistos ho logos,* a phrase in the Pastorals designating a "fundamental," often cited from some creed or hymn).

The reference (3:5) to "deeds done in *dikaiosynē,*" denotes "human righteousness which cannot save" (Ziesler, p. 155), our own "right deeds" that do *not* count before God (Käsemann).[100] But there is no indication of polemic here against "deeds done on the basis of *the law,*" as at Gal 2:16 *ex ergōn nomou* (the same shift has been observed at Eph 2:9), for the sense of "law" is now different (cf. 1 Tim 1:9). Nor is there any reference to "the righteousness *of God*" as the contrast to *dikaiosynē*-done-by-us. Instead, the emphasis is on God's "mercy," on baptism and God's pouring forth of the Spirit, "richly." The antithesis "serves . . . to strengthen the *sola gratia*" (Luz, p. 377), cf. v. 7.

The aorist participle *dikaiōthentes* in v. 7 is the same form as that at Rom 5:1. That fact, among others, prompts Ziesler (p. 155) to opt here for "declare" rather than "make righteous." The following phrase, "by the grace of That One," is reminiscent of Rom 3:24 and 5:15, among other references in Paul, but is also the emphasis that we found heightened in Ephesians. The words "in order that we might become heirs according to hope of eternal life" employ Pauline terms and even preserve his future aspect to salvation. The Pastorals do emphasize a future epiphany of the Lord Jesus Christ (1 Tim 6:14; 2 Tim 4:1; Titus 2:13) in a way Ephesians had not. All in all, a good deal of Paul's doctrine of righteousness/justification has been preserved here, in a setting that prompts some (e.g., Alan Richardson) to speak of "baptismal justification."[101]

181   In the same epistle to Titus a similar statement about salvation and its implications appears at **2:11–14:**

2:11 The grace of God has appeared for the salvation of all persons,

2:12 training (*paideuousa*) us to renounce irreligion and worldly passions and to live sober, upright (*dikaiōs*), and godly lives in this world,

2:13 awaiting our blessed hope, the appearing of . . . Jesus Christ,

2:14 who gave himself for us . . . to purify for himself a people of his own who are zealous for good deeds.

That Christians are to live "uprightly" is, of course, ethical in sense, as is the similar use of the adjective in the list of attributes for an *episkopos:* He must be "upright" (*dikaios*) (**Titus 1:8**). According to 2:11–14, the doc-

---

100. E. Käsemann, "Titus 3, 4–7," *Göttinger Predigt-Meditationen,* 2. Weihnachtstag (1950), pp. 20ff., reprinted in his *Exegetische Versuche und Besinnungen,* Vol. 1 (Göttingen: Vandenhoeck & Ruprecht, 1960), pp. 298–302.

101. Alan Richardson, *An Introduction to the Theology of the New Testament* (London: SCM, 1958), pp. 235–40, especially 238.

trine (*didaskalia,* 2:10) of Christianity is that God's grace in Christ has saved universally; Christians are to live righteous lives, zealous for good works, until Christ comes in glory. Titus 3:7*a* made clear that justification was connected with baptism and is the basis (7*b*) of our future hope. Yet for all this Pauline vocabulary and thought, the author of Titus goes on (3:8), ". . . insist . . . that those who have believed in God . . . apply themselves to good deeds" (unless with *RSV*'s footnote we render, "enter honorable occupations"). The question arises how the author understood his Pauline categories and these statements (which Paul would presumably have never made) to fit together.

182   Alongside these basic passages in Titus and 1 Timothy about what God has done in Christ, we may note a similar one in **2 Tim 1** that is like Eph 2 in using *sōzō* rather than *dikaioō*: this statement is about vocation and "suffering for the gospel according to the power of God

> 1:9   who saved us and called us with a holy calling,
>   not in virtue of our works
>   but in virtue of his own purpose
>   and the grace which he gave us in Christ Jesus ages ago,
> 1:10 and now has manifested through the appearing of our Savior
>   Christ Jesus,
>   who abolished death and brought life and immortality to
>   light through the gospel." (2 Tim 1:9–10)

Jeremias saw here in what he called an ancient liturgical text a terse reference at 9*bc* to Paul's doctrine of justification. Luz senses in 1:8*a* some reflection of Rom 1:16 ("do not be ashamed of . . .") and then in vv. 9–11 an equivalent to the summary of the gospel at Rom 1:17. But the emphases ("save" rather than "justify"; grace, not works) are more akin to what we have seen in Ephesians and Hellenistic Christianity. And the ultimate concern is to guard through the Holy Spirit (1:12, 14) the deposit (*parathēkē*) that has been entrusted till "the Day." A "share of suffering" may be involved (1:8, 12), but one is to "keep the faith" (4:7).

183   In a verse with two uses of our terms, Paul, according to **2 Tim 4:8**, says, "Finally (*loipon*), there is laid up for me the crown of righteousness (*ho tēs dikaiosynēs stephanos*), which the Lord, the righteous judge (*ho dikaios kritēs*), will award (*apodōsei*) to me on that Day, and . . . to all who have loved his appearing." The "righteous judge" here gives crowns to those who have kept faith and loved him to the end, with nothing said about punishing the wicked (such as are listed at 3:2–5, e.g.). The crown, most exegetes hold (e.g., Barrett; Ziesler, p. 155), is "a reward for righteousness," though it can also be taken as an epexegetical genitive, "the crown consisting in righteousness."[102] Ziesler objects that this would make

---

102. So Lock in ICC. Against it may be the word order, with the genitive "of righteousness" in between the article and noun "the . . . crown."

righteousness "thoroughly eschatological," but in the Pastorals that is one clear aspect of salvation (see above, on Titus 3:7). He himself muses that the sense of reward for "my own righteousness" "comes very oddly indeed in a supposedly Pauline letter" (p. 156). Paul had spoken of an "imperishable" crown for Christians at the end of life's race (1 Cor 9:25), and when he spoke of the Thessalonians as a "crown" (1 Thess 2:19), the context was the parousia. References in Revelation to a crown (of life, 2:10, etc.) are eschatological. It is possible therefore that 2 Tim 4:8 has just that sense, of righteousness given as a "crown" at the end.

184 Two references to *dikaiosynē* in virtue-vices lists are surely ethical; Timothy is told, "Pursue righteousness (*dikaiosynēn*), godliness, faith, love, steadfastness, gentleness" (**1 Tim 6:11**), and again, "Pursue righteousness (*dikaiosynēn*), faith, love, and peace, along with those who call upon the Lord from a pure heart" (**2 Tim 2:22**).[103]

Finally, there is that verse about the function of (OT) Scripture which post-Reformation theology treasured because of its adjective *theopneustos:*

All Scripture (is) $\begin{Bmatrix} \text{inspired by God and} \\ or:, \text{inspired by God, (is)} \end{Bmatrix}$ profitable for teaching, for reproof, for correction, and for training in righteousness (*pros paideian tēn en dikaiosynē,*), that the people of God may be complete, equipped for every good work (*pan ergon agathon*). (**2 Tim 3:16**; *RSV* adapted)

The ultimate purpose of Scripture is clear: to bring Christians to "every good work." Of the four previous aims ("profitable for . . ."), the last, like the first, is positive in tone. While "education for *dikaiosynē*," it might be argued, could mean something akin to *didaskalia* (doctrine) about the righteousness of God, there is little in the context to suggest such a sense. The meaning is more likely ethical (Ziesler, p. 155), akin to Titus 2:12—God's grace trains us to live righteously.

185 b. *Conclusions from the exegesis.* How does one describe these findings in the Pastorals on *dikaiosynē*?

(1) There has been preserved the Pauline sense of justification as a past event (Titus 3:7), connected with the Christ-event (1 Tim 3:16), actualized for Christians in baptism, with the gift of the Spirit.

---

103. The variations in such enumerations and even the facts that *dikaiosynē* comes first and that we have the trio "righteousness, faith, love" (with a fourth term each time) are points of which it is difficult to make anything. The virtues list at Gal 5:22 includes *pistis* (trustworthiness) but not *dikaiosynē*. Recently Eduard Schweizer has sought to link God's righteousness and the vices catalogues in Paul; cf. "Gottesrechtigkeit und Lasterkataloge bei Paulus (inkl. Kol und Eph)," *Rechtfertigung* (Käsemann fs), pp. 461–77. His best example, in my judgment, is 1 Cor 6:9–11 (cf. §§ 64–65), preceded as it is by a list of those who do certain vices, "the unrighteous" (*hoi adikoi*), who will *not* inherit God's kingdom. While Schweizer does not discuss the Pastorals or virtues lists, his comment holds (reflecting Käsemann) that God's righteousness does not "remain an abstract" but seeks to become concrete in the trivialities of everyday life (p. 476). Hence such lists as 1 Tim 6:11 and 2 Tim 2:22.

(2) The Pauline emphasis on "grace," which was heightened in Ephesians, continues too (Titus 3:7, 2:11), though as in Ephesians "salvation" becomes the basic term, not justification. "Saved by grace" is in antithesis to "by works" (Titus 3:5; 2 Tim 1:9), but the law is viewed differently from the way it was viewed in Paul's day (1 Tim 1:9). "Faith" is not stressed with justification/salvation; *pistis* tends to be "the faith of the church" (J. Quinn).

(3) Since the future appearing of Christ Jesus is stressed in the Pastorals, *dikaiosynē* does seem to have an eschatological reference at the Day of the Lord (cf. Titus 3:7*b*; 2 Tim 4:8).

(4) In the now lengthening interval between Christ's once and future appearings (cf. 2 Tim 1:10, 4:1) and the period between one's baptism-justification and the judgment, living righteously and doing good works are emphasized (Titus 2:12–14; 1 Tim 6:11; 2 Tim 2:22, 3:16).

186   c. How shall we *evaluate* these developments? Bultmann saw in the Pastorals a continuation of Paul's own thought since grace remains a force shaping life.[104] More negatively, Luz characterizes the situation in the Pastorals, with reference to righteousness/justification, as one where soteriology has been severed from Paul's imminent eschatology and thus relativized so that the several passages on the Christ-event have "more a decorative than a constitutive function" (p. 379). Indeed, the Pastorals no longer succeed in grounding "the imperative" in the "indicative." What is more, the gospel, including expressions of it as "grace, not works," has, while continuing as a factor, become in fact a doctrine that supports the church (including its structures of office), instead of offering a constant critique of it (p. 380).

187   Such an analysis, while viewing the theology of the Pastorals as a further development of Paul's thought but a decline from Paul's own view, did not, of course, exist in the sixteenth century. The Lutheran Confessions readily quote the Pastoral Epistles, e.g., in favor of "the righteousness of reason" (1 Tim 1:9), on baptism (Titus 3:5–8) and even on the proper use of the term "reward" (2 Tim 4:8).[105] But the later history of Lu-

---

104. Rudolf Bultmann, *Theology*, Vol. 2, pp. 183–86. Luz, "Rechtfertigung," p. 379, n. 42, suggests this favorable assessment by Bultmann of the Pastorals results from his "individualizing tendency" in interpreting Paul's doctrine of righteousness/justification.

105. **1 Tim 1:9** is quoted at Ap. 4 (Tappert ed., 110.22)) in support of "civil discipline" or "the righteousness of reason." To Lutheran laity perhaps the best-known passage from the Pastorals is that from **Titus 3:5–8**, the "sure saying" about baptism, quoted in the Small Catechism to explain how water can produce such effects; the answer lies in the connection with the word of God, i.e., life and regeneration in the Holy Spirit; nothing is made by Luther of the phrase "justified by his grace" in v. 7. Cf. also Large Catechism (Tappert, 440.27).

2 Tim 4:8, about "the crown of righteousness," is quoted by Melanchthon in Ap. 4 in explaining that there is no argument about "reward" once it is granted that "we are accounted righteous by faith for Christ's sake and that good works are pleasing to God because of faith. . . . The crown is owed to the justified because of the promise" (Tappert ed., 162. 362–63, the context of which should be consulted).

theranism shared (i) the Pastorals' tendency to make of justification "a doctrine" and to separate it from "sanctification" (cf. Luz, p. 377; "having been justified," Titus 3:7, one then seeks to "live uprightly," Titus 2:12); but (ii) also shared the concern that exegetes like Luz and Käsemann show over the emphasis on the church in Ephesians and the Pastorals becoming dominant over the gospel of justification, so that the critical function of God's *dikaiosynē* against all institutions, including the church, is diminished or lost.

188   d. *Explaining what happened to Paul's theme* of righteousness/justification in the later writings of the Pauline school, Ulrich Luz has recently listed various possible explanations for the changes and indeed diminution in the role *dikaiosynē* (*tou theou*) had played in Paul's writings, especially Romans, when compared with the deuteropaulines:

(1) The Rechtfertigungslehre *never was the center* of Paul's thought, but a polemical peaking of his theology in certain circumstances (so A. Schweitzer, more recently U. Wilckens[106]).

(2) The doctrine was *so complicated* and made *such high intellectual demands* that it could not realistically be carried through. As a later canonical document put it, Paul's letters contain "some things in them hard to understand" (2 Pet 3:16). Is this also true for the author of the Pastorals?

(3) The doctrine was *so tied to situations* ("works of law" vs. faith)

The Formula of Concord, it may be noted, at Epitome III:7 (Tappert, 474.10) lists the deuteropauline emphasis on "by grace" among the *particulas exclusivas* that it especially commends. But at Epitome II:8 (Tappert, 474.11) and in the Solid Declaration (Tappert, 542.19) we can see a severing of justification and "the good works which follow it" (much as in the manner of the deuteropaulines) and an attempt to distinguish "justification" and subsequent "renewal." That "justification is renewal" (a Melanchthonian idea, which, however, is never precisely stated in the Apology) can no longer be allowed as a statement without the explanation that "the renewal which follows justification . . . will not be confused with" it; at **Titus 3:5** Paul is said to have used "regeneration and renewing in the Holy Spirit" in a way that is termed "discriminately"—i.e., as forgiveness and adoption, but distinguished from "renewal."

One may say that the Lutheran development already within the Book of Concord, from CA-Ap. to Formula, parallels in some ways that from Paul himself to the Pastorals.

106. Cf. above, §§ 78–79 and n. 54. Luz, "Rechtfertigung," cites U. Wilckens, "Was heisst bei Paulus: 'Aus Werken des Gesetzes wird kein Mensch gerecht'?" *EKK Vorarbeiten Heft* 1 (1969): 51–77, reprinted in Wilckens' *Rechtfertigung als Freiheit: Paulusstudien* (Neukirchen-Vluyn: Neukirchener Verlag, 1974), pp. 77–109. Wilckens himself says he is concerned with the relationship between Rechtfertigungslehre and ethics; with Schlatter, against Bultmann, he finds their connection in the theme of being freed from the power of Sin, rather than in justification as "gift" in contrast to the principle of human accomplishment. In Romans, Wilckens especially sees an ethical thrust to the doctrine of justification for the specific situation at Rome; cf. further his EKKNT commentary and *The Romans Debate* (above, n. 75). Luz, n. 8, comments re the Pastorals that in a sense "*all* themes of Pauline theology," except paraenesis, recede, but that Luke (Acts 13) and 1 Clement and Polycarp should also be included in attempting to assess what later happened to Paul's doctrine (on the last two documents, cf. *Righteousness and Society*, pp. 88–89).

and Paul's own career (his "conversion" and his battle for Gentile Christians) that it could not be separated from Paul himself and then continued.

(4) The doctrine was *so specifically related to* debate with *Judaism* that it became passé once Christianity, after A.D. 70, became more and more a religion of the Hellenistic world.

(5) It so *rests on Jewish, apocalyptic assumptions* that the doctrine could not really take root where apocalyptic eschatology no longer obtained (the approach of the Käsemann School is especially vulnerable here).[107]

(6) Closely related to (5) is the point that the truth of Paul's doctrine is *so related to* his message of *the nearness,* indeed the *inbreaking, of the eschaton* that, severed from this, it could not be continued as the decades—let alone two thousand years—went by.

(7) The doctrine may have *no longer corresponded to the needs of later generations.* The success of religious proclamation depends on continuing relevance to a period.

189   Of course, each contention may be met or at least blunted. For view (1) by the evidence and whole tenor of this essay, including prepauline and nonpauline usage of the theme. For (2) by the fact that Paul did emphasize the theme and his successors attempted to preserve it (cf. theory 7 also). Against (3) is the fact that situations repeat and the deuteropaulines make more, not less, of Paul himself (cf. Eph 3:1–13, 4:1; 2 Tim 1:8, Paul "the" [chief] Apostle). Against (4) is the continuing relevance of the OT for which Christianity decided, and against (5) and (6) the church's efforts to preserve future eschatology (as in the creeds). Each student of Paul will have to come to his or her own conclusions on these explanations, especially on (7). Luz believes factors (6) and (7) to be the crucial ones in the case of the Pastorals (pp. 380–81). Given the delay of the parousia, with the loosing of the gospel of righteousness/justification from its eschatological context and the need for the church to settle down in society, reduction of the message about *dikaiosyne* to the individual grounding of salvation for "church members" perhaps became inevitable.

190   But one is struck by the fact that the author of the Pastorals did seek to preserve the theme "by grace, not by works" and the future hope of fulfillment, Paul's universal concern, and even the phrase *dikaiothentes tē; chariti* (Titus 3:7), and made them part of a basic teaching on which, as "deposit of faith" (2 Tim 1:12), the church, to use a Reformation phrase, "stands and falls." Indeed, one must ask whether talk of justification as *articulus stantis et cadentis ecclesiae* is not precisely a reflection of the theology of the Pastorals!

---

107. Luz, "Rechtfertigung," cites Günther Klein, "Gottes Gerechtigkeit als Thema der Paulus-Forschung," in Klein's *Rekonstruktion und Interpretation* (BEvT 50; 1969), p. 234. Analogous is the rooting of Jesus' concept of the kingdom of God in Jewish apocalyptic. By the time Paul wrote, *basileia tou theou* no longer carried the original significance for Gentile readers, yet the theme has survived, admittedly with many interpretations over the centuries.

191   One may be a bit more generous than Luz when he says the Pastorals provide a model "not for what the church ought to be but for what it has become" (p. 381). For one ought not to be so much of a purist against "Frühkatholizismus" as to regard all supposed tendencies toward later "declines" in doctrine as a "fall" from a pristine theology of Paul.[108] The burden of our argument has been that Paul himself inherited formulas about "the righteousness/justification of God," and that how one employs this way of putting the gospel varies with situations. Ephesians and the Pastorals made attempts at translating Paul's distinctive message. We may judge them the poorer for their handling of eschatology and of righteousness's critical function against all human achievement, boasting, and even institutions (including the church, so Luz), but the thinning of the earlier richness is probably no worse here than when we have to deal with the OT prophets or Jesus, on, say, the kingdom of God, as we try to have them address new situations—or, one may add, the postreformation restatements of the earlier Lutheran documents from the years around 1530.

C. Some Alternative Central Themes in Paul

192   The case has been made above, by detailed exegetical examination, for the importance of the rise and development of *righteousness/justification* in the Pauline literature of the NT. Certainly in Romans God's righteousness and justification by faith, expressed in a great number of *dikaio*-references and related concepts, provide the central theme; the gospel is expressed in these terms. In Galatians and in part in Philippians the case was similar. The other acknowledged epistles, chiefly because of topics addressed, have fewer references. That the theme is not, however, one developed only polemically late in Paul's career is guaranteed by the prepauline formulas that interpret Jesus and his death in such characteristic OT, Jewish terms. In the later deuteropaulines the theme continues, but with less emphasis in different circumstances. It may be claimed that, of the other NT literature, some reflects favorable reception of Pauline thought (e.g., 1 Pet) and some shows necessary correctives of misunderstood Paulinism (e.g., Jas). That the righteousness of God, *dikaiosynē tou theou,* echoed more widely in early Christianity than in just the Pauline

---

108. The debate on "early Catholicism" in the NT has often run something like this: "Some documents exhibit *frühkatholische* tendencies and therefore are to be treated as of secondary importance, even when in the canon" (so, e.g., Käsemann). "Ah, but you are admitting that such Catholicism is 'scriptural' and therefore equally valid." (Behind these views lurk the canon-within-the-canon dispute and the question of legitimacy of development—was there "decline" or "a fall"? Or is all that is in Scripture of the same weight?) I continue to regard "early Catholicism" in the sense of hierarchical office together with a later sense of sacraments as "medicine of immortality" to be absent from the NT (so Conzelmann). See §§ 315–17.

churches is suggested by references in Matt 6:33, Jas 1:20, and 2 Pet 1:1 (to be discussed in Part IV).[109]

But the attempt, at the Reformation and elsewhere, to make righteousness/justification the center (Mitte) and norm—of the NT and of all theology because it was the center of the center in Romans and Paul—has been resisted even in connection with Pauline theology (however the Pauline corpus is defined), because of scientific (descriptive) reasons as well as confessional ones.

193   Obviously, there are problems in speaking of "the center" for any one's theology unless it is expressly so designated (and followed) by the writer himself. (To use, illogically, the term "*a* center" already brings us to the notion of a constellation of ideas where some themes may shine more brightly than others. No one nowadays would deny such a role to *dikaiosynē* in Paul; "this doctrine is today recognized even across confessional boundaries as an inalienable constituent of Paul's theology," Käsemann, *Romans,* p. 24.)

But do we wish to consider, in defining "central" for our purposes, only the NT documents by Paul (and if so, with or without the pre- and deuteropauline evidence), or (also) to consider evidence for it as "central through later centuries," and/or central in the sense of "useful for us today"? (All of these understandings enter in, I find, in discussions of the issue by even quite careful NT scholars.)

How shall we weigh—more heavily or at a discount—what might be called "constants" in Pauline thought? By these are meant things that he does not so frequently mention but that we can assume were always basic in his thinking, e.g., what some have termed the "substructure" in Paul's theology, like the OT (so C. H. Dodd) or the "warp and woof" in his theological cloth, eschatology and Christology?

Do items have a greater or lesser claim to being "central" if they were inherited by Paul or were uniquely developed by him? For example, is the emphasis on the cross of Jesus "characteristically Pauline," given the fact he inherited and shared a common Christian doctrine of the death of Jesus, or is "by faith, not works" more "characteristically Pauline" because he shaped or at least sharpened the either/or himself?

To take a final question, do we mean by "central in Paul" something

---

109. On the general position above concerning the place of *dikaiosynē* in Paul's theology, cf. Eduard Lohse, "Die Gerechtigkeit Gottes in der paulinischen Theologie," written for a group of Catholic and Evangelical exegetes in 1971, in his *Die Einheit des Neuen Testaments: Exegetische Studien zur Theologie des Neuen Testaments* (Göttingen: Vandenhoeck & Ruprecht, 2d ed., 1973), pp. 209–27; and, more descriptively in Paul, but recognizing the ecumenical and inner Lutheran concerns, Georg Eichholz, *Die Theologie des Paulus im Umriss* (Neukirchen-Vluyn: Neukirchener Verlag, 1972), pp. 215–36. J. Christiaan Bekker, *Paul the Apostle: The Triumph of God in Life and Thought* (Philadelphia: Fortress, 1980), was not published until after this essay was completed. The "coherent theme" he finds is indicated in his subtitle and may be described as "apocalyptic theocentrism" (p. 363). See also below, n. 129.

that is a basic and initial concern of his (like the cross) or an ultimate and final goal toward which all other items in his thought move, like ethics or becoming *teleios* ("perfected," Phil 3:12)? Is "central" what God has already done or what he promises?

194 By this time one may simply wish to eschew any attempt at fixing what is central, and settle for "dominant perspectives" as the greater part of wisdom (so *JBC* 79), but inevitably some perspectives loom "more dominant" than others, and both descriptively, because the Pauline material is there (like Mt. Everest, to be scaled) and for practical reasons in the life of the church and for theology, the attempt must periodically be made.

195 A representative outline of some recent and classical attempts at this task has been suggested by Hans Conzelmann,[110] in the following list:

A. The Righteousness of God
   1. Justification—Reformation, Protestant Orthodoxy, Bultmann, Barth
   2. Reconciliation—much recent NT study; Presbyterian Confession of '67
B. Mysticism
   3. "In Christ"—this could be done either (a) in a mystical way (Albert Schweitzer), individually; or (b) sacramentally, ecclesiologically
C. Heilsgeschichte
   4. "Salvation"—thus many NT scholars

JBC treats eight or so possible concepts among its dominant perspectives (all of them discussed below). One might also organize approaches in terms of:

(1) God's viewpoint—sovereignty and will of God, predestination, God's plan (many examples, Catholic, Calvinist especially; systematic theology, most "orthodox" approaches)

(2) effects on humans—"before and after" (Christ or conversion); cf. Bultmann's "man under sin"/"man under faith"; Luther's anthropological *pro nobis;* pietism; existentialism

(3) effects on the cosmos—"new creation" (in some interpretations); "in Christ" (sometimes); reconciliation and justification (sometimes)

Sam K. Williams (see n. 80 above), terming the question of the "center of Paul's thought" "a scholarly argument not likely to be resolved soon," points to anthropology, Christology, soteriology, as all components, but from his study of Romans finds the thrust there to be "theocentric" (p. 289). Yet Käsemann speaks of the "old conflict" that arises, even with Romans and when justification is regarded as important, when it is "regarded

---

110. Hans Conzelmann, "Current Problems in Pauline Research," *Int* 22 (1968): 171–86; *Theology* (above, n. 42), pp. 155–61.

as the consequence rather than the content of the gospel (so Molland), or
when it is set in the shadow of salvation history and accepted merely as a
specific explanation and application of eschatology (thus, Ridderbos), or
when it is placed in antithesis (Schweitzer) to the receiving of the Spirit
(again, Ridderbos)." After mentioning Christology as another example of
"the theme" of Romans, he adds that this "point of division" on what is
central indicates "the unsolved basic problem."[111]

196   We cannot hope to resolve the issue of the central theme in Paul to
everyone's satisfaction, but even a brief survey of proposed alternatives to
righteousness/justification will show:

(1) some strengths and weakness of each of these (sometimes suggest-
ing the same failings for which *dikaiosynē* is criticized and the appropriateness of a bit more patience with any theme in Paul);

(2) the ways in which each is often linked to righteousness/justifica-
tion, in Paul and sometimes in the sixteenth-century Lutheran confessions;
and thus

(3) the soundness of the Reformation choice in this perspective and
the soundness of our contention that while righteousness/justification is by
no means the only way to express Paul's message, the case for regarding it
as the central one remains a persuasive one.

197   1. *The Gospel.* Because of association later of *euangelion* with the
four NT "good news books" about Jesus' career, it is often forgotten how
Pauline a term "gospel" is. The noun occurs sixty times in the Pauline corpus (only 6× in Mark, 4× in Matthew; never in Luke or John, unless we
count the later book titles), the verb 21× in Paul (never in Mark or John,
just once in Matthew, and 10× in Luke). We can readily agree with Professor Fitzmyer's definition of gospel as "*par excellence* Paul's . . . way of
summing up the significance of the Christ-event, the meaning that the person, life, ministry, passion, death, resurrection, and lordship of Jesus of
Nazareth had and still has for human history and existence" and his list of
its characteristics: revelatory, dynamic, kerygmatic, normative, promis-
sory, and universal—even if we would not stress so much that it was
"Paul's *personal* way of summing up . . . the Christ-event."[112] The term
euangelion in some of the Pauline references probably comes out of earlier
(Hellenistic Christian) use,[113] and his two references to "*my* gospel" (Rom

---

111. Williams (see above, n. 80), in *JBL* 99 (1980): 289. Käsemann, *Romans,* p. 24, citing E. Molland, *Das paulinische Euangelion: Das Wort und die Sache* (Oslo, 1934), pp. 62–63,
and H. Ridderbos, *Paul: An Outline of His Theology* (Grand Rapids: Eerdmans, 1975), pp.
162 and 29–43 respectively (reflecting Albert Schweitzer, *The Mysticism of Paul the Apostle*
[New York: Henry Holt, 1931]).

112. Joseph A. Fitzmyer, "The Gospel in the Theology of Paul," *Int* 33 (1979): 339–50,
quotation from p. 341; reprinted in *Interpreting the Gospels,* ed. James Luther Mays (Philadelphia: Fortress, 1981), pp. 1–13, quotation p. 4, and in *To Advance the Gospel: New Testament Essays* (New York: Crossroad Publ. Co., 1981), pp. 149–61 and 151; cf. *JBC* 79: 27–34.

113. Käsemann, *Romans,* p. 8; cf. the analysis of possible examples in Peter Stuhlmacher, *Das paulinische Evangelium: I. Vorgeschichte* (FRLANT 95; 1968), pp. 207–89.

2:16, 16:25) do not indicate a peculiar version of the good news or one different from that of other apostolic preachers (Cranfield, p. 163). Paul had made "the gospel" his own.

The Lutheran Confessions readily use "gospel" in a variety of ways to refer to what is most characteristic of Christianity. The difficulty in the sixteenth century and in Paul's day was that "gospel" needed to be given greater specificity. Few themes in Paul commend themselves so obviously as the content of "the gospel which he gospelled" (cf. Gal 1:11; 2:2, 5, 14) as does "righteousness/justification by faith, not by works" (Gal 2:16–17). The content of the gospel, put in terms of Romans, is that God's justifying righteousness is being revealed in Christ. One may say "the gospel" is central in Paul, but this is expressed par excellence as righteousness/justification.

198   2. *Christ* can obviously be called Paul's central theme too, the one whom he preaches (1 Cor 1:23) and whom to know Paul counted all previous gains in his life as loss (Phil 3:7–8). "The key concept about which the whole of Pauline theology must be organized is Christ," but then it is added, as "Christocentric soteriology" (*JBC* 79:22). But this is already to grant that Christ becomes important in Paul not so much for who he is but for what he does; as the *JBC* article goes on (after setting aside the Bultmannian interpretation as too anthropological), Paul's Christology is "functional," about "Christ as significant for man" (79:25). In particular that meant for Paul "Christ crucified" (1 Cor 1:23, 2:2), and so the meaning of his death.

Our reasons for not just making Christology Paul's central theme are several. (a) It is now clearly recognized that Paul really contributed little that was new to early Christian christologizing; a great deal of development in the area had taken place prior to and outside of Paul's own work. With passages like Rom 1:3*b*–4 or Phil 2:6–11, he was stressing or sometimes adding to certain accents in the material at hand.[114] (b) In such passages and generally for Paul, the "decisive moment" comes with Jesus' death (and resurrection); his Christology is bound up with the meaning of the cross (and exaltation to lordship). Thus to make Paul's christological emphasis precise we are led into another area of thought, proposal 3, below, about what is central in Paul. (c) In that Paul took over existing christological statements about Jesus and his death that saw their significance in terms of righteousness/justification (Rom 4:25, etc., see above, §§ 60–76), the stage was set for him to use justification as his own specific interpretation of Christology.[115]

---

114. Cf., e.g., R. H. Fuller, *The Foundations of New Testament Christology* (New York: Scribner's, 1965), or Eichholz, *Theologie*, pp. 38–39, 101–232, esp. 196; *JBC* 79: 55, 61.

115. In addition to references above, cf. Käsemann, "The Pauline Theology of the Cross" and "Justification and Salvation History in the Epistle to the Romans," in *Perspectives on Paul* (Philadelphia: Fortress, 1971), pp. 32–59 and 60–78. Eichholz, *Theologie*, p. 38, following Schlatter: "In Paul, gospel and Christology, like gospel and God's righteousness, be-

The Lutheran reformers of course saw "Christ" as often the equivalent of "gospel," and so sometimes talked of Christ as the equivalent of justification too (their particular expression of gospel). It was the need for greater specificity in meaning that carried them further. Obviously, though, justification *sola gratia sola fide* makes no sense without *solus Christus.*

199 The *sola* phrases just mentioned suggest need for comments on *"grace." Charis,* while denoting "graciousness" in Greek and having a background in OT *hesed* and *hēn* (lovingkindness, mercy), is preeminently a Pauline term, even though it has some limited use elsewhere in the NT; cf. James Moffatt, *Grace in the New Testament* (New York: Long & Smith, 1931). It deserves more attention among Pauline perspectives than *JBC* 79 gives it, and more than simply using it to speak of Jesus' death and resurrection as "the event of grace" (Furnish; cf. Bultmann School). In Paul, *charis* especially appears, opposed to law and works, in the company of faith, justification/righteousness/salvation. It is concrete expression of the love of God in Christ (indeed, primary, 2 Cor 13:14), throughout the whole work of God in saving/rightwising persons. There can be no objection in Reformation theology to calling Paul's "a religion of grace" as is often done; setting "grace" in context with the other *sola* phrases and with justification guarantees retention of its Pauline frame of reference and meaning.

200 3. *Jesus' death and resurrection* may, of course, also be claimed as central in Paul (cf. *JBC* 79:68–74). Cranfield (*Romans,* pp. 826ff.) goes so far as to see here the *articulus* on which Christianity stands or falls. Paul always linked the two, as did earlier Christian formulations (Rom 4:25). One does not talk about the cross apart from awareness that Jesus lives as lord; only for gnostics and heretical Christians was it possible to speak of a "risen" Christ while avoiding the note of his passion, suffering, and death (cf. above, § 111, on Phil 3:10, e.g.).

To adopt this third approach might argue, for instance, for *"expiation"* as central in Paul (cf. *JBC* 79:83–89). The Reformers, echoing medieval theology, certainly reveled in this theme; if anything, they stressed "satisfaction" more fully than the NT texts do (e.g., CA 3, especially the Latin text, Tappert 30.3).[116] They saw it, as one may say Paul did, as integral to righteousness/justification.

Our objection again, even to making atonement/expiation/"Christ-crucified" central, lies in the facts that so many of the formulas are pre-pauline, the terms (like *hilastērion,* etc.) are rare, and Paul's interest lies in interpreting and applying their meaning; that comes, both with the formulas and in his own theological work, along such lines as justification and

---

long together; better, they are woven together inseparably"—hence the encompassing character of Paul's Rechtfertigungstheologie.

116. Cf. Peter Stuhlmacher, "Schriftauslegung in der Confessio Augustana," (cited above, n. 11), pp. 196–98.

reconciliation. If one does stress such a theme, then "the cross" (*stauros*), not "blood," is Paul's own term, and that emphasis Reformation theology has made amply important in terms of its *theologia crucis*.

201   4. *Reconciliation*. Because this metaphor, drawn from human relations, rather than the lawcourt (as forensic justification has been taken to be), and used in the Pauline letters to express reconciliation of humanity with God and of persons with each other, has deep meaning in our age of estrangement, it has had wide and growing use in the last several decades. The "Presbyterian Confession of 1967" deliberately chose the categories of "God's Work of Reconciliation" and "the Ministry of Reconciliation," rather than any "justification" language. *JBC* 79:81 terms "the reconciliation of man to God" in Pauline theology "the main effect of Christ's passion, death, and resurrection." Some forty years ago Vincent Taylor called it "the best New Testament word to describe the purpose of the Atonement" (though he tended to include "forgiveness" and other related ideas when expounding it). Perhaps the most striking example is the recent work of Peter Stuhlmacher in making "the gospel of reconciliation (Versöhnung) in Christ" or of "the Versöhnung of God with his creation through the sending of the Messiah Jesus Christ" to be "das Herzstück des Neuen Testaments."[117]

This trend toward "reconciliation" (often away from "justification") is weakened somewhat when we recall the criticism that in German "Versöhnung" often covers both what might be called "expiation-atonement" *and* "reconciliation" (in n. 117 cf. Fitzmyer and Stuhlmacher, and see Fitzmyer, § 368, n. 12, below), and writers even like Käsemann[118] seem to

---

117. Cf. Edward A. Dowey, Jr., *A Commentary on the Confession of 1967 and an Introduction to "The Book of Confessions,"* (Philadelphia: Westminster, 1968), pp. 14–25. J. A. Fitzmyer, "Reconciliation in Pauline Theology," in *No Famine in the Land: Studies in Honor of John L. McKenzie,* (ed. J. W. Flanagan and A. W. Robinson; (Missoula: Scholars Press, 1975), pp. 155–77; reprinted in *To Advance The Gospel,* pp. 162–85. V. Taylor, *The Atonement in New Testament Teaching* (2d ed. London: Epworth Press, 1954), p. 191; *Forgiveness and Reconciliation* (New York: Macmillan, 1941). P. Stuhlmacher and Helmut Class, *Das Evangelium von der Versöhnung in Christus* (Stuttgart: Calwer Verlag, 1979), pp. 17, 44. Stuhlmacher (pp. 5–11) reports a dramatic shift in his views from the days when he was a pupil of Bultmann (and Käsemann): Under the influence of the OT and Jewish backgrounds he has come to see the basis for Paul's Rechtfertigungstheologie to lie in Jesus' atoning death, and this has led him, in light of the OT-biblical themes of "Sühne und Versöhnung," expiation and reconciliation, to take more seriously the historical Jesus and his outlook. Paul's Rechtfertigungsevangelium expresses who Jesus was and where the crown of his messianic work of Versöhnung lay, namely in his substitutionary sacrifice on the cross. All this does not mean that Stuhlmacher, who has done such considerable work on *dikaiosynē theou,* is deserting that theme, but he is viewing it in a greater biblical continuity and with Versöhnung as overarching theme. But see § 201, paragraph 2 as well as P. Stuhlmacher, "The Gospel of Reconciliation in Christ—Basic Features and Issues of a Biblical Theology of the New Testament," *Horizons in Biblical Theology* 1(1979): 161–90.

118. E. Käsemann, "Some Thoughts on the Theme, "The Doctrine of Reconciliation [Versöhnungslehre] in the New Testament," in *Essays in Honour of Rudolf Bultmann: The Future of Our Religious Past* (New York: Harper & Row, 1971), pp. 49–64. What the Greek

be dealing with both together. We have argued that early Christian atonement formulas (using *hilaskesthai*, etc.) lie behind *both* "righteousness/jus-
tification" and "reconciliation" (*apo-katalassō*) imagery. Taylor is guilty of
something of the same thing in lumping together biblical theology concepts like "forgiveness" (for the ministry of Jesus) and "reconciliation" (in
Paul). A more careful tracing of developments is needed.

The importance of "reconciliation" terms in Paul is diminished too
when we compare statistical occurrences with *dikaio*-words (above, § 78:
verb, 27×; noun, 57×):

> *katalassō*, "reconcile"—6× (Rom 5:10 twice; 2 Cor 5:18–20,
> thrice; 1 Cor 7:11, of divorce);
> *katallagē*, "reconciliation" (noun)—4× (2 Cor 5:18–19, twice;
> Rom 5:11, 11:15);
> *apo-katallasso*, a double compound verb, "reconcile"—3×, all in
> the deuteropaulines (Col 1:20 and 22; Eph 2:16).

It can also be seen from these figures that "reconciliation" really occurs in
just two chief passages in Paul's acknowledged letters. In each of these it is
also to be observed that Paul talks about *dikaiosynē (theou):*

> 2 Cor 5:18–21—God "through Christ *reconciled* us to himself,
> and gave us the ministry of *reconciliation;* that is, in Christ
> God was *reconciling* the world to himself, . . . entrusting to
> us the message of *reconciliation.* . . . We beseech you . . ., *be
> reconciled* to God . . ., so that in him we might become *the
> righteousness of God*" (cf. above, §§ 66–68, 95);
> Rom 5:9–11—"now *justified* by his blood, much more shall we
> be saved. . . ." While enemies, "we were *reconciled* to God
> . . .; much more, now that we are *reconciled,* shall we be
> saved. . . ." Through Christ "we have now received our *rec-
> onciliation*" (cf. above, § 142)

202 In my judgment, the development of this theme of reconciliation
should be read, not as starting with Jesus (as Goppelt proposed) but in the
Hellenistic Christian community's experience of God's transforming power in Christ so that it spoke of God reconciling "all things" to himself
through Christ (Col 1:20; 2 Cor 5:19–21), estranged sinners in particular
(Rom 5:10–11), Jews and Gentiles in one body (Eph 2:14–18). Cf. also
Rom 11:15, the rejection of the Jews has meant "reconciliation of the
world." Paul welcomed and used this material, intertwined with justification terminology, but stressed the anthropological as well as the cosmic

---

NT refers to by *hilastērion,* Latin *propitiatio,* "expiation" is expressed in German by Sühne/
Sühnung; what Greek speaks of in terms from *(apo)katalassō,* reconcile, is expressed in the
German Versöhnung.

side (2 Cor 5:18, "God reconciled *us*" interprets "was reconciling *the world*"), and he saw "the ministry of reconciliation" as a task (5:18) paralleling "the ministry of righteousness" (2 Cor 3:9). The interpretation in Col 1:22–23 of the hymn at 1:15–20 stresses the church as the *missionary* body of Christ, and Eph 2:15–16 the church as the place of reconciliation.[119]

This basically soteriological concept of reconciliation is no rival to righteousness/justification but a parallel, in development and use. The meaning is the same. The latter means "peace with God" *without* our doing anything; the former, enmity ended, *before* any effort of ours (Rom 5:1 and 10; Bultmann, *Theology*, 1, p. 287). The Lutheran Confessions recognize this interchange of terms, justification and reconciliation (Tappert ed., 129.161, 544. 30, both Ap. and Formula, SD). The greater number and weightier passages about the former, in Paul and in the other parts of the NT, and above all in the OT, argue for righteousness/justification as the more significant term in biblical theology.

203   5. Another concept that can be used to show the meaning of the Christ-event and therefore the center of Paul's gospel is (a) the term *rescue* or *release* or *redemption. JBC* 79:90–93 speaks of "redemptive liberation" (though that term runs the danger of interpretation along the somewhat different lines of modern "liberation theology"). Involved in Paul are nouns like *apolytrōsis,* "redemption" (7× in Paul; 1 Cor 1:30, Rom 3:24, 8:23, the rest in Col and Eph); *(ex)agorazō,* to "buy (back)" (4 significant cases, 1 Cor 6:19, 7:23; Gal 3:13, 4:5, possibly "sacred manumission" background, cf. H. D. Betz, *Gal.*, 150, n. 117); and *rhuomai,* "rescue" (as at 1 Thess 1:10; Rom 11:26; Col 1:13). The terms are not frequent ones in the NT. They have the advantage of not being encrusted with so many later associations and debates. If used, these terms must be spelled out from Pauline passages as release from, e.g., law, Sin, death, powers and principalities, and self, "for freedom." But then justification dealt with exactly the same concerns. Sacred manumission, moreover, is less a living image today than it is a lawcourt metaphor.

204   (b) *Salvation (sōtēria)* is another term used similarly by some writers to locate the center in Paul's thinking.[120] They take it as salvation *from* such powers as just listed and *for* such things as righteousness and life. As already indicated, it can refer to past, present, or future in Paul (see above, § 147, and n. 97), link with the occasionally used noun "Savior," and possibly relate to a "plan of salvation" on the part of the Father (*JBC* 79:35–51, cf. 52–97; see below, point 9).

---

119. See my survey and bibliography, "Reconciliation," *IDBSup*, pp. 728–29. L. Goppelt's interpretation, "Versöhnung durch Christus," appeared in *Lutherische Monatsheft* 6 (1967): 263–69, reprinted in Goppelt's *Christologie und Ethik: Aufsätze zum Neuen Testament* (Göttingen: Vandenhoeck & Ruprecht, 1968), pp. 147–64.

120. Cf. C. A. Anderson Scott, *Christianity according to St. Paul* (Cambridge Univ. Press, 1927, reprinted 1961); A. M. Hunter, *Interpreting Paul's Gospel* (1955), rev. ed. *The Gospel according to St. Paul* (1966, both Philadelphia: Westminster).

The noun *sōtēria* occurs some eighteen times in the Pauline corpus, *sōtēr* ("savior") twelve (chiefly in the Pastorals), and the verb "to save" twenty-nine times. While therefore a significant term numerically compared to the last two items discussed (release/redeem, reconcile), it may seem colorless until filled with some of the nuances from Paul's more specific images. The Lutheran Confessions (cf. Tappert ed. 548.52) seemingly equate salvation and justification; the latter term fills out what salvation is and means for them.

205   6. Since the turn of the century *the theme "in Christ"* has been a classical contender for the center of Paul's theology (so Deissmann, Albert Schweitzer, James Stewart's *A Man in Christ,* etc.). The statistics (*en* with *Christō,* or *Kyriō,*, or their equivalent, 165× in Paul's letters), the range of usages, and for some people the adjective "mystical" (often with "union" or "incorporation") made for a very attractive case. However, as the *JBC* analysis (79:138) indicates, subsequent studies since Schweitzer have placed the phrase (a) in the context of "faith" and "baptism" (79:125–32), just as, we might add, is true with "justification"; (b) in relation to a host of other phrases, "through, into, with Christ," each with distinct nuances (79:134–37); and (c) have made more precise the various senses of *en Christō,*, so that we can now say some of those 165 cases mean nothing more than "by Jesus Christ" (instrumentally), others have an ecclesial sense (Gal 1:22) or mean simply, adjectivally, "Christian" (e.g., "a man in Christ" = a Christian man). What is more, the "mystical" sense has given way in many instances to an "eschatological" one. We have learned that *en Christō* usually goes with the indicative statements about what has been done for us by God in Christ, and *en Kyriō* with imperatives and elsewhere. We have also observed how "in Christ" ties in directly with righteousness/justification and indeed sometimes has a forensic aspect (e.g., Gal 2:17, above, § 101).[121]

206   The "in Christ" theme had its attractiveness once justification was shunted aside as but the first step in a long process of Christian development after baptism. Obviously the years a believer has "in Christ" loom larger than the "initial moment of justification." Even so, Anton Fridrichsen, while granting that "the caption *en Christō* may be placed above everything St. Paul says," insisted that "a proper understanding of St. Paul must proceed from his teaching about how man is justified by faith in God's act of justification."[122] But once we see that righteousness/justification is more than that, as we have argued above, then the relation to "in Christ" shifts so that the latter is a parallel or, better put, a concomitant phrase, with many nuances, in Paul's theology of the righteousness of God. "In Christ" in certain of its particular senses, especially for our rela-

---

121. Cf. H. L. Parisius, "Über die forensische Deutungsmöglichkeit des paulinischen *en Christō,*" *ZNW* 49 (1958): 285–88. Basic bibliography in *JBC* 79:138 on the theme.
122. A. Fridrichsen, "Jesus, St. Paul, and St. John," in *The Root of the Vine* (cited above, n. 39), pp. 41, 44.

tionship with Christ, was likely Paul's own coinage; this may give it greater significance as something characteristic of his own thought; but it at the same time thus lacks OT and prepauline heritage, such as *dikaiosynē* possessed (which from its OT background in *ṣdq* was also relational). Other matters of content, time, and substance can scarcely be conveyed by a prepositional phrase as well as they can by a *Wortfeld* that includes verb, nouns, and adjective-adverb.

207   (7) Related to (6) are efforts to take *the church* as central in Paul's overall and, it is claimed, mature, thought. This has been done, for one thing, through emphasizing *en Christō,* in its ecclesial sense and the data in Ephesians (cf. Emile Mersch; J. A. T. Robinson, *The Body* [SBT 5; 1952] *JBC* 79:139–44, for summary and bibliography). But compare, against the trend in earlier ecumenical theology to treat "body of Christ" as if it were the *only* NT figure, Paul Minear, *Images of the Church in the New Testament* (Philadelphia: Westminster, 1960), who stresses the many (ninety-six) pictures of the church in Scripture. Moreover, the "body of Christ" metaphor changes from the acknowledged letters of Paul (1 Cor 12, e.g.) to Colossians and Ephesians (where Christ is "head"—this shift is one bit of evidence for designating them as deuteropauline). Professor Fitzmyer observes that, even in the list of "seven unities" (Eph 4:4–6), "Paul never came to speak of 'One Church' *(mia ekklēsia)*" (*JBC* 79:142) (but cf. 4:4 *hen sōma*). He adds that "the ontological reality" that links Christians in union with Christ "is the possession of the Spirit of Christ" (see proposal 8, below).

208   (a) Occasionally the term *covenant* is employed to seek a corporate, ecclesial side in Paul and a center for his thought. We have encountered it at times in regard to righteousness/justification (cf. also *JBC* 79:95). But NT references to "covenant" are rare (*JBC* 79:115), chiefly in traditional material about the Lord's Supper; 2 Cor 3:6–18 may be Paul's own most important references (2×, 3:6, 14). Attempts to read covenant theology into Paul must therefore be treated with great caution. Unlike *ṣdq-dikaiosynē,* here is an OT concept that does *not* come across into NT thought very widely. The reasons may include the facts that in Greek use *diathēkē* most commonly meant "legal document, last will and testament," not "covenant"; legalism in Jewish circles about the covenant made the theme less attractive for Christians like Paul; and in the Roman empire the terminology suggested a secret group probably engaged in politically subversive activity (cf. G. E. Mendenhall, "Covenant," in *IDB* 1, pp. 722–23).

209   (b) Lastly, the term *koinōnia* is sometimes brought to the fore with an ecclesial sense of "fellowship" (most recently G. Panikulam[123]) and made central. Terms from *koinōneō* are common in Philippians (R. P.

---

123. George Panikulam, *Koinōnia in the New Testament: A Dynamic Expression of Christian Life* (AnBib 85; 1979). As an exercise in biblical theology from Paul, Acts, and 1 John, this diss. brings out much about NT ecclesiology from the noun *koinōnia.* Ecclesial "fellowship" is often too easily taken to be the sense, however.

Martin's commentary). But more careful analysis of the objects of "fellow-ship" or, better, "participation" of which Paul speaks, and the relative paucity of references (noun 14×, verb 5×, adjective 5×) in the Pauline corpus makes this no real contender for the central theme. (See below, also, Section D.)

The evidence is sufficient to claim that the community, local and more-than-local, of the church was important for Paul and dare not be ig-nored. It is special pleading to make it central for his theology. I would say the same holds for *baptism* and *Lord's Supper,* the first something *from* (not *for*) which Paul argues, the latter mentioned far less and with less em-phasis and clarity about it than we might suppose (cf. *JBC* 79:128–32 and 145–48 for survey).

210   8. *"The Spirit"* has already been mentioned and rightly so as a prominent theme in Paul. In some scholarly circles (Wernle, J. Weiss, Windisch, the last mentioned more on the basis of sacramentalism, cf. Fur-nish, pp. 245–46, 257, 264–65) Paul's view of the Christian has been inter-preted as one of a "sinless pneumatic enthusiast," and, with many charismatics today, the emphasis would be on the presence of the Spirit in the believer as the heart of Pauline theology. The *JBC* treatment properly links Paul's Pneumatology to his Christology. Lutherans would link both to justification (cf. Rom 8). Both our traditions may often have underval-ued in theology and practice the dynamic of the Spirit, but neither Luther-ans nor Roman Catholics (nor NT scholarship on Paul) is likely to make the Spirit central.

211   Related to the Spirit, (a) *sanctification* has in some Christian tradi-tions been made the be-all and end-all in interpreting Paul (and all of the-ology and Christian life). The adjective *hagios* ("holy, saint[s]") is common in Paul, occurring over 75 times; the nouns *hagiasmos* and *hagiosynē* and the verb *hagiazō* are rare (8×, 3×, 9× in the corpus); see above on 1 Cor 6:11 (§§ 64–65), Rom 6:19 (§§ 145–49), for examples. We have argued against "sanctification" as a further step after "initial justification." It is integral with what God's righteousness involves.

212   Note may be taken here of the occasional effort to make (b) *ethics* the center of Paul's thought, as if he turned to such "practical matters" in his epistles with an obvious sigh of relief after wading through his "theolo-gy."[124] Against such views, Furnish's relating of Paul's theology and his ethics suffices. Particularly with *dikaio*-terms it is clear that the moral-eth-ical is integrated into the theological-forensic.

213   9. Last of all, we come to the proposal that for many Lutherans (e.g., J. Munck, K. Stendahl) as well as others has replaced justification as the organizing principle for Pauline thought, namely *salvation history.*

We may begin by saying that while theology for centuries stressed

---

124. E.g., M. S. Enslin, *The Ethics of Paul* (New York: Harper & Row, 1930, reprinted Nashville: Abingdon, 1962); the paper by Edwin Freed, read to a LCUSA consultation, sum-marized in my introduction to *Lutheran Hermeneutics* (cited above, n. 19), pp. 18–20.

Paul's references to *election and predestination* (Middle Ages, Luther, Calvin), such terms—while not to be disregarded in Paul (cf. above, § 154, on Rom 8:29–30)—are not what modern discussions exegetically focus on.

"The Father's Plan of Salvation History," above all involving the pre-existent Son who after his sacrificial death was exalted (or restored) to lordship is the way *JBC* 79:35–79 describes this perspective on Paul. God's "will" and "purpose" are good Pauline terms. Much can be integrated under a "plan of salvation," including, we may note, *dikaiosynē theou* and the role and destiny of Israel (79:37, 43).

We have argued above that what Paul says about the righteousness of God at work lies at the base of his treatment of Abraham and "persons of faith" like him since Christ, and lies at the heart of Rom 9–11, in righteousness terms, at 10:3–12 (see above, §§ 155–60). In this way Paul's *Rechtfertigungstheologie* gives birth to *heilsgeschichtlich* lines of thought, not vice versa. (Where in *pre*pauline Christianity is much of "salvation history"?) We think it truer to Paul to start with what he says about God's action in Christ and its meaning for sinners than with God in his foreknowledge (in Romans, finally only at 8:29) or in his "choosing us in Christ before the foundation of the world" (so the, perhaps hymnic, perspective of Eph 1:3–14). What many designate as possible salvation history in Paul is better understood as a retrospective statement of faith, in contemplation upon the overall sweep of God's doings in past and future, than as a starting point and center for Paul's Christian experience and theology. What Heilsgeschichte seeks especially to protect—namely, God's role as author or initiator, and the universal scope of what he does—is amply safeguarded, we believe, by righteousness/justification as presented above.

214   The difficulty with the theme of Heilsgeschichte/plan of salvation is that it requires us to read certain terms and modern concepts into Paul. One begins with a certain centrality for "salvation" (see above, point 5b) and, because this must come "in history," then posits a program, a plan, or outline, often with philosophical concerns or views of history from more recent times. "Plan" is, of course, not Paul's word. I am not persuaded by Cullmann that *oikonomia* in the NT period means Heilsgeschichte (in the patristic period, sometimes it does).[125] *Mystērion,* taken against its OT-Semitic, not Greek mystery-cults, background, is more helpful, but then in the sense of "secret" openly revealed by God, in the gospel, through Christ crucified (1 Cor 2:7 in context; cf. *JBC* 79:32–34). That gospel is, of course, especially spoken of by Paul in Romans as the revelation of God's righteousness.

---

125. Against O. Cullmann, *Christ and Time* (rev. ed., Philadelphia: Westminster, 1975) and *Salvation as History* (London: SCM, 1967), cf. J. Reumann, "*Oikomomia* = 'Covenant'—Terms for *Heilsgeschichte* in Early Christian Usage," *NovT* 3 (1959): 282–92; "Oikonomia-Terms in Paul in Comparison with Lucan *Heilsgeschichte,*" *NTS* 13 (1966–67): 147–67; and its companion article, "*Heilsgeschichte* in Luke—Some Remarks on Its Background and Comparison with Paul," *Studia Evangelica* 4 (Texte und Untersuchungen 102; Berlin: Akademie-Verlag, 1968): 86–115.

The proof of the pudding lies in how much we can spin out from Paul of a "plan" of salvation. *JBC* 79:35–79 does it with due balance, emphasizing Christology and eschatology, and without overstressing "church" or "periods of history." For the "salvation" part, however, we must go to other terms (cf. 79:37 righteousness/justification, then 79:80–97).

Others have gone further in their schematizations. J. Munck stressed Paul's own role as *the* Apostle who had a particular *oikonomia* (administration, management) of the *mystērion* in spreading the gospel to the Gentiles (Eph 3:1–13), whose unique function will be to testify before Caesar and who presents himself as a *heilsgeschichtlich* figure like Moses (Rom 9:1–5) as he gathers representative congregations of Jews and Gentiles before Jews again have the opportunity of salvation in God's *Heilsplan* (Rom 11:25–32). T. W. Manson saw Abraham, the law, and Christ as the three great moments in Paul's view of history. C. K. Barrett—to me, persuasively—sees Adam, Abraham, Moses, Christ, and "the Man to come" as the "nodal figures" in Paul's view of history.[126] Rom 5:12–21 allows us to think of segments in human history from Adam to Moses and then after the giving of the law. But further than that it is difficult to go.

215 The "salvation history school" has maximalized such references and others within the framework of "biblical theology." The Bultmannian School has vigorously denied the existence of Heilsgeschichte in Paul, in the name of anthropological, existential interpretation. Gal 3 and Rom 4 have become battlegrounds. The answers lie somewhere between these extremes in approach. The mediating treatment by Ulrich Luz on Paul's understanding of history argues that Paul has no "theory of history" and hesitates even to use the term "Heilsgeschichte," but insists Paul is concerned to talk of God, his sovereignty and righteousness in history.[127] Yet Käsemann allows that, in Rom 4 and elsewhere, "it is impossible to deny that the apostle's message of justification has the dimension of salvation history," but insists this be understood as "the sphere in which God's word is perceptible as promise and gospel, awakening faith or unbelief, and setting man in the conflict between attestation and denial" (*Romans,* p. 255).

Because Heilsgeschichte grew out of the salvation experience of justification on the part of Paul and other early Christians but was not his starting point or so clearly articulated a view, and because modern constructs read in so many other factors, we prefer, while recognizing the legitimacy of salvation history in Paul, not to make it his central theme. Righteousness/justification builds in many of its concerns and points to a

---

126. J. Munck, *Paul and the Salvation of Mankind* (London: SCM, 1959); *Christ and Israel* (above, n. 88). T. W. Manson, in *On Paul and John* (SBT 38; 1963), p. 45. C. K. Barrett, *From First Adam to Last: A Study in Pauline Theology* (New York: Scribner's, 1962).

127. U. Luz, *Das Geschichtsverständnis des Paulus* (BEvT 49; 1968). On Abraham in Gal 3 and Rom 4, cf. the literature cited in Käsemann, *Romans,* pp. 101–02, 106, esp. that by Wilckens and Klein, plus L. Goppelt, "Paulus und die Heilsgeschichte: Schlussfolgerungen aus Röm. iv und i. Kor x. 1–13," *NTS* 13 (1966–67): 31–42.

legitimate place for Heilsgeschichte; to reverse matters and make Heilsgeschichte central seems less likely to include certain aspects like ethics or reconciliation, which have been listed above.

216   10. *Summing up on "Central Theme."* In light of all these proposals, one may wish to interpret Paul simply in light of "dominant perspectives" (cf. Käsemann, *Paulinische Perspektiven* [1969], Eng. trans. n. 115 above). However, as in the *JBC* article, some structure must be adopted to present and work with the varied "perspectives." If Christ is the "key concept," nonetheless Paul's Christology is "functional," and that means "soteriology," and we are then back to choosing among "reconciliation," "expiation," "redemptive liberation," and "justification" (so *JBC* 79:22, 25, 80–97). Careful reading of that article suggests that, in spite of all its minimizing of justification as "not the key to Pauline theology" (79:94), the topic is more pervasive throughout than appears under that heading in 79:94–97, for justification (almost irrepressibly) crops up also at 79:9 (the "new life as the 'justification' of man"), 79:37 (in the Father's plan), 79:71 (with Jesus' death and resurrection), 79:73 (the new relationship created by Jesus Christ). Cf. also 79:13 (revelation), 109 (the law), 127 (faith). If the presentation there on Paul had been able to take advantage of fuller insights since 1967 and were not so directed against the then-popular Bultmannian picture of Paul and his view of justification (cf. *JBC* 79:23–24), the assessment, especially in view of work on OT "righteousness," might be different. One may note in passing that the position in Stendahl's famous article "Paul and the Introspective Conscience of the West" (which seems to me to hit, not Paul, but interpretation since Augustine of which both our confessional traditions are heir) is somewhat reassessed in Professor Stendahl's later comments: he is not against justification but for Heilsgeschichte.[128]

In my own judgment the strongest alternatives to righteousness/justification as the central theme in Paul, apart from the terms "gospel" and "Christ" ("grace"), have been "in Christ" (less so perhaps nowadays) and today "reconciliation" and "salvation history." None of these is really a competitor, for all interrelate. While "reconciliation" may appeal better to today's mind, descriptively it cannot compare on the amount of Pauline evidence. Salvation history is viable only as a modern penchant for history and system is read in and a method of "doing theology from the vantage point of God" is preferred to Paul's mission- and gospel-approach among sinful people. In the absence of a superior or equally strong alternative,

---

128. K. Stendahl, "The Apostle Paul and the Introspective Conscience of the West," *HTR* 56 (1963): 199–215; most recently reprinted in his *Paul Among Jews and Gentiles* (Philadelphia: Fortress, 1976), pp. 78–96. Note, however, also in that volume "Justification Rather than Forgiveness," pp. 23–40, and pp. 129–32 where Stendahl denies that he meant Paul's doctrine of justification was primarily polemical and regrets being forced to choose, as a Lutheran theologian, between justification and salvation history, his real interest for Rom 9–11 and for Christian-Jewish relations. Cf. also Dan O. Via, Jr., "Justification and Deliverance: Existential Dialectic," *Studies in Religion/Sciences Religieuses* 1 (1971): 204–12.

righteousness/justification, rightly expounded, remains a defensible choice by current exegetical standards. Encouragement for this choice comes indirectly from one other unexpected source.

D. "Eschatological Participation" vs. "Covenantal Nomism"

217   1. The avowed *purpose* of a major study project by Professor E. P. Sanders, of McMaster University, is expressed in his subtitle, to make what he calls a "holistic comparison" of "patterns of religion" in Palestinian Judaism (Jewish sources 200 B.C.E.–200 C.E.) and Paul (the seven unquestioned letters, omitting 2 Thessalonians, Colossians, Ephesians, and the Pastorals, p. 431).[129] By a "pattern of religion" he means "how a reli-

---

129. *Paul and Palestinian Judaism: A Comparison of Patterns of Religion* (Philadelphia: Fortress, 1977). The importance of the book is indicated in my paper on "The Augsburg Confession . . ." (cited above, n. 10), pp. 7, 28, and 34, and in N. Dahl's review in *Religious Studies Review* 4 (1978): 153–58. Hans Hübner, "Pauli Theologiae Proprium, Prof. Dr. Hubert Jedin zum 80. Geburtstag am 17 Juni 1980," *NTS* 26 (1979–80): 445–73, offers a critical response to Sanders within the setting of Protestant-Catholic dialogue. Also see Byrne (above, n. 81).

Another book (based on the same seven letters by Paul) which, like Sanders's, seems to reject righteousness/justification as central theme in Paul but which repays further examination is that by J. Christiaan Beker, *Paul the Apostle* (see above, n. 109). Beker locates "the coherent theme of Paul's gospel" in "his apocalyptic world view" (p. x; cf. 181, 260, and passim) and argues for this "coherent apocalyptic theme" as indeed "the truth of the gospel" (pp. 171–72). In reality, Beker at times also views "the apocalyptic world view" as "the fundamental carrier of Paul's thought" (p. 181), which is in its core both christocentric (but not "christomonistic") and theocentric (or, better, theoultimate), pointing to the final "triumph of God" as the center and coherent theme of Paul's gospel (pp. ix, 354–55). As if this concatenation of centers is not ample, Beker also refers to Christ's death as "the redemptive center" (p. 184), his resurrection as "the coherent center of the gospel" (p. 171), and writes that "Paul's center is located in the lordship of Christ as it anticipates the final triumph of God" (p. 260). Justification is therefore mentioned at one point as just one of half a dozen "symbols of salvation" (pp. 256–57), following the outline of Gerd Theissen, "Soteriologische Symbolik in den paulinischen Schriften," *KD* 20 (1974): 282–304. At times, it is structuralism which seems determinative, as when Beker calls the apocalyptic language in which the "primordial experience" of Paul's call to apostleship is expressed the "deep structure," of which the various particular symbols or surface structures, like righteousness and justification, are but expressions in specific situations (pp. 15–16, though his list of examples there does not quite agree with Theissen's).

If, however, Beker's scattered treatments of "justification" and "righteousness" are considered as a whole (pp. 28, 37, 65–69, 71, 74, 78–83, 92, 97, 151, 256–57, 260–71, 275; oddly, the theme is somewhat blunted in Beker's Chapter 4 on Galatians), the result is impressive. Especially when Beker states that "the righteousness of God (and his verdict of justification) constitutes Paul's original hermeneutic of the Christ event" (p. 264) and that Paul employed "the language of justification by faith" not as a rival to a " 'participation' hermeneutic" but so as to integrate and protect "sacramental realism" against "realized eschatology" and so preserve "the apocalyptic perspective of the lordship of Christ" (p. 275), one suspects it does function, in a way that Beker has not openly acknowledged, as "the theme of the gospel" in Paul even beyond Romans 1—4, where he does admit it (p. 78). This is particularly so in that Beker can demonstrate his apocalyptic theme most impressively by the example of righteousness/justification as interpreted by the Käsemann School (pp. 262–64); his effort to see Paul's

gion is perceived by its adherents to *function*" in terms of "getting in and staying in" as members (including the beginning point and end of the religious life involved, and "steps in between"; what systematic theology calls "soteriology," p. 17). Sanders prefers this term "pattern" to "trajectories" because the latter implies sequential development and implicit goal; cf. pp. 20–24 for his critique. For the basic and important (for our concerns) finding in this comparison between Paul and Palestinian Judaism, with which he did find himself to stand in contrast, see 4, below.

218   2. Sanders's book on Paul and Palestinian Judaism is disconcerting for those who champion "righteousness by faith," it would seem, for he clearly asserts this theme to be "inadequate as a *term* to indicate the centre of Paul's theology" (p. 438, even though attention is given to recent German discussion on "God's righteousness," pp. 523–42). Sanders's reasons are these: (1) "Käsemann does not make clear *how* righteousness by faith can be cosmic and not individualistic" (p. 438, n. 41, citing Käsemann's essay "Justification and Salvation History," but not his Romans commentary); and (2) his agreement with Schweitzer that (a) in Galatians, "the doctrine of the righteousness by faith . . . is worked out with the aid of conceptions drawn from the eschatological doctrine of the being-in-Christ" so the latter is basic, and (b) in Galatians, Romans, and elsewhere Paul does not bring into connection with "righteousness by faith" such things as "the other blessings of redemption, . . . the spirit, and the resurrection," and ethics (pp. 438–39, quoting Schweitzer, *Mysticism* [n. 111 above], pp. 220–21).

As for (2a), however, we can now point to righteousness/justification as being not only prior to Galatians but also prepauline (cf. the formulas, above §§ 58–76) and must ask whether a doctrine of "being-in-Christ" is clearly demonstrable before Galatians. Whose cart precedes whose horse? Statement (2b) rests on a caricature by Schweitzer of "the doctrine of righteousness by faith," namely, "all that Christ does to believers is to cause them to be justified" (*Mysticism,* p. 295; quoted by Sanders, p. 439). Readers will have to judge from the evidence above in this paper whether the *dikaio*-passages do not touch on both forensic and ethical senses. Sanders himself (p. 440) grants some passages do link "faith" to ethics and allows that "Schweitzer did not see the *internal connection* between the righteousness by faith terminology and the terminology about life in the Spirit, being in Christ," etc. (what Sanders will call "participationalist" terms).

219   3. *Sanders*'s own detailed *analysis* of Paul finds man's plight to be described as either

"transgression"   or   "bondage,"

---

concerns as "cosmological" yet passionately devoted to extroverted service by the church in this world is, I think, served too by righteousness/justification seen as the core in Paul's theology. For Beker's criticism of some of Sanders's emphases, cf. pp. 14, 236–38, 241–42, 258 n. 5, 268, 286 (especially see note * there, on Sanders's ambivalence about justification), 340, and 362.

and corresponding to each description are two sets of soteriological terms,
"the juristic"   and   "the participatory" (p. 508).
Each set of terms is then spelled out through terms for the following two
categories:

"transferring . . . to the group
which will be saved":
e.g., participation in the
death of Christ,
freedom,
transformation, new creation,
reconciliation,
justification/righteousness
("righteousness" in Paul, he holds, has
no one fixed meaning, pp. 491ff.; we
agree, as shown above)
(For this list of juristic categories, see pp.
464–72.)

"being among the group
which will be saved":
membership in Christ's body,
One Spirit,
"in Christ,"
"to belong to Christ, to be servants of the
    Lord"

(For this list of participatory categories,
see pp. 456–63.)

Sanders contends that, of these two sets of terminology, "the heart of
Paul's theology" is "not primarily concerned with the juristic categories,
although he works with them. The real bite of his theology lies in the participatory categories, *even though he himself did not distinguish them this
way*" (p. 502, italics in the original). However, he has more to say about
justification/righteousness. Sanders goes on that it will not simply do "to
define Paul's own soteriological goal by the term 'righteousness' " because
he shared that term even in the forensic-eschatological sense with Jews and
Judaizers (pp. 505–06). At issue was the *true* righteousness, by law or by
faith (Phil 3:9). Yet even "the general conception that one is saved by faith
was completely common in early Christianity" and Paul's contribution lay
"in the antithetical formulation: by faith and not by works of the law" (p.
519). All this may help prepare us for the surprising statement that "righteousness by faith and participation in Christ ultimately amount to the
same thing" (p. 506). But "it seems necessary to follow Paul's own procedure and to define righteousness by faith by the other categories, those
which we have called 'participatory' " (p. 507). To conclude: "The two
main sets of soteriological terms," Sanders says, "go together"; the "more
appropriate," however, is "the participatory."
220   Parenthetically, as if to "solve" our running debate between the
Augsburg Confession and the Formula of Concord on justification, Sanders remarks that, had Paul been a systematic theologian, he might have
worked both sets of terms into a coherent whole by regarding "righteousness as the preliminary juristic status which leads to life in Christ"; this
occasionally Paul seems to do, as at Rom 5:1. But then Sanders gives what
to him are "weighty arguments" for *not* regarding "righteousness as the
gateway to life" (pp. 506–07). So righteousness/justification in Paul is after

all broader than just a first step, but Paul sowed the seeds for both uses of his terms.

As for the basic issue, it *is* a dispute about terms; see above, the quote from p. 438, righteousness as a *term* is inadequate to indicate the center of Paul's theology. *Materially,* however, it is correct, when defined by "participatory" categories—which is to decide with the CA that justification-/righteousness has a broad sense and means other things as well!

221   *Comment:* I find Sanders's distinction between the two sets of soteriological terms far from clear. Is "juristic" the right word for every item in the lefthand column? Does one not also "participate" in what is listed there as well as in those in the righthand side? Sanders's putdown of righteousness/justification as the center for Paul's theology (p. 438) must not, in any case, be taken as his final word. In a roundabout way he *does* endorse the Reformation choice, for the descriptive phrase of a modern historian of religion, "eschatological participation," was not only a term Paul did not use; it was, of course, not extant in the sixteenth century either, when our forefathers worked with biblical or traditional classically theological terms. One suspects also that it would not move many souls today without considerable explanation. As Sanders surprisingly admits, "the participationist way of thinking is *less easily* appropriated than the language of acquittal and the like" (p. 520, italics added). One may also ask, regarding "participation," should not Pauline uses of *koinōnia* (see above, C. 7 [b] on central themes) have been checked? However one proceeds, "eschatological" must be explained as to the type of eschatology (Sanders rightly includes both "future expectation" and "present guarantee," pp. 447–53).

222   4. However one sums up what Sanders describes as central in Paul, the overall conclusion of the book is that Paul's *pattern of religion* ("eschatological participation") is "an *essentially different type of religiousness from any found in Palestinian Jewish literature*" (p. 543, italics in original), where the pattern turns out to be "covenantal nomism." By this he means "the view that one's place in God's plan is established on the basis of the covenant and that the covenant requires as the proper response of man his obedience to its commandments, while providing means of atonement for transgression" (p. 75, cf. 236 on rabbinic reflection of the pattern). Between all of Palestinian Judaism and Paul a "change of systems" has taken place, and even use of "righteousness terminology" has a different sense in Paul, not as "maintenance of status" but as a "transfer term" (p. 544).

However, Sanders notes, Paul's view was not maintained, and Christianity itself became a "new covenantal nomism," (p. 552). But the Pauline corpus with its message of justification/righteousness (and other ways of putting its subject matter) was available and continues to be, to recall Christianity from time to time back to the Pauline gospel, as the Reformation sought to do.

IV. Righteousness/Justification in Other New Testament Writers

223   The prominence of (God's) righteousness and justification in the OT and postcanonical Jewish literature like Qumran leads us to expect reflections of the theme in other parts of the NT and early Christianity besides Paul and the Pauline school. At the same time, the variety of applications in the OT and developments within Judaism should lead us to expect other possible meanings and avenues of development than that found in apostolic Christianity for spelling out the significance of Jesus' death and the deepening of that significance in Paul and his school. Indeed, we may specifically expect some applications more akin to the OT sense of ethical righteousness (uprightness, justice) and contemporary Jewish uses of the concept.

A. The Synoptic Evangelists, Especially Matthew

224   1. In line with the fact that Jesus did not in his historical ministry use righteousness/justification terminology very much (see I, B, above), the **Gospel of Mark** has nothing of significance for our purposes. Only the adjective *dikaios* appears (2×), once to describe John the Baptist (6:20) and once in Jesus' statement, "I came to call not 'righteous people' (*dikaious*) but 'sinners' " (2:17). Luke 5:32 expands that verse by adding "to repent." Matt 9:13 gives a different context by adding, "Learn what it [Hos 6:6, also at Matt 12:7] means, 'I desire mercy and not sacrifice.' " What does the saying, perhaps from, but certainly colored by, the early church, mean by "righteous ones"? (Cf. *Righteousness and Society,* p. 78.)

The parallel to 17*b* at 17*a,* "Not the well but the sick have need of a physician," has led some to see a background in a (Hellenistic) proverb about the doctor who tends the sick, not the well; therefore, Jesus' mission focuses on "sinners." Others assume terminology of Jesus' opponents to be reflected; they regarded themselves as *dikaioi* (cf. *Pss. Sol.* 13:11; 15:6–7). Commentators under the influence of the doctrine of original sin have struggled to show there really were "no righteous persons" (examples in Haenchen, who adds: such matters were not in the purview of the text).[130] The phrase is certainly to be seen in light of its long biblical history (above, §§34, 36–41); Jesus refers to those in Palestine in his day who were "good, proper, orderly folk," what we call "respectable people" (*TEV*). One may wish to add that 2:17 uses this term in antithesis to "sinners" (cf. Matt 5:45, 13:49; Luke 15:7, 10, etc.) and uses it ironically (Schrenk, *TDNT,* s.v. *dikaios,* 2, p. 189; cf. V. Taylor, p. 207; see above, § 49). J. Schmid says "not . . . ironic" but proceeds to add that the piety of "the just" here is "basically unsound, inadequate, and over-presumptive . . . of no worth before God." Similarly Jeremias: Jesus invites to the "festive meal" even the pious who do not take sin seriously and are more remote from God than are the "sinners."

Of course Mark, like apostolic and Pauline Christianity, lays great emphasis on the cross and Jesus' atoning death (e.g., 10:45). But this is done without *dikaio*-terminology.

225   2. It is doubtful whether *the sayings source Q,* common to Matthew and Luke, contained any reference to righteousness/justification (cf. above, § 49; *Righteousness and Society,* p. 67; one possibility is the verb at Matt 11:19 par. Luke 7:35, in the sense of "vindicated," on which see below). We shall treat any possible examples below under Matthew (§ 227) and Luke-Acts (§ 246).

226   3. For the **Gospel of Matthew** we may assume the use of sources (Mark, Q, "M") by a "second generation" evangelist, perhaps about A.D. 90 (cf. *Peter in the New Testament,* pp. 13–14). More important with the term *dikaiosynē* is the debate over whether the seven instances of the noun in Matthew always have the same sense or vary in meaning. Some hold that it regularly refers to a gift from God (e.g., M. J. Fiedler, summary in Rohde [cited below, n. 134], pp. 90–91). Other writers like Dupont (*Les Béatitudes,* 3, pp. 383–84) and Strecker (*Der Weg der Gerechtigkeit,* pp. 149–58) argue in their monographs that the sense of "ethical or moral conduct that is in keeping with God's will" always obtains; in part, this view is a reaction to past efforts to "paulinize" exegesis of Matthew. We are more impressed with the argument of J. P. Meier that since in the OT (and Paul) *dikaiosynē* does not always have just one sense but can refer to both the saving activity of God and to man's moral conduct, we ought to be open to

---

130. Ernst Haenchen, *Der Weg Jesu: Eine Erklärung des Markus-Evangeliums und der kanonischen Parallelen* (Berlin: Töpelmann, 2d ed., 1968) p. 111, cf. 113–14. Josef Schmid, RNT, *The Gospel according to Mark,* trans. and ed. Kevin Condon (New York: Alba House, 1968), p. 67. Vincent Taylor, *The Gospel according to St. Mark* (London: Macmillan, 1959), p. 207. J. Jeremias, *New Testament Theology, Part One, The Proclamation of Jesus* (London: SCM, 1971), pp. 119, 147, 251.

either possibility in a document so rooted in OT-Jewish thought as Matthew is. Each case must be decided on its own merits in context.[131]

227   a. If the one (Q) case of *the verb* at 11:19*b* means "wisdom is vindicated" (*edikaiōthē*) by her deeds"—with reference to Jesus, christologically in Matthew, reflecting "the deeds of the Messiah" at 11:2 (E. Schweizer)—the other one at 12:37, which is unique to Matthew, carries an even more juridical sense of "be justified" in contrast to "be condemned":

> on the day of judgment . . . ,
> by your words you will be justified (*dikaiōthēsēᵢ*),
> and by your words you will be condemned (*katadikaiōthēsēᵢ*).

The section in Matthew deals with Jesus' defense against the charge that he casts out demons by Beelzebul (12:24). The immediately preceding verses come from Q (12:33–35 par. Luke 6:43–45) about the good or evil tree/person bringing forth good or evil fruit/things/words (34*b*). Matthew expands this in vv. 36–37 with a statement about the judgment and justification, typically OT/Jewish and even rabbinic (Schmid, p. 212) in thought. The sentiment that words, not works alone (Grundmann, p. 331), especially "careless words" (12:36, cf. Sir 23:15; especially against the Spirit, 12:31–32), determine one's fate at the judgment is reminiscent of the logia on denial or confession (Matt 10:32–33 par. Luke 12:8–9, Mark 8:38). Words are "works."

228   b. Many of the uses of *the adjective dikaios* in Matthew (17×) are routine, having the OT/Jewish (and regular Greek) sense of "what is right" 20:4), or "the righteous" (13:43 = Dan 12:3), specifically in the sense of OT worthies (23:29, "the monuments of the righteous"; 13:17, "prophets and righteous men") or applied to an individual of the past ("innocent Abel," "innocent blood," 23:35) or the present (1:19, Joseph, a "just man"; cf. Ziesler, p. 140, and *Mary in the New Testament* [cited above, Preface, n. 2], p. 84). Pilate's wife speaks of Jesus as "that righteous (innocent) man" (27:19). From the same background is explicable the an-

---

131. John P. Meier, *Law and History in Matthew's Gospel* (AnBib 71; 1976), pp. 76–79, reiterated in *The Vision of Matthew* (New York: Paulist, 1979), p. 225. Other literature: Georg Strecker, *Der Weg der Gerechtigkeit: Untersuchungen zur Theologie des Matthäus* (FRLANT 82; 1962); summary in *Righteousness and Society*, pp. 68–69. G. Bornkamm, G. Barth, H. J. Held, *Tradition and Interpretation in Matthew* (Philadelphia: Westminster, 1963). W. Trilling, *Das Wahre Israel: Studien zur Theologie des Matthäusevangeliums* (Erfurter Theologische Studien 7; Leipzig: St. Benno Verlag, 1959; Munich, 1964). Benno Przybylski, *Righteousness in Matthew and His World of Thought* (SNTSMS 41; 1980), diss. McMaster Univ. (E. P. Sanders). Bultmann, *Theology*, 2, p. 8.
      Commentaries on Matthew: A. H. McNeile, 1915; F. V. Filson (HNTC; 1963); J. Schmid (RNT, 5th ed. 1965); W. Grundmann (THKNT; 1968); Eduard Schweizer (NTD; cited from trans., *The Good News According to Matthew* [Richmond: John Knox, 1975]).

tithesis between "the just" and "the unjust" (*adikous,* at 5:45, parallel to "the good" and "the evil"; cf. on the latter group also Luke 6:35, "the ungrateful and the selfish") and between "the righteous" and "the evil" (13:49).

229   c. The seven examples of *the noun dikaiosyne* thus turn out to be the decisive ones for ascertaining Matthew's thought on righteousness/justification. We shall examine them by their order in the book, noting also verb and adjective examples in passing, even if they have been characterized above already. If Ziesler is correct, while in Matthew the verb at 11:19 is "demonstrative" (meaning "vindicate") and at 12:37 is "declaratory" (he shies away from calling it "forensic" but does refer it to acquittal at the last judgment), "the noun and adjective . . . always have an ethical content. 'Righteousness' is always something one *does*" (p. 141, cf. 128ff. and 142). But by Meier we have been warned about such "monochromatic" interpretation.

230   (1) After the reference to Joseph as *dikaios* (1:19), Matthew's first use of *dikaiosyne* comes at **3:15** in a dialogue inserted into the baptism scene (3:13, 16–17 par. Mark 1:9–11). To John's objection that Jesus should instead baptize him, Jesus replies, "Let it be so now. For thus it is fitting for us to fulfil all righteousness (*plerosai pasan dikaiosynen; RSV*)." Most commentators agree that "the doing of God's will is certainly intended" (cf. E. Schweizer's excursus on the term, pp. 53–56). But "will" in what sense? Ziesler probably speaks for many when he classifies the verse under "man's righteousness" in the sense of "right conduct" as performed by disciples, partly on the grounds that both Jesus and John the Baptist are involved ("fitting *for us*"); it is therefore exemplary for Christian disciples (pp. 133–34). Montefiore went further in this direction with his sense of "fulfil every righteous ordinance" (cited by Ziesler, p. 133).

On the other hand, some point to the verb "it is fitting" as virtually equivalent to the Greek *dei,* "it is necessary that," and thus the idea of divine necessity (cf. Grundmann, p. 97), and still others to the verb "fulfil" as expressing completion of a personal relationship, involving God's will ethically (H. Ljungman), or as expressing fulfillment of prophecy and of God's plan (cf. Meier, p. 79, among others). Either way a *heilsgeschichtlich* sense is apparent. Cullmann went so far as to see the sense as "acquire pardon for all" (*Baptism in the New Testament* [SBT 1; 1950], pp. 18–19). One probably cannot reach a decision on 3:15 without either a rigid theory on uniform Matthean use or the allowance that overtones of both senses could be there in light of the further uses of *dikaiosyne* in the book. Cf. on 21:32 below.

Five of the uses of our term occur in the Sermon on the Mount, where there is also found the reference to the *dikaioi* and *adikoi,* the just and unjust, on both groups of which God in his generosity sends his rain and sun (5:45).

231   (2) Matthew's fourth beatitude, with its parallel, runs thus:

5:6 Blessed are those who hunger   Luke 6:21 Blessed are you that
and thirst after righteousness   hunger now,
(*tēn dikaiosynēn*),
for they shall be satisfied.   for you shall be satisfied.

The form of these macarisms should be recalled: they are eschatological promises about what God will do (hence *TEV,* "God will satisfy them fully"). While "hunger and thirst" is an OT pairing (Amos 8:11; Isa 55:1) and could be from the earlier form in Q (and even from Jesus), the direct object "after righteousness" is much more surely a Matthean addition than a Lucan omission; Matthew makes the promise precise with a favorite term of his (5:10, 20; 6:33). What does "righteousness" mean?

The sense of "justification" (Str-B, 1, p. 201) is dismissed by Ziesler (p. 133) in favor of "man's life of obedience to God's will" (citing Strecker among others). But from the OT background of "righteousness" as God's eschatological salvation and vindicating activity and the content here of eschatological promise concerning something God gives, the sense called for at 5:6 is that of a gift from God of salvation, his eschatological victory (cf. Meier; *JBC*). For all the interest Matthew has "in bringing God's righteousness to practical fruit in his community" (5:20), he cannot forget the OT sense of "God's eschatological act" (Schweizer, pp. 91–92). Ziesler senses this when he calls it finally both "gift and demand."

232   (3) At **5:10** we have an eighth beatitude found only in Matthew.

Blessed are those who are persecuted for righteousness' sake (*heneken dikaiosynēs*), for theirs is the kingdom of heaven.

This beatitude repeats verbatim in its promise the first beatitude (5:3). The content of v. 10*a* on persecution echoes that of vv. 11–12. The reference to "righteousness" is typically Matthean and seems almost certainly redactoral (Schmid, p. 82). Indeed, the whole verse may be Matthew's own work, though the idea does appear elsewhere (cf. 1 Pet 3:14) and so could be traditional.

The view is common that righteousness here is "something demanded of men by God" (Ziesler, p. 142, but modified by "probably"; cf. 133). Cf. Grundmann, p. 132: "Rechttun." Schmid adds, it consists "in der treuen Nachfolge Jesu." Use of the noun without any article here (contrast 5:6) suggests to Schweizer (p. 96) and others "the various forms of expression in which 'righteousness' becomes concrete."

John L. McKenzie (*JBC* 43:32), however, sees something further: "Persecution for righteousness' sake is persecution that is endured in order to maintain good relations with God by obedience to his will.... *The expansion identifies Jesus with righteousness.* He replaces the Law as the one and sure means by which one maintains good relations with God" (italics added). But following Jesus brings persecution.

233 (4) Clearly **5:20**, a logion unique to Matthew, contrasts the *dikaiosynē* of Jesus' disciples with that of the scribes and Pharisees and calls for a "higher righteousness":

> For I tell you, unless your righteousness exceeds that of the scribes and Pharisees, you will never enter the kingdom of heaven.

The verse stands as a superscription over the antitheses that follow (5:21–48) illustrating by specimen examples the way of life called for among disciples. Verse 5:20 speaks of entry into the kingdom (cf. 5:19), but "no more as in the three previous verses of the law" (Schmid, p. 89). What was said of old in the Mosaic law is now to be "fulfilled" both by sharpening or radicalizing it (antitheses 1, 2, 4) and sometimes by abolishing it (antitheses 3, 5, 6). In Matthew this is the first time Jesus' teaching refers to the scribes and Pharisees. While many commentators take "their righteousness" and "yours" to indicate a "good" and "the better" righteousness (Schlatter, for example), one must remember Matthew's final opinion on these groups (in his own day) as expressed massively in the "woes" of chap. 23 ("outwardly righteous, inwardly full of lawlessness," 23:28). Not "Pharisaic righteousness carried to a higher degree" but a different sort of obedience is implied.

Agreed, "your righteousness" here is comprehensive; centered not in more laws but in the double command to love God and the neighbor (22:37–39; cf. Schweizer); it is "the conduct of a man which is in agreement with God's will, which is well pleasing to him and right" (G. Barth, in *Tradition and Interpretation in Matthew*, p. 139, cited with approval by Grundmann, p. 152). We have here the first of the "entry-sayings" in Matthew about going into the kingdom, this one with a condition about righteousness. (Isa 26:2 is sometimes cited as a prototype for entering into Jerusalem and the temple after Yahweh's victory: "Open the gates that the righteous nation which keeps faith may enter in.") But whence this righteousness? Ziesler (pp. 133–34), who firmly classifies 5:20 under "man's activity" as "Christian behaviour," adds the possibility—"unless one supposes that 5:6 implies it is also God's gift."

One probably must come down on the side of obedience response and righteous behavior in life for 5:20, but the sense of gift as well as demand echoes in the passage, at least from 5:6.

234 (5) At **6:1** *dikaiosynē* is used in a typically Jewish sense: "Beware of practicing your piety (*dikaiosynēn*) before men." It denotes "religious, moral, and compassionate activity in general" (Ziesler, p. 134). Almsgiving, prayer, fasting (6:2–18) illustrate the point. In line with usage in Judaism, it may be that at 6:1 we have what had become a technical term for almsgiving (*JBC* 43:43; note the textual variants; see also §96 above, on 2 Cor 9:9–10).

235   (6) **6:33** more clearly inclines to the sense of divine gift.

6:33 But seek first his kingdom and his righteousness (*tēn basileian* *kai tēn dikaiosynēn autou*), and all these things shall be yours as well.	Luke 12:31	Instead, seek his kingdom, and these things shall be yours as well.

The context is admonition against anxiety (6:25–34). Instead of being anxious (*merimnaō*) about various aspects of life, or seeking (*epizēteō*) the way the Gentiles do for such things (6:32), the "little-faith" disciples (6:30, a favorite word in Matthew to describe disciples, cf. 8:26, 14:31, 16:8) are admonished to seek (*zēteō*) God's kingdom and righteousness, with the promise that "he will provide you with all these other things" (*TEV;* passivum divinum). Luke's "instead" is toned down to "first" (but there is no "second" or "third"). The Greek suggests that Matthew has added *kai tēn dikaiosynēn* to the original Q statement (Trilling, among others, cited in Kertelge, *Rechtfertigung,* p. 46).

As at 5:20, *dikaiosynē* here has to do with the righteousness required for entry into the kingdom. Ziesler lays out the possible meanings, though his line of argument is not always clear:

God's own righteousness	*or*	righteousness which pleases God, of which he is the standard.
"Vindication," when the kingdom comes in the *future* (McNeile, Stuhlmacher). But. . . .		Ziesler, holding the kingdom is *present* in Matthew, takes it therefore as "righteousness which God wants and believers practise" (Hill, Descamps). But he goes on,

"Further, *prostethēsetai* ['it will be added'] points to righteousness as God's gift, and not only the object of man's search; this may not make man's righteousness identical with God's, but does suggest that God is its source" (p. 135). He finally compares it with Jas 1:20 ("the anger of man does not work with the righteousness of God"). All this discussion by Ziesler is under the heading of "man's righteousness," and both passages are listed under "Christian behaviour"; yet elsewhere he terms righteousness at 6:33 "both demand and eschatological gift" (pp. 143, 170)!

236   Because 6:33 is the only place in Matthew (and one of just three in the NT apart from Paul; cf. Jas 1:20 and 2 Pet 1:1) where "righteousness *of God*" occurs (*autou* = the Father, v. 32, and God v. 30), Kertelge treats the verse. He interprets it thus: By this addition the idea of striving after "the kingdom" [cf. the Q logion] as an eschatological gift is supplemented and protected in the thought of Matthew from the danger of being misunderstood in an enthusiast (*schwärmerisch*) way. Matthew makes us attentive not to overlook the demand in the present that lies in the gift of God. "Righteousness" designates "the righteousness which is demanded by God for entry into the kingdom," "the right condition of life before God" (cf. 5:20). At the same time it is a person's own righteousness (cf. 5:20, 6:1), admittedly not maintained on one's own but that granted by God to man as eschatological possibility (cf. 5:6—its gift character is not excluded by its aspect as a "present" entity). In this way the Jewish works-character of the righteousness of the "righteous" is basically broken, i.e., christologically, for the fulfilling of the law has lost its meaning as basis for righteousness through the fact that it is now oriented to the work and person of Jesus (pp. 46–47). So Kertelge's wrestling with this difficult verse.

G. Strecker, to take another opinion, sees in 6:33 a condition in the present ("seek righteousness") for the future consequence of the kingdom; "the way to the *basileia*" leads "only over *dikaiosyne*" (p. 155). W. Grundmann insists, however, on distinguishing God's righteousness here from "your righteousness" (5:20, 6:1) and the noun in an absolute sense (5:6, 10). He relates 6:33 to 6:10b, the third petition in the Lord's prayer, unique to Matthew, "Thy will be done"; hence, the coming of God's kingdom is carrying through his will, doing righteousness lets one enter the kingdom (p. 217; cf. Schlatter).

237   The verse must be interpreted first as Matthew constructed it and then in the context where he used it. "God's righteousness" is plainly parallel to "God's kingdom." As the beatitudes show, the kingdom (5:3,10) is God's future eschatological gift. So also is righteousness (5:6). In that the kingdom is both present and future in Matthew, so also is righteousness. Because of the situation Matthew addresses, battling against both (Jewish) legalism and a (Hellenistic, charismatic) tendency to say "Lord, Lord" but not do the will of God (cf. 7:15–23 and Bornkamm-Barth-Held), he, naturally from his Jewish-Christian background, stresses judgment-to-come and the need for righteousness to be manifested in every walk of life. Accordingly his gospel is strong on imperatives and response to God's will. Meier, who believes 6:33 presents righteousness, like the kingdom, as a divine gift, relates the verse also to that Matthean addition to the parable of the Wicked Tenants,

> Therefore I tell you, the kingdom of God will be taken away from you (Jews) and given to a nation (*ethnon*) producing fruits of it (21:43).

The theme of fruit-bearing, so common in Matthew (e.g., 7:17–20; 12:33) means fruits of righteousness, from "good trees." The kingdom is a gift, but moral living (fruit) follows.

Käsemann has argued that 6:33 is the key to this whole section of Matthew.[132] By redaction Matthew makes precise his sense of God's righteousness as identical with the kingdom that is God's gift, future but also

---

132. E. Käsemann, *Matthäusevangelium*, lectures, Göttingen, 1957, mimeographed student notes, pp. 75–76.

at hand. In this kingdom the demand for radical obedience is rooted (4:17), in both its present aspects and future promise. From this verse the surrounding wisdom sayings (6:26, 28–30) and proverbial material (6:27) are to be understood.

238   Before we come to the final *dikaiosynē* reference in Matthew, a host of other *dikaio*-passages appear. Most of them have been discussed or noted above: **9:13,** "I have not come to call the righteous . . ."; **11:19,** "Wisdom is justified by her deeds"; **12:37,** "by your words you will be justified . . ."; **20:4,** "whatever is right." A triple reference at **10:41,** at the end of the "missionary discourse" as the twelve are sent forth, calls for some comment:

> 10:40 He who receives you receives me, and he who receives me receives him who sent me.
>
> 10:41 He who receives a prophet because he is a prophet shall receive a prophet's reward,
> and he who receives a righteous man (*dikaion*) because he is a righteous man (*eis onoma dikaiou*) shall receive a righteous man's reward (*misthon dikaiou*).

Ziesler is content to limit the reference here to "the pious, God-fearing, upright people *of the OT*" (p. 138, italics added), but the reference is certainly in Matthew to itinerant missionaries of the Jesus-movement. True, "prophets and righteous men" is a designation for OT worthies (Matt 13:17, 23:29), but wandering prophets, "righteous men," and other sorts of leaders like "wise men and scribes" (23:34) must have been part of the leadership and the missionaries of Matthew's church. On the basis of 13:43 and 49, "the righteous" has been taken as a designation for all of Jesus' disciples. Käsemann sought to refer the term to members of the community while "prophets" refers to leaders, but Schweizer's analysis of the Matthean community resists that distinction; he takes "die Gerechte" to be members of the Matthean church who by their teaching and actions live a life that is exemplary according to God's commands. The verse says that whoever shows hospitality to such a follower of Jesus will receive an appropriate reward (from God).[133]

239   (7) At **21:32** one senses we have a key passage, but a baffling one. "For John came to you in the way of righteousness (*en hodō; dikaiosynēs*), and you did not believe him." The verse occurs in a parable, on the Two Sons (21:28–32), unique to Matthew, set in the Jerusalem ministry of Jesus as a "last appeal" to Israel to repent. V. 31 concludes that "tax collectors and harlots" who first said no but afterward repented will go into the king-

---

133. E. Schweizer, *Matthew*, pp. 253–54; *Matthäus und seine Gemeinde* (SBS 71; 1974), pp. 156–57. Käsemann, *Exegetische Versuche und Besinnungen* (cited above, n. 100), Vol. 2 (1964), pp. 89–90; = "The Beginnings of Christian Theology," in *NT Questions of Today,* trans. W. J. Montague (Philadelphia: Fortress, 1969), pp. 90–91.

dom before those (21:23, the chief priests and elders) who said yes to the father's command but did not obey. V. 32 is a Matthean addition (Schmid, p. 303), perhaps based on tradition (cf. Luke 7:29–30, discussed in B, below, "the tax collectors justified God" by accepting John's baptism, the Pharisees and lawyers rejected God's purpose by not doing so), is linked to the parable by the phrase "afterward repented" (21:29, 32) and to 21:23–27, which is on the Baptist whom the authorities have not believed. **240** What is meant by "John came to you in the way of righteousness"? Ziesler's interpretation, presented under "man's righteousness" (pp. 131–32), considers the sense to be simply that John came "with the message of righteousness" about the standard God demands for one's way of life, or possibly "a double reference to John's preaching and to his own exemplification of it." For the former are McNeile, Schrenk in *TDNT,* and Schmid; for the latter, Strecker. The phrase has OT antecedents in wisdom literature (e.g., Prov 8:20, "I walk in the way of righteousness, in the paths of justice"; 12:28, "in the path of righteousness is life"; cf. 2 Pet 2:21); hence the possibility that John (and Jesus) came as righteous men or teachers of wisdom as well as demanding righteousness (3:2, 8; 5:20). Ziesler's main question is whether "righteousness" here has a Christian connotation or not; answer: yes, for in Matthew the Baptist belongs in tandem with Jesus, not in a period prior to the "time of Jesus."

McKenzie (*JBC* 43:147) takes the phrase differently: not that "John led a righteous life," but "he showed a way by which men could become righteous," by repentance and the work of faith (tax collectors and publicans "believed" John). Is a fourth way possible: in light of what is widely acknowledged to exist, a Matthean view of salvation history (cf. Strecker, M. Punge, R. Walker) to see "the way of righteousness" as a *heilsgeschichtlich* expression? Righteousness has always been God's will. His people Israel have turned their history into an *Unheilsgeschichte* (21:33–43; 22:1–10), and the church is now "true Israel" (21:43). But a situation where Gentiles without the OT knowledge of God's will for obedience and righteous conduct are crowding into the church (cf. 22:11–13 and the demand for fruit-bearing) causes the evangelist to emphasize the imperatives, especially regarding righteous conduct. "The way of righteousness" is thus the course of Heilsgeschichte culminating in the Baptist and Jesus as salvation—but also, as the context here shows, a call for righteous response.

In this setting, 21:43 suggests a salvation-history sense, which in Matthew is not without the moral imperative.

241 Matthean *dikaio*-terminology concludes with four references in chap. 23 to the OT righteous (23:29, 35 twice) and the scribes' and Pharisees' hypocritical righteousness, and two in the "parable" of the sheep and goats. At 25:37 and 46, Schweizer takes the reference to be to members of the Matthean community; the more likely interpretation is that pious pagans (*ta ethnē*) are spoken of, who are judged on their treatment of Christians (perhaps missionaries) or of all the poor, with whom the Son of man identifies. If the parable of the Laborers in the Vineyard (20:1–16, which

134 OTHER NEW TESTAMENT WRITERS

Schweizer says presents "the surprising righteousness of God") "protects us against righteousness through works," 25:31–46 (the Sheep and the Goats) protects us against "righteousness through intellectualized theology" (p. 480). **Matt 27:19**, Jesus as "that righteous man," we have already noted.

242   d. *Summing up.* Righteousness cannot be said to be a major theme in Matthew, and compared to "kingdom" its usage is limited. However, it emerges as an emphasis not from the Jesus-tradition or sources but from "Matthew" himself (the evangelist, his school, or the particular community tradition with which he works). Therefore it is important.

Moreover it is related to certain particular interests of his: moral conduct, seen against an OT background (5:20); the continuity and interrelatedness of Jesus and John the Baptist (and with the prophets and righteous of Israel's past history); as part of Matthean Heilsgeschichte (21:32) and of eschatological promise (5:6), closely related to the kingdom (6:33), the theme of fulfillment (3:15); the church community (10:41; 13:43, 49); and faith (21:32; cf. also H. J. Held on *pistis* as "trust," according to Matthew—the *oligopistoi* are those who have understanding but not trust, as at 14:31, and these "little-faiths" are at times referred to as "the righteous").

On the other hand, Matthew does not exploit every occasion that he could to drag in the term. In the formula quotation of Zech 9:9 at 21:4–5, for example, a possible reference to Jesus as *dikaios* is omitted. At 23:23 (par. Luke 11:42) the list of "weightier matters of the law" that scribes and Pharisees neglect includes "justice and mercy and faith(fulness)," but the Greek for "justice" is *krisin.* The same word occurs at 12:20 in the citation of Isa 42:3, "till he brings justice to victory," but Matthew makes nothing of it, nor do we.

243   While many of the *dikaios*-usages reflect an OT sense of "the righteous," in contrast to "unrighteous" people, and the verb examples both times fit the OT sense of judgment and vindication, the noun passages fall into a pattern, we would conclude, like this:

God's eschatological *gift of salvation*—5:6, 6:33,
       possibly with a sense of *salvation history*—3:15, 21:32
the response of the disciples in terms of *moral conduct* and how
       one lives—5:10, 5:20, 6:1; perhaps 3:15, 21:32.

Cf. *Righteousness and Society*, p. 70; Meier, pp. 77–78. In a number of cases both senses seem involved (3:15, 21:32, perhaps even 5:20 and 6:33).[134]

---

134. Meier cites in support of his conclusion studies by Wrege, Frankemölle, and Kratzer, plus M. Fiedler's diss. on righteousness in Matthew, best summarized in Joachim Rohde, *Rediscovering the Teachings of the Evangelists* (Philadelphia: Westminster, 1968), pp. 47–112, where other studies like Punge's on salvation history in Matthew are treated. Fiedler sees *dikaiosynē* in Matthew as a polemical concern in controversy with Pharisaic Judaism.

It is for that reason that Strecker has invented the term "imperatival indicative" to describe Matthean theology. The situation in Matthew's church is such that one does not just present the indicative and then the imperative, as in the Sinai Covenant or Paul, but one addresses the imperative again and again to believers lest they fail to obey or bear fruit and so, like Israel of old, lose the kingdom. But, against Strecker, useful as the terminology is, it must be urged that Matthew is addressing a community and its leaders who already know the story of Jesus culminating in cross and resurrection (and Matthew does not truncate Mark's theology of the cross), a community of the baptized who experience forgiveness at the Lord's Supper (only 26:28 in all the NT makes this connection). Thus the indicative stands behind the community and this gospel book. Far better is Conzelmann's comparison of Matthew and Paul: Where Paul speaks of righteousness as God's gift and of faith as the human response, Matthew sees the kingdom as the gift and righteousness as the response.[135] But even this must be qualified somewhat: Righteousness in Matthew also has the sense of gift at times, and Matthew is not without emphasis on faith. The theology in Matthew is thus different from, but not contrary to, that of Paul; it is what might be expected in another type of Christianity, strongly oriented to the Jesus and OT-Jewish traditions, and developing its account of the meaning of the cross through narrative, rather than through early Christian atonement formulas.

B. Luke—Acts

244 Like Matthew's, Luke's is a gospel based on sources (Mark, Q, special materials including "L"), late in the first century, by an editor-evangelist with a clear theological program of his own. Unlike Matthew, he does not particularly reflect Jewish-Christian background and is able to present his story of the ongoing gospel and emerging church in a second volume, rather than having to telescope it into his story of Jesus as Matthew did. The major question for us is whether his moderate use of *dikaio*-terminology (less than in Matthew, more than that in Mark or John; see chart below) shows Pauline influence.

	dikaiosynē	*dikaios*	*dikaioō*	
Mark	—	2	—	
Matthew	7	17	2	
Luke	1	11	5	+ *dikaiōma, dikaiōs* 1× each
Acts	4	6	2	
John	2	3	—	

---

135. H. Conzelmann, *Theology*, p. 149.
That Paul and Matthew are in full agreement is emphasized by Peter F. Ellis, *Matthew:*

245   1. In *Luke's Gospel*[136] the only example of *dikaiosynē* occurs in the Benedictus at **1:75:** God's oath to Abraham was to grant us that, delivered from enemies, we might serve God "in holiness and righteousness," i.e., right conduct in an OT sense. The adjective is used several times in the infancy narrative to describe pious Israelites—Zechariah and Elizabeth **(1:6)** and Simeon **(2:25).** Related, in our judgment, is the phrase at **1:17** in the angel's message to Zechariah, that his son-to-be, John,

> 1:17 will go before him [God] in the spirit and power of *Elijah,*
> *to turn the hearts of the fathers to the children* (Mal 4:5–6)
> and the disobedient to the wisdom of the just (*dikaiōn*),
> to make ready for the Lord a people prepared.

Outside the opening chapters the same usage is found at **23:50,** in describing Joseph of Arimathea as "a good and righteous man." That the last four references mean "waiting for the incarnation" (Descamps, David Hill) is rightly rejected by Ziesler (pp. 138–39). The passages themselves characterize the persons as "walking in all the commandments and ordinances (*dikaiōmasin*) of the Lord blameless" (1:6), "looking for the kingdom of God" (23:51), and in contrast to the "disobedient" (1:17).

That Jesus came to "call not the righteous but sinners to repentance" **(5:32)** has been noted above. To repent is a theme of the sermons in Acts (2:38, 3:19, 5:31, etc.).

246   **7:29** has been noted with reference to Matt 21:32 above. In the midst of his account of Jesus' testimony to John the Baptist, Luke inserts parenthetically

> 7:29 (When they heard this all the people and the tax collectors
> justified [*edikaiōsan*] God, having been baptized with the
> baptism of John;

His Mind and His Message (Collegeville, MN.: Liturgical Press, 1974), pp. 154–55, though his understanding of "law" in each theologian is oversimplified.

While many factors in the makeup of Matthew are still disputed, such as the degree to which the split with Judaism has already taken place, redaction criticism has made many points of the gospel clearer. That 7:15–23 is directed against antinomians who appeal to their charismata (7:21–22, they prophesy, cast out demons, etc.) rather than to good works in the Jewish-Christian sense is clear from G. Barth's study in *Tradition and Interpretation* (cited above, n. 131), even though Rohde and Kümmel are unconvinced of this "second front" on which Matthew fights. In interpreting the Sermon on the Mount too much cannot be made of 5:3–10 (or v. 12), the beatitudes, as promises, on which, along with 5:13–14 as indicatives, the imperatives that follow rest (so Jeremias). Ironically, NT scholars who are Lutheran in background (Bornkamm and pupils, Jeremias, Stendahl, J. D. Kingsbury) have been among the leaders in helping us appreciate Matthew's Gospel in its own terms.

136. Recent, useful **commentaries on Luke** for our purposes are rare; but cf. A. R. C. Leaney (HNTC; 1958); K. H. Rengstorf (NTD; 1962); E. Earle Ellis (NCB; 1966, rev. ed. 1974); J. Schmid (RNT; 1960); W. Grundmann (THKNT; 2nd ed., 1961); F. W. Danker, *Jesus and the New Age* (Clayton, MO: Clayton Publishing House, 1972); and I. Howard Marshall (New International Greek Testament Commentary; Grand Rapids: Eerdmans, 1978).

7:30 but the Pharisees and lawyers rejected the purpose of God
for themselves, not having been baptized by him.)

Ziesler (p. 129) takes it in a declaratory sense, citing commentators for either the meaning "recognising God's righteousness in the mission of John" or "recognising God's just demands on them." Since the phrase contrasts with "rejected God's purpose for them" (v. 30), the sense is even better put as "acknowledged God's justice," or "vindicated God" or even "accepted God's righteousness" (cf. BAGD, *dikaioō,* 2). In Luke the reference doubtless links with **7:35** (par. Matt 11:19), which rounds out the section: "Wisdom is justified (*edikaiōthē*) by all her children," i.e., is "shown right by results," i.e., "persons changed" (Ziesler, p. 128). We have already suggested "vindicate" as the sense (above, §§ 225, 227). Luke sees the vindication of God in the response of publicans and others to John's baptism and to Jesus as the "friend of publicans and sinners" (7:34).

In what is likely Lucan redaction linking the lawyer's answer identifying the two great commands (10:25–28) and the parable of the Good Samaritan, the lawyer, in asking "Who is my neighbor?" is described as "trying to justify" himself (*thelōn dikaiōsai,* **10:29**). That is, show that he is in the right. The same sense is involved in **16:15**, Pharisees are "those who justify yourselves before men" (*hoi dikaiountes,* the participle is probably connative, "try to show yourselves right"), that is, in public.

Routinely OT in sense are **12:57** ("judge what is right," *to dikaion;* also good Greek sense); **14:14** (in a macarism, those who host the poor, maimed, lame, and blind "will be repaid at the resurrection of the just"); **15:7** (" 'righteous' persons who need no repentance"); **20:20** ("spies who pretend to be sincere," *dikaious*).

In the crucifixion account the penitent thief rebukes his companion who had railed at Jesus: "Do you not fear God, since you are under the same sentence of condemnation (*krimati*)? And we indeed justly (*dikaiōs*) . . . , but this man has done nothing wrong" (**23:41**, unique to Luke). The centurion's words at Jesus' death are not a confession, "This was truly God's son" (as in Mark and Matthew), but the assertion, "Certainly this man was innocent" (*dikaios,* **23:47**). If in Matthew the statement of a pagan woman, Pilate's wife, was that Jesus was *dikaios* in the sense of "innocent" (27:19; cf. 27:4, 24 *athōos*), the soldier's testimony has the same forensic sense of "not guilty" legally (a Lucan concern); it does not necessarily suggest the "Righteous One" of early Christology (cf. above, §§ 57, 60), which we do meet in Acts. Cf. Ziesler, pp. 137–38.

247   We have saved till last the most significant passage, the parable of the Pharisee and the Publican (18:9–14), a passage that may reflect Pauline usage and on which Lucan evidence in Acts is pertinent. When Luke introduces it **(18:9)** with the explanation that Jesus told this parable "to some who trusted in themselves that they were righteous (*dikaioi*) and despised others," we have the same sense of the adjective as at 15:7, cf. 20:20, 5:32. The Pharisee rejoices that he is not like the *adikoi* (v. 11). But at the end of

Jesus' parable it is said of the humble, self-effacing tax collector, "I tell you, this man went down to his house justified (*dedikaiōmenos*) rather than the other," the proud, boastful Pharisee (**18:14**). Ziesler calls the verb "declaratory," but hesitates as to whether it means "simple forgiveness" (Descamps), "judicial absolution" (Schrenk, *TDNT*), or, as he decides (with Hill, G. Klein, and others), comes "close to Paul's 'justification' " (p. 129). In *Righteousness and Society* (pp. 75–77) it has been argued, considering the Acts evidence (below) that genuine Pauline influence is slight, that the parable can be accepted as basically from Jesus, and the sense of the verb is "find favor" (so Jeremias; *TEV,* "in the right with God"; the key text cited by Jeremias, 2 Esdr 12:7, uses "find favor" in parallel with "be accounted righteous"). That allows for a teaching by Jesus in a Jewish setting where "find favor" is a parallel to "be accounted righteous," preserved in L material, and used by Luke, but not paulinized. But the Acts material must be considered.

248   2. In the *Acts of the Apostles*[137] Lucan usage, partly dependent on source material, runs the gamut from routine Greek and OT-Jewish senses for *dikaio*-terms to clearly Christian, theological meanings. At issue is whether Acts reflects Paul's teaching concerning justification or, for that matter, much characteristic Pauline doctrine at all.

a. Traditionally the author of Acts was regarded as Luke, a companion of Paul (cf. the "we" sections in Acts, and Col 4:14, Phlm 24, 2 Tim 4:11), who therefore should have accurate knowledge of the apostle's premier teachings. This theory remains in some quarters "still a plausible hypothesis" (*JBC* 45:2). At the least, however, Luke has a distinct program of Heilsgeschichte in mind as he employs his sources (cf. *Peter in the New Testament,* pp. 9–10, 39–40). Further critical scholarship has posed major questions about authorship by a companion of Paul, in part on the basis of whether he is really acquainted with "the most pregnant features of the historical Paul" (Kümmel, p. 181); in company with Conzelmann, Haenchen, Marxsen, Vielhauer, Evans, O'Neill, and others, Kümmel, e.g., concludes, "Acts cannot have been written by a companion of Paul" (p. 184). The suggestion that Acts was written from a knowledge of Paul's *letters* (but not by a traveling companion; cf. M. S. Enslin, *Reapproaching Paul* [Philadelphia: Westminster, 1972], pp. 24–27), simply heightens the question of how much this author understood Paul.

---

137. The commentary situation on **Acts** is more satisfactory than that on Luke; cf., among others, F. J. Foakes-Jackson, K. Lake, H. Cadbury, *The Beginnings of Christianity,* vols. 4 and 5 (London: Macmillan, 1933); H. Conzelmann (HNT; 1963); E. Haenchen (MeyerK 1965; the trans., *The Acts of the Apostles* [Philadelphia: Westminster, 1971] is cited above). Further, Philipp Vielhauer, "On the 'Paulinism' of Acts," in *Studies in Luke-Acts* (Essays presented in honor of Paul Schubert), ed. L. E. Keck and J. L. Martyn (Nashville: Abingdon, 1966; reprinted Philadelphia: Fortress, 1980), pp. 33–50, especially 41–42; originally in *EvT* 10 (1950–51): 1–15, and reprinted in Vielhauer's *Aufsätze zum Neuen Testament* (Theologische Bücherei 31; Chr. Kaiser, 1965), pp. 9–27; trans. originally in *Perkins (School of Theology) Journal* 17 (1963): 5–17.

249   Specifically with regard to justification, views on Luke's knowledge of Pauline theology have been classified by Menoud[138] (pp. 210–17) in three camps:

(1) Luke knew this terminology and was well acquainted with other aspects of the Apostle's thought (the traditional view). Involved are the exegetical difficulties we shall note below and the fact that so many other features of what is characteristically Pauline are missing. For example, reconciliation (*katallagē* terms), "in Christ," Paul's concept of Sin (rather than "sins") or of the law and even of the cross (atonement; Luke inclines to a "martyr theology") are even *less* represented than "righteousness/justification" is.

(2) Luke misunderstood Paul and altered his ideas (so, many nineteenth-century exegetes; Vielhauer, E. Schweizer, G. Klein). On the other hand, commentators like Loisy, *The Beginnings of Christianity* (Lake-Cadbury), and even Haenchen and Conzelmann (references in Menoud) reject the view.

(3) Luke presents only hints or hazy reflections of Paul's theology; he has some of Paul's words but not the thought (U. Wilckens, Haenchen, Conzelmann).

It is, of course, also possible to claim (4) that the writer of Acts knew nothing of Paul's specific teachings but simply reflects strands from common apostolic Christianity that also appear (more and otherwise developed) in Paul.

Menoud concludes himself that, though Luke emphasizes the unity of thought in speeches by Paul, Peter, and Stephen, he had actual "threads . . . spun by Paul" to weave into the cloth and so gives us "a faithful reflection of the Gospel of Paul" (pp. 217, 223).

250   The prize exhibit for many scholars in this debate has been a passage not using any *dikaio*-term but thought to echo Paul: at the "Council of Jerusalem," Peter says to the "apostles and elders,"

> 15:10 Now therefore why do you make trial of God by putting a yoke upon the neck of the disciples which neither our fathers nor we have been able to bear? [Cf. Gal 5:1, 3:19].
>
> 11 But we believe that we shall be saved through the grace of the Lord Jesus, just as they will [cf. Gal 2:16, 5:6, 6:15; Rom 3:9, 22, 24].

---

138. Philippe H. Menoud, "Justification by Faith According to the Book of Acts," in Menoud's *Jesus Christ and the Faith: A Collection of Studies,* trans. Eunice M. Paul (Pittsburgh Theological Monograph Series 18, ed., Dikran Y. Hadidian; Pittsburgh: Pickwick Press, 1978), pp. 202–27, originally in *Foi et salut* (cited above, n. 20), pp. 255–76, and reprinted in Menoud's *Jesus-Christ et la Foi* (1975). To his survey add Martin Hengel, *Acts and the History of Earliest Christianity* (Philadelphia: Fortress, 1980), p. 67, who finds "un-Pauline 'Paulinism' " with regard to "justification by faith alone" at Acts 13:38–39 and 15:11.

While commentators claim, "Paul could not have said it better," Menoud (pp. 205–10) compiles an impressive case for *pre*pauline thinking and expression here. The "yoke" symbol is an OT one (also Matt 11:29–30). The expression "saved by grace" (*sōzō*, not *dikaioō*) is deuteropauline or common early Christian; Paul "never uses the expression *dia tēs charitos tou Kyriou Iēsou*" (p. 208). The conceptualization is neither Pauline nor Lucan at points (e.g., the law as a collection of commands and prohibitions that nobody has ever been able to keep; cf. also Haenchen, p. 446, nn. 3 and 4). One should not label 15:10–11 "Paulinism put on the lips of Peter," but "common Christianity" (for v. 10, Menoud thinks, second-generation Gentile Christianity; for v. 11, older material, perhaps actually echoing Peter). Note also the possibility that 15:6–11 (or 12) is from a source (early?) about a meeting separate from the "council" (15:13ff.; *Peter in the New Testament*, pp. 53–54; *JBC* 45:72–77).

All in all, we are dubious about genuine knowledge of Paul's distinctive teachings, including righteousness/justification on the part of the author of Acts, let alone comprehension and accurate reflection of them in what he writes. But Acts may reflect common Christian views both from the author's own day (perhaps ca. A.D. 90) as well as from early days. This is particularly impressive if we accept the view that salvation/justification (by grace) through faith was general in Christianity and that Paul shaped it against "works of the law" (E. P. Sanders; cf. above, § 219).

251   b. Some of the evidence in Acts represents quite normal use of *dikaio*-words; e.g., **4:19** (is it "right in the sight of God"?); Cornelius was "an upright (*dikaios*) and God-fearing man" (**10:22**); or, the reverse, Elymas the magician is addressed as "enemy of all righteousness" (*dikaiosynēs*, **13:10**). We are in a familiar OT orbit when (**17:31**) Paul, in his Areopagus address, says God "has fixed a day in which he will *judge the world in righteousness* by a man whom he has appointed"; the italicized words reflect Pss 9:4, 96:13, 98:9. Haenchen (p. 526) speaks of "retributive justice," Ziesler (pp. 130–31) of God as judge, though with hints of the "righteousness of the Messiah." Related therefore is the statement at **10:35** in Peter's sermon to Cornelius that "in every nation any one who fears God and does what is right (*ergazomenos dikaiosynēn*) is acceptable to him" (related to God's "impartiality," 10:34, i.e., there are no racial barriers to salvation [Haenchen, p. 351]; the reference reflects the centurion's devout life and almsgiving, 10:2). Likewise with **24:15**, "there will be a resurrection of both the just and the unjust (*dikaiōn kai adikōn*)," Paul before Felix, reflecting Pharisaic belief (cf. 23:6–8).

It is when we examine the sermons in Acts (cf. above, §§ 56–57) that we encounter more significant uses. At **3:14** Peter refers to Jesus as "the Holy and Righteous One" who was killed; at **7:52**, Stephen, to the martyred prophets who announced "the coming of the Righteous One whom you have now betrayed and murdered"; at **22:14** Ananias of Damascus says that "the God of our fathers appointed you . . . to see the Just One

. . ." on Damascus Road. In each case *ho dikaios* is a christological title (see above, § 57). That he is "innocent" and "conforms to God's will" is obvious (Ziesler, pp. 136–37). Descamps "infers the saving righteousness of God" (cited ibid., p. 137, n. 1); *JBC* (45:45) brings in the servant (Isa 53:11). We think it a prepauline title that fed into the "atonement formulas" (above, §§ 57–76), which are not, however, found in Acts.

In Paul's speaking with Felix the governor about "faith in Christ Jesus" (24:24), the Apostle emphasized, to the alarm of Felix, "justice and self-control and future judgment" (**24:25**). The first and third items, *dikaiosynē* and *krima*, it would be attractive to take in a more Pauline sense, but the presence of *enkrateia* suggests that "justice" is a moral term here, and the schema a typically Lucan one of ethics and judgment (*Righteousness and Society*, p. 76).

252   This leaves the most disputed passage, **13:39**. In the first lengthy sermon by Paul that Acts reports, at Pisidian Antioch, the climax is,

> 13:38 Let it be known to you, therefore, brethren, that through this man [Jesus] forgiveness of sins is proclaimed to you,
> 39 and by him everyone that believes is freed from everything from which you could not be freed by the law of Moses (*apo pantōn hōn ouk ēdynēthēte en nomō; Mōüseōs dikaiothēnai, en toutō, pas ho pisteuōn dikaioutai*).

The verb *dikaioō* is thus used twice, in the sense of "be freed" (*RSV;* cf. BAGD, 3c), or "exonerate" (Haenchen, p. 413). In Paul, Rom 6:7 is most usually compared, "he who has died is freed from sin" (same verb, perfect tense, plus *apo,* as here). There is wide agreement that the verse represents "a specific Pauline outlook" (*JBC* 45:68), "an incontrovertible reference to the theology of Paul" (Menoud, p. 2). Let us grant that the verses do not mean to say the law justifies in some respects, but by Jesus one is justified or freed from what the law could not handle (Haenchen, p. 412, n. 4, "a doctrine that an incomplete justification through the law is completed by a justification through faith" was "foreign" to the author of Acts; Ziesler, p. 130, n. 1; Menoud, pp. 211–12). Let us also agree with Ziesler that "be quit of/saved from" and therefore *RSV*'s "be freed" is a satisfactory rendering of the verb *dikaioō.* The question is whether the sense is Pauline.

For one thing, v. 39 seems to be paralleled with v. 38; and to explain "forgiveness of sins" by *dikaiosynē tou theou* is not found in Paul's own letters (comparable are only Col 1:14 and Eph 1:7 in the deuteropaulines). Forgiveness is a prime Luke-Acts category; it is explained here by *dikaiousthai apo,* being liberated from what the law could not free from. Any link to Jesus' atoning death is lacking; the link here is to Jesus' resurrection (cf. also 5:31, 10:43) or perhaps the forgiveness Jesus exhibited already during his earthly ministry (cf. Luke 7:47–49, e.g.). Indeed, "sins" (pl.) is untypical of Paul himself. One may ask whether the concept of believing is the same as in Paul; Harnack saw here in Acts "partial justification," not by faith *alone* but by faith *also;* on the whole, cf. Vielhauer, "On the 'Paulinism' of Acts."

If these are agreed "facts" as Menoud says, it is over the inferences that we vary. He himself believes 13:38–39 *is* in conformity with Pauline thought and a genuine reminiscence of Pauline teaching. I am not persuaded either of that or of Menoud's larger theory that Luke got the idea of a *two*-volume presentation from 2 Cor 5:18–21 (redemptive action accomplished by Christ, proclamation of it in the world). As we have observed, the most widespread view in critical circles is that Luke means to reflect Pauline theology in a phrase he knew to be his, but without its substance or detail.

Another proposal is possible: that Luke reflects here not Paul's specific doctrine known from his letters but a general widespread early Christian view that one is rightwised by faith; for a Jewish audience in the synagogue, Paul can even be allowed to say it is rightwising "from everything from which you could not be saved by the law of Moses" (according to a then prevalent view of the law), and that this is synonymous with "forgiveness of sins." Paul's own antithesis, "by faith, not by works of the law," need not be emphasized (even if the writer knew it), for that issue was no longer a live one in Luke's day.

253   3. *Summary on Luke-Acts.* Since evidence for reflection of Pauline theology in Acts is not impressive, we need not call Luke 18:9–14 a "paulinizing" of a parable.

Luke-Acts knows the *dikaio*-terms not merely in routine usage of the Greek world but especially where Luke writes "biblically" as in Luke 1–2, in the OT sense of piety and uprightness or righteousness. Since he writes on Jesus, using sources that did not stress righteousness/justification, it is not surprising that he does not emphasize the theme in his gospel, and if he was not a colleague of Paul, it is not surprising that he gives but echoes at best of it from Paul's own thought. Since Luke's view of Jesus' death is different, it is natural for him not to spell out its meaning in terms of the atonement formulas about righteousness/justification.

But Luke-Acts does demonstrate how pervasive the terms were from OT roots. False claims at being *dikaios* were opposed (Luke 10:29, 16:15, 18:9, cf. 5:32). God's righteousness is vindicated (Luke 7:29), through Jesus and the response of sinners and publicans to him (Luke 7:35). He is "the Righteous One" (Acts 3:14, 7:52, 22:14). That he taught how the humble and self-effacing, in contrast to the boastful, get to be "justified" is recorded (Luke 18:14). Through Jesus one is justified in the sense of freed or exonorated, in ways the law of Moses could not provide (Acts 13:38–39). There is also ample reference to future resurrection of the "just (and unjust)" (Luke 14:14; Acts 24:25), future judgment (Acts 17:31), and ethics in light thereof (Acts 24:25).

This is not Paul's view, but a different sort developed in Gentile

Christianity, from the gospel and OT traditions, but in light of the Christ-event.

C. The Gospel of John and the Johannine Corpus

254   The Fourth Gospel presents a type of Christianity that is different from either the Pauline or Synoptic sorts. Though rooted in the Jesus-tradition and at many points quite in touch with Semitic, OT, and Palestinian backgrounds, it is finally the result of a process of theological reflection in a Hellenistic Christian world, in the 90s A.D., by a school connected with the "beloved disciple." Neither "the kingdom of God" (of the Synoptics) nor "the righteousness of God" (Paul) is prominent; for other themes like "eternal life" (not without links to Paul and the Synoptics) have come to the fore. The cross is central, as "the hour," but the hour of vindication and triumph, not just suffering. "Church" and "Ministry" are minimalized, Christology is maximalized. "Faith" does not occur as a noun (in the corpus only at 1 John 5:4, and Revelation, 4×), though the verb *pisteuein* does, and "grace" only in the Prologue (John 1:14, 16, 17).

In this very different version of "the good news," *dikaio*-terms occur but seldom, and then along lines representing a somewhat different development of OT usages. We will treat the Fourth Gospel and then the epistles (examples only in 1 John, which obviously relates to the Fourth Gospel School), and then the very different apocalypse, Revelation.

	dikaiosynē	*dikaios*	No examples of the verb *dikaioō*
John	2	3	
1 John	3	6	
Revelation	2	5	*dikaiōma* 2×

255   1. The *Gospel of John*[139] refers first, using our terms, to the judgment Jesus exercises as *dikaia:* "My judgment is just" (**5:30**), because it seeks to do the will of the Father. To those who dispute his authority and his use of it (e.g., in healing on the sabbath, 7:23) he urges, "Do not judge by appearances, but judge with right judgment" (**7:24,** *tēn dikaian krisin krinete*). In passing, Jesus' prayer at **17:25** addresses God as "righteous Father" (*pater dikaie*); it is the only epithet in the prayer except for "holy" (v. 11). All three adjective uses are conventional ones. Typically Johannine in Christology and eschatology is the fact that the righteous Father (Ziesler, p. 136, is straining the passage to make him here specifically "Judge") has committed judgment, already now, into the hands of Jesus

---

139. **On John:** Bultmann (MeyerK; trans., Philadelphia: Westminster, 1971); C. K. Barrett (1955; rev. ed., 1979); Raymond E. Brown (AB, two vols., 1966, 1970), among others.

(Paul spoke indifferently of the judgment seat of God or of Christ, Rom 14:10, 2 Cor 5:10 respectively).

256 Both noun occurrences cluster in a Paraclete saying during Jesus' upper room discourse. When the *Paraklētos* comes,

> 16:8 that one will convince the world of sin and of righteous-
> ness (*dikaiosynēs*) and of judgment (*kriseōs*):
> 16:9 of sin, because they do not believe in me;
> 16:10 of righteousness (*dikaiosynēs*), because I go to the Father,
> and you will see me no more;
> 16:11 of judgment, because the ruler of this world is judged.

The work of the Paraclete will involve setting the world straight with regard to Jesus: Failure to believe in him as God's revelation is sin; he turns out to be *dikaios* because God is going to exalt him whom men have killed; the judgment that stands is not the one men have made of Jesus but the one that declares God is condemning Satan, the prince of this world (cf. 12:31; 14:30). Obviously in view is the passion drama, culminating in the cross, and the victory God will work in it. *JBC* 63:151 brings out the triple contrast:

> who was guilty of sin: Christ or his executioners?
> who was just: Christ or his traducers?
> who finally stands condemned: Christ or his enemies?

But in what does the *dikaiosynē* consist that God's victory at Jesus' cross will make clear, that the Paraclete will press home? Ziesler, though recognizing difficulties, says, "Christ's *character* as vindicated by God in his exaltation (v. 10)," and adds "this Christ-righteousness is the true righteousness, as opposed to man's erroneous ideas of righteousness" (p. 131, italics added). He also quotes the broader sense suggested by Descamps (*Les justes,* pp. 89–92): innocence, moral righteousness, and victory over sin, with Christ's righteousness as the source of the Christian's justification (p. 131, n. 1; p. 143), but calls the text unable to sustain all this. We believe that Ziesler is too concerned to see here the moral sense of "character," and Descamps too prone to search for imputation patterns. This passage refers to vindication of Jesus by God's exalting him after the cross, thus reversing the opinion of his enemies. The roots are in OT usage of the term. The sense here of "vindicated" is akin to that we found at 1 Tim 3:16 (see above, § 61; *Righteousness and Society,* p. 73; cf. Ziesler, pp. 154–55).

There is an even broader background, suggested by Théo Preiss:[140] in the juridical and even courtroom terms so prominent in John. *Paraklētos* is such a word ("advocate"). "Judgment" is prominent (5:30, *passim;* 16:11).

---

140. Théo Preiss, "Justification in Johannine Thought," in *Life in Christ* (SBT 13; 1954), pp. 9–31; summary in *Righteousness and Society,* pp. 73–74.

"Witness/witnessing" is a frequent theme. We probably have reflected a version of the OT cosmic lawsuit theme: *dikaiosynē* comes when God reverses the seemingly dominant view of the world; "the heavenly Judge who is to condemn us has come to die and rise again to justify his enemies" (Preiss, p. 30; cf. *Righteousness and Society*, pp. 73–75).

257 The Fourth Gospel thus once echoes OT use of "righteousness/justification terminology," not in a Pauline, but in an OT way, for declaring the meaning of Jesus' death. To this extent, it is akin to the "atonement formulas." The First Epistle adds further evidence for this view in Johannine circles.

258 2. The thought at John 17:25 of God as a "righteous Father" is echoed in *1 John*[141] **1:9** when it is said that God is *dikaios* with reference to the way he saves us in Jesus Christ.

> 1:9 If we confess our sins, he is faithful and just (*pistos estin kai dikaios*), and will forgive our sins and cleanse us from all unrighteousness (*adikias;* cf. 5:17 "all *adikia* is sin").

Though it is "the blood of Jesus his Son" that "cleanses us from all sin" (1:7), the referent of "he" in v. 9 is most likely God (vv. 5, 6) whom we make "a liar" if we say "we have not sinned" (v. 10; cf. 5:10). The description of God as "faithful and just" is OT language (Exod 34:6–7; Deut 32:4). He has provided expiation through Jesus (1:7; cf. 2:1–2, below). Since sin is a continuing fact even for the believer (1:8, 10), forgiveness and cleansing (what Paul could call "rightwising") must continue for those who "walk in the light" of God. Ziesler classifies 1:9 under "God as saving," though noting some commentators see "notions of judgment as well" (p. 136). Both aspects, plus possible reference to God's fidelity to his covenant (A. E. Brooke, ICC, p. 19), reflect the OT sense of *ṣdkh*.

259 1 John **2:1** assures "anyone who sins" that "we have an advocate (*paraklēton*) with the Father, Jesus Christ the righteous (*Iēsoun Christon dikaion*)." Ziesler seeks to interpret this as a reference to his "ethical character" and, while allowing the possibility (Descamps, pp. 67–68, 142–45), in the "strong soteriological note" present, of "the saving righteousness of God," declines to link this with *dikaion*. We think the slogan-like phrase (cf. Phil 2:11 *Iēsous Christos kyrios*) reflects the early christological title of "the Righteous One" and, like similar slogans (cf. 1 Pet 3:18), deals with the atonement; cf. 2:2, "He is the expiation (*hilasmos*) for our sins." The "salvation" note is strong here.

260 Ziesler's classification may be more accurate for **2:29**, "If you know that he [Jesus, not God; cf. 2:28] is righteous (*dikaios*), you may be sure that every one who does right (*pas ho poiōn tēn dikaiosynēn*) is begotten of him [God; cf. 3:9]."

---

141. **On 1 John:** A. E. Brooke (ICC; 1912); C. H. Dodd (MNTC; 1946); Bultmann (MeyerK; 1967; cited from Hermeneia 1973).

What "doing righteousness" (2:29) means is further clarified by **3:7** and **10:**

> 3:7 He who does right (*ho poiōn tēn dikaiosynēn*) is righteous (*dikaios*), as he (lit., "that one") is righteous (*dikaios*). . . .
> 3:10 . . . whoever does not do right (*dikaiosynēn*) is not of God, nor does he love his brother.

"Righteousness" is something one does, like "truth" (1:6). It does involve the ethical (what Ziesler calls "Christian behaviour," p. 133), above all practice of the love-command. This dynamic Johannine idiom need not involve supposed correction of a "misunderstood Paulinism" where some were taking "righteous" in a religious, but not moral, sense (as C. H. Dodd thought, MNTC, p. 72). It combats rather a gnostic perversion that ignored deeds in the world. The question is how, since God is righteous (1:9) and Christ is righteous (2:1), the believer who does righteousness comes to be righteous (3:7), "just as That One [Jesus] is." The answer of the epistle lies not only in the role of Jesus Christ as expiation (2:2) and intercessor (2:1) and our participation in and through him with the Father (1:3, 6) but also in the Johannine idea of being begotten of God: "Every one who does righteousness has been begotten of him" (2:29); "every one who has been begotten of God does not keep on committing sin . . . , he is not able to continue sinning because of having been born of God" (3:9). The Christian loves his Begetter (God, Christ) and all the fellow-children born of God (5:1). What elsewhere (in Paul) might be the forensic side of righteousness/justification, prior to the ethical on our part, is expressed in 1 John by the figure of new birth—though expiation wrought in Christ is common to both ways of putting the message.

The final use of *dikaios* in 1 John is a passing reference to the Cain and Abel story: the former's deeds were evil, the latter's were "righteous" (**3:12**).

261 Like the Fourth Gospel, 1 John depicts God as righteous. His is a saving righteousness, in Christ. *Dikaio*-language is used, as in early Christian creedal slogans (though not in the Fourth Gospel) in connection with his work of expiation. Because of birth from God and participation in (or fellowship with) Christ, the Christian can be described as *dikaios;* therefore he "does righteousness" and loves not the world but the community of brothers and sisters.

262 3. The *Book of Revelation*,[142] a proclamation of Christ's lordship and imminent triumph, amid persecution conditions, ca. A.D. 96, presented in the genre of apocalypse (with prophetic and epistolary features), uses *dikaio*-terminology only in its closing chapters. A number of the examples are in hymns praising God, very much in the OT vein:

---

142. **Revelation:** R. H. Charles (ICC; 1920); E. Lohse (NTD; 1960).

15:3 Great and wonderful are thy deeds,
O Lord God the almighty!
Just (*dikaiai*) and true are thy ways, [cf. Ps 145:17, Deut 32:4]
O King of the ages!

16:5 Just (*dikaios*) art thou in these thy judgments [Pss 119:137; 145:17]

16:7 True and just (*dikaiai*) are thy judgments [Pss 19:10; 119:37]

19:2 His judgments are true and just (*dikaiai*) [same references].

As in 1 John, such references carry over to Christ, who is described at **19:11** as the warrior who comes on a white horse:

He who sat upon it is called Faithful and True
and *in righteousness he judges* and makes war.

The italicized words, *en dikaiosynē₁ krinei*, derive from Ps 96:13 (of God) and/or from Isa 11:4 (the messianic king from David's line). As in the gospel of John, he is judge.

263 Finally there is the admonition at **22:11**—

Let the evil doer still do evil,
and the filthy still be filthy,
and the righteous still do right
(*ho dikaios dikaiosynēn poiēsato eti;* variant verb *dikaiōthetō*),
and the holy still be holy.

The first line comes from Dan 12:10, *ho adikōn adikēsatō* (cf. also Ezek 3:27). The third line parallels it, employing the very common biblical contrast of *adikos/dikaios* (Ziesler, p. 213, calls them and *adikia/dikaiosynē* "true antonyms"); the predicate uses the expression found in 1 John about "doing righteousness." Lines 2 and 4 are contrasting parallels around the adjectives *rhuparos/hagios* and their cognate verbs. The sense as in Daniel is that in the limited time before the End, when there is no more opportunity for repentance, the evil person will continue in wickedness, the righteous and holy person in doing good—and each will bear the consequences at the judgment soon (cf. vv. 12, 14–15).

264 Revelation's few references are thus oriented to God as righteous, in his judgment, now and to come; and to Christ, who likewise judges, reflecting also the old Holy War theme and the note of vindication for God and his people that the OT attached to our terms. There is no concern to show how one becomes righteous through Christ; the message is "Hold on, in doing righteousness," till the End.

265   4. *Overall, for the Johannine corpus* one is impressed at how much of the usage of *dikaio*-terms and conceptions is to be explained from the OT. God is righteous, in judgment and salvation. So is Christ, as judge (John 5:30), expiation (1 John 2:1–2), and as divine Warrior (Rev 19:11). God's people are to "do righteousness" (1 John 2:29, 3:7, 10; Rev 22:11), above all by loving "because he first loved us" (1 John 4:19, cf. 4:10; John 13:34).

Of the emphases from what I would call the major passages in each book on *dikaio*-terms—John 16:10, vindication; 1 John 2:1, with 1:9, salvation, and 3:7,10, ethical response; and Revelation, judgment—they can indeed be grasped in their unity only from an OT background. Specifically Christian is the linking of this salvation victory to the cross of "Jesus Christ the righteous one," as in early creedal formulas.

D. James[143]

266   The document known to us as the Letter of James, the author of which calls himself simply "a servant of God and of the Lord Jesus Christ" (1:1), is no epistle but rather paraenesis of the Jewish wisdom-tradition type, barely clothed in letter form, and is not by any brother of Jesus, according to most of modern scholarship (against the traditional, though by no means constant, view that this James was the James mentioned at Mark 6:3 par., 1 Cor 15:7, etc.; cf. Kümmel, pp. 405–06, on the patristic tradition here). Characterized by alliteration (1:2), paronomasia (1:1–2; 2:4), and even a line of Greek hexameter (1:17), the work especially reflects the Hellenistic wisdom tradition (stressed by Dibelius). A Christian community setting is sometimes indicated (1:1, 2:1, and 5:7–8 are the only references to Christ; but see also 1:18, 21 on baptism), and sayings of

---

143. **James:** Joseph B. Mayor, *The Epistle of St. James* (London: Macmillan, 2nd ed., 1897). J. H. Ropes (ICC; 1916). M. Dibelius (MeyerK, 9th ed. rev. by H. Greeven, 1957; 11th ed. trans. in Hermeneia, 1976, is cited above). F. Mussner (HTKNT; 1964). C. Leslie Mitton, *The Epistle of James* (London: Marshall, Morgan & Scott, 1966).

On **2:14–26**, history of exegesis, cf. Dibelius-Greeven, Hermeneia, p. 174, n. 132, and Mussner, p. 146, n. 3, for bibliography; see esp. Paulus Bergauer, *Der Jakobusbrief bei Augustinus und die damit verbundenen Probleme der Rechtfertigungslehre* (Vienna: Herder, 1962; cf. Dibelius-Greeven, p. 53, n. 204).

Further, on the contents of 2:14–26 and the issues posed by the verses, Georg Eichholz, *Jakobus und Paulus: Ein Beitrag zum Problem des Kanons* (TEx 39; 1953); *Glaube und Werke bei Paulus und Jakobus* (TEx 88; 1961). J. Jeremias, "Paul and James," *ExpTim* 66 (1954–55): 368–71. E. Lohse, "Glaube und Werke. Zur Theologie des Jakobusbrief," *ZNW* 48 (1957): 1–22, reprinted in and cited from his *Einheit des Neuen Testaments* (cited above, n. 109), pp. 285–306. Max Lachmann, *Sola Fide. Eine exegetische Studie über Jakobus 2 zur reformatorischen Rechtfertigungslehre* (Gütersloh: Bertelsmann, 1949). Willi Marxsen, *Der "Frühkatholizismus" im Neuen Testament* (Biblische Studien 21; Neukirchen: Neukirchener Verlag, 1958), pp. 22–38; summary in his *Introduction to the New Testament* (Philadelphia: Fortress, 1970), pp. 229–31. W. Nicol, "Faith and Works in the Letter of James," *Neotestamentica* (Pretoria) 9 (1975): 7–24. James Burtchaell, "A Theology of Faith and Works: The Epistle to the Galatians—A Catholic View," *Int* 17 (1963): 39–47.

Jesus (paraenetic, of the wisdom variety) appear to be reflected at 2:5, 12–13, 3:18 (cf. the beatitudes of Matt 5:3, 5, 5:7, 5:9, respectively).

We reject the views that James rests on a Jewish *Grundschrift* (A. Meyer) or that it is an antignostic polemic of the second century A.D. (Pfleiderer). The thesis of Bo Reicke (in AB), that the author writes ca. A.D. 90 "to admonish the recipients to Christian patience" in the face of "social discontent and political aggressiveness" (p. 6), has not widely commended itself. An early date (and authorship by a brother of Jesus) has continued to have defenders (Michaelis: the oldest, extant Christian writing; G. Kittel; F. Mussner reasons the document must have appeared after Romans, which he says James reflects, but stems from a time before Paul's letters were collected and from a time when there was Jewish Christianity such as speaks here, therefore A.D. 60–70; cf. the list of scholars holding such views in Kümmel, p. 407, n. 9). But the arguments against any date in the forties and against a brother of the Lord as author and against even a date prior to 70 are strong (so Kümmel; Marxsen's *Introduction;* cf. also *JBC* 59:1–5). Further precision as to setting can best come only after analysis of contents.

267   1. *The eight instances* of *dikaio*-vocabulary in James begin at **1:20** with one of the few cases outside the Pauline corpus in the NT of "the righteousness *of God*" (cf. Matt 6:33; 2 Pet 1:1). Kertelge (p. 47) sees here "dependence on late Judaism," and Stuhlmacher (p. 192) a reflection of the apocalyptic tradition. Therefore it need not be picking up a Pauline term but one common in Judaism and Christianity.

a. What does James mean in a section on "hearing and doing" (1:19–21) when he says, ". . . be slow to anger,

1:20 for the anger of man does not work the righteousness of
  God (*orgē gar andros dikaiosynēn theou ouk ergazetai*)"?

Surely implied is "the righteousness which God demands" (Ziesler, p. 135), specifically at the judgment (Kertelge, p. 47). This *dikaiosynē* "is something which comes about precisely through the action of human beings" (Dibelius, p. 111), though, as in Jewish thought, our writer does not distinguish terminologically "God's work" and "human obedience" (Stuhlmacher, p. 192); hence Schrenk (*TDNT*) and Ziesler (p. 135, cf. n. 7) place the passage under "God's, and not man's, righteousness." Perhaps the contrast between "God's wrath" and "God's righteousness" (which as "judgment" and "salvation" go together already in the OT; cf. above, § 123, on Rom 1:17–18) lurks behind the verse. In any case, human *orgē* blocks righteoueness *coram Deo.* "God's righteousness" here means "his unshakable fidelity to what is right" as norm for human conduct; cf. *Righteousness and Society,* p. 80; Stuhlmacher, pp. 192–93, who remarks that James is like the targumist on Deut 33:21 who forgot the sense of the original: Deut 33:21, "with Israel he (God) executed . . . *sidqat Yhwh,*" read as a plural and interpreted as "Yahweh's saving deeds" (Stuhlmacher, pp.

142–45; cf. above, §§ 35, 40), became in the Targum, "he did righteousness before God" (so Stuhlmacher, pp. 182–83; cf. Ziesler, p. 121).

Given the OT-Jewish background here, it is precarious to see Jas 1:20 as a specific reaction to Paul's usage of the phrase "righteousness of God." Dibelius speaks for many when he writes that at most

> it is conceivable that Paul's formulation, turned completely upside down in meaning and deprived of its depth, reappears here as a common Christian watchword for a life which is "righteous" in the true sense. In this case, a religious language influenced ultimately by Judaism would have brought about this recoloration.

(P. 111, the first sentence cited approvingly by Kertelge, p. 47, together with the comment: this would mean, as is apparent, "that the author of the epistle of James has not understood or no more understands the Pauline use of the formula *dikaiosynē theou* and has now interpreted it back again in the sense of the meaning which it had in late Judaism.")

268   b. Closely related in sense to 1:20, in the opinion of most commentators, is **Jas 3:18**, an "isolated saying" (Dibelius) in a section on the works and good conduct of a person who is wise and understanding (3:13ff.). The concluding admonition is, "The harvest of righteousness (*karpos de dikaiosynēs*) is sown in peace by those who make peace" (*RSV*).

The final phrase should be taken not, however, as a dative of agent (as in *RSV*, "by") but as a dative of advantage (Dibelius, p. 215, a conclusion he terms "now generally accepted") as in *NAB*.

The harvest of justice is sown in peace for those who cultivate peace. The passive verb suggests "is sown *by God*," as in the beatitudes, especially Matt 5:9, to which 3:18 is often compared. Admittedly, "harvest of righteousness" is still ambiguous: *dikaiosynēs* as a genitive of origin would mean "fruit which comes from righteous conduct" (*JBC* 59:25, as "reward" for such conduct), but as a genitive of definition it would mean "fruit which consists in righteousness"; Ziesler (p. 136) inclines to the former, Dibelius apparently to the latter: "righteousness is sown and harvested only in peace." In either case, the sense is ethical. There is a similarity to Phil 1:11, but there it was "fruits of righteousness" that come about "through Jesus Christ" (above, § 108). Jas 3:18 stands more clearly in the wisdom-paraenetic tradition of 3:15–17, peaceable conduct being one of the "good fruits" (v. 17) of the "wisdom from above" (cf. Mussner, p. 175).

269   c. The two instances of the adjective *dikaios* may be noted before tackling the chief passage. In the admonitions against the rich who, in spite of the threat of the judgment (5:3), have unjustly oppressed the laborers, James concludes, **5:6**, "you have condemned (*katedikasate*), you have killed the righteous man (*ton dikaion*); he does not resist you."

The verse must first and foremost be seen in the OT-Jewish tradition of "the righteous sufferer"; it is a general accusation of how the rich regularly oppress and martyr the poor and pious (cf. Wis 2 esp.; ample references in Dibelius, pp. 239–40, 39–45). Ziesler wishes to refer it further to "the Christian righteous" (p. 141), which the context calls for, but other scholars have seen here a veiled reference specifically to the martyrdom of Stephen (Mussner, p. 198) or even of James the brother of the Lord (assuming pseudonymous appeal to his fame; so Greeven, in Dibelius, p. 240, n. 58). The big question is whether one is to see here an identification of Jesus with "the righteous one." Mussner (p. 199) feels he is "surely not to be excluded," and certain church fathers definitely took 5:6 christologically. However, in view of the lack of such references in James and the context of the passage, it is a wiser decision, with Mayor (p. 155), to take "the righteous person" generically, and not read in a reference to Jesus (so Mitton; Reicke; *JBC*). This sense is borne out by a final use of *dikaios:*

5:16, "The prayer of a righteous man (*dikaiou*) has great power in its effects." The context is prayer for one another, especially in illness. We may discard attempts to see here righteous intercessors in heaven (like Elijah in later tradition, cf. v. 17, for the reference to him there is to his prayer on earth, not his translation into heaven) or James the Just; "any devout person in the traditional Jewish sense" is meant (Dibelius, p. 256; Mussner, p. 229, who adds, prayer is effective when it is by a person who fulfills God's will). The seemingly tautologous verbal expression contains in Greek the same participle found (of faith) at Gal 5:6, *energoumenē,* here coupled with *ischuei;* there is no connection with the Galatians passage suggested by the commentators. Almost always they take it as a middle voice here (as in Gal 5:6). (Exception: Schlatter, passive, "when it is made active [by God].") Its sense: as an adjective ("energetic prayer," Dibelius), or causally, "because it is active," or temporally, "as soon as it comes to God and is heard by him" (Mussner, p. 228). The verse echoes Prov 15:29, "The Lord . . . hears the prayer of the righteous."

270   d. In the little treatise at **2:14–26** on faith and works the verb *dikaioō* occurs three times, and the noun once in a quotation of Gen 15:6. James is arguing against a person who says "I have faith" (*pistin echein*) but who has not works (*erga,* 2:14). When such a person says to a brother or sister (i.e., a fellow Christian, Mussner, p. 131, n. 2) who is ill-clad or hungry, "Go in peace, be warmed, be filled [by God? the first phrase is typically Jewish]," such words are of no use; such "faith" does not save the speaker but, without works, is dead. Then follows a diatribe development of the theme.

v. 18a, *Hypothetical opponent:* "You (sing.) have faith and I have works." The reply to this position that "some specialize in faith, others in works" (*JBC* 59:20) begins presumably in 18b—though Dibelius calls "the problematic v. 18, one of the most difficult New Testament passages" and admits the reply could commence only in 19 or even in 20 (pp. 154, 151). There is even debate whether 18a is not affirmation of something previously said (so Mussner, "It is *rightly* said . . .," cf. Dibelius, pp. 156–68). Assuming a response to 18*a* begins in 18*b,* the dialogue runs:

> *Reply:* "Show me your faith apart from your works, and I by my works will show you [sing., as throughout] my faith (18*b*). You believe that 'God is one' [Deut 6:4]; you do well! [irony] Even the demons believe—and shudder (v. 19)! Do you want to be shown, you foolish fellow, that 'faith apart from works is barren'? (v. 20, cf. v. 17)."
>
> *Reply continued—scriptural proof* (vv. 21–23): "Our father Abraham" (a title used by Jews and Christians, cf. Rom 4:12), whom apparently the opponents of James had invoked,
>
> was he not justified (*edikaiōthē*) by works (*ex ergōn*), when he offered his son Isaac upon the altar (Gen 22)?

Of course. The conclusion is, "Faith was active along with (*synērgei*) his works, and faith was completed (*eteleiōthē*) by works." Thus the Scripture (Gen 15:6, LXX, as is quoted at Gal 3:6 and Rom 4:3 by Paul) was fulfilled (*eplērōthē*) which says,

> "Abraham believed God, and it was reckoned to him as righteousness (*eis dikaiosynēn*), and he was called 'friend of God' (cf. Isa 41:8, 2 Chr 20:7)."

Then the author speaks in his own person (vv. 24–26): "you (pl., as in 2:14–16) see that a person is justified (*dikaioutai*) by works and not by faith alone (*ex ergōn . . . ouk ek pisteōs monon*)." *Further example* (v. 25): In the same way (*homoiōs*), was not also Rahab the harlot justified by works (*ex ergōn edikaiōthē*), when she received the messengers and sent them out another way (cf. Josh 2)? [The example is meant to be parallel to that at v. 21, but it limps in that, unlike the case of Abraham, there is no mention in the Joshua story of "rightwising" as there is in Gen 15:6, and the author in James omits any reference to the pagan woman's faith—though Heb 11:31 salutes it—and he likewise omits any epithet like "friend of God." Very likely there was a fuller "Rahab tradition" in Judaism that he passes over in making his main point, "justified by works." Cf. Dibelius, pp. 166–67.]

The author's overall conclusion is then restated (cf. vv. 20 and 17), embellished with a simile the precise force of which the commentators debate: "For as the body apart from the spirit is dead, so faith apart from works is dead." (2:26) In this anthropological comparison, "spirit" means the breath of life, as at Gen 2:7 and elsewhere in the OT.

271 The thrust of 2:14–26 is to oppose, scripturally, those who teach "faith alone" (v. 24), that one's faith apart from any works can save (2:14). Our treatise replies that faith by itself, apart from works, is barren (v. 20) and totally dead (vv. 17, 20), for one's faith is shown by works (v. 18*b*).

The point of the scriptural "proofs" is—in the case of Abraham—that "a person is justified by works and not by faith alone" (v. 24), though when the Rahab example is given it is said simply that she "was justified by works" (v. 25). That faith is assumed throughout, even in v. 25, is made clear by the closing analogy: body *and* spirit, faith *and* works. And finally the passage defines how *pistis* is being used: It denotes mere intellectual belief, that "God is one."

It is possible, even likely, that James here reflects a Jewish exegetical tradition about Abraham found in the synagogue (Dibelius, pp. 165, 168–74). It may specifically be conjectured that some (esp. vv. 21–23) of the diatribe stems from such origins. But how does James use it in a Christian setting?

272   2. The *history of Christian exegesis* of Jas 2 (cf. Mussner, pp. 148–50) really begins with Augustine's concern over relating it to Paul's doctrine of justification. In earlier centuries James had difficulty in claiming a place in the canon, partly because of doubts about authorship; these doubts were resolved by the late fourth century, though Jerome's uncertainties echoed down to the time of Erasmus and Luther (cf. Kümmel, pp. 405–06; Alfred Wikenhauser, *New Testament Introduction* [New York: Herder & Herder, 1958], pp. 474–75). Augustine's solution to "contradictions" between Paul and James on faith and works was that Paul referred to works that preceded faith, James to those that follow faith. (He is right at least on James.) Augustine further distinguished between "dead faith," which even demons have (Jas 2:19), and the faith that justifies, which (Gal 5:6) is active through love.

> Homines autem non intelligentes, quod ait ipse Apostolus, *Arbitramur justificari hominem per fidem sine operibus legis* (*Rom.* III, 28); putaverunt eum dicere sufficere homini fidem, etiamsi male vivat et bona opera non habeat. Quod absit ut sentiret Vas electionis: qui cum dixisset quodam loco *In Christo enim Jesu neque circumcisio aliquid valet, neque praeputium;* max addidit, *sed fides quae per dilectionem operatur* (*Galet.* V,6). Ipsa est fides quae fideles Dei separat ab immundis daemonibus: nam et ipsi, sicut dicit apostolus Jacobus, *credunt et contremiscunt* (*Jacobi* II, 19); sed non bene operatur. Non ergo habent istam fidem ex qua justus vivat, id est, quae per dilectionem operatur, ut reddat ei Deus vitam aeternam secundum opera eius. Sed quia et ipsa bona opera nobis ex Deo sunt, a quo nobis et fides est, et dilectio, propterea idem ipse Doctor Gentium, etiam ipsam vitam aeternam gratiam nuncupavit. (*de gratia et libero arbitrio* VII. 18, *PL* 44. 892).

From "A Treatise on Grace and Free-Will," trans. P. Holmes and R. E. Wallis, *The Works of Aurelius Augustine,* Vol. 15, ed. M. Dodds, *The Anti-Pelagian Works of St. Augustine,* Vol. 3 (Edinburgh: T. & T. Clark, 1876), p. 32: Unintelligent persons, indeed, with regard to the apostle's statement: "We conclude that a man is justified by faith without the deeds of the law [Rom 3:28]," have thought him to mean that faith is sufficient for a man, even if he lived a bad life, and has no good deeds to allege. Impossible is it that such a character should be deemed "a vessel of election" by the apostle, who, after declaring that "in Christ Jesus neither circumcision availeth anything nor uncircumcision," adds the important statement, "but faith which worketh by love" [Gal 5:6]. It is such faith which severs the faithful children of God from unclean devils,—for even these "believe and tremble," as the Apostle James [2:19] says, but they do no good works. Therefore they possess not the faith by which the just man lives,—the faith which operates through love in such wise, that God recompenses it according to its works with eternal life. But inasmuch as we have even our good works from God, from whom likewise comes our faith and our love, therefore the selfsame great teacher of the Gentiles has designated "eternal life" itself as his gracious "gift."

Others, including Aquinas (*Sup. epist. s Pauli* in Rom. 3:28), repeated that solution on works before and after faith.

273   Luther's solution is often said to have been simply that of "canonical criticism": He demoted James to a tertiary level, barely still within the NT canon (stressed by Mussner, pp. 42–46). His judgment of James was that it was "a right strawy epistle," but (for he did have some good things to say of it) that was spoken in comparison with Romans, Galatians, Ephesians, and 1 Peter. Moreover, it was a judgment arising not merely out of controversies then or even out of content criticism, that James has little to say about Christ, but it stemmed from an opinion that James was the work of no apostle or brother of the Lord but rather of "some good pious man who took some sayings of the apostles' disciples and threw them thus on paper"; he added, devastatingly, someone "unequal to the task" (1522 Preface, rev. 1545, to James).[144] In that opinion on the origins of James, Luther did not stand alone in his day, for contemporaries like Erasmus and Thomas Cardinal de Vio, Cajetan, shared such doubts about the authorship of James. Historical criticism and content thus combined with the Reformation situation to produce Luther's estimate of James, and often thereafter Lutherans felt they had to have a low opinion of the document and Catholics a high one.

---

144. *WA,* Deutsche Bibel 7, pp. 344, 384; cf. *WA,* Table Talk, 3, No. 3292a; trans. in Philadelphia ed., *Works of Martin Luther,* 6, pp. 477–79, and, slightly rev., in W. G. Kümmel, *The New Testament: The History of the Investigation of Its Problems* (Nashville: Abingdon, 1972), pp. 23–26. German also in Mussner, pp. 43–46. Cf. also Kümmel, "The Continuing Significance of Luther's Prefaces to the New Testament," *CTM* 37 (1966): 537–81.

274   Since the sixteenth century James has been variously assessed not only on the faith-works issue and authorship question but also as a touchstone on the question of "canon within canon" (cf. Stuhlmacher, pp. 191–92). Without adopting Augustine's solution, a host of exegetes have come to speak of James as a necessary counterbalance or sequel to Paul (so A. Schlatter; Jeremias, p. 371, "James ch. 2 has its full right to stand by the side of Paul" or "to stand after Paul"). Soren Kierkegaard, it may be remembered, favored texts from James for his meditations and conjectured that Luther "in our age" and situation would have dragged James into greater prominence.[145] Ecumenically, Max Lachmann, in 1949 proposed, against the background of the unity yet tension that runs through Scripture and through the history of theology, an emphasis beyond the Reformation's "justification through faith alone" on Jas 2 as a demand for concrete realization of faith in personal existence. Georg Eichholz (1961) argued, on the basis of different understandings of "faith" in Paul and in James, for the importance of the latter as a "counterbalance" to misunderstandings of Paul.

275   Yet it remains a fact that many exegetes are convinced that for all these efforts at bringing Paul and James together there exists "only a theological alternative and never a 'both/and' " (Stuhlmacher, p. 194). "Whenever 'James is understood not as a correction but as a basis' there is a theological misuse of scripture"; thus "we are summoned to a criticism of James from the perspective of the gospel, not concerning his practical word but his theological form" (W. G. Kümmel, *Introduction,* p. 416, quoting Marxsen and Paul Althaus[146]).

    3. *James in situ, and Paul.*

276   a. We have already excluded (§ 266 above) the "early dating" solution that suggests that there is no conflict because James wrote before Paul articulated his doctrine of justification. That hypothesis runs into difficulties not only for the reasons for which critics have usually rejected it, such as the Hellenistic style of James (which the "secretary hypothesis" scarcely solves), but also the fact that *dikaio*-language had been applied long before Paul, in "atonement formulas" (something missing in James);

---

145. *For Self-Examination and Judge for Yourselves!* trans. W. Lowrie (New York: Oxford Univ. Press, 1941), p. 49: "Imagine Luther in our age, observant of our situation. Doest thou not believe that he would say again, 'The world is like a drunken peasant: when you help him up on one side of the horse, he falls off the other!' Doest thou not believe he would say, 'The Apostle James must be dragged a little into prominence—not in behalf of works *against* faith, . . . but in behalf of faith, in order . . . that the need of grace may be deeply felt.' " (I doubt that Luther would refer to the *apostle* James, but the CA and other Lutheran statements, certainly in the spirit of Luther, have repeatedly emphasized that faith is a strong, active mighty thing, expressing itself in life—though it is not these deeds that save or justify.)

146. Paul Althaus, "Die Gerechtigkeit des Menschen vor Gott (Zu der heutigen Kritik an Luthers Rechtfertigungslehre)," in *Das Menschenbild im Lichte des Evangeliums* (fs E. Brunner; Zürich: Zwingli, 1950), p. 46; cf. G. Schrenk, in *TDNT,* 2, p. 201, who contrasts similarly the "underlying practical motif" and the "theologically vulnerable formula in 2:23" of James.

the theme of rightwising by God's grace is not just Paul's later invention. Moreover, the epistle shows no reflection of Paul in its view of the law, nor of Jesus' own critique of the law for that matter. A date toward the end of the first century seems most likely, on all counts (so Kümmel, p. 414; Marxsen; Schenke-Fischer, *Einleitung*[147]: between 80 and 90). The author was a practical churchman, bent on providing simple, chiefly ethical advice.

277 The opponents against whom he writes in 2:14–26 are clearly Christian; who else would speak of "faith alone" as a means to righteousness/ justification? The phrase is found nowhere in Judaism, not even at Qumran (Stuhlmacher, p. 193, n. 1). The issue is an inner-Christian one (seen by Lohse, among others, stressing 2:24). But Paul himself and his pupils whose writings are extant in the canon never spoke of *ex pisteōs monon* (though the sense, we suggested, was implied, in contrast to "works of the law"); never understood faith the way 2:19 does, as mere head-belief; and never saw the Christian simply "having faith" without expression in life and conduct of God's will. What James seems to set in contrast is not works and faith but "living faith" and "dead faith" (*JBC* 59:19); the latter idea can only be a grotesque parody of what Paul taught.

278 We may point out also that just as "faith" is differently understood by Paul and by James, so also "works" is a term differently employed. For the former it was "works *of the law*" that were opposed as a means of salvation; Paul could use "work" in a more positive way for the Christian response (see above, §§ 125–29). For the latter, "works" are what Christians are to do, faith being presupposed. What James calls "works" Paul calls "fruit" (of the Spirit, or of righteousness, Gal 5:22; Phil 1:11). Each writer operates in a different situation: Paul opposed Judaizers and legalism, on the one hand, and gnosticizing libertinism on the other; James did not see Pharisaic or Christian emphasis on the law as the way of salvation as a problem, but saw only the menace of those who prated of "faith alone" with no life or deeds to match. The situations can be put in chart form thus:

	The Gospel means	
	vs. Legalism	Justification by grace	vs. Libertinism
PAUL:		through faith, resulting in fruit of the Spirit	
	in opposition to "works of the law" as a way of salvation after accepting Christ		in opposition to failure to "walk by the Spirit," filled with "the fruits of righteousness"

147. Hans-Martin Schenke, Karl Martin Fischer, *Einleitung in die Schriften des Neuen Testaments, II. Die Evangelien und die anderen neutestamentlichen Schriften* (Gütersloh: Gütersloher Verlagshaus Gerd Mohn, 1979), p. 240.

JAMES:		Justification (by faith, assumed) out of which arises	
	(not an issue) The author holds to a "nomistic optimism" [148]	"works" that show that one is justified	in opposition to those who say "faith alone"

279   But who are these opponents who taught thus about the lack of any need for "works," so that "only faith" is necessary, in the sense of belief in God? There is widespread scholarly opinion that Paul's own views are not meant, nor those of the Paulinists whom we meet in the canonical writings. But it is conceivable that other later followers of Paul, exaggerating a part of his teaching, came to some such view as the author of James vehemently opposes. He fights "a Paul who has become formalized," a mere "shadow Paul" (Eichholz, 1953, p. 38). To what extent Paulinists actually perverted the Apostle's views, and to what extent James had misunderstood their formulas, is impossible for us today to tell.

280   It is speculative, but possible in my opinion, to argue as Marxsen does that the author of James wrote to *defend* Paul's own teaching on justification and faith, and that he sought to do so against these pseudo-Paulinists by carrying their views to their most absurd limits: "faith" is merely to say the *shema,* one needs "only faith," even if it leaves other Christians naked and starving while one mouths pious platitudes about what God will do. Our author took particular pains to make his case on scriptural grounds. That his chief example is Abraham is to be explained not on anti-pauline polemical grounds but because the opponents probably appealed to Paul's use of Abraham, and James was able to make use of an existing Jewish tradition that taught that Abraham's faith (Gen 15:6) was a work, as was, par excellence, his testing at the sacrifice of Isaac (Dibelius, p. 170; indeed, Paul himself in Galatians may have been opposing that view of Abraham, cf. H. D., Betz, *Galatians,* pp. 139–40). The use by James of the Rahab tradition is less happy or complete as an argument, for, like the Abraham story in Jewish tradition, it functioned to show that the OT figure was "justified by works" whereas James wants to score the point "faith *and* works." James thus hoped to preserve by his formula "faith and works" what Paul had said through "faith" (including "obedience," fruit of the Spirit, the process of faith working itself out in love). (So Marxsen; cf. *Righteousness and Society,* pp. 83–86; *JBC* 59:21; similarly Burtchaell [as in n. 142], pp. 46–47.)

---

148. The phrase is that of Rolf Walker, "Allein aus Werken: Zur Auslegung von Jakobus 2, 14–16," *ZTK* 61 (1964): 162. Walker argues, in light of Jas 1:22–27, 2:10–26, that "faith" in our passage means *Gesetzesfrömmigkeit,* devotion to the law. His point is that piety and works need to be combined, one must not talk about "the royal law of liberty" but do nothing about what it implies. Such a sense, of course, removes any element of attack against Paul or Paulinism.

281   We cannot tell how James's strategy worked out in his own day. It was successful to the degree that if there was a group that taught such a caricature of faith, it never flourished in normative Christianity (Gnostic Christianity might be another matter). (Cf. Eph 2:8–10 as another way of handling the matter.) And never in the Reformation or elsewhere was such a view against works taught; in the sixteenth century the CA raised to amazing prominence in Articles 6 and 20 the fact that "faith is bound to bring forth good fruits." But Augustine's solution of the supposed contradiction came only at the expense of Paul's real teaching, and ever since then we have had attempts that are all too easy in harmonizing and homogenizing Paul and James, when we should instead recognize the different situations in which they spoke and the different use of some of the same words they employed.

282   It is probably too much to call James "a Paulinist," though he does present a view on justification/righteousness that is as prominent as any other theme in his epistle. He was working, though, to defend what Paul took to be central, righteousness/justification, involving faith—a faith that is expressed obediently to God in service of the brother and sister in life. The Jacobean corrective does have something "indispensable" to say to Christianity, especially regarding "the life solidarity of the community" (Kümmel, p. 415, citing J. B. Souček "Zu den Problemen des Jakobusbriefes," *EvT* 18 [1958]; 466) and as a warning against a "spiritualizing Paulinism."

283   But the corrective, like the pseudo-Pauline perversion, dare not be mistaken for what is original and central. Justification lay at the heart of Paul's message; for James it was but one among several theologoumena. Paul could speak, like James, against those who claimed to "have all faith" yet who lacked love—they are "nothing" (1 Cor 13:2). But his view of justification was broader than that of a forensic event (Stuhlmacher, p. 194), and spanning past, present, and future with the doctrine, he was concerned about more than showing by one's works that one was righteous (cf. Ziesler, pp. 128–29). But James protects the Pauline view at a point where it has seemed vulnerable in application, as the history of theology demonstrates.

E. Other New Testament Writings

284   A few examples of our terms remain to be considered in Hebrews (9×, plus *dikaiōma* 2×); 1 Peter (5×), and 2 Peter (8×). While Hebrews was long considered part of the Pauline corpus of letters (cf. Kümmel, p. 393), doubts about Paul's authorship had already emerged by the time of the Reformation, though Trent and the Pontifical Biblical Commission as recently as 1914 claimed it was Paul's (cf. *JBC* 72:28). More recently almost all exegetes, Roman Catholic included (cf. *JBC* 61:2–3), have recognized not only an authorship other than Paul's but also increasingly a type of theology distinct from anything else in the NT. That Peter is himself the author of 1 Peter has been widely denied, and that the apostle wrote 2 Peter has even more commonly been rejected (cf. *Peter in the New Testament,* pp. 16–17). If Hebrews has been removed from the Pauline corpus by modern scholarship, 1 Peter has sometimes been declared "Pauline" on the basis of content!

These documents are often termed "general or catholic epistles," aimed at early Christianity in general. That is truest of 2 Peter, untrue of 1 Peter if the author (Peter) really wrote it to the provinces in Asia Minor mentioned at 1:1, and untrue of Hebrews, which seems addressed to a specific but elusive community. Hebrews is really a homily, with a letter-like conclusion (13:22–25 esp.). Dating of all these documents remains disputed. We may place Hebrews and 1 Peter between 80 and 95 (unless the latter is Peter's own work, from before 67), and more confidently locate 2 Peter in the second century, as late as 140–150.

285   1. *Hebrews*[149] must not be read in the shadow of Paul, where church tradition has long placed it. Though absence of the doctrine of the *iustificatio impiorum* has often been used to help show that Hebrews is *not* by Paul, we must now, however, ask (with Grässer) whether there is not some sort of Rechtfertigungslehre of a different sort in Hebrews.

286   a. The modest use of *dikaio*-terms in Hebrews surely points in a nonpauline direction.

> At **1:9** the author quotes from Ps 45:7, applying it to God's Son,
> Thou has loved righteousness (*dikaiosynēn*) and hated lawlessness (*anomian*);
> therefore God, thy God, has anointed thee. . . .(*RSV*)

The quotation means that the Son "loved justice," obediently fulfilling God's will (Westcott; Ziesler, p. 131).

At **5:13** the phrase *logou dikaiosynēs* occurs in a paraenetic section where the audience is being told it still needs "milk" (elementary doctrines

---

149. **Commentaries on Hebrews:** Franz Delitzsch, *Commentary on the Epistle to the Hebrews,* trans. T. L. Kingsbury, 2 vols. (Edinburgh: T. & T. Clark, 1868, 1870). B. F. Westcott, *The Epistle to the Hebrews* (London: Macmillan, 1889). James Moffatt (ICC; 1924). Hans Windisch (HNT; 1931). H. Montefiore (HNTC; 1964). F. F. Bruce (New International Commentary on the New Testament; Grand Rapids: Eerdmans, 1964). Otto Michel (MeyerK; 12th ed., 1966). George Wesley Buchanan (AB; 1972).

See also Erich Grasser, "Rechtfertigung im Hebräebrief," in *Rechtfertigung* (Käsemann fs, 1976), pp. 79–94. On Luther, cf. Helmut Feld, *Martin Luthers und Wendelin Steinbachs Vorlesungen über den Hebräerbrief. Eine Studie zur Geschichte der neutestamentlichen Exegese und Theologie,* Veröffentlichen des Institutes für europäische Geschichte Mainz 62 (Wiesbaden, 1971); Kenneth Hagen, *A Theology of Testament in the Young Luther: The Lectures on Hebrews* (Studies in Medieval and Reformation Thought, 12; Leiden: Brill, 1974). Luther's lectures on Hebrews in 1517–18 (*WA* 57/3) were formative in his development. At this time Luther accepted Pauline authorship (by 1522 he was dubious). Though his lectures have been interpreted as exhibiting the "Reformation breakthrough" on the sense of *iustitia dei passiva,* Luther also showed a profound emphasis on "promise," "faith" (as personal certitude), and "covenant" in Hebrews.

of Christ) and is not ready as yet for "solid food" (advanced teachings for the mature): "Every one who lives on milk is unskilled in (*apeiros*) the word of righteousness." If *logos* means "doctrine," then there is a possibility of taking the phrase as a reference to a Rechtfertigungslehre, even in a Pauline sense (cf. Westcott, p. 134), but the exegetes have long preferred to interpret it in the sense of "discourse," and so, continuing the metaphor of v. 13*b* about a child, as "speaking rightly or intelligently" (so already Delitzsch, pp. 263–65; Michel). Ziesler (p. 135) opts for "principle of righteousness" or "moral truth," citing F. F. Bruce and H. Montefiore, who in their commentaries depend in turn especially on H. P. Owen.[150] While this line of interpretation seems simply to suggest "moral discernment" (v. 14, Ziesler), it masks Owen's claim that Hebrews assumes three stages of "ascent" in Christianity:

1) childhood—instruction in "first principles" (cf. 6:1, *logos tēs archēs*);

2) maturity—ethical perception, moral *askēsis; logos dikaiosynēs,* 5:13;

3) "solid food"—the doctrine of Christ's high priesthood, *logos parakleseōs,* 13:22.

This tripartite scheme seems to us to be forced. The *logos dikaiosynēs* does have to do with the advanced teaching of the author, but that certainly includes Christology (above all of Jesus as our High Priest) and could involve the moral aspects also. (The interweaving of christological confession, as at 3:1, 4:14, etc., and exhortation, as at 2:1–4, 3:1–13, 4:14-16, 5:11–6:20, is typical of Hebrews.)

287 In the chapters about the high priesthood of Jesus—reflecting what may be an early Christian hymn at 5:7 (or 5)–10 (so G. Schille, G. Friedrich) and quotations from Pss 2:7 and 110:4—we have a reference at 7:2 to the name of Melchizedek as "by translation, king of righteousness" (*basileus dikaiosynēs*), a phrase (developed here for application to this prototype of Jesus) that suggests "righteous king" (so Jos. *J. W.* 6.10.1. §438) or "dedicated to righteousness" (*Righteousness and Society*, p. 87), unless with Luther (*WA* 57/3: 187–88) one sees in "righteousness" and "peace" ("king of Salem" = *eirēnē*, v. 2) the gifts of justification or at least typical messianic blessings (Isa 9:5–6; *JBC* 61:38).[151] Ziesler finds "no real clue to the connotation" here (p. 131). Grässer (pp. 85–86) sees a messianic-priest-

---

150. H. P. Owen, "The 'Stages of Ascent' in Hebrews V. 11–VI. 3," *NTS* 3 (1957–58): 243–53. Thereby rejected was Spicq's view that Paul's doctrine of justification was meant. With *diakaiosynēs* as an obj. gen., Owen means "moral standard" that a person "can apply to each concrete situation of life" by "a series of correct moral choices" (p. 244). This established, he then allows that the phrase can also mean "right speech" or discourse. Owen is obliged to allow, however, that the author of Hebrews skips over stages 1 and 2, even though his hearers are deficient there, so as to get to stage 3!

151. J. A. Fitzmyer, " 'Now This Melchizedek . . .' (Heb. 7, 1)," *CBQ* 25 (1963): 311–14, reprinted in his *Essays on the Semitic Background of the New Testament* (London: Geoffrey Chapman, 1971; SBLSBS 5; 1974) pp. 229–33.

ly horizon, and would relate the "word of exhortation" (13:22) of the *auctor ad Hebraeos* to the *logos dikaiosynēs* (5:13) as a teaching on proper faith and life for the *dikaioi/teleioi* (see below, §§295–97, on the latter term).

288 The section on the ministry of the Levitical priests (9:1–10) with which that of Christ will be contrasted (9:11–10:18) twice uses *dikaiōma* in the plural for Levitical "regulations": **9:1,** "The first covenant also had regulations for worship," which are described in some detail and are said to be sacrifices "which cannot perfect the conscience of the worshiper" (v. 9) but which **(9:10)** "deal only with food and drink and various ablutions, regulations for the body imposed until the time of reformation," i.e., when Christ appeared and "entered once for all into the Holy Place" (9:11–12). The Old Covenant of Moses with its ordinances is thus declared at an end; the blood of Christ now purifies consciences to serve the living God, he is therefore mediator of a new covenant (9:14–15).

289 At **10:38** the author uses a passage familiar to us from Paul, Hab 2:4, but with v. 3 of the quotation also (contrast above, §121, on Rom 1:17):

10:36	For you have need of endurance, so that you may do the will of God and receive what is promised.
10:37	"For yet a little while,
(= Hab 2:3)	and the Coming One shall come and shall not tarry;
10:38	but my righteous one shall live by faith (*ho de dikaios*
(= Hab 2:4)	*mou ek pisteōs zēsetai*),
	and if he shrinks back,
	my soul has no pleasure in him."
10:39	But we are not of those who shrink back and are destroyed, but of those who have faith and keep their souls.

This is not Paul's use of Hab 2:4 but one closer to the original OT sense. (That Hebrews' use of Hab 2:4 rests on a Palestinian Jewish tradition of exegesis is quite possible, cf. Michel, pp. 364–65.) There is no interest here in rightwising but rather in "the Christian righteous" living by faith "yet a little while" until the End, enduring till the promise is fulfilled (cf. 3:6, 14, 6:11; "promise," 4:1, 6:12, 8:6, 9:15, 10:36, etc.). Being righteous connects with faith, but *pistis* almost in the sense of "faithfulness" (Ziesler, p. 143). 10:36–39 is the high point of this paraenetic section (10:19–39); it also directs us to the famous chapter 11, on faith.

290 After his definition that "faith is the assurance of things hoped for, the conviction of things not seen" (a definition different from any sense of *pistis* in Paul), our author uses *dikaio*-words in several of his illustrations:

11:4 By faith Abel offered to God a more acceptable sacrifice than Cain, through which [i.e., his faith, cf. Michel, p. 384] he received approval as righteous (*emartyrēthē einai dikaios*), God bearing witness by accepting his gifts.

"Faith" is prominent here, and so is "being testified by God as righteous," but it is scarcely justification by faith in Paul's sense (as Descamps suggested, *Les Justes,* 226ff.); this is not Paul. It is not the straight OT narrative either, for Abel is not called "righteous" there. (For the closest parallel in Scripture, see Matt 23:35 and 1 John 3:12, above, §§241, 260, on Abel as *dikaios,* in the sense of innocent or righteous.) Ziesler seems to me to be dealing with the passage in Pauline terms when he writes, "It is still really justification by works, yet righteousness does arise from the faith" (p. 143). We have here, it should rather be said, an *interpretation* of Gen 4:4 (Grässer, p. 81), yet a way of thinking that is more OT-like than Paul's on being righteous (Michel, p. 384), a way of thinking where apparently God "recognizes him as such because he is" (Grässer, contra Luther's eisegesis here).

291　There is one other bit of evidence on 11:4, however: The *Tg. Neof.* explains that at the root of the differences between Cain and Abel was a *doctrinal* dispute! The two brothers agree that the world "was created by mercy" but differ over whether the world is (Abel) or is not (Cain) "governed according to the fruits of good works." Cain further denies the judgment; "there is no judge," no other world, no rewards for the just or retribution of the wicked, all matters Abel affirms. It was over this dispute that Cain slew him (so *Tg. Neof.;* cf. M. McNamara, *The New Testament and the Palestinian Targum to the Pentateuch* [Rome: Pontifical Biblical Institute, 1966], pp. 156–60; Buchanan, p. 185) . If this line of interpretation lies behind 11:4 (and possibly 1 John 3:12), then "faith" meant or included "right belief" in Hebrews 11!

292

>　　**11:7**　By faith Noah, being warned by God concerning events as
>　　yet unseen, took heed and constructed an ark for the saving
>　　of his household; by this he condemned the world and be-
>　　came an heir of the righteousness which comes by faith (*tēs*
>　　*kata pistin dikaiosynēs egeneto klēronomos*).

The final clause sounds extremely Pauline ("heir," "righteousness by faith" [Ziesler, p. 135, thinks "*kata pistin* is equivalent" to Paul's *ek pisteōs*], and also "for saving," [*eis sōtērian*]; cf. Westcott, p. 357, and Michel, p. 388, who does not exclude the possibility that "Hebrews and Paul concur in the doctrine of Gerechtigkeit"). But *kata pistin* is never found in Paul. For the verse there is a straight OT background (Gen 6:9, Noah was the first person in the Bible designated "a righteous man"). He "acquires" or "attains" the promise by his attitude of faith (*TDNT,* 3, p. 785, Foerster, on *klēronomos*). As with other examples, we seem to have, not Paul's understanding of faith and rightwising, but the OT-Jewish exegetical tradition, understood afresh in our author's Christian perspective. Especially is this apparent in the long Abraham example (11:8–19), where there is no mention of Abraham believing God and that reckoned as righteousness (Gen 15:6), but the climax is (as in Jas 2:21) his offering up of Isaac (v. 17).

293 **11:33** Summary statement about Gideon, Barak, etc., six OT names plus "the prophets" who through faith "conquered kingdoms," etc., nine verb phrases, among which is "enforced justice" (*RSV;* Greek *ērgasanto dikaiosynēn*), literally "worked righteousness" in the sense of "did what is right" (cf. Ps 15:2; Acts 10:35; Jas 1:20 in Luther's rendering, "was vor Gott recht ist"). It is uncertain whether the author has specifically in mind Samuel (1 Sam 12:4) or David (2 Sam 8:15, in the sense of "administered justice"). Grässer (p. 82) speaks of *institia operata* (*fide* or *iuxta fidem*) here. Buchanan, who has argued that "by faith" throughout chap. 11 refers to creed, confession, tradition, Scripture, or God's word (see on 11:4 above), senses a change in meaning here. Instead of *pistei,* "by faith" (18×, vv. 3–31), we get in v. 33 (and v. 39) *dia* (*tēs*) *pisteōs* (cf. v. 13, *kata pistin,* as in v. 7). Therefore Buchanan suspects a source here, perhaps poetic (cf. Michel, pp. 415–16). The phrase about *dikaiosynē* is not Pauline, nor is it antipauline, but OT idiom (Hebrew *ʿāśâ ṣĕdāqâ*), to "do righteousness" (Delitzsch).

294 **12:11** uses a "now/later" contrast to sum up the teaching of 12:3ff. on discipline (*paideia*) and suffering. In the form of a wisdom statement, there is a future promise: "For the moment all discipline seems painful rather than pleasant; later it yields the peaceable fruit of righteousness (*karpon eirēnikon . . . dikaiosynēs*) to those who have been trained by it (*gegymnasmenois,* by *paideia*)." The genitive is one of apposition: the fruit rich in peace, namely, righteousness (Grässer, p. 85; Michel, p. 446). One is reminded of Jas 3:18 (cf. §268 above). Ziesler (p. 133), as so often, sees "Christian behaviour" here, but more likely eschatological gifts are meant for those who endure.

295 The final reference is at **12:23** in the list of things at which the author's addressees have arrived: You have come (*RSV,* here adapted) to

> 12:22 Mount Zion, the city of the living God, the heavenly Jerusalem,
>   innumerable angels in festal gathering,
> 12:23 the assembly of the first-born who are enrolled in heaven,
>   a judge, the God of all,
>   spirits of just men made perfect (*kai pneumasi dikaiōn teteleiōmenōn*),
> 12:24 to Jesus, the mediation of a new covenant, and
>   the sprinkled blood that speaks more graciously than the blood of Abel.

We are here in a long paraenetic section encouraging those slack Christians who are being addressed in Hebrews to "run the race that is set before us" (12:1), with discipline (12:3–11), looking to Jesus "the pioneer and perfector of our faith" (12:2). The several admonitions of 12:12–17 (which amount to a responsibility to "press on," in peace and holiness, to "obtain the grace of God") are here undergirded by a law/gospel contrast, between the old Israel at Sinai (darkness, gloom, fear before the living God) and the ecclesia of Jesus at a contrasting mountain, Zion. The contrasting scenes, details of which often elude us and which were probably intended by the writer to be allusive, set in opposition to each other two mountains, two "mediators" (Moses and Jesus), two covenants, and much more. The eschatology seems of the "realized" variety ("you have not come to" [v. 18–21] but "you have come to . . . ," [vv. 22–24]), but Hebrews is notorious for the way it speaks of the "now" time while still pointing to a future event of fulfillment (9:28, closest NT reference to a "second coming;" cf. 12:26). Perhaps the vision in 12:22–24 is in part proleptic, related to the author's concern to rouse his hearers to how crucial Christian confession and living in the present moment are, via both admonitory threat and comforting promise. God is judge, but we have Jesus' gracious blood!

With "spirits of just persons made perfect" we have the added problem of whether OT saints are meant (cf. chap. 11) or the Christian(s) (dead); Ziesler, pp. 140, 143, does little more than reflect this perplexity.

296   Older commentators had no difficulty in saying that these *dikaioi teteleiōmenoi* are "the righteous" who have been vindicated by God at the judgment and "perfected" in the sense of realizing the end for which they were created and attaining the purpose of their calling (Delitzsch, 2, p. 352, who sees involved all the righteous of both covenants, from Abel on; Westcott, p. 416, who refers to "departed saints," still only "spirits" for whom the judgment "has been in part triumphantly accomplished," and he adds "in virtue of the completed work of Christ"). It should be noted that "to perfect" (*teleioō*) is a favorite category of Hebrews (2:10; 5:9; 7:19, 28; 9:9; 10:14; 11:40, on perfecting through Christ, which the law could never accomplish; cf. G. Delling, *TDNT* 8, pp. 82–83, a LXX usage employing cultic terminology, "to put someone in the position in which he can come, or stand, before God").

297   Modern commentators are more aware of roots in Judaism, apocalyptic or rabbinic, behind the phrase (as with others in 12:18–24, Michel, p. 460). The word "spirits" for the dead occurs in Enoch (22:3ff., 108:3; cf. Wis 3:1, "the souls of the righteous"). Cf. Heb 12:9, God is "the Father of spirits" (Michel, pp. 442–43, 466). But one may go further and find in Enoch a division between "the spirits of the righteous" and sinners or "spirits of men who were not righteous" (Enoch 22:9, 13; 41:8; 103:3–4). Commentators like Windisch (p. 114, cf. Michel, pp. 467–68; cf. also Przybylski, *Righteousness in Matthew* [cited above, n. 131], p. 46) go further and see a Jewish parallel to *dikaioi teteleiōmenoi* in the *gĕmûrîm ṣaddîqîm,* the "perfectly righteous" (Sifre Deut 307 on 32:4; 40 on 11:12; *t. Qiddušin* 1:15, *t. Sanhedrin* 13:3); the phrase contrasts with the person who is "perfectly wicked" (rāšāᶜ gāmûr) and in Tannaitic literature suggests the ṣaddîq gāmûr is "righteous" but may still commit (minor) transgressions.

Grässer concludes that our phrase at 12:23 refers to "the OT pious, who on the basis of their earthly righteous conduct (Rechtverhalten) are in heaven perfected," for whom Enoch (11:5) is prototype.

Michel proceeds more cautiously. It was said in 11:40 that the OT figures mentioned in chap. 11 "should not be made perfect apart from us." Therefore we have an option at 12:23:

Either (dikaioi) teteleiōmenoi, from rabbinic gĕmûrîm, denotes the (OT) righteous on whom God's judgment has already fallen (cf. chap. 11), the pious who have received the testimony that they are righteous,	or they are Christians (Christian dead), who through the passion of Christ have been perfected (2:10, 5:9).
"To perfect" is eschatological (cf. 11:40); the participle is like an adjective.	Then the sense of teleiousthai is soteriological; the participle is passive ("having been perfected") at 12:23. But then how does this phrase at 12:23c relate to 12:23a, about "the ekklēsia of the first-born"? But v. 24 (Jesus' blood, covenant-mediator) point in a soteriological direction.
The prior phrases in 12:22–23ab tilt it in the direction of apocalyptic description.	

Exact meaning is difficult to decide. As the passage stands, it seems to encompass the OT righteous and Christians in a promise of perfect righteousness, related to God's promise and what he has done once for all in Jesus at his death, a kingdom-status (12:28) that Christians have, even though they still must "run the race."

298 b. What type of theology is this, so far as righteousness/justification is involved, where "rightwising" is never spoken of (dikaioō is unused in Hebrews), but there is talk of "the righteousness which comes by faith" (11:7), but "faith" has its own particular sense of firm assurance about things hoped for (not "trust" and "obedience," as in Paul) and "righteousness/justice" is something OT saints "worked" (11:33) or a "fruit" that Christians who hold on amid sufferings and discipline attain (12:11)?

Our author knows a "word of righteousness" (5:13), but that has to do as much with moral exhortation as with a foundation in what Christ the great high priest has done "once for all." (We do have a document that stresses Jesus' passion and death, but that talks of his exaltation, rather than his resurrection.)

There is a sharp contrast between the old and new covenants, Moses vs. Christ, to a degree not unlike Paul (in Gal 3, e.g.); a law/promise contrast (cf. 7:19, 28; 9:22; 10:1), dear to the Lutheran reformers. The (dikaiōmata of the old covenant cannot save (perfect) worshipers (9:1, 10).

But though Hebrews speaks of persons being righteous (12:33), connected with faith, perhaps even right belief (11:4), the author shows no in-

terest in developing Hab 2:4 as Paul does (cf. Heb 10:36–39), and uses
Abraham as an example of faith with more emphases on Gen 22 (cf. Jas
2:21) than on 15:6 (cf. Paul).

Yet Hebrews insists our "consciences" are "purified . . . to serve the
living God," so that we can "draw near . . . in full assurance of faith" (after baptism) only on the basis of "the blood of Christ," the great high
priest (9:14, 10:22; cf. the cultic depiction of the death of Christ in chap. 9,
including the term *hilastērion* at 9:5, the only NT reference to the "mercy
seat" besides Rom 3:25; and 13:9–14).[152]

299   Grässer (pp. 88–91) contends that Hebrews, in completely different language from Paul, sets forth the same gospel, indeed Rechtfertigungslehre, but in terms of the *conscientia perfecta ex opere Christi* (*per
hostiam suam*, 9:26). Christ alone is the way (10:19–20) to living service of
God in a kingdom we have received in a grace to which we are to hold fast
(12:28, *NAB*).

Vielhauer[153] speaks similarly of "two parallel interpretations" in Hebrews' doctrine of the self-offering of Christ the high priest and Paul's
treatment of the atoning death of Jesus in his doctrine of justification. This
is especially true if we parallel to the points we have made in discussing
Paul—namely, that righteousness/justification is (a) not just a matter of
the individual but of the community or "the corporate," and (b) is not to
be limited to a first step in salvation, followed by "sanctification"—the
facts that in Hebrews being "perfected" includes being "sanctified" (10:10,
14) and "the One who sanctifies and those who are sanctified are all of one
(origin)" (2:11).

300   Paul and Hebrews present the gospel differently, in settings that
are different for each author. They share in common, however, the following:

(1) the theology of the early Christian "atonement" emphasis on the
death of Christ;

(2) an unfolding of the meaning of that death *ephapax* ("once for
all") as "good news";

(3) both use *dikaio*-language, Paul to a greater degree;

(4) both connect it with "faith" (but in different senses of *pistis*);

(5) both reflect OT-Jewish backgrounds for righteousness/justifica-
tion, but different strands thereof; Paul is more innovative and makes new
applications or senses, Hebrews in its usage is more akin to usages in Matthew and James.

But read in his own right, the author of Hebrews exhibits in his treatise yet another way of presenting the Christ-event and its meaning in such
dikaio-terminology.

---

152. H. Koester, " 'Outside the Camp': Hebrews 13.9–14," *HTR* 55 (1962): 229–315.
153. *Geschichte der urchristlichen Literatur. Einleitung in das Neue Testament, die
Apokryphen und die Apostolischen Väter* (Berlin: de Gruyter, 1975), p. 250.

301   2. *1 Peter.*[154] As noted above (§284), the Pauline character of this document has increasingly been noted by some recent scholarship. Cf. especially Schenke-Fischer, *Einleitung* 1, 201–02. This does not mean Paul himself was involved, but the Paulinist School.

Among the pieces of evidence for "Paulinism" are the emphasis on and portrayal of the death of Christ; some of the paraenesis, especially the Haustafeln material (cf. 2:13–17 with Rom 13:1–7); and use of the OT (only 2:4–10 and Rom 9:25–33 in the entire NT use the same combination of texts from Isa 8:14, 28:16, and Hos 1–2)—though, of course, all this could stem from common apostolic Christianity; and more specifically, the use of *en Christō* (3:16, 5:10, 14), the concept of baptism (1:23, 2:2; cf. Rom 6:3ff., Col 2:12, Eph 2: 5–6), participation in Christ's sufferings prior to glory (cf. Rom 8:17), and emphasis on *charis* ($10\times$) and reference to *charisma* (4:10), not to mention the use of *dikaio*-terms, which we are exploring.

It is probably going too far to claim the pseudonymous writer of 1 Peter originally wrote PAULUS at 1:1 and that another hand changed three letters to read P*ETR*US (Schenke-Fischer, 1, p. 203), but the conclusion is a fair one that "no other primitive Christian line of thought has worked so strongly in the letter and its ideas as the Pauline tradition" (ibid., p. 202, though n. 5 adds the tradition found in James is the next strongest influence! In part, the persecution situation found in 1 Peter helps to explain some of the similarities to James).

The alternative, if one holds to Peter's authorship and an earlier date than we have proposed, must be even stronger appeal to common apostolic traditions shared by Peter and Paul (cf. *JBC* 58:4).

One other preliminary: Schrenk (*TDNT* 2, p. 199) proposes a unitary meaning in 1 Peter for "righteousness" when he says "*dikaiosynē* is always the doing of right as acceptable conduct" in this epistle. Ziesler is more balanced: some passages may suggest justification (pp. 144–45), but elsewhere (especially with the noun, p. 133), "Christian behaviour" is meant. A paragraph in *Righteousness and Society* (p. 87) argues that in the references in 1 Peter a pattern of "indicative followed by the imperative" appears. To establish any of these views, each passage must be considered individually.

302   a. *The Passages.* At **2:23** in a christological passage (set in turn in a Haustafeln section on slaves submitting to their masters but enduring suffering, 2:18ff.), the suffering Christ is described as one who, when reviled, "trusted to Him who judges justly" (*paradidou de tē, krinonti dikaiōs*). This *RSV* rendering refers to God as the judge. A variant reading in a few lectionary texts, the fathers, and the Vulgate (*tradebat autem iudi-*

---

154. **Commentaries on 1 Pet:** E. G. Selwyn (cited above, n. 43). F. W. Beare, *The First Epistle of Peter* (Oxford: Basil Blackwell, 1947 cited here; 3d ed. 1970). Bo Reicke (AB; 1964). K. H. Schelkle (HTKNT; 1964). L. Goppelt, MeyerK; 1978).

canti se iniuste), becomes a reference to Pilate (hence R. Knox, "gave himself up into the hands of injustice"); it was championed as a reading by Harnack but is simply an interesting scribal error (perhaps influenced by 2:19; cf. Beare, p. 123; not even listed in the UBSGNT or Metzger's *Textual Commentary*).

The passion emphasis of 2:21–23 (in what may be a hymn fragment, 2:22–25; cf. Goppelt, pp. 204–07) is carried over into **2:24,** using language from Isa 53:4, 12 (italics below) about Christ,

> who *bore our sins himself* in his body on the tree,
> in order that we might die to sins and live to righteousness (*tē̜ dikaiosynē̜ zēsōmen*); *by* whose *stripes we are healed.*

The final phrase reminds Beare (p. 124) so much of Rom 6:10–14, 18–19 that he says it "clearly reflects dependence." What Ziesler sees as "Christian behaviour" here (p. 133), though he also terms it "the consequence" of "the familiar (Pauline!) theme . . . of dying and rising with Christ" (p. 143), Beare presents with the emphases reversed: "Moral influence" is "subordinated to . . . the effective power" of cross and baptism. Selwyn (p. 181) terms "righteousness" both "the goal and motive of the new life." Schelkle (pp. 85–86) speaks of righteousness not attained by our own efforts, but "always for Christ's sake." There is actually no phrase in Romans quite like what we find here at 2:24; the closest may be 6:10–11, about "living to God," and 6:18–20, "slaves/free (with reference) to righteousness" (above, §145). In context at 2:24, "righteousness" stands in contrast to "sins" (note the plural, uncharacteristic of Paul himself), and vv. 18–21*a* give it a behavioral sense; but the passion reference to the just God, the death of Jesus (and, to anticipate 3:18, Jesus as "the Righteous One") point to soteriology. On a grammatical basis, with the dative one of reference, the sense probably tilts to the meaning "live for righteousness," i.e., for what is right in God's sight (cf. BAGD, *zaō* 3b; cf. Rom 6:10), to which one gives oneself (Goppelt, p. 210).

303   1 Peter **3:12** is part of a quotation of Ps 34:17 in a passage (3:8–12) that at the conclusion of the Haustafeln section enjoins unity and love upon the entire community.

> 3:12   For the eyes of the Lord are upon the righteous (*dikaious*),
> (= Ps and his ears are open to their prayer.
> 34:17) But the face of the Lord is against those that do evil.

The OT psalm, attributed to David, spoke of the afflictions of the righteous person (in the OT sense) and how Yahweh delivers that person. Ziesler, p. 141, calls attention to the application here to "the Christian righteous, those who live in obedience to Jesus, and so receive his verdict of approval." Goppelt, more contextually in 1 Peter, points to those who, on the basis of their being born anew, live aright (2:24) as "the righteous."

But their obedient living especially involves steadfastness in suffering, as the next section makes clear.

3:14–17 emphasizes how the conduct of Christian believers should put their revilers to shame, specifically with the promise,

> **3:14** even if you do suffer for righteousness' sake (*dia dikaiosynēn*), you will be blessed (*makarioi*, cf. 3:9).

Matt 5:10–11 (and hence *verba Christi,* Selwyn thinks, transmitted in the catechetical process) is an underlying beatitude cited by all commentators. We noted above (§232) the widespread view that righteousness at 5:10 means in effect "doing the right" as disciples (hence Goppelt here, Recht-verhalten)—unless "righteousness" at 5:10–11 is identified with Jesus. At 3:14 (cf. 2:24) "suffer for righteousness" could mean virtually "suffer for God (and Christ)," the righteous Judge (and Righteous One) respectively.

The reference at **3:18** to Christ as the Righteous One (*dikaios*) who "died [or suffered] for sins once for all (*hapax;* cf. Hebrews)," has already been discussed above as an early Christian "atonement formula" (§60, above). It is the language of Isa 53:11, "the righteous one, my servant, shall make many to be accounted righteous" (cf. *JBC* 58:20), perhaps in terms of the OT "sin-offering" (cf. Selwyn, p. 196). This is the passage that Ziesler (p. 144) argued "it is possible to take . . . in terms of justification." It is obviously a seminal passage for the section and the entire document (cf. 4:1; 2:21).

Finally there is **4:18,** a quotation of Prov 11:31, in a summary section about rejoicing in "suffering as a Christian" (4:16), even in the face of judgment.

> 4:18 If the righteous man (*ho dikaios*) is scarcely saved, where will the impious and sinner appear?

This is said in support of the point that judgment must begin with the household of God, and if there, "what will be the end of those who do not obey the gospel of God?" On it is based the admonition (4:19) to "do what is good and trust themselves to a faithful Creator." What does 1 Peter mean by "the righteous man" (i.e., so Schelkle, p. 126, the Christian)? Ziesler (p. 141), one of the few commentators to take up the matter, sees a "double note, ethical-forensic." Goppelt, p. 315, finds in the term the person who lives a life based on the gospel, whose word and deed depend on faith (cf. 3:12, as treated by Goppelt).

304 b. *Summary.* In a persecution situation, the author writes, reflecting many common early Christian and Pauline views, to urge steadfastness as suffering and judgment draw near. God "judges justly" (2:23). Christ, the Righteous One, died for our sins (3:18, 2:24) so that we might "live to righteousness" (2:24). Our author can use OT quotations about the righteous (Ps 34:17, Prov 11:31) but understands these to refer to Christians who are righteous (3:12; 4:18). In their present situation Christians can be described as those who "suffer for righteousness" (3:14, for the right, or possibly for God). Undefined is how one gets to be *dikaios,* but grace is prominent, there is an obvious connection with the death of Jesus, and the readers are "in Christ" (5:14). Faith plays a role (1:5, 7, 9, 21; 5:9) in standing firm and attaining salvation. If Ziesler is right, 3:18 and 4:18 hint at forensic justification.

Lacking is the verb *dikaioō* or rightwising, but as a development of Paul's theology of the cross in a new situation 1 Peter can be said to show the ongoing importance of righteousness/justification in another type of (Pauline?) NT Christianity.

305 3. *2 Peter.*[155] Probably the latest book to be written that got into the canon (and that only after slow and delayed recognition, cf. Kümmel, pp. 433–34), 2 Peter is a document from the first half of the second century (Reicke, p. 144, was willing to go as early as A.D. 90; *JBC* 65:4, to the late first, early second century), written against false teachers, probably Gnostics (chap. 2), in defense of early Christian apocalyptic eschatology (chap. 3, the "scoffers" deny the unfulfilled promise of Christ's parousia). A *defensor fidei,* writing in the name of "Symeon Petros" and recounting first-hand experiences like the Transfiguration on "the holy mountain" (1:16–18), also reflects a type of Hellenized Christian piety, where faith begins and love caps a chain of virtues (1:5–7) and where one aims at escaping the "corruption" or "defilement" that is in the world (1:4; 2:20) in order to become "participants in the Divine Nature" through *epignōsis* (1:3–4).

2 Peter also makes special appeal to Paul (3:15–16) and thus is a Pauline as well as a Petrine testament (cf. Knoch). It makes considerable use of key early Christian terms and themes, including some of those of Paul's letters, like "faith" (1:1, 5), "grace" (3:18; 1:2), and even righteousness/justification terminology, but the overall profile and content of Christianity here differs from anything we have met before.

306 a. *Relevant passages in 2 Peter.* The opening eloquent but quite general address uses *dikaiosynē tou theou* and thus, along with Matt 6:33 and Jas 1:20, is but one of three such examples of the phrase in the NT outside the Pauline letters.

> **1:1** Symeon Peter, slave and apostle of Jesus Christ, to those
> who have obtained a faith of equal standing with ours in the

---

155. **Commentaries on 2 Pet:** J. Mayor, *The Epistle of St. Jude and the Second Epistle of St. Peter* (London: Macmillan, 1907). C. Bigg (ICC; 1901). J. Moffatt (MNTC; 1928). K. H. Schelkle (HTKNT 13/2; 1964). Bo Reicke (AB; 1964). E. M. Sidebottom (NCB; 1967). W. Grundmann (THKNT; 1974). Otto Knoch, *Die "Testemente" des Petrus und Paulus. Die Sicherung der apostolischen Überlieferung in der spätneutestamentlichen Zeit* (SBS 62; 1973), on Acts 20:18–35, 2 Timothy, 2 Peter, and 1 Clement, in light of Vatican II, on apostolic traditioning. E. Käsemann, "An Apologia for Primitive Christian Eschatology," in *Essays on NT Themes* (SBT 41; 1964), pp. 169–95. Tord Fornberg, *An Early Church in a Pluralistic Society: A Study of 2 Peter* (Coniectanea biblica, NT series 9; Lund: C. W. K. Gleerup, 1977). Jerome H. Neyrey, "The Form and Background of the Polemic in 2 Peter," *JBL* 99 (1980): 407–31.

righteousness of our God and Savior Jesus Christ (*en dikaio-
syne₍ tou theou hemon kai soteros Iesou Christou*). (*RSV*
adapted)
RSV note: Or *of our God and the Savior Jesus Christ.*

The address is general, not geographical. Commentators who see here a reflection of Symeon's speech at Acts 15:7–11, cf. v. 14, suggest the Gentiles
are meant as those who have obtained a faith now like that of the Jewish
Christians; Moffatt, p. 176, points out, however, that the distinction is
probably between apostles and "ordinary Christians who owed their faith
to the apostolic preaching (iii.2)" (so also Bigg, p. 250, citing J. A. Bengel);
this would be in line with the view of apostleship and office in the letter, as
Käsemann (175ff.) and others develop it (see below).

In any case the "faith" involved seems *"fides quae creditur,* the aggre-
gate of apostolic teaching handed on to succeeding generations" (*JBC*
65:7; Schelkle, p. 185; cf. Jude v. 3); "*right* confession" (Bultmann, *Theology* [see above, n. 15] 2, p. 136). Fornberg (p. 97, n. 2) does question, however, whether this widespread interpretation of *pistis* here need be
assumed; was our later distinction between *fides quae* and *fides qua* developed as yet in the early church?

307   Two textual details demand attention. The 1611 *KJV* had "the
righteousness of God and our Saviour Jesus Christ," following MSS,
which read an article before "saviour" as well as before "God," so that *two*
divine persons were involved. All editors today read it with a single article[156] before the hendiadys "God and savior," and understand it, as in the
RSV text, to refer to Jesus Christ. (V. 2 shows that the author can distinguish "God" and "Jesus Christ our Lord.") Thus Jesus is referred to as
"our God and savior," and most commentators (cf. Fornberg, p. 142) note
the increasing tendency in the period (e.g., in Ignatius, *Ephesians* 18.2) to
call Christ "God." Second, instead of *en dikaiosyne₍,* MS Sinaiticus has *eis
dikaiosynen,* a correction, Kertelge thinks (p. 47, n. 134), which was meant
to reflect more fully a Pauline understanding of the phrase.

What is the meaning of "those who have obtained a faith of equal
standing with ours *en dikaiosyne₍* of our God and savior Jesus Christ"?
One cannot overlook the point that the old formula *dikaiosyne (tou) theou,*
with its OT, indeed perhaps apocalyptic, background, for "God's saving
righteousness," has here become a "righteousness of *Jesus Christ* our God
and savior" (word order changed in English to bring out the christocentric
emphasis; the Greek begins like the earlier phrase and then becomes a reference to Christ). This use of "God" as a christological title (cf. Schelkle,
p. 185) overturns Ziesler's classification of 1:1 as "*God's* righteousness, not
Christ's" (p. 130, for he simply follows V. Taylor in holding that the NT

---

156. Papyrus 72 (iii/iv cent.) reinforces this point even in its variant reading, *tou theou
Iesou tou kyriou hemon* (Grundmann, p. 67).

does not ever call Jesus "God").[157] The reference to Christ also renders dubious the definition of *dikaiosynē* here as "God's just government of the Christian community" (Ziesler, p. 130, following *TDNT*), a sense that would be quite singular.

Most recent commentators find in *dikaiosynē* here a just and even-handed treatment by God (or Christ) that sees to it that all persons, Jew and Gentile, every believer, get the same equal faith. It is not "faith *in* the righteousness of our God" but "faith attained by or on the grounds of his justice."[158]

308   Käsemann (p. 173) goes a step further. He speaks of addressees here "who through the justice of our God and (of the?) Saviour Jesus Christ share our faith and enjoy equal privilege with ourselves." That, as just noted, makes of *dikaiosynē* a kind of fairness or divine impartiality and philanthropy (Stuhlmacher, *Gerechtigkeit,* p. 202). Käsemann then goes on to the notion that in 2 Peter the apostles serve as *source* whence the gift they have received overflows to other Christians, and that that happens with justice (in the sense of *aequitas,* so also Grundmann, p. 66), leveling out inequities in salvation history (p. 174). (In this sense, Schrenk's *TDNT* statement cited above could apply, "das göttliche Walten in der Führung der Gemeinde.") In this view of Käsemann's we have an example of Pauline concepts having become Hellenized; "saving righteousness" has become "equalizing justice." Most Catholic scholars and some Protestants reject a good deal of Käsemann's reading of 2 Peter, especially the extreme contrasts he finds when he describes it as, through and through, a document from the viewpoint of "early Catholicism" (Frühkatholizismus), where

> the messenger of the Gospel has become the guarantor of the tradition, the witness of the resurrection has become the witness of the *historia sacra,* the bearer of the eschatological action of God has become a pillar of the institution which dispenses salvation . . . (p. 177).

---

157. Against that view, cf. Raymond E. Brown, "Does the New Testament Call Jesus 'God'?" *TS* 26 (1965): 545–73, reprinted in Brown's *Jesus God and Man* (New York: Macmillan, 1967), pp. 1–38, esp. p. 22 on 2 Pet 1:1. James M. Reese, "The Principal Model of God in the New Testament," *Biblical Theology Bulletin* 8 (1978): 129, sees 2 Pet 3:18 ("in the knowledge of our Lord and Savior Jesus Christ") as parallel evidence at the end of the document for referring 1:1 at its beginning to Jesus as God.

158. At 1:1 only a few commentators see present the Pauline doctrine of justification; Schelkle (p. 185. n. 1) names J. Felten (1929) and J. Michl (1953). Sidebottom, p. 104, says "perhaps," but "more probably" it means that "second generation faith is as good as that of the first." Mayor, p. 81, noted Eph 1:15 as an analogy (*pistin en tō, kyriō, Iesou*) but rejected "faith in the righteousness of Christ as our justification" for the sense. Ziesler, p. 130, allows that 1:1 "may refer to God's saving righteousness" but opts for "God's just government." Moffatt (MNTC, p. 176) is typical of the usual view: "by the equity of our God and saviour Jesus Christ."

Is the evidence there to sustain such a view, especially as regards 1:1? Granted, "a faith of equal standing *with ours (hēmin)*" may refer to "us apostles and eye-witnesses" (3:2; 1:16), rather than to "us Jewish Christians" in contrast to you Gentiles (as in Eph 2:11ff.), but this "we-style" (cf. 1:1–14, 16, 18; 3:15), while referring to the apostles (including Paul, apparently) and the apostolic age, surely means at times to include the hearers in the same privileges (1:1*b*, 4, 16*a*, 19; 3:18) through the sharing of the promises (1:4; 3:13) or through the word (1:19, especially as related to and in Scripture, 1:20). Schelkle (p. 184, n. 2) specifically warns against a *Gegenübersetzung* of apostles and laity. The "faith . . . obtained" reminds one of Paul's "gospel, which you received, in which you stand" (1 Cor 15:1) and "the grace in which we stand" (Rom 5:1). If it is faith like Peter's (and the other apostles'), then it is not just a matter of content (for the phrase of Jude 3 is *not* repeated here, "transmitted to the saints once for all") but also involves an element of personal appropriation (*fides qua;* cf. 1:5, the only other use of *pistis* in the document).

309   Is *dikaiosynē* here merely *aequitas*? One could be more confident if the phrase were "righteousness/justice *of God.*" The fact is, our author has created a new phrase, "(the) righteousness/justice of *Jesus Christ* our God and savior." Attractive as it would be to say that he preserves the apocalyptic sense of *dikaiosynē tou theou* as part of his effort to defend primitive Christian apocalyptic, evidence is lacking in 2 Peter to encourage us to take the phrase as an apocalyptic *terminus technicus*. But what, then, could our author be reflecting in this phrase at 1:1? Since he knows (and defends) Paul (3:15–16), is it not possible that he has taken a Pauline term and recast it christocentrically? Possible candidates for his starting point in the Pauline corpus are Rom 3:5 ("the justice of God," subjective genitive, possibly taken as *aequitas*) or Rom 1:17, 3: 21, 22, 25. I find Rom 3:22 the most likely candidate, *dikaiosynē de theou dia pisteōs [Iēsou] Christou,* as background for *dikaiosynē tou theou hēmōn kai sōtēros Iēsou Christou.* The concept of faith at Rom 1:12 could even lie at hand to explain 2 Pet 1:1, for Paul spoke of imparting spiritual gifts "to strengthen you" at Rome, i.e., better and more carefully put, "that we may be mutually encouraged by each other's faith."

310   If *defensor fidei* is trying to reflect a Pauline theme, heightened christologically, at the beginning of his treatise, the sense of 1:1 would be

> to those who, on the basis of the righteousness of our God and savior Jesus Christ, have obtained a faith equal to ours.

(The preposition *en* I take as "on the basis of" or "by," a sense that holds in the *aequitas* translation too; cf. Moffatt in n. 158.) In an unexplained way, Christ's *dikaiosynē* provides the access for entree by the Christian readers into the apostolic faith. This peculiar phrase warrants further study by others.

311 Insignificant for our purposes is **1:13**, "I think it right (*dikaion*) . . . to arouse you by way of reminder. . . ."

Of greater interest are the Noah and Lot references in chap. 2, where the author asserts the doom of the contemporary false teachers in light of OT examples. The framework of the argument runs,

> **2:5** If God did not spare the ancient world, but preserved Noah,
> a herald of righteousness (*dikaiosynēs kēryka*) . . . ,
>
> **2:7** and if he rescued righteous Lot (*dikaion*) . . . ,
>
> **2:9** then the Lord knows how to rescue the godly from trial and
> to keep the unrighteous (*adikous*) under punishment until
> the day of judgment.

The general contrast is that between the righteous and the unrighteous (Ziesler, p. 213). The false teachers are in the latter group, cf. 2:15, "forsaking the right way . . . , they have followed the way of Balaam, . . . who loved gain from wrongdoing (*adikias*)" and 2:13 where they are described as *adikoumenoi misthon adikias,* a wordplay meaning "damaged in respect to (i.e., cheated out of) the reward of unrighteousness."[159] To call Noah "a herald of righteousness" (2:5), in "the world of the ungodly," reflects not only the OT designation of him as righteous (Gen 7:1) but also the tradition that he preached repentance (*Jub.* 7.20–39; Jos. *Ant.* 1.3.1 §74; *1 Clem.* 7.6). It presumably means he announced God's just will and demand (Schelkle, p. 208, citing Wis 10:4, Sir 44:17, Philo, and Sibylline Oracles as evidence for a haggadic tradition; Grundmann, p. 93, adds more references, including *Gen. Rabba* 30 [18b]).

To speak of Lot as "righteous" (2:7) reflects not only the story contrast to "the licentiousness of the wicked" (2:7b) but usage at Wis 10:6 ("a righteous man" whom Wisdom rescued; cf. also *1 Clem.* 11:1). One may also compare Matthean usage (1:19; 23:29, 35) and Tannaitic use of *ṣaddîq* for OT worthies (Przybylski, p. 44). The 2 Peter account goes on parenthetically concerning Lot,

> **2:8** for by what that righteous man (*ho dikaios*) saw and heard as
> he lived among them, he was vexed in his righteous soul
> (*psychēn dikaian*) day after day with their lawless deeds.[160]

---

159. See BAGD, s.v. *adikeō* 2b and the literature cited there; Moffatt, "done out of the profits of their evil doing."

160. An alternate rendering is suggested by Schelkle for 2:8, attractive if the article *ho* is omitted (with MS Vaticanus) before *dikaios*: "for he was righteous with reference to seeing and hearing," i.e., in what people saw and heard of him; therefore "living among a people of lawless deeds, he was vexed in his righteous soul." This would refer to "inner" (8b) and "outer" righteousness (8a). Cf. the Vulgate's *aspectu enim et auditu iustus erat.* But reading *ho dikaios* and taking the dative as instrumental, Schelkle then adopts, with the majority of exegetes, the sense of the *RSV* above. Is this a case where the Vulgate rendering has encouraged a later distinction between "inner" and "outer" righteousness?

We thus have a threefold repetition about Lot as righteous, reflecting a strand of rabbinic interpretation that exalted him, in contrast to another line of rabbinic exegesis that looked at him unfavorably as a sinner because of Gen 19:30–38 (references in *JBC* 65:15). It seems idle to debate, with Ziesler (p. 140), whether "righteous under the old or the new covenant is intended." Our author is citing examples of those in the ancient world whom God delivered as "righteous" or "godly" persons, in contrast to the unrighteous and ungodly who received punishment. As in the OT, righteousness is in relation to a norm for conduct and relationships that God has revealed, relative to the time and situation. (All the examples in 2:4–10 are from the period described in Genesis, which is prior not only to Moses but even to Abraham.)

312   The condemnation in 2 Peter 2 against the false teachers and the Christian converts whom they hope to lure into their system warns (2:20) that if people, after escaping "the defilements of the world through the knowledge (*epignōsis*) of our Lord and Savior Jesus Christ," become again entangled and overpowered, "the last state has become worse for them than the first" (cf. Matt 12:45, applied now to apostates). Then the statement,

> **2:21** For it would have been better for them never to have known the way of righteousness (*epegnōkenai tēn hodon tēs dikaiosynēs*) than after having known it to turn back from the holy commandment delivered to them.

The thought is reminiscent of Heb 6:4–6, better to remain unconverted than to fall from faith afterward (Schelkle, p. 218). "Faith" is designated as "the way of righteousness" and the "holy commandment." The former phrase is reminiscent of Matt 21:32, which we took (§§239–240) as a salvation-history description of the course in which John the Baptist and Jesus came, according to God's will; the alternative there was "with a message about what God demands." Ziesler, here as at Matt 21:32, assigns the phrase under "man's righteousness" and specifically with the sense of "Christian behaviour" for 2:21 (p. 133). In 2 Peter there are obvious affinities to "the way of truth" (2:2)[161] and "the right way" vs. the "way of Balaam" (2:15). *Defensor fidei* probably means here by "the Way of righteousness" Christianity itself; note that one comes to know it through *epignōsis* (cf. 1:3, 8; 2:20), and compare "the Way" as a designation for early Christianity (Acts 9:2, etc.). For our author it included "faith" as a

---

161. Grundmann, pp. 89–91, calls attention in connection with 2 Pet 2:2 and 21 to the similar phrases in the *Apocalypse of Peter* (Akhmin fragment 22, 28; Hennecke-Schneemelcher, *New Testament Apocrypha* [Philadelphia: Westminster], Vol. 2 [1965], pp. 672 and 676) about those in "the place of punishment" who "had blasphemed the way of righteousness." He suspects a common tradition of ultimately wisdom origins. "Way" denotes a Lebenslehre, not "teachings as theory and action as practice" but interaction of the two.

bundle of doctrines (*fides quae*) and as an ethic of moral living, not libertinism (such as the licentious "errorists" show, 2:12–19). His illustrations in 2:4–10 do not suggest that the prepatriarchal figures there had the same *epignōsis* but simply that they illustrate how God always dealt with those righteous (according to current standards) in contrast to the unrighteous.

By the "holy command" (note the singular) "delivered" to us (cf. Jude 3) he does not mean the OT Mosaic code or "an unevangelical works righteousness" (Schelkle, p. 218)—though the line of argument and situation vs. the Gnostics "helped to recommend the O.T. with its decalogue and ethical teaching to the church" (Moffatt, p. 200)—but "the commandment of the Lord and Savior through your apostles" (3:2), which in turn seems to embrace doctrines, like the parousia, as well as ethics.[162] The apostles (3:2), especially Paul (3:15) and Peter (1:1, 16), are links or channels for making known knowledge of "the Way of righteousness."

313 Finally, at 3:13, in a section (3:11–13) after the scoffers have been refuted for their notion that things just go on and there is no longer hope that the Day of the Lord will come, our author uses apocalyptic to undergird his appeal for "lives of holiness and godliness" (v. 11). Christians are to wait for (and even hasten, perhaps by prayer, missionary endeavor, and repentance) "the Day of God" when heavens, earth, and all its works shall be dissolved by fire (an expectation widespread in apocalypticism and in Stoicism). Then the author says:

> **3:13** According to God's promise we wait for *new heavens* and *a new earth* in which righteousness dwells (*en hois dikaiosynē katoikei;* the italicized words of the translation are from Isa 65:17 and 66:22, perhaps the "promise" intended).

One point of the last four words in the verse is to indicate that in the promised future the unrighteous will have no place (Reicke, p. 182). That reinforces and leads into the admonition to proper living ("a clean, honest life," Moffatt, p. 210) while we wait (3:11, 14). Analyzed from the standpoint of *diakio*-terminology, this assertion on the new heavens and earth as "the home of justice" (*NEB;* cf. *Righteousness and Society,* pp. 91–92) may also reflect, as Ziesler insists (p. 143), a righteousness "clearly by God's creation, . . . more corporate than individual, and in a new world rather than in the present one"; in this way it serves as promise for those who seem to see the *adikoi* now in triumph; God will right things one day! We have a place and status depicted where God's people will finally be delivered, but this apocalyptic vision of what God will do serves in turn to encourage the orthodox church community to "wait" and "be zealous" therefore (3:14; cf. *Creation and New Creation,* p. 89). Schelkle (p. 230)

---

162. Cf. G. Schrenk, "The Christian Message as *entolē* in the Conflict against Gnosticism and Libertinism (the Johannine Writings and 2 Peter)," *TDNT,* 2, pp. 553–56, especially 555 (2 Peter moves closer to the *nova lex* of the postapostolic fathers).

goes further than seeing here just a reference to God's justice or to "the righteous persons" who will dwell in the new age. Because "righteousness" is so often a feature of the messianic age and "the Righteous One" a designation for the messiah (cf. *TDNT,* 2, pp. 186–87), he suggests that the righteousness unobtainable in this age that will come when the messiah returns is meant. Cf. Isa 32:1, 16–17 and Enoch 46:3, "the Son of man, who has righteousness, with whom righteousness dwells." It is a state or condition, connected with a Person, by God's promise.

314 b. *Summary* on "righteousness/justification" terms in 2 Peter— the document conceives of a way of righteousness and truth (2:21, 2) that included Noah, who heralded the righteousness God wills (2:5) and in which righteous Lot (2:7–8) walked, in contrast to the unrighteous and their lawless deeds in the prepatriarchal period. It is now a Way of righteousness attained by knowledge and faith on the basis of "the 'righteousness of God,' our God and savior Jesus Christ" (1:1), its teaching-and-manner-of-life differing sharply from that of the current false teachers. Eschatologically, God promises a new heavens and earth where "righteousness dwells" (3:13), i.e., when in the messianic age the righteous shall dwell around their Lord, who has "come," amid the conditions of *shalom* and justice envisioned in apocalyptic tradition.

The usage here is not Paul's, though it may seek to reflect some of his themes (3:15–16). It is not the OT and apocalyptic notion of vindicating, saving righteousness at the judgment, though something of that spirit underlies the book. It is not "rightwising" or "justification," but hints of that Pauline sense may lie behind our phrase at 1:1. What is involved? There is a suggestion of Heilsgeschichte, how God preserved Noah (2:5), rescued Lot (2:7), and has granted us great promises (1:4), which he will fulfill. Above all, in a new situation, facing (Gnostic) false teachers, our orthodox author has developed righteousness terminology in new ways as part of his attempt to translate the gospel in a pluralistic Hellenistic culture, reaching out to elements of it he deems acceptable while polemically rejecting other trends (Fornberg, pp. 146–48). *Dikaio*-language thus plays a varying but often important role from some of the oldest verses in the Bible (like Judg 5:11[163]) through the final book composed in the NT.

315 c. *A note about Frühkatholizismus.*[164] The *JBC* article on 2 Peter,

---

163. K. Stendahl: "perhaps the oldest piece of tradition in the whole Bible," the roots for "Paul's concept of justification" (*IDB* 1, p. 425).

164. **On 2 Pet and Early Catholicism,** cf. Käsemann, "Apologia" (n. 155 above); Fornberg (as in n. 155), pp. 3–6; Schelkle, HTKNT 13/2 on 2 Peter, "Exkurs: Spätapostolisches und frühkatholisches Zeugnis," pp. 241–45.

Further literature (Protestant): Käsemann, "Paul and Early Catholicism," in *New Testament Questions of Today* (Philadelphia: Fortress, 1969), pp. 236–51. W. Marxsen (n. 143 above), *"Frühkatholizismus,"* and his *Introduction,* pp. 242–44. G. Klein, "Der zweite Petrusbrief und der neutestamentliche Kanon," *Ärgernisse. Konfrontationen mit dem Neuen Testament* (Munich: Kaiser, 1970), pp. 109–14. U. Luz, "Erwägungen zur Entstehung des Frühkatholizismus," *ZNW* 65 (1974): 88–111. Siegfried Schulz, *Die Mitte der Schrift. Der*

in its discussion of "authenticity" and "canonicity" (which a decision for pseudonymity "does not prejudice," cf. Schelkle, pp. 245–48), observes:

> Today in German Lutheran circles the question of the place of 2 Pt in the canon has been reopened on the ground that the epistle shows objectionable signs of "early Catholicism." (65:2)

The term and issue of Frühkatholizismus crop up in discussions not only of 2 Peter but also of other NT books and reflect debates between—and among—Protestants and Catholics on Christian origins.

The term itself, Frühkatholizismus, which appears already in the nineteenth-century analyses by F. C. Baur and A. Ritschl (cf. also Rudolf Sohm) of late and post-NT developments (cf. Schulz), has been used by Käsemann and Marxsen, among others, to describe a Christianity with some or all of the following features: faith as *fides quae creditur,* a bundle of doctrines expressed in creeds; ministry as an office, indeed as priesthood; (monarchical) episcopacy, and thus hierarchical structures; a canon of inspired Scriptures; sacraments conceived as "medicine of immortality" and tied, like the Spirit, to the structures of a (hierarchical) ministry; the breakdown of eschatology as a focus of faith or concomitant of all doctrines and life, so that it becomes one doctrine among many, concerning "the last things"; and an appeal to some or all these elements of orthodoxy against heresies and heterodoxy. The term "early or incipient Catholicism," on the way to the patristic church, is frequently contrasted with the *Urgemeinde* or primitive Christianity.

316   Käsemann and others have tarred 2 Peter, among other documents, including Acts, with the brush of "early Catholicism," meaning for them a decline or deviation from earlier Christianity and its gospel, if not a "fall" in theology and practice from prior norms (e.g., in Paul on soteriology, or John in Christology and ecclesiology). But since 2 Peter and other such documents are in the canon, the admission of such development reflected within the church's collection of Holy Scripture has been hailed as significant by others: " 'Early catholicism' thus has a definite foothold

---

Frühkatholizismus im Neuen Testament als Herausforderung an den Protestantismus (Stuttgart: Kreuz, 1976). H.-J. Schmitz, *Frühkatholizismus bei Adolf von Harnack, Rudolph Sohm und Ernst Käsemann* (Themen und Thesen der Theologie, Düsseldorf: Patmos, 1977). C. Bartsch, *"Frühkatholizismus" als Katagorie historisch-kritischer Theologie, Eine methodologische und theologiegeschichtliche Untersuchung* (Studien zu jüdischem Volk und christlicher Gemeinde 3; Berlin: Institut Kirche und Judentum, 1980).

Roman Catholic discussions: F. Mussner, "Frühkatholizismus," *TTZ* 68 (1959): 237–45. H. Küng, "Der Frühkatholizismus im Neuen Testament als kontroverstheologisches Problem," *Theologische Quartalschrift* 142 (1962): 385–424, reprinted in *Das Neue Testament als Kanon: Dokumentation und kritische Analyse zur gegenwärtigen Diskussion,* ed. E. Käsemann (Göttingen: Vandenhoeck & Ruprecht, 1970), pp. 175–204.

within the canon—an important point which . . . has far-reaching implications for contemporary ecumenical discussion."[165]

Käsemann uses 2 Peter in order to fulminate against a canon containing such "testimony to the onset of early Catholicism," against an eschatology "concerned only with . . . the triumphal entry of believers into the eternal kingdom and with the destruction of the ungodly," and against a church that "identifies the Gospel with her own tradition" (p. 195). Similarly G. Klein. On the other hand, Schelkle (pp. 244–45, cf. 237) reproaches Käsemann for holding to a *sola scriptura* that is not *tota scriptura* and states himself that "2 Pet 3:15 begins the Roman-Catholic Church in the NT, the pillars and teachers of which are Peter and Paul as Roman princes of the apostles"; the concern of the Catholic exegete is to show that what happens here is not a perversion of what was original and true, but "genuine, valid development" (p. 245).

317 The question must, in honesty, be raised whether many of these features of "early Catholicism" do not have some earlier roots, even in Paul, and whether everything Käsemann sees in 2 Peter is really there. As a general rule, NT documents should be read in their own right, and not in light of later patristic emphases. 2 Peter does represent developments that are late and almost singular within the NT, but "Frühkatholizismus" and "frühkatholisch" may not be helpful or even appropriate descriptive terms.[166]

We would agree with Conzelmann's judgment[167] that the "catchword" Frühkatholizismus runs the danger that one thinks there can be found "a pure, original form of Christianity" behind later accretions. He refuses to equate the term with either the presence of "tradition" (*paradosis*) or "a fixed ordering of the ministry—even though this may already have a monarchical head. It first appears where the ministry has the quality of communicating salvation, where the working of the spirit and the sacrament are bound up with the ministry." The theology of Luke-Acts, another storm center, he does not therefore label as "early Catholic." We would do well to avoid it for 2 Peter, unless very carefully defined.

318 One recent treatment (Schenke-Fischer, 2, p. 328) sums up thus on 2 Peter. Its struggle against gnosis and its attempt to anchor Christian faith in history, especially Jesus' work, was and is necessary. But its lines of solution—including uncontested certainty about salvation, the abandoning of the world to corruption, and the preservation of the inheritance as a

---

165. Reginald Fuller, *The New Testament in Current Study* (New York: Scribner's, 1962), p. 95. Cf. above n. 108.

166. So H. Riesenfeld, "Criteria and Valuations in Biblical Studies," *Svensk exegetisk årsbok* 39 (1974): 78–79, cited with approval by Fornberg, p. 6.

167. H. Conzelmann, *Theology*, pp. xvi, 289–90. *History of Primitive Christianity* (Nashville: Abingdon, 1973), pp. 19–20. The quotations that follow in the paragraph above are from *History*, p. 20, and *Theology*, 290.

static possession assured through a Lehramt (O. Knoch says, through "the binding of all exposition to the church and the church, indeed, of Peter," p. 80)—come into question when compared with "the center of the NT, the message of Jesus about the reign of God, the Pauline doctrine of Rechtfertigung, and the Johannine proclamation about Christ." The question is whether 2 Peter, along with his offer of a solution, does not lead us on the wrong track (*einen Irrweg*). "In agreement with his intent and recognizing his difficult historical situation, we should seek after other ways to preserve the inheritance of the primitive Christian kerygma."

V. Summary Reflections over Righteousness / Justification as Expression of the Gospel

A. Die Mitte der Schrift

319   Beneath the surface of Catholic-Protestant discussion of scriptural material, and indeed in the debate over 2 Peter, often lurks the idea of "a canon within the canon"[168] and Catholic fears over it and therefore counterclaims for *"tota scriptura."* Typical is the comment that "Käsemann's solution [to the realization that there is 'early Catholic' material in the NT] has been to fall back on the canon within the canon or 'the center of the NT' " (*JBC* 67:94). Therefore this much abused and misunderstood term about the canon calls for some comment.

320   "Canon within the canon" seems to stem from Luther, rather than the Lutheran symbolical books. It is well known how Luther, in his practical work of translation, had to make decisions on text and canon. For the OT he followed the Hebrew; for the New he arranged the 27 books in his 1522 NT in such a way that James, Jude, Hebrews, and Revelation (not 2 Peter!) were printed at the end of the corpus, on unnumbered pages. This

---

168. The most important recent essays are probably in Ernst Käsemann, ed., *Das Neue Testament als Kanon* (n. 164 above), and Inge Lønning, *"Kanon im Kanon": Zum dogmatischen Grundlagenproblem des neutestamentlichen Kanons* (Forschungen zur Geschichte und Lehre des Protestantismus, Reihe 10, Band 43; Munich: Kaiser, and Oslo: Universitetsforlaget, 1972). Additional literature surveyed by Wolfgang Schrage, "Die Frage nach der Mitte und dem Kanon im Kanon des Neuen Testaments in der neueren Diskussion," in *Rechtfertigung* (Käsemann fs, 1976), pp. 415–42. Note, among other articles, H. Küng (as in n. 164 above); E. Haible, "Der Kanon des Neuen Testaments als Modellfall einer kirchlichen Wiedervereinigung," *TTZ* 75 (1966): 11–27; E. Schweizer, "The Need for a Canon within the Canon," in "Scripture-Tradition-Modern Interpretation," in his *Neotestamentica* (collected essays; Zürich & Stuttgart: Zwingli, 1963), pp. 208–10, and "Kanon?" *EvT* 31 (1971): 339–57.

latter choice reflected a doctrinal judgment that ranked books on the basis of the principle that "Christum treiben" (to "drive Christ" before our eyes) makes a book canonical, though there were other important factors in the case of James, for example (see above, § 273) or, e.g., the matter of the exclusion of "second repentance" in Hebrews (cf. 6:4–6, 10:26, 12–17).

To be precise, Luther rated NT books on three levels:

    I. John, Paul, 1 Peter, 1 John
    II. Synoptics, Acts, 2 Peter, 2–3 John
    III. James, Jude, Hebrews, Revelation[169]

Admittedly involved in his decisions were not only historical-critical factors but also a theological principle, which was *not*, however, "justification" but "Christ."

321 The Lutheran Confessions not only lack this classification scheme of Luther, they fail to include any list of "canonical books." Indeed, "canonical" is not used as a term. In the Confessions, as we have seen (§§ 1–23, above), "justification" is employed preeminently as expression of what the gospel is, though (especially in the CA and Ap.) in a broad sense and in conjunction with other expressions like "reconciliation" and "forgiveness of sins."

Lutheran orthodoxy spoke, as the church fathers had, of biblical books as *homologoumena* and *antilegomena* (books "acknowledged" and "disputed"), meaning by the latter books in the canon such as those Luther had doubts about, but later Lutheran dogmaticians accepted the authority of these "deuterocanonical" books too.[170]

322 Modern usage of "canon within the canon" tends to appear to be—and hence the Roman Catholic fear, as expressed above—a downgrading of certain books in the canon below others, the elevation of Paul to the peak of the whole NT, and the use of "justification" to judge documents in the Pauline corpus and the rest of the NT. Käsemann's analysis of 2 Peter lends credence to that fear when he says:

> The heart and motive force of the Pauline proclamation is the doctrine of justification. . . . Pauline eschatology . . . proclaims the sovereignty of God in the doctrine of justification. . . . II Peter has lost all real understanding of this 'He comes in triumph'; it is determined by the expectation of something impersonal—the divine nature. The sub-section has become the main subject; the Judge of the world has become the instrument of the apotheosis of the pious man. ("Apologia," pp. 182–83)

---

169. *WA,* Deutsche Bibel 7, p. 384.
170. Cf. Robert D. Preus, *The Theology of Post-Reformation Lutheranism* (St. Louis: Concordia, 1970), pp. 305 and 386, n. 148; cf. p. 31.

In the name of the whole Bible, Catholics fear the selection process, *sola pars scripturae* (Küng, p. 199), and the Sachkritik-functioning of "justification *sola fide.*"

323 It may be remarked that criticism of the "canon within the canon" principle can come from Protestants as well (e.g., H. Diem; cf. Schrage, pp. 421–24). Gerhard Maier's *The End of the Historical-Critical Method* is an onslaught against Luther's principle (which he dismisses as not binding because not in the Confessions) and against Käsemann; extremely put, "Whoever makes justification of the ungodly his focal point on which all theology should be based, and stamps this as the 'specifically Christian,' banishes important lines and basic thoughts of Scripture into powerless darkness" (p. 40). (For summary and response to Maier, cf. Stuhlmacher, *Historical Criticism*, pp. 66–71.[171])

324 The fact remains, however, that all Christians, and each confessional tradition, and most individual systematic theologians and exegetes do operate with a "canon inside the full canon," certainly in practice and often in theory.[172] The NT not only follows upon but stands above the Old, in authority and in revealing God in Christ and the Spirit. As regards Christology, the Fourth Gospel and Paul are the mainsprings for later normative Chalcedonian formulations. In ecclesiology, Matthew and Ephesians exert particular influence. For ethics, the Sermon on the Mount, 1 Cor 13, and (especially, we have noted in Roman Catholic thought) Gal 5:6 with Jas 2:14–26 have been influential. Even in the new three-year lectionary, where the effort was made to give a certain proportional balance to all books of Scripture, there are large areas omitted or underrepresented and others overemphasized, all on the basis of certain principles of selection. (Particularly unfortunate is the tendency not to hear the OT in its own right.[173])

325 The point is well taken that "in practice the Church does not accept the whole NT as equally normative" (*JBC* 67:97). That means, among other things, Raymond Brown cautions, that we ought to be particularly concerned "to pay more attention to Scripture when it disagrees with what we want to hear," remembering that "the Church itself stands under the judgment of Scripture" (cf. *Dei Verbum* 2.10; *JBC* 67:97 and 96).

For the Protestant, the aim is not to find "Frühprotestantismus" in the NT (the phrase is Haible's, pp. 13–14; it would not occur to most Lutherans). For all concerned, the goal is not to be "more neutestamentlich

---

171. W. Maier, *The End of the Historical-Critical Method,* trans. E. W. Leverenz and R. F. Norden (St. Louis: Concordia, 1977). P. Stuhlmacher, *Historical Criticism and Theological Interpretation of Scripture,* trans. R. A. Harrisville (Philadelphia: Fortress, 1977). Maier does end up accepting "Christ" as the center and heart of Scripture; cf. my comments in *Lutheran Hermeneutics* (cited above, n. 19), pp. 5–6, and nn. 13–19.

172. John P. Meier, *The Vision of Matthew* (cited above, n. 131), p. 226, suggests that for Matthew the OT prophets, not the law, were "the canon within the canon."

173. Cf. Arland J. Hultgren, "Hermeneutical Tendencies in the Three-Year Lectionary," in *Lutheran Hermeneutics* (cited above, n. 19), pp. 145–73, especially 152–53.

than the New Testament,"[174] but to allow the breadth which the NT does for faith and life, while reflecting in our days its emphases and centralities.
326 But we live in a day in NT scholarship when various answers are being given to the question of a central criterion for the NT. As Schrage outlines options, there are (1) Jesus and his message (Jeremias; E. Stauffer, who regards Paul as a decline from Jesus); (2) the creedal formulas of the early church (H. Schlier, R. J. Dillon, and others); (3) anthropology as the constant (H. Braun); (4) Christ (Vögtle, von Balthasar, Reicke), though in what sense "Christ" (who can even function *contra scripturam*) may need further definition.[175] Other answers doubtless exist; cf. the list just for Paul of what is "central" (above, §§192–216).
327 The Lutheran claim, in dialogue about justification, as regards Scripture and its center, can be put something like this. Assuming (cf. §§1–3, above) that the word of God, in particular the gospel of God, stands supreme over the church (and Scripture too), and that the apostolic gospel is preeminently witnessed to in the NT, which is the oldest written precipitate of testimony to the "Christ-event" (which is, in turn, centered in Jesus' death on the cross, resurrection by God, and exaltation as Lord), we are confronted repeatedly, at least for each age or generation, with the task of stating as clearly as possible what this gospel/word of God is according to the NT.

The gospel can, of course, be expressed in many ways in differing situations in the NT.[176] According to Jesus during his ministry, the good news

---

174. Hans Küng, *Structures of the Church* (New York: Thomas Nelson, 1964), p. 164, cf. pp. 154–69.

175. Details in Schrage (see n. 168 above), pp. 429–42, who himself argues for *Christus justificans* or *Christus pro nobis*. Literature on each option:

(1) J. Jeremias, *The Problem of the Historical Jesus* (FBBS 13; 1964); E. Stauffer, *Jesus, Paulus und wir* (Hamburg: Friedrich Wittig Verlag, 1961).

(2) H. Schlier, "Kerygma und Dogma," in *Die Zeit der Kirche* (Freiburg: Herder, 2nd ed., 1958), pp. 206–32; *Besinnungen auf das Neue Testament* (Freiburg: Herder, 1964), pp. 15–16; *Das Ende der Zeit* (Freiburg: Herder, 1971), pp. 302ff. Richard J. Dillon, "The Unity of the Gospel in the Variety of the Canon," *Catholic Theological Society of America Proceedings* 27 (1972): 85–115 (traditional statements of the gospel's central truth served as a *regula fidei* for proclamation).

(3) Herbert Braun, "The Meaning of New Testament Christology," in *God and Christ: Existence and Province* (*JTC* 5; 1968), pp. 89–127, and "Hebt die heutige neutestamentlich-exegetische Forschung den Kanon auf?" in *Das Neue Testament als Kanon* (cited above, n. 164), pp. 219–32.

(4) Anton Vögtle, "Kirche und Schriftprinzip nach dem Neuen Testament," *Bibel und Leben* 12 (1971): 153–62, 260–81; Hans U. von Balthasar, "Einigung in Christus," *Freiburger Zeitschrift für Philosophie und Theologie* 15 (1968): 171–89, esp. 187; Bo Reicke, "Einheitlichkeit oder verschiedene 'Lehrbegriffe' in der neutestamentlichen Theologie?" *Theologische Zeitschrift* 9 (1953): 401–15.

176. To present the different ways the OT and NT have of expressing the "good news" is the aim of the "Word and Witness" program of the Lutheran Church in America, used in over 2,000 congregations in the United States and Canada; cf. F. R. McCurley, Jr., and J. Reumann, *Understanding the Bible* (Philadelphia: LCA Division for Parish Services, 1977; rev. ed., Fortress Press, 1983).

was that "the kingdom of God is at hand" (Mark 1:14 and elsewhere). For the apostolic kerygma it was "Jesus' death and resurrection." In John's gospel it is "eternal life." In Paul we have seen a variety of ways of expressing the gospel, including (first in our list) "justification."

328 Because the Augsburg Confession, for good reasons in the sixteenth century, was oriented to Paul and his letter to the Romans (along with John, for Christology), Lutherans have been accustomed to seeing justification, so central in that epistle, as above all *the* expression of the gospel. Doubtless they have been too quick at times to read justification-terms into other biblical writings and have used it in a heavy-handed way as a standard. But their experience has been that justification *sola fide propter Christum* has served well in keeping God's work in Christ uppermost, to his glory, and that as "the doctrine of doctrines," justification can have a salutary effect for framing all other beliefs and guiding practices of the church.

But it must also be remembered that the CA and Apology interchange justification with other NT expressions as ways of stating the Gospel. Further, with the growth of historical study of Scripture, Lutheran exegetes and theologians have been as concerned as any to let the different uses of *dikaio*-language and alternate ways of proclaiming the gospel in other books of the Bible come to expression.

329 Put as simply as possible, the center of Scripture is "the gospel." The gospel, as it is appropriately expressed in each situation or document—Paul, Matthew, John, James, etc.—is the norm and standard for each part of Scripture.[177] Whether in terms of chronological priority (prepauline and Paul), bulk of references, spread of usage (OT, Pauline corpus, Matthew, 1 Peter, James, Hebrews, 2 Peter, etc.), an impressive case can be made for righteousness/justification terminology in terms of its continuity and centrality as a scriptural theme.

330 The conclusion of this paper is that the prevalence of righteousness/justification thought, even and especially when viewed under the impact of modern biblical scholarship, is even more impressive than the sixteenth-century confessors probably assumed, and certainly more varied than most Lutherans have realized. Appropriate to each document where such terms occur, and as the prime expression of "gospel" in the NT's first major theologian, Paul (with whom only John can compare in importance), it has a sound claim for centrality in Scripture. To this extent it functions as Mitte and Norm, directly in some parts of the NT and indirectly in others, with variations from Paul in meaning in certain authors, and on occasion conspicuous by its absence.

---

177. The appropriateness of the expression of "gospel" to *each* book or part of the Bible in its historical setting I have stressed in "Exegetes, Honesty and the Faith: Biblical Scholarship in Church School Theology," *Currents in Theology and Mission* 5 (1978): 16–32, esp. pp. 30–31.

B. Résumé on Righteousness/Justification

331   1. *Method:* Our survey has sought to examine every example of *di-kaio*-terminology in the NT (plus some using *adikos,* etc., with attention to problems like "good works," of concern to the dialogue), against the background of OT usage.

All cases of *dikaio*-nouns, verb, adjective, and adverb, from the root term *dikē,* "justice, punishment, vengeance" (cf. *TDNT* 2, pp. 178, 192; *NIDNTT* 3, pp. 352–53) require consideration because, even though our English translations may mask the fact with a variety of renderings, the Greek reader would be struck by the sameness of terms involved. Thus connections may then strike one, in working with the original languages, connections among what we speak of as "righteousness," "justification," "upright(ness)," "judgment," "vindication," "acquittal," "requirement," and even "liberation from." Perhaps even more might have been done with related terms like *adikos* and *ekdikeō* ("execute justice, punish, avenge").

332   This method of procedure, involved as it has been, is desirable because the *secondary literature,* in spite of the excellence of many recent monographs, is often *limited* to a single biblical author (Paul, Matthew), or book (Sam K. Williams's article on Romans, see n. 80) or a particular phrase like "righteousness *of God"* (so Stuhlmacher and Kertelge) or a specific area of controversy (Paul vs. James), or is set within a particular problematic (Ziesler's attempt to solve the difference between the Reformation and Trent by using for all biblical passages the categories of "forensic" and "ethical," and finding a key in his claim, p. 85, that in the intertestamental literature the verb is forensic, while the noun and adjective are "almost wholly ethical"; this pattern he then finds in the NT, e.g., pp. 163, 185, 212, so that Protestantism is right on the verb and Catholicism on the noun/adjective, pp. 1, 212). Even the sophisticated study by Pryzbylski on Matthew, with its conclusion that Matthean usage is to be explained best from Jewish usage (Qumran and Tannaitic: *dikaiosynē = ṣedeq; dikaios = ṣaddîq; eleēmosynē,* "almsgiving" = *ṣĕdāqâ;* all usages are to be taken in the sense of "the demand of God upon man to live according to a certain norm, the law," p. 105, yet Matthew, we are told, does teach that salvation is a gift of God, *sola gratia*—if not through *dikaio*-terms, then rather through the verb *eleeō,* as at 9:27, 15:22, 17:15, 20:30–31, and in verses like 1:21 and 26:28, so p. 106), may be termed "flawed" because of his decision not to treat the verb in his Jewish sources on the grounds that *dikaioō* does not play "a significant role" in Matthew (p. 7; it does occur at 11:19 and 12:37). The decision is surprising after his criticisms of Ziesler and Fiedler on methodology, pp. 6–7, and his own references to verb forms (e.g., p. 136, n. 174, where it is noted that in 1QH the verb *sdq* means "man can become righteous only by means of God's grace"; p. 143, n. 144; and cf. pp. 108–10, where both noun and verb are used to ascertain the meaning of "disciple"). The ancients did not limit their concept of something just to nouns or verbs; the full picture emerges

only from all the evidence. Proper use of the "word study method" therefore calls for examination of all pertinent terms in the context of the passages where they occur.

333   Finally, regarding methodology, we have often made sharper distinctions between "prepauline, Paul, and postpauline," e.g., than many discussions have been accustomed to offer. While some of this analysis is problematical, it does allow us better to explain variations in meaning for *dikaio*-terms and to suggest the likely course of development, with its ups and downs, for righteousness/justification in the NT.

334   By and large our account has been limited to the canonical literature. For extracanonical Christian developments, which generally take the form of understanding *dikaiosynē/dikaioō* as "justice" in an ethical sense, as something the Christian *does*, cf. *Righteousness and Society,* pp. 86–93, and the paper by Robert Eno for this dialogue (e.g., in the patristic centuries there was "development of a theology which taught salvation by God's grace but which was . . . in danger of viewing the Christian life as a new form of law").

336   2. *Findings.* (See chart, § 335.) Against a background of wide usage in the ancient Near East, "righteousness" terminology, centering around the root *ṣdq* in Hebrew, provides a rich and basic OT theme, related to the covenant, worship, ethics, and eschatology in Israel, in her view of God, salvation, creation, and wisdom. Particularly important was "the righteousness of God," not only as a norm for relationships and in forensic situations (at the judgment) but also for God's saving actions. The terms also find frequent reference with regard to human beings, especially in the sense of moral and ethical "uprightness," in relation to God's norms for a situation, in relationships with one another, and with God.

337   Such OT usage continued, with further development of its own, in the emerging forms of Judaism, especially in connection with (distributive) justice and moral living (so, in the rabbinic sources) but also for God's judgment and forgiveness/justification of those deeply conscious of their sins (so Qumran).

338   Though neither Jesus nor the kerygma in Acts made particular use of the righteousness/justification categories, the little creeds and slogans of the early church about Jesus' death and its meaning (cf. Dillon, above, §326, n. 175 [2], on the importance of these) readily employed the theme: Jesus is the Righteous One who died for the unrighteous, who was then vindicated by God; he is "righteousness for us," in him we are rightwised; the "Christ event" of cross and resurrection was "for our justification," so that we might become "the righteousness of God." In this pre- and nonpauline Christian theologizing, which reflects in turn the central NT concepts, lies the basis for important future lines of development.

339   Paul took over this terminology. He uses it soteriologically, christologically, and in ethical teaching, in his eschatologically-charged theology. Righteousness/justification comes into special prominence in the

335 (Chart on "Findings")
THE DEVELOPMENT AND IMPORTANCE
OF RIGHTEOUSNESS/JUSTIFICATION
IN THE NEW TESTAMENT WRITINGS

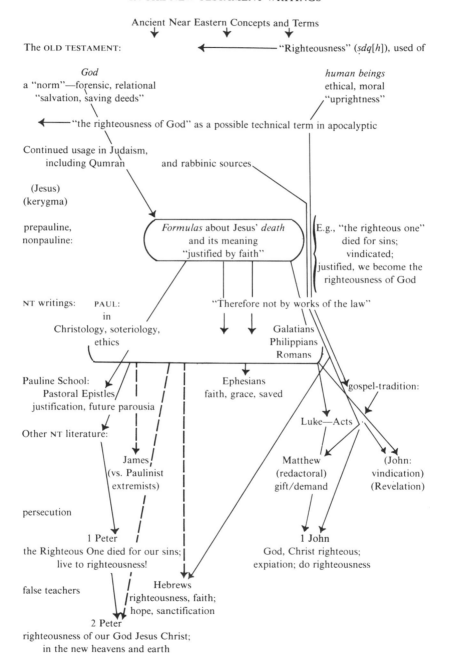

Ancient Near Eastern Concepts and Terms

The OLD TESTAMENT: ←———————— "Righteousness" (*sdq*[*h*]), used of

God
a "norm"—forensic, relational
"salvation, saving deeds"

human beings
ethical, moral
"uprightness"

←——"the righteousness of God" as a possible technical term in apocalyptic

Continued usage in Judaism,
including Qumran   and rabbinic sources

(Jesus)
(kerygma)

prepauline,
nonpauline:

Formulas about Jesus' *death*
and its meaning
"justified by faith"

E.g., "the righteous one"
died for sins;
vindicated;
justified, we become the
righteousness of God

NT writings: PAUL:
in
Christology, soteriology,
ethics

"Therefore not by works of the law"

Galatians
Philippians
Romans

Pauline School:
Pastoral Epistles
justification, future parousia

Ephesians
faith, grace, saved

gospel-tradition:

Other NT literature:

Luke—Acts

James
(vs. Paulinist
extremists)

Matthew
(redactoral)
gift/demand

(John:
vindication)
(Revelation)

persecution

1 Peter
the Righteous One died for our sins;
live to righteousness!

1 John
God, Christ righteous;
expiation; do righteousness

false teachers

Hebrews
righteousness, faith;
hope, sanctification

2 Peter
righteousness of our God Jesus Christ;
in the new heavens and earth

188

letters to the Galatians and to the Philippians. What the polemical situations there bring to the fore is not "justification by faith" (for that was more widespread apostolic Christianity), but "by faith" in contrast to "by works of the law" (as urged by the "Judaizers"). In Romans Paul most comprehensively puts the gospel he proclaims into terms of "God's righteousness" and our justification. Righteousness is revealed in the gospel as saving power from God, given in Christ through faith to persons under sin who are brought, each one, "into Christ," "unto sanctification," in a community of faith, ultimately to salvation in all its fullness. There are frequent overtones of the corporate nature of this righteousness, far beyond the individual believer, as God's faithfulness to his whole creation, to Jew and Gentile alike (i.e., all human beings).

340   The later (deutero)pauline literature continued to emphasize righteousness/justification, each document in its own situation. Ephesians, though devoid of any apocalyptic setting, stresses "salvation" ("saved," rather than "justified") "by grace through faith," with the corporate-ecclesiastical and ethical aspects strong. The Pastoral Epistles preserve Paul's formula "justified by grace" through Christ in contrast to "works done by us in righteousness," and reintroduce the factor of future fulfillment so prominent in Paul. The imperative to "live righteously" is accelerated too.

341   In the Pauline evidence a new "pattern of religion" can be seen, using righteousness/justification categories as prime concepts, a pattern different from anything current in Judaism and one not sustained in Christianity in ensuing patristic centuries.

342   The prominence that the early Christian creedal expressions of the gospel gave to righteousness/justification terms, and that Paul and his school developed, has not been retrojected into the gospel tradition to any extent. Luke preserves one parable from Jesus about the publican who was "justified" with God; Acts speaks of Jesus as "the Righteous One" through whom people are "justified" (forgiven, freed, in believing, from what the law could not free people). Matthew has his own redactional usage of "righteousness" to denote both ethical demand and, we suggested also, the gift and even perhaps the way of salvation. John's few uses of the term "righteousness" echo the OT: God vindicates Jesus. The First Epistle of John speaks more fully of how God is righteous and how Jesus Christ, the Righteous One, is expiation for our sins and cleanses us; we are therefore to "do righteousness." Revelation emphasizes, amid apocalyptic judgment, our holding fast in doing righteousness.

343   Hebrews has its own way of stressing Jesus' death "once for all" while employing "righteousness" and "faith" terminology, indeed even speaking of "the righteousness which comes by faith." One can see why centuries of tradition linked Hebrews with the Pauline corpus, yet also why modern scholarship brings out different nuances in this effort to proclaim the same gospel along lines of cultic, priestly thought and of sanctification.

344   While James has often been pitted by later theologians against Paul, we found James an attempt to speak in simple, practical terms against a kind of Paulinism that had misinterpreted "faith alone" in a one-sided way. In such a situation, where salvation by "works of the law" after accepting Christ was not the immediate threat it had been in Paul's day, James sought, by the formula "faith and works," to defend that which had been Paul's concern.

345   1 Peter, as a document "Pauline" in thought, shows the ongoing importance of righteousness/justification in a time when believers suffer (persecution) "for righteousness' sake." Christ, the Righteous One, died for our sins, so that we might "live to righteousness," grace being prominent for those "in Christ."

346   2 Peter, in yet another type of situation, conceives of a "way of righteousness" going back to prepatriarchal times; a "faith of equal standing" for apostles and people, for Jews and Gentiles, on the basis of the " 'righteousness of God,' i.c., our God and savior Jesus Christ"; and the promise of the new heavens and new earth where righteousness dwells. Thus at the outer edge chronologically of the NT canon, we hear echoing one of the oldest biblical themes, from the OT and in earliest post-Easter Christianity, God's righteousness, now thoroughly christologized, and still the object of fulfillment to come from God.

C. Retrospect and Reflection

347   Righteousness/justification as a scriptural theme has, of course, its limitations and drawbacks. It is, for example, not found in any form in some books of the Bible and dare not be interpolated in its Pauline sense into authors not demonstrably in contact with Pauline theology. Its forensic aspect makes it less welcome to the modern mind than certain other NT expressions for salvation and allows it to fall prey to legalistic lines of interpretation.

But almost no concept is featured in *every* book of the Bible. The considerable spread of righteousness/justification as a theme among NT writers in varying situations is far greater than one might have supposed, and few concepts have had a history of development over so many biblical and Christian centuries. What is more, God as judge and the lawsuit, lawcourt motif have an abiding value, which we lose at our peril theologically. What God does in his dispute with Israel or judgment of Jew and Gentile—or, better, has done for us in Jesus Christ—is what is significant.

348   The Lutheran experience testifies that justification by grace through faith as the exemplary expression of the gospel has been salutary for theology and church life in directing attention to God's work for us and our response to him in the world. What is present in such prominence biblically and what often existed in our common prereformation tradition regarding God, namely righteousness/justification, Lutherans have in their massive use of this theme[178] found to be beneficial, a blessing, and something indispensable.

The Reformation choice of justification as central in the CA can then be supported by considerations of fidelity to the experience of Luther and others and their study of Scripture (not just Romans and Galatians but also Isaiah and Psalms), and also of their desire to be biblical while being ecumenically irenical at Augsburg. And what better NT book on which to rest a claim than Romans, the starting point ever so often for developing a systematic theology?

349 But contemporary biblical investigation makes the case for righteousness/justification even stronger and more intriguing, we have found, in Paul, the rest of the NT and even the OT, than the Reformation fathers may have suspected. While Lutherans today are impressed with the soundness of the choice made in 1530 by CA 4 and find it bolstered by the fact that it existed as an expression of the gospel prior to Paul and by its development afterward, they also recognize that elsewhere the gospel could be—and was—expressed in other ways and that even Paul had varied concepts in which to put God's good news. But that the gospel of God stand supreme, and that it is, in their experience and so often exegetically, spelled out paradigmatically as justification, is their concern, testimony, and commitment.

350 Lutherans have chosen to be a bit like the hedgehog in the Greek poet's contrast, "The fox knows many things, but the hedgehog knows one big thing."[179] (No implications about Catholic "foxes," or Sir Isaiah Berlin's use of the contrast!) The "one big thing" they have found in Scripture and experienced to be of greatest value in the church is justification. There are "many other things" that Jesus did (John 21:25), many other things that the apostles preached and Paul taught (cf. 2 Pet 3:16). But this "one needful thing" they have chosen, the word of God as good news in terms of God's rightwising power for salvation and life.

351 Once again: Righteousness/justification is not, for Lutherans, simply "a 'theology of the threshold,' " as the Anglican H. E. W. Turner says he was taught at school, but it is rather the whole and the heart of the gospel, that norm in all relationships, such as *ṣdq* was in the OT. Turner's

---

178. For a recent example, cf. Wilfried Härle and Eilert Harms, *Rechtfertigung: Das Wirklichkeitsverständnis des christlichen Glaubens* (Uni-Taschenbücher 1016; Göttingen: Vandenhoeck & Ruprecht, 1979). Its "systematic unfolding" of the doctrine of justification touches on ontology, anthropology, economic theory, ethics, history, and eschatology. Its outline of the biblical base (pp. 16–40), while confined to Paul, is suggestive in its treatment of how his prior understanding was reshaped by the kerygma (formulas) of the (Hellenistic) church and by the revelation of Christ to him.

179. Archilochus, *poll' oid' alōpēx all' echinos hen mega.* Text in Ernest Diehl, *Anthologia Lyrica Graeca* (Leipzig: Teubner), Vol. 1, 2d ed. (1936), frag. 103. Cf. I. Berlin, *The Hedgehog and the Fox: An Essay on Tolstoy's View of History* (New York: Simon & Schuster, 1953).

rather surprising discovery, in dialogue with Scandinavian Lutherans at Helsinki (in 1952), was the "important consequences in Christian Spirituality" that "Justification by Faith Alone" has; as he put it,

> Positively these include a relationship to God which includes commitment and surrender as an indispensable ingredient, the understanding of the Christian life (which includes Christian conduct) as a response to God's saving initiative in Christ, with the marks of gratitude, dependence, and responsive love. Negatively it stands as a beacon light against any attempt by the Church to absolutize itself, to turn itself from a penultimate into an ultimate, to forget that it is still *in via* and not yet *in gloria,* the pilgrim people of God.[180]

This "one big thing," righteousness/justification, Lutherans find to be the gospel and the doctrine of doctrines, ever God's power to salvation.

---

180. H. E. W. Turner, "Justification by Faith in Modern Theology," in *New Testament Christianity for Africa and the World: Essays in honour of Harry Sawyerr,* ed. Mark E. Glasswell and Edward W. Fasholé-Luke (London: SPCK, 1974, pp. 100 and 111.

The Biblical Basis of
Justification by Faith:
Comments on the Essay
of Professor Reumann

──────────────────────────────**2**

Joseph A. Fitzmyer, S.J.

352   We are all indebted to Professor John Reumann for a masterful and comprehensive survey of the biblical data related to the Reformation emphasis on justification by grace through faith. It contains many points of clarification that will spark further discussion among us and also relates much modern scholarly study of justification in the OT and the NT to our ongoing dialogue. His characteristic thoroughness leaves us all in his debt.

My comments on his paper will point out (1) issues that are easily agreed on or that would find little disagreement from modern Roman Catholic theologians or exegetes; (2) areas that perhaps need further clarification; and (3) problems of interpretation that may still seem divisive. Rather than single out elements in Reumann's discussion that could be classified under these three headings, I prefer to comment on his material in the order in which he has presented it from one or another of these three viewpoints. My aim, then, is not so much to present a rival Roman Catholic discussion—which would be very repetitious, because of the vast amount of agreement that I find with Reumann's treatment of the biblical material—as to advance our ecumenical dialogue on this issue of fundamental importance. Nor is it my aim to play at bibliographical one-upmanship; Reumann has covered the biblical material to be cited very well, and only in rare instances shall I call attention to items of further interest. I also realize that I am reacting to his essay from a personal Roman Catholic viewpoint; my colleagues may want to react a little differently at times.

I

353   Regarding the preliminary paragraphs (§§1–4), I make the following comments:

(1) Roman Catholics will agree that:

(a) "The gospel stands as norm and rule over the church, Ministry and ministries, bishops, councils, pope, and all the life of God's people" (§1). This is a point of agreement that is found in the Malta Report.[1]

(b) The gospel "sets forth what God has done for us in Christ" (§1).

---

1. See "The Gospel and the Church," in *Evangelium—Welt—Kirche: Schlussbericht und Referate der römisch-katholisch/evangelisch-lutherischen Studienkommission "Das Evangelium und die Kirche", 1967–1971* (ed. H. Meyer; Frankfurt am M.: O. Lembeck; J. Knecht, 1975), #20, 33 (pp. 40, 43). Cf. *Worship* 46 (1972): 332, 335; LW 19 (1972): 262, 264.

(c) The "gospel" or "word (of God)" is the "oral proclamation of the message from and about God" (§2).[2]

(d) Even that " 'the word of God' [is] supreme over the church and, indeed, over the Bible" (§2)—provided, in the latter case, it is recognized that God's word is not known to us independently of "the Bible" (= the *written* word of God).

(e) Even that the principle *ecclesia semper reformanda* is to be applied to "the restatement of doctrine in new situations . . ." (§§2, 5). This has been admitted in principle in "Teaching Authority and Infallibility in the Church" and in *Mysterium ecclesiae*.[3]

(f) Even that the law/gospel contrast (§3) is a valid aspect of "the word of God," although this contrast has not been one that has normally received Roman Catholic emphasis.

354   (2) Further clarification would be needed before I agree that "the gospel is expressed above all as 'justification' " and that the latter is "the article on which 'rests all that we teach and practice' " (§1 quoting CA 4 and Smalcald Articles II.I:5). I realize that further clarification is offered by Reumann below (§§5, 7–23, cf. 327–30, 348, 350–51).

II

355   Regarding Reumann's introduction, which reviews the Reformation claim (§§5–23), I readily acknowledge the problems mentioned in his note on methodology and biblical terminology (§§24–26); one always has to keep those in mind in this sort of discussion.

(1) Roman Catholics will agree that:

(a) Justification/salvation "rests solely on 'the entire Christ' in his obedience, not on our love or virtues; it means forgiveness of sins, and also repentance, with love and good works following" (§11, quoting Formula, Epitome III:3–11).

(b) The concept and nature of justification can be admitted as described (§12), as excluding "all confidence in our *works and merits*" (§13), when these are understood as coming solely from us, and that the conditions of justification are not our works but "God's gift, Christ's righteousness [even though this last term is not particularly a NT way of putting it, much less a way that Roman Catholics would phrase it], and faith" (§14).

(c) In a sense one can consider justification to be "the same thing" as *regeneratio, vivificatio,* even reconciliation, salvation, forgiveness of sins, since all these aspects of the relationship between God and human beings

---

2. Here "gospel" is being used in the sense of "the word of God," as the latter was understood in Vatican Council II, *Dei Verbum* #2–4. For an earlier Roman Catholic use of "gospel" as a comprehensive term, see the Council of Trent, session IV, *Decretum de libris sacris et de traditionibus recipiendis,* par. 1: ". . . puritas ipsa Evangelii . . ." (DS 1501).

3. See *TS* 39 (1979): 143; or *Teaching Authority and Infallibility in the Church* (cited above, Editor's Note, n. 1), p. 44. See also *Acta Apostolicae Sedes* 65 (1973): 396–408, esp. pp. 402–03; trans. in *Catholic Mind* 71 (no. 1276, Oct. 1973): 54–64, esp. pp. 58–59.

come ultimately from God himself (who is the sole origin of that relationship) through the work of Christ and his Spirit/grace; they are all appropriated by human beings solely by faith, understood indeed not as something excluding "word or sacraments but solely . . . any claim of merit on our part" (§§15, 12). But I should prefer, at least on biblical grounds, to distinguish these aspects of God's action in us, recognizing that they are biblical images that describe different formalities of one complex whole (viz., the relationship itself). I am happy to note the "series of steps" set forth (§15, from SD, III:17–28) that tend to recognize some difference of aspect. (More on this later.)

(d) "The only essential and necessary elements of justification" are those listed, provided "faith" is understood as described above at the beginning of c, even though the "narrow" definition of it is transcended (see further below).

(e) Art. 4 of CA (as quoted above, §19) contains a genuine understanding of "justification," as far as it goes.

356   (2) I should require further clarification on the following points:

(a) Where does one find that the "biblical usage of justification terms may reflect both a 'broader' and a 'more narrow' sense" (§15)? The difficulty is the phrase "justification terms," which immediately implies that in *biblical usage* all of those mentioned in II/1c above enjoy a fluidity or can without further ado be understood as "justification terms." Where in the Bible is "justification" understood as "a broad 'salvation' term"? This will be sensed especially as a problem in the interpretation of Pauline passages.

(b) What is meant by " 'the eternal and essential righteousness' of God . . . connected with the indwelling of God in the believer, which follows upon justification . . ." (§17, referring to *SD* III:54–58)? Is this only another way of saying what Luther meant by *iustitia Dei* as *iustitia aliena*? If so, how can it then be that which "God manifests toward the impenitent and despisers of his Word" (§17, quoting *SD* XI:86)?

(c) What does the "fluidity" that existed "around 1530" (§21) and in "subsequent theological and exegetical treatment" in the Lutheran tradition mean for us in this dialogue? Is such fluidity more normative than later, less fluid formulations (e.g., in Lutheran Orthodoxy)?

III

357   Reumann has done well to include a consideration of OT teaching on righteousness (§§27–48) because, even if the biblical basis of the Reformation emphasis on justification by grace through faith is more immediately derived from Pauline teaching, Paul himself insisted that "the righteousness of God has been manifested apart from the law, although the law and prophets bear witness to it" (Rom 3:21). And he asks, "Do we then overthrow the law by this faith? By no means! On the contrary, we uphold the law" (Rom 3:31), i.e., we uphold the teaching of the OT itself. Hence, no understanding of justification in the NT is really possible with-

out some comprehension of its OT background and that of intertestamental literature prior to it.

358 When it comes to comments on Reumann's presentation of the OT data on *ṣdq* and its cognates (§§28–48), I should like to make the following points:

(a) In general, I should have preferred a more separated treatment of the Hebrew data, the LXX usage, and the pertinent material of the intertestamental literature, because Paul is more clearly influenced by the Greek OT than by its original form and because the treatment of *sedeq*, etc., in Qumran literature, for all its surface resemblance to Pauline justification, is at once a development of certain OT ideas and yet not quite that of NT justification.

359 (2) I am in basic agreement with Reumann's presentation (§§27–36) of Hebrew *sedeq* as a comprehensive relational idea, expressing at times the relationship of God to human beings and the world and at times that of human beings among themselves (whether as kings and commoners [Jer 23:5], or as neighbors and brothers/sisters). But it is not possible to leave it merely as "relationship" (*pace* Cremer et al.); it needs further specification, be it societal, or even judicial.

(a) Hence, I agree with Reumann's insistence on the relational idea of *sedeq* as both ethical and forensic, depending on the contextual use of it. In its first appearance in the Bible it is used of Noah in an ethical sense (Gen 6:9, "Noah was a righteous man ['*îš ṣaddîq*], blameless [*tamîm*] in his generation, and he walked with God")—said of an individual in an obviously pre–Mosaic–law context. However, the piel and hiphil conjugations of the verb *ṣdq* were often used in the OT with a forensic connotation, "declare to be righteous, in the right, acquitted," in a context suggestive of God's tribunal. This is the "delocutive" use of the verb.[4]

If the ethical meaning of *ṣaddîq*, "righteous" (etc.), could be understood in the OT without reference to the Mosaic law (e.g., Gen 6:9; 7:1; 15:6; 18:19), i.e., as conducting oneself in a right relation with God or human beings, it came in time to designate a mode of conduct consonant with the covenant and to express a specific covenantal relationship (Isa 54:9–17; Hos 2:18–19) or one consonant with the Mosaic law (e.g., Isa 51:7 [Israel as *yōdĕ'ê sedeq, 'am tôrātî*, "(those) knowing righteousness, the people of my law"]). Covenantal characteristics of "fidelity," "steadfast love," "loyalty" were associated with it (e.g., Jer 9:24; Ps 143:1–2), as was the "observance" of the Mosaic law (e.g., Ezek 18:5–9). These modes of understanding flesh out the skeleton of "righteousness" as relational, giving it both a societal and a judicial nuance.

(b) I also agree with Reumann's analysis of *sedeq* as applied to God (§35). Not only is he the "Righteous One" (Isa 24:16, probably intended in an ethical sense), but he too judges with righteousness (Ps 9:9, 96:13, 98:9; Isa 11:4; cf. Lev 19:15), clearly affirmed in forensic contexts. To such pas-

---

4. See D. R. Hillers, "Delocutive Verbs in Biblical Hebrew," *JBL* 86 (1967): 320–24.

sages I should relate the idea of Yahweh's *rîb,* "lawsuit," with Israel (Jer 12:1, etc.). I should prefer, however, to emphasize that *ṣedeq* becomes the quality or attribute par excellence that describes Yahweh's activity toward his people and the world, because it was to be understood as the quality par excellence that was to characterize the conduct of Israelites and human beings in general.[5] In the long run, that too is the reason why, if ancient Canaanites had venerated a god *Ṣedeq* in their pantheon (I agree with Reumann's explanations, above, §31 of the theophoric names, *Malkî-ṣedeq,* "My king is Ṣedeq," *'Adōnî-ṣedeq,* "My lord is Ṣedeq"[6]), the Israelites insisted that 'Yahweh is our Ṣedeq/our righteousness' (*Yhwh ṣidqēnû,* Jer 23:6). In this instance, however, it is not easy to decide about the nuance of *ṣedeq* that would have been intended.

(c) I also agree that Yahweh's vindication of his people finds expression at times in his "triumphs" (*ṣidqôt Yhwh,* Judg 5:11). This may, indeed, be part of the "holy war" theme; but it may also be part of the *rîb*-theme, mentioned in III. 2.b above, i.e., Yahweh's victories in a lawsuit with Israel (i.e., in a forensic context); see 1 Sam 12:7; Mic 6:5.

(d) I also agree with Reumann that Yahweh's vindication of his people is eventually cast in terms of "salvation," especially in postexilic writings; in this vein I should stress those passages cited by him (above, §§35, 37, 38; cf. Ps 98:2 [*yěšû'ātô/ṣidqātô*]; Neh 9:6–37; Ezra 9:6–15). Here Yahweh's righteousness and other covenantal qualities are extolled in the salvation of a remnant; postexilic Israel stands before Yahweh's tribunal and sings of his deliverance, brought about in a saving judgment.

360   (3) As can be seen from the comments made so far, I am in basic agreement with Reumann's analysis of the OT data. Here I should like to stress one aspect of the data a little more than he has done—this is not really a point of disagreement. In the matter of God's righteousness and the relationship it expresses between him and humanity (or the world), one must stress the priority of God's activity toward sinful human beings, Israel or the world in general. It is not merely that "no living human being is righteous" before him (Ps 143:2), but that Yahweh gratuitously seeks out faithless Israel and will not let it go off from him. Listen to Hosea's prophecy, "I will heal their faithlessness; I will love them freely, for my anger has turned from them" (14:4); or earlier, "I will make for them/you a covenant on that day with the beasts of the field . . . , and I will betroth you to me forever; I will betroth you to me in righteousness and in justice, in steadfast love, and in mercy" (2:18–19).

361   (4) I am, however, somewhat skeptical about Yahweh's righteousness in its alleged relation to creation and cosmic order in the OT. True, Daniel in his prayer exclaims that "Yahweh our God is righteous in all the

---

5. To borrow an expression from later Scholastic theology, predication by the *via positiva* and *eminentior* was at work here.

6. See my discussion of these names in *Essays on the Semitic Background of the New Testament* (London: Chapman, 1971; reprinted, SBLSBS 5, 1974), pp. 229–31.

works that he has done" (*kî ṣaddîq Yhwh ʾĕlōhênû ʿal kol maʿăśāyw ʾăšer ʾāśáh,* 9:14). But does "all the works that he has done" enable us to extend "righteousness" to such things as creation, the cosmic order of the universe? When Reumann (§47) says, in dependence on Reventlow, that "all of God's acts may thus be seen in the OT as Rechtfertigungsgeschehen," I hesitate. Earlier (§32), Reumann had referred to H. H. Schmid in a similar vein. But the only OT passage to which he referred was Jer 31:35–36, which may indeed refer to Yahweh's fixed order of the cosmos, but it contains no mention whatever of his *sedeq* (or any of its cognates). Moreover, apropos of §47, I fail to see how Yahweh's *sedeq* is involved in his gracious election of persons such as Abraham (Gen 12:2–3), or in the kerygma of the Deuteronomist's history. Reumann himself seems to be skeptical of this approach (see §48), and I share that skepticism. Certainly, none of the OT passages cited in §47 call for a consideration of the *cosmic* dimension of justification.[7]

What I am concerned about in this regard is the tendency in some modern discussions of either God's "righteousness" or of "justification" in both the OT and the NT to sever the relationship (rightly found in these concepts) from its judicial moorings. If one detects that the notion of *sedeq* does undergo a shift in postexilic writings toward a way of expressing God's salvific bounty or activity toward sinful humanity or sinful Israel (see §359, III. 2.d above), it is still something that he exercises in a judicial setting; it is his salvific bounty or activity manifested in a just judgment— and that differs from a manifestation of his power in creation or in governing the universe.

362   (5) When the OT message of God's righteousness and justification was translated into Greek, the complex of *sedeq*-terms significantly found expression in Greek words of the stem *dik-*, which carried its own philosophical nuances, chief among which was the idea of conformity to a norm (usually the obligations of polite society). Covenantal obligation and obedience to the Mosaic law were then seen to be more of a norm than might have been detected in the Hebrew tradition itself. Reumann has cited (§41) two ways in which the LXX usage has been characterized. Even though this usage is scarcely divested of judicial nuances, *dikaiosynē* is at times strikingly used to render other covenantal qualities of Yahweh: *ʾĕmet*, "fidelity" (Gen 24:49; Josh 24:14; 38:19, etc.); *ḥesed*, "steadfast love" (e.g., Gen 19:19; 20:13; 21:23). This mode of translation is undoubtedly influ-

---

7. Perhaps a contrast might be permitted here, in order to point up the difficulty; though it is drawn from Pauline theology and not from the OT, it is intended solely as a way in which a cosmic dimension has been found in Pauline thinking, which it might not otherwise have had. Consider Rom 11:15 ("the reconciliation of the world") or 2 Cor 5:19 ("God was in Christ reconciling the world to himself"). Here the effect of the Christ-event viewed as *katallagē,* "reconciliation," has a scope not limited to human beings (i.e., anthropological), but concerns even the *kosmos* (hence cosmic). If we had OT passages of a similar nature, in which Yahweh's "righteousness" were given a cosmic dimension, then the cosmic consideration of Rechtfertigungsgeschehen might have some plausibility.

enced by the postexilic understanding of *ṣedeq* in its relation to "salvation."

363   (6) As for the development of *ṣedeq*-ideas in the intertestamental literature of the Jews, I agree with Reumann's introductory description of the conviction among the Essenes of Qumran about their utter sinfulness in the sight of a righteous God: "God's absolute righteousness is heightened alongside human depravity" (§42). Here one detects a noteworthy advance of emphasis over most OT passages. Not only does one find in this literature the precise term *ṣedeq 'ēl,* "the righteousness of God" (1QM 4:6)—Paul's term (e.g., Rom 1:17), which is never found exactly in the OT, despite its emphasis otherwise on God's righteousness[8]—but even sentiments that resemble Paul's insistence that "all have sinned" (Rom 3:23) and that human righteousness comes gratuitously from God alone (cf. Rom 3:20). Reumann has appealed to the *Manual of Discipline* (1QS 11:2–6, 12–15) as an example of Qumran thinking that comes remarkably close to that of Paul. One could also appeal to the Thanksgiving Psalms (1QH 4:30–31; 15:12–25). But I am not happy with the Vermes translation of 1QS 11 that he uses; it is a bit too "Christian" for my understanding of the text. *Mišpāṭî* is simply not the equivalent of "justification" in lines 2, 5, 12, 14.[9] It should rather be translated simply as "judgment." This may deprive it of some of the resemblance to Pauline thinking, but it also preserves its transitional value. I agree with Reumann (§42, quoting Ziesler) that the nuance of the effect of God's righteousness in these texts is both forensic and connotative of moral renewal. But it is not yet the same as Pauline "justification," even apart from the lack of any mention of *faith.* It provides, however, an interesting stage in the development of ideas among Palestinian Jews in the last pre-Christian centuries. If the members of that Qumran community could refer to themselves as "sons of righteousness" (1QS 9:14; cf. 1QH 2:13), it is because of their conviction of God's favor and righteousness manifested toward them.

364   Similarly, I share Reumann's hesitation about Vermes's translation of the important passage in the Pesher on Habakkuk (1QpHab 7:17–8:3), which I should rather translate as follows (more closely relating it to the words of the prophet themselves):

["But the righteous one because of his fidelity shall find life"]:
The interpretation of it concerns all the observers of the law in
the house of Judah, whom God shall deliver from the house of

---

8. The closest one comes to a similar expression in the OT is *ṣidqat Yhwh* (Deut 33.21). This, however, becomes in the LXX, *dikaiosynēn kyrios epoiēsen,* "the Lord has wrought righteousness."

9. See P. Benoit, "Qumran and the New Testament," *Paul and Qumran: Studies in New Testament Exegesis* (ed. J. Murphy-O'Connor; London: Chapman, 1968), pp. 1–30, esp. p. 27; J. Jeremias, "Justification by Faith," *Central Message* (cited above, n. 24), pp. 51–70, esp. pp. 66–69.

judgment because of their struggle and their fidelity to the Teacher of Righteousness.

Vermes has unfortunately loaded the word *'ĕmūnātām,* "their fidelity," with the Pauline connotation of *pistis* (which Paul derived from the LXX, investing it with his own nuance). Even though "fidelity" and "righteousness" occur together here, it is still a far cry from the Pauline sense of justification by grace through *faith.*[10]

IV

365   I have little to criticize in Reumann's treatment of justification as a notion used by Jesus during his ministry. It is difficult to judge about this matter in Stage I of the gospel tradition because the major occurrences of the terms *dikaiosynē* and *dikaioun* are probably all to be attributed to Stage III of that tradition, viz., to the redactional activity of the evangelists (as Reumann recognizes, §49), or possibly to the earlier tradition of Stage II. Not even Matt 6:33 ("his kingdom and his righteousness") is necessarily to be traced back to Jesus himself.

366   I am again skeptical about attempts to understand Jesus' preaching of the kingdom as a proclamation of *ṣedeq* in a cosmic sense or even to relate the eschatological aspects of the two ideas, justification and kingdom (à la Jüngel). They both have eschatological dimensions, but that does not mean that justification and kingdom have the same comprehension. Similarly, Jesus' fellowship with sinners at table can be "an implicit expression of the acceptance of sinners" (§50), but it is not yet understood as "justification by grace through faith" (which, for Paul at least, depends on Christ's resurrection [Rom 4:25], as Reumann himself eventually acknowledges (§§53–54).

367   "Justification" is one of the ways of describing an effect of the Christ-event. It may, indeed, be ultimately rooted in a teaching of Jesus (such as his kingdom-preaching calling for repentance) or in his conduct with sinners, but that seems to be about as far as one can go in discussing "justification" as an element of Stage I of the gospel tradition. Jesus would certainly have been affected by OT ideas on *ṣedeq* and perhaps even by the thinking about it among Jews of the last centuries in pre-Christian Palestine. But we cannot be more specific. For just as it is difficult to trace the use of "gospel" back to Jesus himself, so too the understanding of it as the message of "justification by grace through faith." These come rather from

---

10. See further my article, "Habakkuk 2:3–4 and the New Testament," *To Advance the Gospel: New Testament Essays* (New York: Crossroad Publ. Co., 1981) pp. 236–46; reprinted from *De la loi au Messie: Le Développement d'une espérance: Etudes d'histoire et de théologie offertes à Henri Cazelles* (ed. J. Doré et al.; Paris: Desclée, 1981), pp. 447-55. Cf. J. G. Janzen, "Habakkuk 2:2–4 in the Light of Recent Philological Advances," *HTR* 73 (1980): 53–78.

a reflective summary of Jesus' own impact on his disciples in word and deed.[11]

V

368   Reumann rightly stresses (§§56–57) that there is no clear evidence that "justification by faith" formed part of the early Christian kerygma, but that when "justification" or "righteousness" emerged in early prepauline Christian teaching, it formed part of the reflective *homologiai,* "creedal summaries" or "confessional slogans," even though some of these early summaries also lack attempts to encapsulate the effects of the Christ-event[12] in terms of justification. I therefore agree that there is evidence in the prepauline strata of the "use of justification/righteousness terminology" especially in presenting the meaning of the cross and the resurrection. When, however, one looks again at some of the *homologiai* and prepauline material that Reumann has discussed, one may react with a bit of reserve about some of his suggestions.

369   That 1 Pet 3:18 is such a creedal summary with justification terminology (§60) I can agree. But I note that the term "righteous" is applied to Jesus himself (probably in the OT sense), who died for our (the *adikoi*) sins to bring us to God. There is here no indication that he "justified" us; if we had only this *homologia,* we would scarcely suspect its relation to a "doctrine of justification." It says, in fact, more about Jesus' sacrifice as a once-for-all suffering for sin than about *adikoi* achieving a status of righteousness before God. It could just as easily be understood in terms of remission of sins (*aphesis hamartiōn*), redemption, or reconciliation—other effects of the Christ-event.

370   Similarly, the hymn embedded in 1 Tim 3:16, which contains justification and faith terminology, is patently *christological,* not soteriological. The "justification" of Jesus may be forensic and connote an eschatological vindication of him in a lawsuit setting, but it says nothing about the effect of his justification on human beings (even through faith).

---

11. See further "The Gospel in the Theology of Paul," *Int* 33 (1979): 339–50; reprinted, *To Advance the Gospel,* pp. 149–61; *Interpreting the Gospels* (ed. J. L. Mays; Philadelphia: Fortress, 1981), pp. 1–13.

12. Here and elsewhere in his essay, Reumann speaks of the "doctrine of the atonement" or of the "atoning death" of Christ. I realize that he is using these terms generically, as a sort of abbreviated way of speaking about what I should prefer to call the "Christ-event" (the complex of Jesus' passion-death-burial-resurrection-exaltation-intercession). I note this because for me "atonement" is, in a specific sense, merely another way of saying "reconciliation," and both of these terms (or ideas) express an effect of the Christ-event under an image that differs from that of "justification." See further my article "Reconciliation in Pauline Theology," *No Famine in the Land: Studies in Honor of John L. McKenzie* (ed. J. W. Flanagan and A. W. Robinson; Missoula, MT: Scholars Press, 1975), pp. 155–77; reprinted, *To Advance the Gospel,* pp. 162–85.

371   It may be that 1 Cor 1:30 ("Christ Jesus, who became wisdom for us from God, righteousness-and-sanctification, and redemption") is "a prepauline formula" (Reumann, §62) or a "liturgical fragment" (Käsemann [as cited above, n. 45], p. 53—*dato, non concesso*), but it has none of the clear evidence for an appeal to an earlier tradition such as one finds in 1 Cor 15:3–5 (to which Reumann appeals). Moreover, both Käsemann and Stuhlmacher merely assert that it is such, whereas Kertelge (p. 302) does not list it among the prepauline material that he discusses. If, on the other hand, it is a Pauline formulation, it means no more than that Christ has become for us the source of righteousness (coming from God), and the mode of that righteousness is here left unspecified; in effect, it amounts to an abstract christological affirmation that is only beginning to verge on the soteriological.[13] It scarcely provides the basis for "the close identity of Christology and justification" (E. Gaugler, cited by Reumann, §62).

372   The first clear prepauline fragment mentioning the justification of human beings through Christ is 1 Cor 6:11; I have no difficulty with this current estimate. But I hesitate to agree with Reumann that the terms, "washed, sanctified, justified" were originally synonymous (§64) or that *edikaiōthēte* here means "simply the 'forgiveness of sins,' " as Bultmann maintains (§65). This again conflates parallel NT images or figures used to describe diverse effects of the Christ-event, which should be kept distinct, and explains a genuine Pauline image ("justification") by one ("forgiveness of sins") that is only doubtfully Pauline (see §400 below) or even Lucan (see Reumann §252).

373   I hesitate about the alleged prepauline character of 2 Cor 5:21, *pace* E. Käsemann et al. This appears to be a too easy way of solving a problem in Pauline theology. This happens to be the earliest instance in the genuine Pauline letters of *dikaiosynē theou,* and here it is said that Christians "become" it;[14] for this reason this assertion does not neatly fit into what may be a slightly Procrustean notion of Pauline justification. I can understand Conzelmann's desire to relate it to 1 Cor 1:30; but just as Paul there spoke of justification by using an earlier rhetorical formulation about Christ Jesus having been (God's) "righteousness" for us, so too here he can rhetorically sum up the Christian experience, speaking of our having become "God's righteousness." Reumann (§68) does well to note that there is "no explanation" in the passage about *how* the effect of justification is brought about. I hesitate to explain "justification" as "new creation," since that again violates the autonomy of the diverse Pauline images. God's power (*Macht*) is indeed one; but the diverse aspects under

---

13. I am also puzzled by NT scholars who bracket together "righteousness-and-sanctification" and isolate them from "redemption" in the same verse. Reumann's formulation (§63) about Christ as God's righteousness who brings us justification/sanctification/redemption is certainly more adequate.

14. Here one finds a basis in the NT for Luther's *iustitia aliena,* which he otherwise wanted to use throughout the interpretation of Romans.

which Paul has viewed the effects thereof in human life are another matter. Since the imagery draws on Paul's own varied background, whether Jewish or Hellenistic, I hesitate to lump them all together. Similarly, I hesitate to extend the cosmic dimension of reconciliation (5:19) to the righteousness mentioned in this passage.

374   As for the prepauline formulas in Romans, I have no objection to the consideration of either 4:24–25 or 3:24–26a as such. I should prefer to regard the former as a confessional slogan rather than a kerygmatic formulation (see above). It may also well reflect Isa 53:5, 6, 12, and the parallelism of its formulation stresses only *one* global effect of the Christ-event. Though I made no use of the suggestion that Rom 3:24–26a incorporated a prepauline formula in my commentary on that passage in Romans,[15] I now have no difficulty with that interpretation of it. It is certainly a more plausible explanation of the anomalies in the passage than that of either Talbert or Fitzer (that it is postpauline).

375   Apropos of Reumann's summary (§76), I am ready to admit that there are traces of prepauline confessional material in the NT that speak of "justification" as an effect of the Christ-event. I can agree with Käsemann that it is not a Pauline invention and with Reumann that it was part of apostolic faith—how *commonly* a part may be judged by my reservations expressed above about how successfully the Reumann net has brought in the catch.

VI

376   When one comes to the genuine Pauline writings, it is clear that one finds in these an affirmation of justification, and, as H.D. Betz points out, it is an understanding that Paul shares with early Jewish Christianity. He does not differ with them on the doctrine of justification by faith, but on its implications for Gentile Christians (above, §80). However, the absence or presence of the Pauline affirmation of it in different letters creates something of a problem. It is not that justification by faith "was unknown to him in Thessalonica" (ibid.), but rather that he saw no need to formulate an effect of the Christ-event in terms of it in that church situation; there is simply no trace of a Judaizing problem in the early letter—even letters—to the Thessalonians. Under pressure from that problem in certain early Christian communities Paul came to see the need to adopt the earlier Christian formulation of justification and join to it its explicit relation to grace and faith. It may be that consideration of the Judaizing problem has been given too much weight in the past, as Reumann suggests, but I am reluctant to admit the emergence of full-blown "justification by grace through faith" in Paul's ministry without impact from that problem.

377   Apropos of 1 Thessalonians, Reumann cites 2:10 and 5:8. I fail to

---

15. See *JBC* 53:39–41; this was written before Reumann's article on the passage (*Int* 20 [1966]: 432–52) had appeared.

see how 2:10 can be used seriously as evidence, even if Paul did teach justification by faith in that community. After all, it says only that "our behavior was holy, righteous (*dikaiōs*), and blameless," in a statement of Paul
about his own conduct—each of the three adverbs could be understood
solely in an OT sense! Similarly, I fail to see the relevance of 1 Thess 5:8 to
the question of justification by faith, even if it does reflect Isa 59:17.
"Righteousness" occurs in Isaiah, but the breastplate has become in Paul
"faith and love."[16] If Paul did indeed teach justification by faith to the
Thessalonians, it is difficult to think that he is alluding to that teaching in
these images of 5:8. To me it is much more of a problem to explain why it
is that only in 1 Thess 1:3 (and in 2 Thess 1:11!) Paul relates *pistis,* "faith,"
to *ergon,* "deed, work." Even if *ergon tēs pisteōs* is best explained as a subjective genitive, "a deed arising out of faith" (above, §83), which I should
prefer, it is still strange that in the later letters, when the problem of the
Judaizers has surfaced, *pistis* is never again so related to *ergon,* and *ergon
tēs pisteōs* is studiously avoided—undoubtedly because of the connotation
that *ergon* has by then acquired because of *erga tou nomou,* "deeds of the
law" (Rom 3:28) or even *erga* alone (Rom 4:2).

378   Apropos of 2 Thessalonians, Reumann rightly cites only 1:5–6 and
notes that the picture is forensic (p. 45), since God's judicial righteousness
is referred to. But I find the comment of E. Best, which Reumann quotes,
reading far more into Paul's statement than I should be willing to admit.
In vv. 3–4 Paul speaks of the Thessalonians' "faith, love, and patience,"
but in vv. 5–6 what is promised to them ("the kingdom of God," and
"rest") will be granted not on the basis of their faith, but because of their
affliction. I can readily admit with Reumann (ibid.) that 2 Thessalonians
reflects the OT and prepauline background of justification, but I find nothing in either letter to the Thessalonians that is distinctively Pauline in this
regard.

379   When one comes to the letters written by Paul during what Reumann calls his "mature years" (§85), the doctrine of justification by faith
clearly emerges. Reumann's preliminary remarks (§§85–88) are acceptable, even though I prefer a slightly different chronological ordering of the
letters in this period.[17] Though Paul shared justification with other elements of apostolic, especially Jewish, Christianity, we find *his emphasis* on
it in this period because of the perverting "gospel" (not really a gospel)
that was being preached by his opponents in Galatia and elsewhere.[18]

---

16. Note there the joining of "faith and love" that will appear again in 2 Thess 1:3. Cf.
Gal 5:6, where their relation is expressed differently.

17. For my preferred dating of the Pauline letters of this "mature" period, see *Int* 32
(1978): 310.

18. I too would insist on the diversity of Paul's opponents, even among those who were
Jewish Christians; those in Jerusalem and Antioch were not the same as those in Galatia. But
I see no reason to include the possibility of Gnostics or Jews among those causing trouble in
Galatia (see Reumann, §98); cf. *JBC* 49: 7. Reumann (§100) thinks that Paul's opponents in

Paul's "earlier" views have to be respected as such and not minimalized, as Reumann rightly acknowledges (§88). I can agree that Paul's "eschatology emphasizes the decisive thing that God has done in Christ (which Paul can variously describe with regard to the cross and the resurrection), and [that] it regularly looks forward to a consummation to come, in the fullness of which Christians do not yet participate" (§88). But the same degree of "emphasis" on justification is not found in 1 Thessalonians (or 2 Thessalonians) as is found in Galatians, Romans, or even parts of Philippians, in these and other writings of his mature years. In this regard, I do not find Paul's "theological stance" that consistent in emphasis.

380 Apropos of Reumann's discussion of 1 Corinthians (d[1]), I think that he rightly stresses the significance of the occurrence of justification phrases (1:30; 6:11) apart from any debate with Jews or Jewish Christians over the law. But Paul's use of the earlier formulas also appears here significantly without any reference to *pistis,* "faith." This stands in contrast to the use of an earlier formula in Rom 3:24–26a, where a reference to faith is clearly introduced (v. 25). As I read the 1 Corinthian passages discussed by Reumann, I see Paul summing up the Christ-event under the image of justification/righteousness, using indeed earlier formulas, to cope with the eschatological problems of that community.[19] But they have not yet acquired the specific relation to faith and grace that they will get when the Judaizing problem forces him to cope with it. There is, indeed, a sense in which "the message of the cross does not differ from that of justification in, e.g., Romans" (§91), because the latter expresses one valid aspect of that message, viz., the destruction of human *kauchēsis,* "boasting" (1 Cor 1:29). But I am not sure that all the imagery of the "message of the cross" can be reduced to merely that.

381 As for the passages that deal with justification in 2 Corinthians, I can in general agree with Reumann's treatment of them (§§92–96). In the course of it he introduces a summary of the interpretation of righteousness proposed by the Käsemann School (§93). No one will criticize the first three points (that the "righteousness of God" is a term inherited from Judaism, that it denotes not only a gift from God, but also God's power, that it expresses God's loyalty to the community and even to creation). But it may be an exaggeration to say that "God's righteousness" is "the theme of Paul's *whole* proclamation and theology" (ibid.; emphasis mine). Acceptable too is the idea of God's righteousness pressing human beings into its service (a military aspect), "the ministry of righteousness" (2 Cor 3:9). When Reumann states (§95) apropos of 2 Cor 5:21 that through God's ac-

---

Galatia were insisting "on circumcision and acceptance of the Mosaic torah as necessary for salvation." But does this mean *all* of "the Mosaic Torah" or not? As I read Galatians, the opponents were Judaizers who were trying to impose on the Gentile Christians only *some* Jewish practices (circumcision, observance of feast days, possibly reverence of angels [if that is what *stoicheia tou kosmou* (4:2, 9) is supposed to mean]). Hence Paul writes, "I testify to every man who receives circumcision that he is bound to keep the whole law" (5:3).

19. I find Barrett's explanation of 1 Cor 1:8 (cited above, §90) to be eisegetical.

tion in Christ we become "new creatures," reconciled to God, having a *diakonia* of reconciliation, and forgiven, this can be accepted, as long as one remembers that in this whole passage (5:16–21) Paul is employing *various* figures or images, which express different aspects or effects of the Christ-event, *without necessarily equating them.* I agree with the characterization present in the passage of the result as "corporate, not individualistic." Moreover, "reconciliation" may here be treated as cosmic in its dimensions, but that cosmic character is not described by Paul as part of the other effects.

382   As for Paul's Letter to the Galatians, I find myself in agreement with the vast majority of Reumann's interpretation of the passages dealing with righteousness/justification. On one problem, however, I should like to have seen a little more discussion, viz., the distinction between "declare righteous" and "make righteous." I agree, *dikaioun* has to be understood in a juridical or forensic sense. Reumann finally opts specifically for "a declarative sense" (§100, relying on H. D. Betz). But the alternative is not simply the ethical sense, about which J. A. Ziesler writes. Though I was initially fascinated by Ziesler's distinction,[20] I have come more and more to see its inadequacies and tend to agree with much of Reumann's reaction to Ziesler's analysis of individual instances in the NT. Yet the issue is whether or not one can leave *dikaioun* solely with the declarative denotation.[21] Is God's word, spoken in a verdict of acquittal, efficacious or not, i.e., does it terminate or not in a real change in the human beings so addressed? Or, to put it in terms of Käsemann's thinking, is the "power" (*Macht*) of the righteous God effective in his declaration? If we admitted above (§359, [2a]) that the piel and hiphil of Hebrew *ṣdq* were delocutive, we also have to realize that the Greek contract verb *dikaioun* used in the LXX belongs to a class that is normally factitive in meaning (e.g., *dēloun,* "make clear"; *douloun,* "enslave"). Since patristic times *dikaioun* has been understood by Greek interpreters of Paul to mean "make righteous." Indeed, this even seems to be suggested by Rom 5:19 itself (see below). Here one may recall the OT notion of God's word as effective (Isa 55:10–11). Yet it is not merely that God's creative power "makes" the sinner anew (that would be to confuse the images again!), but rather that God's declarative justifying power even makes the sinner righteous.

383   I further agree with Reumann's insistence on the present and future aspects of righteousness. In the expression "the hope of righteousness" (*elpida dikaiosynēs,* 5:5), the genitive is appositional, expressing a sure hope "based upon God's promise and not upon our doing the works

---

20. See *TS* 34 (1973): 154–57.

21. Perhaps one should recall here the debate between B. M. Metzger (*Theology Today* 2 [1945–46]: 561–63, esp. p. 562) and E. J. Goodspeed (*JBL* 73 [1954]: 84–92, esp. pp. 86–91). Neither Goodspeed nor Metzger is Roman Catholic or Lutheran! Cf. *JBC* 49:18.

of the law," or even based on "justification" running "through the whole life of the believer and beyond" (§104).

384   In the controversial passage (Gal 5:6) *pistis di' agapēs energoumenē,* "faith working itself out through love," faith is produced in a human being by God's "power" and its *energeia* is not exhausted in it but even produces love, or "the response-in-love of those in Christ," i.e., "actions of loving service" of Christians (§105). I too have often toyed here with the meaning of *agapē* as expressive of God's love for human beings. But in view of 1 Thess 5:8; 2 Thess 1:3 (see my n. 16 above), I prefer to think of it as Spirit-inspired human love, without which no real faith exists. Even though V. P. Furnish (*Theology and Ethics,* cited above, n. 73, p. 203) considers that the "two renderings are complementary" (quoting A. E. Garvie, *ExpTim* 55 [1943–44]:97), I see no reason to invoke the nuance of God's love here,[22] even if one must guard against the later Latin interpretation of this verse as reflecting what Paul would have meant.

385   The Lutheran fear (expressed in §106), however, does not tell us how *agapē,* apparently felt by Paul as a necessary complement of genuine faith (and not just a detachable caboose), is to be related to the "sole sufficiency of God's deed in Christ as the basis of human salvation." Paul certainly does not mean that human beings can be justified by love alone; but can they be without it? Similarly, the "last word" written by Paul in his own hand in the letter's postscript, though it reiterates the gospel that he has been defending, sums up the meaning of "the cross" indeed, but it does so without any explicit reference to righteousness/justification or even to faith. To me, at least, it shows that "the cross" can be expressed without such recourse and that it has other aspects significant for human existence and salvation than merely justification by grace through faith.

386   As for the treatment of Philippians by Reumann, I have no real differences to mention. I too would understand 1:6 in the light of Paul's general teaching on justification. In Reumann's analysis of Phil 3:9–11 (§§110–111), I am happy to see his emphasis on the Christian's need to participate in the sufferings of Christ, even though he never explains what that participation means. Is it something beyond faith? Last, Reumann should have included some comment on the controversial verse in 2:12–13, about working out one's salvation in fear and trembling, even if it contains no explicit righteousness/justification terminology; it is not without its impact in the doctrine of justification.

387   Apropos of Romans, I have no problem with Reumann's structural analysis of the letter (section a). Concerning the theme of Romans (§§117–21), I have always preferred the interpretation of the "righteousness of God" (1:17) as a subjective genitive. This means that it would be understood as a quality or attribute in God (as in Rom 3:5 and *throughout*

---

22. But I am puzzled by Reumann's reference (§105) to Gal 5:14, 22–23 as referring to "works" that "gain satisfaction." This is unclear.

the rest of Romans; but differently from 2 Cor 5:21 [thus agreeing with Reumann about judging each passage in its context, §119]).[23] This is to differ with both "the Reformation view" and "the Catholic view," as cited by Reumann (ibid.), and to agree basically with Käsemann and others. But I insist that this quality must be understood as the dynamic power in God effecting through Christ's cross the justification of human beings—thus paraphrasing Reumann and limiting it to that effect, not confusing the Pauline image of justification with the doubtfully Pauline (and certainly Lucan) image of the "forgiveness of sins," and seeing no need to introduce into it other effects (such as "new life" or "redemption").

388   In the interpretation of *ek pisteōs eis pistin*, "through faith unto faith" (Rom 1:17), I fail to see much difference between the view that it expresses "growth in faith" (which Reumann rejects, §120) and that of the "continuing activity to which the person is to respond with continuing faith" (which Reumann adopts from Kertelge, §120).[24] While I further agree with Reumann's interpretation of the use of Hab 2:4 against Strobel (§121), I am not convinced that the use of this OT passage is derived by Paul from "common primitive Christianity." I see no evidence for such a judgment. That it is also used in Hebrews does not necessarily point in that direction; that usage could depend on Paul.

389   Reumann's treatment of "God's wrath" (Rom 1:18) is comprehensively handled, and I find no difficulty with his dependence on Käsemann's interpretation of it. "God's wrath" is not part of the gospel message for Paul, and that is suggested by the separate use of the Greek conjunction *gar.*

I was happy to see Reumann's distinguishing (§124) of God's *dikaiokrisia*, "righteous/just judgment" (2:5), which affects the wicked, from his *dikaiosynē*, by which he justifies the sinner. The former has often been used (mistakenly) to enhance the latter with the idea of God's vindictive justice.

390   In the crucial passage of Rom 2:6–11, which speaks of God rendering impartially to everyone according to his works, Reumann's treatment well sums up the variety of interpretations that have been used. I cannot agree that the passage has reference only to Jews and Greeks (= pagans) with no reference to Christian believers; the difficulty is that Paul is once again indulging in a generalization, as is his wont so often. On the other hand, I tend to agree with Käsemann (as cited by Reumann, §125) that the doctrine of judgment according to works has to be understood in the light of Paul's doctrine of justification, that at the bar of God's judgment what holds for the believer is the gift and power of his righteousness,

---

23. In adopting the subjective genitive, I am ruling out only the objective genitive, not the genitive of author or origin (which I cannot distinguish very much from the subjective genitive; see Reumann's line-up [§119]). Cf. my n. 14 above.

24. For the growth or progress sense of such an expression, one might also compare 2 Cor 3:18 (*apo doxēs eis doxēn*).

received by faith. In these verses there occur the phrases *ergou agathou,* "good deed" (v. 7, "well doing," *RSV*) and *panti tō$_i$ ergazomenō$_i$ to agathon,* "everyone who does good" (v. 10, *RSV*). This seems to suggest that even for the believer something more than just faith will be a factor in judgment. On the other hand, Reumann may be right in relating these expressions to the *ergon tēs pisteōs* of 1 Thess 1:3; 2 Thess 1:11 (see §§125, 83, 377 above), but I am not sure that the phrase in the Thessalonian context refers to the same thing as here. Significantly, Paul does not speak of the *ergon tēs pisteōs* here in this judicial context.

391   At the bottom of §129 Reumann admits that Protestant exegesis has gone far in recognizing that (and how) Paul speaks of a judgment based on works. It is also good to learn that "God's judgment in the service of justification *by God* is now more widely recognized" (ibid.). It would be good to learn, however, how such a "good deed" of a justified Christian is related to the "working out" of faith through love (Gal 5:6).

392   I agree with Reumann that the "righteousness of God" in Rom 3:5 expresses an attribute and that the genitive is subjective (§§130–31). I can also agree that *dikaiosynē theou* is a "declaration of the power of God working itself out forensically in the sphere of the covenant" for all human beings (Käsemann, quoted by Reumann, §133); indeed, it is God's victory over a rebel world (11:32) through his justification of the ungodly (4:5).[25] But I should want to insist that in Pauline thinking it is a "rebel world" of *human beings,* without any subtle connotation of a cosmic dimension. Hence I find it difficult to agree with point (6) (§133) that "righteousness/ justification in Paul has a cosmic side." It is, indeed, necessary to offset the individualistic emphasis often put on justification (perhaps under the influence of Phil 3:9); but that means only that one must insist more on the *corporate* aspect of justification. Yet "corporate" does not, without further ado, say "cosmic."[26] As I read Paul, justification is in his letters totally anthropological, in a corporate as well as an individual sense. (But if Reumann, Käsemann, and other present-day Lutherans can admit this sense of *dikaiosynē theou,* does this not mean an abandonment of Luther's own position on a crucial point of interpretation, "Die Gerechtigkeit die vor Gott gilt," "the righteousness by which we are made righteous by God"?[27])

393   I find myself in general agreement with Reumann's analysis and explanation (§§135–38) of the heart of Paul's gospel in Romans (3:21–31). In particular, I am most sympathetic to his treatment of the efficacious character of God's forensic declaration of justification, and to his adoption of Käsemann's understanding of God's effective declaration resulting in an

---

25. In referring to *dikaiosynē theou* as an "attribute" in God, I do not imply a static quality. Rather I "attribute" to him such a justifying "power" and see no contradiction between his righteousness as a power to justify and an attribute of his.

26. See further my n. 7 above and the article cited in n. 12.

27. See "Lectures on Romans, Scholia," 1:17, LW, Vol. 25, p. 151; cf. "Preface to . . . Romans" (1546), LW Vol. 35, p. 371; "Preface to . . . Luther's Latin Writings" (1545), LW, Vol. 34, p. 337.

"eschatologically transformed existence," even though I wish that he had used some other mode of expressing it than "transformed." For this is to confuse the Pauline images again. "Transformation" (*metamorphoun,* 2 Cor 3:18) is an independent image, derived from a Hellenistic mythological background, and carries none of the juridical overtones of "justification."

394   On the treatment of Abraham in Rom 4 (§§139–41) as one justified by faith and not by works, a few comments are in order. In addition to the passages cited from Jewish literature in the late pre-Christian centuries and Jewish-Christian literature (§139), one could refer to Sir 44:19–21, which presents a significant understanding of Abraham, which Paul may have thought necessary to counteract. When he speaks of Abraham's righteousness not being based on his works, he speaks generically and says *ex ergōn,* "by works" (Rom 4:2), not qualifying them as *erga tou nomou,* "works of the law." He modifies his statement, in part, because he realizes that the Mosaic law was not yet given, but in part too because he differs from the contemporary Jewish view that even considered Abraham as "keeping the Law of the Most High" (Sir 44:20 [Greek *nomon:* Hebrew *miṣwôt*]). Instead, Paul prefers to follow the sequence of the story in the Book of Genesis itself, where no *erga* are mentioned in the verse about Abraham's justification and where such a work of the Law as circumcision comes in only later than the promise itself. Yet because Paul has phrased the statement about Abraham's justification generically, as not based on works (*ex ergōn*), his phraseology gave rise to an early misunderstanding, as the Epistle of James makes clear (2:24). There the author seeks to correct a caricature of Paul's teaching on justification by faith.[28] It should further be remarked that though Paul speaks here of *epangelia,* "promise" (Rom 4:13, 14, 16, 20), he does not relate it in this passage to *euangelion,* "gospel" (but cf. Rom 1:2; see also Eph 1:13; 3:6).[29] Reumann has rightly stressed the significance of Abraham's justification as opposed to all human boasting.

395   Should not a little more have been made of the "covering up" of sin in Rom 4:6? Is this not somehow involved in the Lutheran emphasis on *simul iustus et peccator?* (In this regard one may note the significant translation of Hebrew *kappōret,* "mercy seat" [Lev 16:13] in a Qumran text by *ksy',* "covering, lid," which reveals that at least some Palestinian Jews in pre-Christian centuries understood the word in this sense, though some modern OT commentators tend to shy away from it.[30])

396   In 4:13 Paul makes use of a contemporary Jewish understanding of the world as having been created for the sake of Abraham; at least what is

---

28. See further below, §413.

29. See "The Gospel in the Theology of Paul," pp. 347–48; *To Advance the Gospel,* p. 157.

30. See further my article "The Targum of Leviticus from Qumran Cave 4," *Maarav* 1 (1978): 5–23, esp. pp. 15–17.

here termed the "inheritance" of the world by Abraham becomes in later rabbinic traditions even the "creation" of the world for his sake, so that he may inherit it.[31] *Kosmos* is used here, but this should not be misunderstood. Abraham was to inherit "the world" because of his righteousness sprung from faith (the genitive in *dikaiosyne tēs pisteōs* (4:11) is not appositional, but one of origin). This does not mean, however, that God's righteousness has thus taken on a cosmic aspect; it rather means that the whole world of human beings, Jew and Greek alike, would be able to share in Abraham's inheritance (righteousness from faith).

397   More would have to be said about the relation of chap. 5 to the whole of Romans, and likewise about the relation of justification to reconciliation (and even sanctification), than Reumann has devoted to these topics in §142. Rom 5:1 has to be taken more seriously; and I hesitate to "blame" Paul for what he may well have intended and actually written. I say this, even though I agree with Reumann about justification not being merely "a past action." Similarly, the significance of *dikaioi katastathēsontai,* "will be made righteous" (5:19, *RSV*) should have been given more elaborate treatment. It is complicated by the sense of the parallel *harmartōloi katesthēsan,* "were made sinners" (by one man's disobedience). In what sense will they be "made righteous" (declaratively or effectively)?

398   In general, I agree with Reumann's discussion of Romans 6 in §§144–50, and in particular with his disagreement with K. P. Donfried about the three stages, past justification, present sanctification, and future salvation. In Pauline thinking they represent rather three effects of the Christ-event, each of which has a past, present, and future aspect.[32] More has to be said about the way Paul speaks of "salvation" in Romans as a whole; here Reumann has obscured the issue somewhat. But the real problem is how to relate the past, present, and future aspects of such effects of the Christ-event; I see them as aspects of a many-sided reality (the Christ-event in human history), which Paul describes under different images, each having eschatological nuances, both "realized" and "futurist." The attempts made in the past to erect these images into theses or into a categorized *ordo salutis* have resulted in casting Pauline thinking into a straitjacket that it was not meant to wear.

399   Reumann's interpretation of Rom 7–8 is acceptable; I agree with his interpretation of the *egō* in chap. 7 (§151) and with his christological interpretation of Rom 8:4 (§152). Apropos of 8:30, I should only query

---

31. See Str-B, 3, p. 209.

32. Briefly put, there is no passage in Romans—in contrast to other letters—where "salvation" is spoken of clearly with either a past or a present reference. The noun *sōtēria* is used in 1:16; 10:1, 10; 11:11, undefined as to time; only in 13:11 does it imply a future reference. The verb *sōzein* is normally found with a future reference; thus, 5:9 (explicitly contrasted with *dikaiōthentes nyn*); 5:10; 10:9, 13 [= Joel 3:5 LXX]; in three instances it is used of the future conversion of the Jews (9:27 [= Isa 10:22 LXX]; 11:14, 26). Only in 8:24 is the past found, *tē elpidi esōthēmen,* "with hope were we saved." But the added prepositional phrase gives it an unmistakably future connotation.

how *dikaioun* "covers everything" (§154), when it is clearly one step in Paul's description, the climax of which emphasizes God's foreknowledge or preferably the glorious destiny of the predestined, called, justified Christian. In his treatment of chaps. 9–11, I query again the "cosmic" sense of God's righteousness (§155); it is rather "corporate."[33] I find no major problems in Reumann's discussion of the ethical parenesis of Rom 12:1ff. (§§161–62). This brings us to the end of his excellent treatment of the *dikaio*-language of the uncontested Pauline letters. I am not, however, happy with Reumann's implied contention (§163) that the discussion so far has shown that "the theme of *dikaiosynē*" is "*the* expression of the gospel" (his emphasis); this is far from clear (see below, §425).

VII

400   As for the deuteropauline letters, Colossians and Ephesians, I have only a few comments on Reumann's otherwise acceptable treatment of them. More stress should have been given to the concept of *hē aphesis tōn hamartiōn/paraptōmatōn*, "the forgiveness of sins/transgressions," in these letters (Col 1:14; cf. Eph 1:7 [possibly Col 2:13 is related to this idea, but the verb there is *charisamenos,* "having forgiven," *RSV*]). This image for an effect of the Christ-event is strangely absent from the uncontested letters of Paul, unless one would want to find it in the (highly controverted) word *paresis* of Rom 3:25.[34] In these letters the use is clear, and that is why I have queried the definition of justification in terms of it by some commentators (see §§355 (1c), 366, 372 above). The image is different, being derived from commerce or bookkeeping, not a lawsuit, and denoting the remission of debts. I should also give more stress to "reconciliation" than Reumann has in Col 1:19–21 or Eph 2:11–18; the development of this theme in these letters is not surprising in view of the diminished role that justification plays in them. Here too one finds both the anthropological and the cosmic aspects of reconciliation, just as one found them (perhaps in a less developed form) in Rom 11:15 and 2 Cor 5:19. Käsemann would regard the cosmic notion as prior to and the source of the anthropological; but it is really the other way round.

401   Specifically apropos of Ephesians, I note the similarity of terminology in Eph 2:4–9 with that of justification passages in the uncontested letters of Paul. But just as Reumann admits that the passage is devoid of *dikaioun*-terminology, I find it hard to think that this passage has anything to do with "justification."[35] Here one detects rather a vestigial development. The Judaizing problems have disappeared, and forms of christologi-

---

33. Note in §160 Reumann's reference to Kertelge's hesitation about the creation emphasis in Rom 9:19–21, invoked by Müller. I share that hesitation too.

34. *Paresis* was translated as "remission" in §136, as I also translated it in *JBC,* art. 53, §40; see further discussion there.

35. Unless, of course, one wants to disregard the difference in biblical images involved.

cal and ecclesiological teaching have come to the fore. Hence it is not surprising that the roles of "grace" and "faith" are now found to be applied to other effects of the Christ-event (such as salvation). Indeed, the *vestigia* of *diakaio*-language that are present lack the distinctive Pauline nuance—one of the reasons why some commentators find it hard to admit that Ephesians is genuinely Pauline. Each instance of such language can be understood in an ethical sense (which Reumann himself admits in one way or another) and can be explained solely from an OT or a Hellenistic background; no example is uncontestably Pauline in its nuance. Last, the comparison of *ex ergōn* (Eph 2:9), in §174 (2), should really be made with Rom 4:2, instead of with the phrase *ex ergōn nomou* (cf Gal 2:16, 3:2, 5; Rom 3:20, etc.), precisely for the reason that I mentioned above (§394).

402 Detailed comments on justification in the Pastoral Letters will be left to my colleague, J. D. Quinn (below, §§428–37), save for one remark, apropos of §187. Where in the NT does one find a basis for the assertion about "the critical function of God's *dikaiosynē* against all institutions, including the church"? It may well be missing in the Pastorals ("diminished or lost"); but where does one find it elsewhere, even (presumably) in the uncontested letters of Paul? I can think of Rom 3:27–28, where Paul speaks about human boasting, either of Jew or Greek, falling under the critical regard of God's righteousness. But is it not anachronistic, indeed divisive, to extend this to "all institutions, including the church"?[36]

VIII

403 Part C in Reumann's paper (§§192–216) deals with "Some Alternative Central Themes in Paul." From what has been said above, I can agree with his position about the rise and development of righteousness/justification in the early Christian community's experience, when he sees little of it that can be traced back to Jesus himself, little of it in the early kerygma, but some of it found in the prepauline confessional formulas (recall my qualifications on some of the passages, §§368–75). I have further no difficulty with Reumann's view of justification as "the central theme" of Romans, Galatians, and part of Philippians (§192). There was little occasion to use it in writing to the Thessalonians and Corinthians; but there was a real need to adopt it from earlier tradition in the writing of Romans, Galatians, and part of Philippians. One has to allow for some difference of emphasis even in this important element of Pauline teaching. If I still continue to think that Paul developed his distinctive teaching on justification by grace through faith under pressure from a Judaizing problem, I should

---

36. I say this, even if I have admitted above (§391) that I was glad to learn that "God's judgment" was being more widely recognized in the "service of justification." After all, "justification" implies a judgment coming from the divine tribunal about human beings; but the extension of *dikaio*-terminology to that of *krinein*, applied even to human institutions, is what bothers me.

not regard it as developed only "late" (Reumann, §192) in his career (see my n. 17).

404   I am also prepared to admit with Käsemann that justification is an "inalienable constituent of Paul's theology" (*Romans,* p. 24; cited by Reumann, §193). It is one of the "dominant perspectives" of Pauline theology (*JBC* 79:22–97, esp. 80–97). When I wrote my sketch of that theology, I was reacting against the Bultmannian approach, which regarded it as mainly an anthropology. I sought to counteract that characterization of it by describing Paul's theology as mainly a "Christocentric soteriology" (*JBC* 79:22; see Reumann, §202). If I were writing that sketch today, I would hesitate between retaining that designation or summing it up under "gospel" (which I did set out as of prime importance in *JBC* 79:27–34).[37]

405   Summing up Paul's theology under "Christ" seems to Reumann (§198) not to recognize clearly enough "that Paul really contributed little that was new to early Christian christologizing." I find this a bit strange— and it runs through much of modern NT scholarship. Why is only that which Paul contributed on his own to be labeled "Pauline theology" or "Pauline christology"? To my way of thinking, the prepauline passages in Rom 1:3–4, 3:24–26a, 4:24–25; Phil 2:6–11 become just as much part of Paul's theology as what he may have contributed on his own. In taking over existing christological statements about Jesus and his death, even those that saw their significance in terms of righteousness/justification, he often gave them an emphasis they did not previously have (e.g., the appropriation of the effect of Christ's death and resurrection as justification *through faith* and *as a free gift of God*). Both the inherited aspects and the new aspects form his christocentric soteriology and thus become the content of his gospel, not however the sole content.

406   In lining up the effects of the Christ-event as envisaged by Paul, I should certainly give the first place today to justification—and no little reason for this pride of place would be Reumann's exposé thus far.[38] I would see it as the most important of the dominant perspectives, which may be numbered (today) about ten: (1) justification, (2) salvation, (3) reconciliation, (4) expiation, (5) sanctification, (6) freedom, (7) liberation, (8) transformation, (9) new creation, and possibly (10) forgiveness of sins, depending on how one regards *paresis* in Rom 3:25 or judges the Pauline authorship of Col 1:14 (*hē aphesis tōn hamartiōn*) or Eph 1:7 (*hē aphesis tōn paraptōmatōn*).[39] To me, these images form a group that Paul uses to describe the effects of the Christ-event, what Christ Jesus did for human be-

---

37. Note that Rom 1:16–17 equates the "gospel" with "God's power" and says that "in it" (or possibly "by means of it") God's righteousness is revealed. It does not, however, equate "the gospel" with "God's righteousness."

38. As I indeed have in the revision of my article "Reconciliation in Pauline Theology"; contrast the original (see my n. 12 above), p. 156, and the revision, pp. 163–64.

39. I have often toyed with adding another image: *doxazein,* "glorify" (see Rom 8:30); but that is really a form of "transformation" stated in different language.

ings *ephapax,* "once for all" (Rom 6:10). In each case one has to explain its origin or background (Hellenistic or Jewish), its meaning for Paul, and the phase of Christ's existence to which it may have been primarily or originally applied. As a group, however, they form the content of the "gospel" for Paul. Yet they are not to be facilely equated.

407 In the light of this I admit that I overstressed reconciliation and downplayed justification in the past. The stress on reconciliation was owing to the confusion engendered by Käsemann's article, which stated that the "doctrine of reconciliation . . . does not even exist in Paul" ([art. cited above, Reumann, n. 45], p. 51). Admittedly, reconciliation does not occur as frequently in Paul's letters as justification/righteousness. But I am not sure that its importance is solely to be attributed to its appeal to moderns because of present-day estrangement (Reumann, §201). There is a problem in the interpretation of Rom 5:1-11, to which I alluded above (§397), which needs more elaborate development than there is space for here. What precisely is the relationship between justification and reconciliation in that passage? Käsemann would have us believe that it teaches reconciliation in the service of justification; it might be just the other way round.

408 E. P. Sanders's work may be regarded as another attempt to find the "central theme" in Pauline theology. Though I am sympathetic with his attempt to shift the emphasis in the study of this theology from "righteousness by faith" as the essence or "center" of it, I cannot agree, any more than Reumann can (§§217-22), that it is to be found in eschatological participation in Christ. This minimizes the content of the Pauline gospel, confuses the objective and subjective aspects of the experience of the Christ-event, and is no more intelligible to modern readers of Paul than justification.[40] My greatest difficulty with Sanders's presentation, however, is not so much with his attempt to understand Paul as it is with the claim that his use of rabbinic material in his holistic comparison, restricted by him to Tannaitic writings, can be used as representative of the "Palestinian Judaism" with which Paul would have been in contact. He states that his "principal concern" is with the "material from the Tannaitic period," which he dates "from before 70 c.e. to Rabbi (R. Judah ha-Nasi)" (*Paul and Palestinian Judaism,* p. 63). "Two large assumptions" are the basis of his presentation, the dating of anonymous material of the halakic midrashim to the Tannaitic period and the by-and-large reliability of sayings attributed to rabbis of what he calls the "Jamnian period or later (from 70 c.e. on)." But neither assumption is wholly acceptable. In dating the Tannaitic material, Sanders is following J. N. Epstein and J. Neusner, whose pioneering work in this regard is to be lauded, but it is only a beginning and needs far more detailed study than either of these scholars has devoted to it. The problem here is something like that of the sayings attributed to Jesus in the Synoptic Gospels. In the latter case we have finally got some

---

40. Reumann senses this too (§221).

Christians to realize that not everything that is attributed to Jesus or put on his lips by evangelists, writing at least a generation later, was necessarily said by him. But, alas, we have not yet got users of the rabbinic material, whether Jews or Christians, to realize that not everything attributed to rabbis of early generations was necessarily uttered by them. Sanders rightly queries "the antiquity of the Targums as we have them" and the pertinence of their data to his study (pp. 25–26); but he strangely works with the assumptions that the Tannaitic and Jamnia material is earlier. I personally am skeptical about any of it being prior to R. Aqiba (end of the first third of the second century A.D.) and consider most of it as coming from the time of R. Judah the Prince (at the beginning of the third century—*attributions* of some material to earlier rabbis (even of the first century A.D.) notwithstanding. Here my disagreement is with Sanders, and not with Reumann; the whole question of the relevance of rabbinic material for the interpretation of Pauline writings needs serious, new assessment. Hence, though I might want to rephrase some of Reumann's criticism of Sanders's thesis in minor ways, I find myself in basic agreement with him.[41]

IX

409   My remarks on righteousness/justification in other NT writers will be brief, since Reumann's treatment of these passages is, in general, quite adequate, and my disagreements are minor. Save for the Epistle of James, the bearing of these passages on the Reformation claim has been of less influence than what has been treated so far.

410   In his treatment of the Matthean material, especially of the Matthean use of the noun *dikaiosynē,* he has adequately handled the various interpretations of the seven passages where it occurs. At 3:15, in Jesus' statement to John the Baptist about the need "to fulfil all righteousness," even if there is an allusion to "divine necessity," "God's will," or Heilsgeschichte, the sense of "righteousness" does not transcend the ethical demand of OT teaching. There is scarcely a nuance of justification by faith here. The Matthean addition of "righteousness" to the fourth beatitude (5:6) probably does refer to God's gift of eschatological vindication/justification, by way of contrast. However, the addition to the eighth beatitude on persecution is probably intended to refer only to the righteous activity expected by God of Christian disciples. Similarly, in 5:20, where the righteousness expected of them has to be more than that of the scribes and Pharisees, and probably not just more in degree but of a different sort, the extent to which an allusion is made here to the gift of righteousness may be debated (I am skeptical). On the other hand, *dikaiosynē* in 6:1 does not transcend the OT sense of upright ethical conduct expected of the Jew.

41. See further J. Nesuner, review of Sanders's book, *History of Religion* 18 (1978): 177–91.

The Matthean addition of "righteousness" to the seeking of God's kingdom (6:33) might sound as though it were counseling a striving to achieve an upright status before God. But that would be to miss the nuance of gift connoted in the verse itself. One does not seek one's own righteousness, but God's, i.e., his eschatological vindicating gift. (Just how is not said.) Here Matthew by his addition has equated "kingdom" and God's "righteousness." Apropos of 21:32, I prefer G. Strecker's interpretation that John's way of righteousness means his preaching and example. Finally, I agree with Reumann's summation on the Matthean use of righteousness-terminology (§§242–43), noting only that its relation to "faith" (e.g., 21:32) is not yet expressive of the Pauline emphasis and that Matthean theology is much more of an "indicative [adj.] imperative [noun]" than an "imperatival indicative" (so G. Strecker). Yet even granted that "righteousness" in Matthew sometimes has the sense of gift, the stress is on the ethical understanding of it. But it would be interesting to know how Reumann would relate the Matthean usage and emphasis to other Matthean ideas, such as "reward" (*misthos*, 5:12, 46; 6:1, 2, 5, 16; 10:41–42) and the distinctively Matthean parable of the sheep and the goats (25:31–46). "Righteousness" itself enters into some of these very passages.

411   I have no disagreement with Reumann's rapid survey (§§244–47) of the passages in the Lucan gospel, not even with the interpretation of the parable of the toll collector and the Pharisee (18:9–14), where the "justification" of the former probably means no more than his "finding favor" in God's sight, as in 2 Esdr 12:7; there is no need to invoke any "paulinizing" of the parable. As for Acts, it may be noted that the espousal of the traditional identification of the author of the gospel and Acts as Luke today (see *JBC* 45:2) in no way implies that he must have had "accurate knowledge" (Reumann, §248) of the Apostle Paul's teachings, or that he had ever read Paul's letters.[42] Even if Luke were a sometime associate of Paul, Acts displays a striking absence of knowledge of basic Pauline teachings; and what little of them it has ("hints or hazy reflections," Reumann, §249) has been shaped to suit Luke's own thesis.[43] That is why Luke characteristically makes Peter sum up Christian belief in terms of being "saved through the grace of the Lord Jesus" (15:11), a nonpauline way of putting it.[44] I agree with Reumann's assessment of the Lucan use of *dikaio*-words in Acts (4:19; 10:22, 34–35; 13:10; 17:31; 24:15), and especially with that in the sermons (3:14; 7:52; 22:14; 24:24). As I see it, the way that "forgiveness of sins" and *dikaiōthēnai/dikaioutai*, "acquitted," are used in 13:38–39 is a prime example of the Lucan fashioning of Pauline terminology to suit his own proclamation. Though I do not share the common negative

---

42. See my commentary *The Gospel according to Luke I–IX* (AB 28; Garden City, NY: Doubleday, 1981), pp. 47–51.

43. In *JBC* 45:74 I called attention to the echo of Paul's words on Peter's lips in Acts 15:11, but I specifically referred to the Lucan Paul of Acts 13:38–39 (comparing Gal 5:6, 6:15; Rom 3:24).

44. But cf. Eph 2:5, 8.

view of Luke's handling of the significance of Jesus' death in the gospel and Acts, I agree with Reumann's assessment of the last passage (§252); but I am not fully convinced about the last proposal in §252. Luke's view is, indeed, "not Paul's view" of righteousness, but one that developed in its own way in Gentile Christianity, from both the gospel and OT traditions, in the light of the Christ-event (see Reumann, §253).

412 I have nothing to criticize in Reumann's handling (§§254–61) of the material from the Johannine gospel or Epistles;[45] similarly for the Book of Revelation (§§262–64). Reumann has rightly stressed the heavy influence of the OT understanding of "righteousness" in these NT books, as well as the dependence on early creedal formulas.

413 Any discussion of justification in the NT must eventually cope with the Epistle of James, and Reumann has devoted a good number of pages to this NT writing (§§266–83). Not only have I nothing basic to criticize in his treatment of this epistle, but I was pleasantly surprised to find that he as a modern Lutheran NT interpreter would come so close to my own Roman Catholic understanding of it. For I too find it hard to think that this epistle rests on a Jewish *Grundschrift* or that it is the earliest of NT writings (§266). It would be mind-boggling to think that this writing would have recorded for Christians of later centuries the earliest reaction to the Christ-event that has been preserved. Though I may date the composition of the epistle a little earlier than does Reumann, I have often quoted the same statement of W. G. Kümmel (see Reumann, §275) that the epistle can rightly be understood only as a corrective to something in early Christianity and cannot be regarded as a basis of later developments.[46] James' "indispensable task in the canon can only be achieved where someone as a Christian has already heard the message of Jesus or of Paul, and through James has his vision sharpened for the exhortation to the work which grows out of faith."[47] In agreement with Reumann, I maintain that the epistle is not a refutation of Paul himself or of direct Pauline teaching. The problem to which Jas 2:14–26 addresses itself is a caricature of Pauline teaching, born (most likely) of Paul's tendency to express things generically—to speak of *ex ergōn* (Rom 4:2) or *chōris ergōn* (Rom 4:6), "works" (without a modifier), when he really meant *erga tou nomou,* "works of the law."[48] This generic mode of speaking may have given rise in the early church to a wider understanding of his teaching, perhaps even to a certain antinomianism, against which James writes and maintains that "faith by itself, if it has no works, is dead" (2:17). In this

---

45. Save that I am not sure that the "perversion" envisaged in 1 John 3:7–10 is necessarily "Gnostic" (Reumann, §260).

46. This has to be stressed even if one detects in the epistle a certain affinity to the teaching of the Matthean Gospel; there are echoes in it of the same tradition that was eventually embodied in that gospel.

47. W. G. Kümmel, *Introduction to the New Testament* (rev. ed.; Nashville: Abingdon, 1975), p. 416.

48. See above, §394.

epistle the understanding, then, of faith, works, and the example of Abraham all differ from the real Pauline understanding of them. For James "faith" (at least in this passage) is an intellectual assent to monotheism (2:19), "works" are those that follow faith (2:17), and Abraham's justification is measured by his offering of his son Isaac on the altar (2:21), whereas for Paul "faith" which may begin with a "hearing" (*akoē*) of the word, involves the commitment of the whole person (*hypakoē pisteōs,* often translated as "obedience of faith," Rom 1:5); or "faith working itself out through love" (Gal 5:6), "works" are the *erga tou nomou* of Jewish observance, and Abraham's justification is measured by his faith (understood as a prime OT example of the commitment that Paul preaches). So I can only say "amen," when Reumann writes: "What James seems to set in contrast is not works and faith but 'living faith' and 'dead faith' (*JBC* 59:19); the latter idea can only be a grotesque parody of what Paul taught" (§277).

414   I have no problems with his treatment of Jas 1:20; 3:18; 5:6, 16. I should only stress a little more that James is certainly following a Jewish exegetical tradition (Reumann, §271), with which Paul is making a complete break.[49] Moreover, the fact that *ek pisteōs monon,* "by faith alone," occurs in Jas 2:24 alone in the NT, makes me uneasy with the importation of it into the translation of Gal 2:16 (as Reumann did in §99) or of Rom 3:28 (as Luther did in his translation of 1522). I am aware of Luther's defense of his insertion,[50] of the tradition of using it before him,[51] and of the possible meaning of the Greek *ean mē* that would justify it.[52] But because it is not a *Pauline* usage—he never added *monon* to any statement about justification by faith—but Jacobean, I as a modern NT interpreter, concerned to respect the nuances of differing NT writers, should prefer not to introduce it into a Pauline text. This is admittedly a minor issue, one that is scarcely church-dividing.

415   Concerning Reumann's treatment of Hebrews, I have a few comments to make, most of which are minor; but one is of some substance, since it affects the overall interpretation of the epistle.

Doubts about the Pauline authorship of Hebrews may well have "emerged by the time of the Reformation" (§284), but it should be recalled that its authorship was unknown even in the time of Eusebius: "But who wrote the Epistle, in truth God knows" (*Hist. eccl.* 6.25, 13); and he even knew that some ascribed it to Clement of Rome, and others to Luke. Despite the western church tradition, I agree that Hebrews "must not be read in the shadow of Paul where church tradition has long put it" (Reumann, §285). Moreover, that "some sort of Rechtfertigungslehre of a different sort" from Paul's can be recognized in Hebrews is vaguely enough ex-

---

49. Ibid.

50. "On Translating," LW, Vol. 35, pp. 185, 188, 195, 196.

51. It is found in one form or another in Origen, Hilary, Basil, Chrysostom, Augustine, Cyril of Alexandria, Bernard, Thomas Aquinas.

52. Cf. Gal 1:19 (?); Phil 3:9; Eph 2:8–9; Tit 3:5.

pressed to agree with; but see further §417 below. For the application of Ps 45:7 to Jesus as God's Son applies "righteousness" to him only in an OT ethical sense, and the (debated) use of the same word in 5:13, in a context of milk-drinkers and inexperience, scarcely transcends the meaning of "principle of (ethical/moral) righteousness." The use of Hab 2:3–4 in Heb 10:37–38 may, indeed, differ from the Pauline use of it in Gal 3:11 or Rom 1:17 and be closer to the original meaning of *pistis* = *'ĕmûnāh*, "fidelity/ faithfulness," but the author's introduction of the definite article (*ho*) into the quotation of Hab 2:3 before the particle *erchomenos* not only personalizes it ("the Coming One") but produces a meaning that is hardly "closer to the original OT sense" (Reumann, §289).[53] The collocation of *dikaios* and *pistis* in the quotation from Habakkuk, however, enables the author of Hebrews to proceed to his elaborate description of faith and its OT heroes and heroines in chap. 11. But in what sense does he understand *pistis*? To this I shall return below. Otherwise, I tend to agree with Reumann in his interpretation of Heb 11:4, 7, that both verses represent a "more OT-like" way of thinking than Paul's on being righteous (§290) or "the OT-Jewish exegetical tradition, understood afresh in our author's Christian perspective" (§292).[54] No further comments need be made on Heb 11:33; 12:11, 22–24.

416   Reumann finally asks (§298), "What kind of theology is this, so far as righteousness/justification is involved. . . ?" He proceeds to formulate his answer in §298–300. But I should prefer to give a slightly different nuance to the answer, since I do not agree with him that *pistis* in Hebrew 11 is simply to be understood as the "firm assurance about things hoped for" (§298; at §290, he made use of the similar *RSV* translation). Here he has unquestioningly taken over a translation of *elpizomenōn hypostasis* from the *RSV* or other modern translations (e.g., *NAB, NIV*). It gives to *hypostasis* much more of subjective meaning, "assurance," than I can concede; this meaning is used by many because of the parallelism with *elenchos* in the following phrase and because of *plerophoria*, "full conviction" of 10:22. Having always been a bit uneasy with that understanding of *hypostasis*, I was happy to see H. Koester's discussion of this noun in *TDNT*, a bit of which I may be permitted to quote:

> Whereas all patristic and medieval exegesis presupposed that *hypostasis* was to be translated *substantia* and understood in the

---

53. See further the articles mentioned in my n. 10 above.

54. I find it difficult to agree that the interpretation of the Cain and Abel scene of Gen 4 found in *Tg. Neof.* 1 "lies behind 11:4" (*pace* M. McNamara et al.). It may be a sixteenth-century copy of an older targum; but how much older? The editor, A. Díez Macho, claimed in his introduction to Vol. 1 (*Génesis*, p. 95*) that the targum "pertinece ya a la época neotestamentaria"); but none of the arguments advanced for such an early date have been seen to be convincing (see *CBQ* 32 [1970]: 107–12; A. D. York, "The Dating of Targumic Literature," *Journal for the Study of Judaism* 5 [1974]: 49–62. In particular, the mode of thinking and contrast used here (mercy vs. fruits of good works) is characteristic of a much later Jewish tradition. Can one find it in any Jewish texts in pre-Christian centuries?

sense of *ousia*, Luther's translation introduced a wholly new element into the understanding of Hb. 11:1. Faith is now viewed as personal, subjective conviction. This interpretation has governed Protestant exposition of the passage almost completely, and it has strongly influenced Roman Catholic exegesis. It has also had a broader effect. Yet there can be·no question but that this . . . understanding is untenable. The starting-point of exposition must be that *hypostasis* in Hb. 11:1 has to have not only a meaning like that in Greek usage elsewhere but also a sense similar to that it bears in the other Hb. references. It should also be noted that *hypostasis* here is parallel to *elenchos* and that it occurs in a sentence full of central theological concepts. Now as regards *elenchos* it is evident that this does not mean subjective nondoubting nor does it have anything at all to do with conviction; it bears the objective sense of "demonstration". . . . In the first instance, then, the *elenchos* of *pragmata ou blepomena* is the proof of things one cannot see, i.e., the heavenly world which alone has reality, whereas in Hb. everything visible has only the character of the shadowy and frontal. If one follows the meaning of *hypostasis* in Hb. 1:3, then *hypostasis elpizomenōn* bears a similar sense: it is the reality of the goods hoped for, which have by nature a transcendent quality.[55]

If this then is the meaning of *pistis* in Hebrews 11, and I am inclined to agree with Koester that it is (and would interpret other passages in the epistle in the light of it), then obviously it is a sense of *pistis* that differs considerably from the Pauline. But then it removes *pistis* from an emphatic subjective understanding—and especially the implied connection it has with "conscience" in Reumann's answer (§§298–99).

417   As I understand the teaching of Hebrews, the effects of the Christ-event can be summed up as "purification" (1:3; 9:14; 10:2), "perfection" (10:14; implicitly 9:9; 10:1), "salvation" (2:3, 10; 5:9; 6:9; 9:28), "sanctification" (2:11; 10:10, 14, 29; 13:12); "redemption" (9:12, 15), "expiation" (2:17; implicitly 9:26); "forgiveness" of sins (10:18; implicitly 9:22), and possibly also (new) "life" (10:38; 12:9) and a "washing" (10:22). These are what Jesus, the Son and the eternal high priest, has achieved once for all for human beings who believe. In some of these passages there is even an explicit reference to an effect on their consciences and an awareness of sin (9:14 [in contrast to the Old Covenant, 9:9]; 10:22 [in contrast to 10:2]). The "faith" of those so involved is explicitly mentioned (10:22), and the example of the OT heroes and heroines bolsters that involvement and sheds light on the meaning of *pistis*. But if the author of Hebrews sees the Christian believer affected in these ways by the Christ-event—and even on the level of conscience—he never casts it in terms of "justification" or be-

---

55. "*hypostasis*," *TDNT* 8 (1972), pp. 572–89, esp. 586–87.

ing made righteous by Christ. This is no longer part of his view of the Christ-event, as it was very much part of Paul's. Reumann admits (§298) that the verb *dikaioun* never occurs in Hebrews; nor does the noun *dikaiōsis* (and when *dikaiōma* occurs [9:1, 10], it has an entirely different connotation, "regulation"). Moreover, in the four places in which *pistis* and *dikaio*-terms are used together (10:38 [=Hab 2:4]; 11:4 [of Abel], 7 [of Noah], 33 [of Gideon et al.]—significantly, not of Abraham!) the terms have a sense closer to OT usage than to Paul's (as Reumann himself admits, §§290–93). Consequently, I can agree with Grässer's summary of the teaching of Hebrews as "conscientia perfecta ex opere Christi (per hostiam suam)" and can even add "mediante fide." But is it really a Rechtfertigungslehre—except in a broad sense, such as that which Reumann has used in speaking of a "doctrine of the atonement" or of the "atoning death" of Christ?[56] I should prefer not to speak of it as such. Similarly, I should not like to think of "the gospel" as limited to either the Pauline Rechtfertigungslehre or Hebrews' "conscientia perfecta ex opere Christi." There is much more to it than what is expressed by either of these teachings. In the light of these remarks I can agree in general with the parallels between Paul and Hebrews (set forth by Reumann, §300). But I should stress that they are at most parallel *aspects of the gospel* (not "the gospel"). Similarly, the author of Hebrews does exhibit "in his treatise yet another way of presenting the Christ-event and its meaning" (§300), but with a "modest use of *dikaio*-terms" (§286).

418   I have no real disagreement with Reumann's treatment of the *dikaio*-passages in 1 Peter. I too recognize the influence of Pauline disciples in the composition of this letter; the author says that the letter has been written "through Silvanus" (5:12), which could be a reference to a sometime companion of Paul (see 1 Thess 1:1), but there is no way to be sure that the same person is meant. Moreover, just as Reumann has stressed, the heritage behind some of the passages discussed might just as easily be that of common apostolic Christianity. And he does right to mention that the mode in which "one gets to be *dikaios*" is left "undefined" (§304).

419   In the treatment of 2 Peter I can easily go along with much of what Reumann has written (§§305–18). One aspect of the letter should perhaps have been stressed a little more, viz., its reference to Paul in chap. 3. For it is this latest writing in the NT that clearly alerts us to the problems that some parts of the church in the early second century were experiencing with the Pauline letters (by now probably collected in a corpus). Though the author refers to "our beloved brother Paul" and to the "wisdom given to him" that is found "in all his letters," yet "there are some things in them that are difficult to understand, which the unlearned and unstable twist to their own destruction, as they do with the rest of the Scriptures" (3:15–16). It would obviously be wrong to restrict the "some things" to the Pauline doctrine of justification by faith, but the statement

---

56. See my n. 12 above.

provides a background for the caricature of Paul's teaching on the subject against which the Epistle of James inveighs in chap. 2.

420   Reumann's discussion of 2 Pet 1:1 is balanced (§§306–10) and comes up with a plausible solution. I too would stress the OT background of the teaching against the false teachers in chap. 2, but I also realize that what *dikaio*-language is present in the letter is a development beyond both that of the OT and that of Paul. Reumann's summary in §314 is adequate. As for Frühkatholizismus in 2 Peter, I react much as does Reumann to Käsemann's exaggerations, and can only agree that "we would do well to avoid it for 2 Peter, unless very carefully defined" (§317).[57] However, I am not sure that I should want to go along with Schenke-Fischer that 2 Peter leads Christians along "the wrong track (*einen Irrweg*)" (Reumann, §318). Even apart from the Frühkatholizismus question, 2 Peter is part of the canon, and as such stands over Christians of every generation not only as part of the inspired word of God, but also as an encapsulation of the gospel. I am not sure that it does not—in its own way—preserve some of "the inheritance of the primitive Christian kerygma."

X

421   Reumann's discussion of the canon within the canon (§§319–25) in the course of his summary reflections is well done; point for point, I could only say "Amen."[58] And his recommendation to "allow the breadth that the NT does have for faith and life" is to be respected, "while reflecting in our days its emphases and centralities" is eminently reasonable. I should only emphasize the word "its" in the last clause.

422   As for the "central criterion for the NT" (§326) or *die Mitte der Schrift,* I resonate positively to Reumann's suggestion that it be considered as "the gospel." That the gospel be considered "the norm and standard for each part of Scripture" (§329) is likewise acceptable, provided that it is recalled that the gospel is not known to us independently of the written Scriptures (see §353 (1d) above). In saying this, I again understand "gospel" as the same as "the word of God," as does Reumann (§327; see §353 (1c) above), and I admit that it can "be expressed in many ways in differing situations in the NT" (§327) and that Paul has a variety of ways of expressing it, "including (first in our list) 'justification' " (ibid.), without, however, implying thereby that it is the essential way. It is first because of the quantitative abundance of its occurrence in his mature letters. But it must be specified that for Paul this means "justification by grace through faith," a specification that will not always be present, even when the gospel

---

57. See further J. H. Elliott, "A Catholic Gospel: Reflections on 'Early Catholicism' in the New Testament," *CBQ* 31 (1969): 213–23.

58. Though Reumann probably does not intend the equation of "deuterocanonical" and the *antilegomena,* it should be recalled that only some of the ancient *antilegomena* acquired deuterocanonical status in the Roman Catholic canon, not all of them.

may be summed up as justification/righteousness in other NT passages. Moreover, though pride of place is thus admitted for "justification" as an expression of the gospel in Pauline writings, one has to recognize that even he has "alternate ways of proclaiming the gospel" (§328), which may resemble the "interchange" of justification with other NT expressions or images that is found in the CA and the Apology. But the variety of NT images is normally respected by modern "NT scholarship" (§326), which warns us against regarding this interchange as equation (e.g., that "justification" is "the forgiveness of sins") in the NT itself.

423 Reumann has, indeed, shown that righteousness/justification is more prevalent in NT teaching than has normally been suspected in earlier centuries or among earlier commentators, and that it is an image of prime importance for an expression of the Christ-event or even the gospel. But his own exposé in this book has sought to set carefully the sense in which righteousness/justification is to be understood in the various passages of the NT in which it occurs. It is not always the specific nuance of Pauline "justification by grace through faith," which received the emphatic emphasis of Martin Luther and his followers in the sixteenth century. This emphasis cannot be allowed to dwarf other legitimate expressions or aspects of the gospel.[59]

424 As for Reumann's résumé (§§331–46), I have little to add to what I have already set forth. He has done well to isolate prepauline, Pauline, and postpauline materials, even if I have expressed some hesitation about how certain we can be about the prepauline material in every passage treated or what role it plays in Pauline theology once it has been incorporated into one of his letters. I have already expressed my hesitation about the relation between "creation" in the OT and God's righteousness and about the pertinence of some NT passages (which depict Jesus as the Righteous One, vindicated by God, and dying for the unrighteous), none of which passages have ever been divisive between our churches. The "pattern of religion" expressed in the Pauline categories of righteousness/justification (§341) may well have been less sustained in ensuing patristic centuries; but I am not sure that they were not sustained at all.

425 Reumann has indeed shown "the considerable spread of righteous-

---

59. Having admitted this, I should prefer to state this matter a bit differently. If the "gospel" may thus be understood as the norm for Christian faith for believers of all generations, this may seem in the long run an inadequate way of stating what that norm really is. "Gospel" may well be admitted to be *die Mitte der Schrift*. But I prefer to regard as the norm of Christian belief for the generations after the primitive community the impact of the historical Jesus of Nazareth (through his person, deed, and word) along with the variety of images and expressions of that impact recorded for us in the different NT writings. The two have to be kept in tandem: the historical Jesus and the NT distillate. For Christians of later generations have no channel or pipeline to Jesus that prescinds from that distillate. As a Roman Catholic interpreter, I would naturally include the dogmatic tradition, but only insofar as it is a genuine development of and remains in dynamic contact with that distillate. For it is the *norma normata*. See further "Belief in Jesus Today," *Commonweal* 101 (1974): 137–42.

ness/justification as a theme among NT writers in varying situations" (§347) and that it is "far greater than one might have supposed," and does well to stress the theological loss, if God as judge and the lawsuit, lawcourt motif were to disappear from Christian thinking. But in this last passage of summary references to righteousness/justification, abundant as he has shown them to be, he passes too quickly to "justification by grace through faith" (labeled even as "the exemplary expression of the gospel," whereas I should prefer to say "an exemplary expression of the Pauline gospel"). The Reformation choice did properly restore an emphasis to an aspect of NT theology in the historical church that had been sadly neglected—an emphasis derived from the greatest NT writing, Paul's letter to the Romans. Under such emphasis the Council of Trent eventually gave recognition to it too.

426 That contemporary biblical investigation makes the case for righteousness/justification even more intriguing than our forebears would have suspected, I can agree. When Reumann says, "While Lutherans today are impressed with the soundness of the choice made in 1530 by CA 4 and find it bolstered by the fact that it existed as an expression of the gospel prior to Paul and by its development afterward, they also recognize that elsewhere the gospel could be—and was—expressed in other ways and that even Paul had varied concepts in which to put God's good news," I have to ask for a clarification: Does the "gospel prior to Paul" mean precisely "justification by grace through faith"? My impression of CA 4 is that this is what is meant there.

427 Finally, there is one aspect of this problem of justification in NT teaching that needs to be emphasized from my point of view. Reumann has done a superb job in summarizing and commenting on the various NT passages dealing with *dikaio*-language. He has discussed well and fairly the Pauline passages that speak of justification by grace through faith and not by works of the law. He has not hedged in the discussion of the eschatological dimension of justification, of its relation to faith working itself out in love (Gal 5:6), or of its relation to Jas 2:14–26. But there is an aspect of NT teaching that has gone untouched in his paper, an aspect that cries out for some treatment, viz., the question of NT teaching on "reward" and "merit" in Christian life, and its relation to justification and salvation. It is the question that Jas 2:14–26 was trying to address (in its own way), that Phil 2:12 hints at, and that various gospel episodes inculcate. But we cannot fault him for not having done everything.

The Pastoral Epistles on Righteousness

————————————————————————————————**3**

Jerome D. Quinn

428 In the second Christian century the Pastoral Epistles (PE hereafter)[1] were already being read in the order Titus, 1–2 Timothy, and in a single collection, separate from that of Pauline letters to churches.[2] They may well have appeared originally in precisely the form of an epistolary rather than as individual letters.[3] In any event they were in circulation in the second Christian generation, perhaps as early as A.D. 85.

429 Paul, his apostolate, the tradition of his teaching, dominate the PE. Out of the framework of a last missionary journey by the apostle, their author makes his case for what will bring authentic continuity with Paul and unity among sharply divided Christian congregations.[4] The PE open in the Letter to Titus with the Pauline directives for churches in which Jewish Christians are the dominant element. The correspondence with Timothy turns to the congregations in which converts from paganism predominate (see 1 Tim 2:3–7) and closes with the Pauline last will and testa-

---

1 Background for summary observations that appear below can be found in other essays that I have published. The following footnotes will cite these studies by using the letter of the alphabet that here precedes each one. The translations from PE are my own.

A "P⁴⁶—The Pauline Canon?" *CBQ* 36 (1974): 379–85.

B "Ministry in the New Testament," in *Biblical Studies in Contemporary Thought* (ed. M. Ward; Somerville, MA: Greeno-Hadden, 1975), pp. 130–60.

C "The Last Volume of Luke: The Relation of Luke-Acts and the PE," in *Perspectives on Luke-Acts* (ed. C. Talbert; Edinburgh: T. & T. Clark, 1978), pp. 62–75.

D "The Holy Spirit in the PE," in *Sin, Salvation, and the Spirit* (ed. D. Durken; Collegeville, MN: Liturgical Press, 1979), pp. 345–68.

E "On the Terminology for Faith, Truth, Teaching, and the Spirit in the PE: A Summary," in *Teaching Authority and Infallibility in the Church* (cited above, Editor's Note, n. 1), pp. 232–37, 342–44.

F "Paul's Last Captivity," in *Studia Biblica 1978* (ed. E. Livingstone; Sheffield: *Journal for the Study of the New Testament,* 1980), 3, pp. 289–99.

G "Jesus as Savior and Only Mediator (1 Tim 2:4–6)," in *Foi et culture à la lumière de la Bible* (ed. Pontifical Biblical Commission; Torino; Elle di Ci, 1981), pp. 249–60.

H "Parenesis and the PE," *De la loi au Messie* (Cazelles fs; cited above, Fitzmyer n. 10), pp. 495–501.

2. See Quinn, A.

3. See Quinn, C, pp. 63–64, 68–72.

4. See Quinn, F, pp. 292–97.

ment of Second Timothy. Thus the PE submit a Pauline *aggiornamento* for a second generation of believers. The apostolate of the Paul of history ended with his execution. The PE offer a "translation" of that ministry and its teaching, consciously aiming at extending Paul's apostolate and offering a doctrinal synthesis to believers who had never seen or heard the Apostle, to whom he had never written. There is no convincing evidence that the author of this correspondence actually quotes the letters that the Apostle had sent on occasion to particular congregations.[5] The PE are rather like a net that has been dropped into a living stream of Pauline Christian practice and teaching, perhaps a stream that flowed from a congregation that the Apostle had instructed (Rome?). The resulting catch is offered for wide consumption.

430 The practical doctrinal synthesis that the PE submit is evidently shaped by and adapted to the needs of believers who now had a history, a past that was simultaneously beyond their immediate experience and yet was profoundly influencing their daily decisions and existence.[6] For the PE, that past speaks with the voice of Paul, a voice that still insists on the Apostle's understanding of righteousness and its relation to faith and works. The Paul of history had addressed his teaching to relatively recent converts to the Christian faith. The PE translate that teaching for congregations that now include not only new converts (1 Tim 3:6) but also an older generation with a younger one that had been reared in Christian homes (cf. Titus 1:6; 2:2–7; etc.). The needs of the new generation include a need for Paul.

431 The characteristic emphasis of the PE appears when one contrasts their positive teaching on righteousness, using the *dik*-cluster of Greek terms, with their single reference to unrighteousness, *adikia*, in 2 Tim 2:19. The rest of the Paulines exploit the antithetical *adik*-terminology much more often. Such verbal dialectic is not particularly congenial to an author who is already contending with terminological grassfires (cf. Titus 1:10–11 with 3:9 and 1 Tim 1:6–7) and who at this point in 2 Timothy is taking issue with those who "quibble over words" and whose "profane drivel" (2 Tim 2:14, 16) is emptying the resurrection of its true meaning. His riposte to this teaching (*logos;* 2:17) is to take up a catena of texts, already traditional among believers, " 'The Lord knows those who are his' and 'Let everyone who names the name of the Lord *depart from unrighteousness*' ". The italicized phrase may have been adapted from Sir 35:3 (cf. 7:2); in *Testament of Dan* 6:10 it appears in the form, "Depart therefore from all unrighteousness and cleave to the righteousness (*dikaiosynē*) of the law of the Lord."[7] In both texts the reference is to human acts prescribed or interdicted by the torah, and the PE are capitalizing on a similar line of thought

---

5. See Quinn, C, p. 66.
6. See Quinn, B, pp. 149–51, 155–58; G, pp. 249–50.
7. See n. 9 on 2 Tim 2:22.

as their author stonewalls the doctrine of those whose conduct[8] does not correspond with their profession of Christian belief. These men deny the final resurrection of all because that is inextricably bound to the final judgment of all, and their conduct would not pass muster in that setting where "the Lord knows those who are his." The drastic judgment that the God of Israel inflicted on the rebellion of Korah against Moses (cf. LXX Num 16:5) is a paradigm for the judgment that the *Kyrios,* the risen Lord of the church, has in store for those who resist the authority and teaching of Paul (cf. 2 Tim 3:8–9).

432   In this perspective the emphasis of the PE on the good conduct of all classes of believers becomes intelligible. The new Pauline presbyter-bishops are to be selected for their virtues, familial and personal. They are to be "sensible, upright (*dikaion*), devout, self-controlled" (Titus 1:8).[9] Thus, with Titus (Titus 2:1, 7–8), they will instruct believers, old and young, men and women, free and slaves, to make visible in their daily conduct "the grace of God" intended "for all human beings" (Titus 2:11). That grace had dawned in the life and death of Jesus "to set us free from every wrong (*anomias*) and to cleanse for himself a people of his very own" (2:14). The "fine conduct" (*kaloi ergoi,* 2:7, 14; 3:8, 14) of this people with their Pauline ministry, disciplined by this grace to "disown godlessness and worldly lusts and to live in a sensible, honest (*dikaiōs*), godly way" continues to reveal in human history, "in this present age," (Titus 2:12) what the terminology for righteousness actually signifies. Genuine Christian conduct is not antinomian and it stops the accusations of unbelievers who claim it is (Titus 2:8, 10; 1 Tim 3:7; 6:1).[10] For the PE, moreover, good deeds are not enough; they must be visibly good and attractive (*kala* as distinct from *agatha*).[11] The actual conduct of believers is thus keryg-

---

8. See 2 Tim 3:1–5, noting particularly the denial of the *dynamis* that must enliven godliness, i.e., the power of the resurrection (cf. 1 Tim 1:12–13 with 2 Tim 2:1; 4:17) and the Spirit (cf. the *pneuma . . . dynameōs* of 2 Tim 1:7 and Quinn, D, p. 361).

9. In this same connection, it is notable that the first obligation of the one who shares the Pauline ministry is to "pursue upright conduct (*diōke de dikaiosynēn*)" (1 Tim 6:11; 2 Tim 2:22). The language is Septuagintal (Prov 15:9; cf. Sir 27:8; Deut 16:20) and denotes something more than a superficial moralism, for Isa 51:1 puts those who pursue *justice* (*hoi diōkontes to dikaion*) into parallel with those who seek *the Lord* (*zētountes ton kyrion*). The righteousness of the God of the patriarchs (cf. Isa 51:8) is the "indicative" behind and beyond these imperatives. The provocative and programmatic essay of Lloyd Gaston, "Abraham and the Righteousness of God," *Horizons in Biblical Theology* 2 (1980): 39–68, ought to be studied in this connection, as well as J. W. Olley, *'Righteousness' in the Septuagint of Isaiah: A Contextual Study* (SBL Septuagint and Cognate Studies Series; Missoula, MT: Scholars Press, 1979), pp. 96–101. On "pursuing righteousness" in Rom 9:30–31, see Reumann, above, §156.

10. On the apologetic purpose of the NT Haustafeln, see A. J. Malherbe, "Hellenistic Moralists and the New Testament," *Aufstieg und Niedergang der römischen Welt* (ed. H. Temporini; Berlin: de Gruyter, forthcoming). I am grateful to Professor Malherbe who shared with me this important study while it was still in MS.

11. In the PE the plural "works (*erga*)" are usually qualified as *kala* (Titus 2:7, 14; 3:8, 14, etc.), only once as *agatha* (1 Tim 2:10). That this emphasis is indeed characteristic of PE

matic, i.e., it proclaims to unbelievers the gospel of Christ's death for our sins and his resurrection for our justification (cf. Rom 4:25).

433 Christian deeds precede and are the setting for the Christian word, "the message meant to be believed," *pistos ho logos* (Titus 3:8a). The unbeliever is attracted by the changed conduct of those who once were as he still is. He asks why and how this happened. The answering word, the *logos,* is an ecclesial confession of faith in the gospel as Paul taught it.[12] The formulation is certainly no quotation of an extant Pauline letter; yet it no less surely proclaims Paul's gospel on the total gratuity of the righteousness bestowed by the Spirit and baptism. The church, which believes that God did not save us "because of deeds (*ex ergōn*) that are righteous (*en dikaiosynē*), deeds that (*ha*) we performed ourselves" (Titus 3:5), has outlived the controversies that dictated the language of Galatians and Romans. In the crabbed Greek of this passage "works" are qualified not with the Pauline "of the law"[13] but with the Septuagintal *en diakaiosynē*.[14] The righteousness in question is biblical, i.e., righteousness as the OT (see 2 Tim 3:15–16) and first-century Judaism conceived it, an obedient performance of the commands of the one God. The performance of such works, precisely as our own, merely human response to the divine will, emphatically did not bring God's salvation to his people.[15] That salvation appeared in the person of one whose name means "savior,"[16] one through whom the Father's righteousness and mercy touch and heal inwardly those who believe and are baptized. "God's was the grace that made us upright" (Titus 3:7).[17] With this phrase the language and the conceptualization of "the

---

can be seen in contrasting the usage of the other Paulines, which never qualify *ergon* with *kalon* (though see Gal 6:9). The connotation of visible attractiveness that the Greek *kalos* suggests is exploited in the argument of Wis 13 where the works (*erga*) of God can lead human beings to the Creator "because the things that are seen are beautiful (*hoti kala ta blepomena,* 13:7)." Here in PE that argument is applied to the *kala erga,* which the Savior God produces in his people, works intended to attract unbelievers to the God who wills the salvation of all.

12. See Quinn, D, p. 347; E, pp. 232–33.

13. Though this omission does not make the statement unpauline, as the usage in Rom 9:11–12 illustrates.

14. This phrase occurs over forty times in the LXX, especially in the Psalms and Isaiah; it recurs in PE in the description of the usefulness of the OT Scriptures (2 Tim 3:16). None of the other Paulines uses exactly this phrase, though an expanded form of it occurs in Eph 4:24, 5:9, as well as in the canticle of Luke 1:75. The other NT uses of *en dikaiosynēi* (Acts 17:31; 2 Pet 1:1; Rev 19:11) apply it to God and/or Christ.

15. See Deut 9:5–6; note that the already emphatic *hēmeis* is further emphasized by its final position.

16. See Quinn, G, pp. 251–53.

17. Literally, "made upright by the grace of that one [i.e. of the God who saved us and who has been mentioned previous to Jesus Christ]." The link between saving mercy and righteousness in biblical Hebrew passed into LXX Greek (cf. LXX Isa 45:25, 46:13, 51:1–8; Gaston and Olley as cited in n. 9; qualifying C. H. Dodd as cited in Reumann, n. 22). On the meaning of *edikaiōthē en pneumati* in the prepauline hymnic fragment of 1 Tim 3:16, see Quinn, D, pp. 353–55.

message meant to be believed" coincide certainly with that of the Paul of Romans and Galatians, as Reumann has explained (cf. above, §§180, 182, 185, 190). The church that used this confession was as firmly committed to the Pauline explanation of the relationship between genuine holiness and merely human acts as it was committed to the seriousness and missionary importance of the visibly good conduct that the Spirit prompted in those who had "put their faith in God" (Titus 3:8b).[18] The Paul of history had to counter charges that his teaching about justification encouraged evil acts (cf. Rom 3:8 with 6:1, 15). The author of PE was compelled to explain why the conduct of believers was (and ought to be) attractively good.

434   The polemical reference in Titus 3:9 to "wranglings about the law (*machas nomikas*)" implies that the "works of the law" against which Paul had inveighed (Gal 2:16) were still like red-hot coals under the gray ashes of the previous generation. The problem of law and its relation to the Christian believer is addressed formally[19] when the PE turn from the predominantly Jewish-Christian congregations envisioned in Titus to the congregations of predominantly Gentile origin who are expected to hear the correspondence with Timothy. That was the context in which the Paul of history had addressed the problem. The PE retain that setting as they propose the true Pauline teaching about the law (1 Tim 1:8–11) in contrast to the strange teachings propounded by some Christians who want to be "rabbis" (*nomodidaskaloi:* cf. 1 Tim 1:3, 7). Paul's "gospel" (1 Tim 1:11) is the measure for any "wholesome instruction" (1 Tim 1:10)[20] about the application of the OT as "law" to Christian living. "Fine (*kalos*) as we know the law (*ho nomos*) is, there is still the question of using it lawfully (*nomimōs*). That involves knowing that the law (*nomos*) is not laid down for an upright person (*dikaiō̦*); rather it is for lawless (*anomois*) and refractory persons . . ." (1 Tim 1:8–9). The upright person here, "set free from every wrong (*anomias*)," is one of the community of believers, described above in Titus 2:14, who stand by the Pauline interpretation of the OT.[21] With the Paul of Romans the PE affirm that the law, like the creation of which it is part, is manifestly and attractively good (*kalos;* cf. 1 Tim 4:4).[22] But like the rest of creation too, the law can be misused as a tool in "the workshop

---

18. See Quinn, D, pp. 352–53.

19. The concentration of *nom*-terminology in 1 Tim 1:7–9 is not found elsewhere in the PE.

20. See Quinn, E, pp. 235–36; G, pp. 257–60.

21. Cf. the emphatic first personal plural address of Titus 2:11–14 with the *oidamen* of 1 Tim 1:8. The upright person (*dikaios*) of 1 Tim 1:9 is not simply a "good citizen" (*NEB*) but a good Christian.

22. On the sense of *kalos,* see my n. 11; note that for Rom 7:12–16 the law is holy (*hagios*), spiritual (*pneumatikos*), and fine (*kalos*); its commandment is holy and righteous and good (*hagia kai dikaia kai agathē*). From this adjectival cope around the law the PE pull a single thread, *kalos,* which is woven, as noted above, into their description of *erga.*

of sin."[23] The law is itself subject to law (*nomimōs*).[24] What is the anterior principle, universal in character,[25] that enables a believer to make legitimate use of the torah? How can a Christian be *amicus legis*?[26] On the presupposition, the PE respond, that he recognize for whose sake law is laid down.[27] It is not meant for an upright person, i.e., for those made upright by God's grace (see Titus 3:7 above). Law is for the lawless as grace is for the upright.[28] In connection with this passage of 1 Timothy, Clement of Alexandria adduces Heraclitus's saying, "They would not know the name of Right, if these things [i.e. the opposite] did not exist."[29] He adds that "Socrates says that law was not produced for the sake of the good."[30] Antiphon (v cent. BC) is cited to the same effect.[31] The concept was in the air in first-century Latin circles.[32] A passage in *Enoch* may witness to its circulation in Hellenistic Judaism in the same period.[33] The PE set the Pauline ecclesial confession, "Fine as we know the law is," within the horizon of current Hellenistic and Roman explanations about the purpose of law in

---

23. Käsemann, *Romans,* p. 205; cf. p. 198.

24. Cf. 2 Tim 2:5 with the unique LXX use in 4 Macc 6:18. As often in the PE, the term has been chosen as much for its sound in the *nomos* wordplay of this passage as for its meaning.

25. C. Spicq (EBib, 4th ed. 1969), p. 331, has called attention to the anarthrous nouns in 1 Tim 1:9a.

26. Thus Ambrosiaster on Rom 2:12 (*PL* 17.67).

27. The passive suggests that the saying applies to the divine lawgiver of the torah (*kalos ho nomos*) as well as to the action of human legislators.

28. Clement of Alexandria cites 1 Tim 1:7–8 to explain why he has said that "both the law and the gospel are the energy (*energeia*) of the one Lord who is 'the power and wisdom of God' " (*Stromata* 1.27, text ed. O. Stählin, *Clemens Alexandrinus, Zweiter Band* [Die griechischen christlichen Schriftsteller der ersten drei Jahrhunderte 15; Leipzig: Hinrichs, 1906], p. 108; cf. 7.2 [Stählin, p. 8]).

29. *Stromata* 4.3 (Stählin, p. 252); H. Diels, *Die Fragmente der Vorsokratiker* (5th ed.; Berlin, 1934–38), #23; Eng. trans., K. Freeman, *Ancilla to the Presocratic Philosophers* (Cambridge, MA: Harvard Univ. Press, 1948), p. 26.

30. *Nomon heneka agathōn ouk an genesthai;* the source of this saying is not extant.

31. Stobaeus, IX. 15 (ed. C. Wachsmuth, 3, p. 349), *ho mēden adikōn oudenos deitai nomou,* "the one who does no wrong needs no law."

32. See Ovid, *Metamorphoses* 1:89–90, on that golden age when humankind *sine lege fidem rectumque colebat,* and Tacitus, *Annales* 3.26, on the eruption of evils that brought it about that men *leges maluerunt.*

33. In *Enoch* 93.3–4, Enoch says, "I was born the seventh in the first week while justice and righteousness still lasted. And after me in the second week great wickedness will arise. . . . a man [Noah] will be saved . . . and he [Noah/God] will make a law for sinners." The translation is by M. A. Knibb, *The Ethiopic Book of Enoch* (Oxford: Clarendon, 1978), 2, pp. 223–24 (for the text, see 1, p. 349). Neither a Greek nor an Aramaic text is extant at this point, though the fragments of 4QEnAram[g] 1. iv (J. T. Milik, *The Books of Enoch* [Oxford: Clarendon, 1976], p. 361, cf. pp. 265–67) by and large correspond with the Ethiopic Enoch 93.9–10 (see Knibb 2, p. 14). This view concerning who needs law appears in other words in Philo *Legum Allegoriae,* 1.93–94, and perhaps in the expansion of the MT that occurs in LXX Esther 5:1f (cf. the still later version of Vulgate Esther 15:13).

For second-century Christian development of the same principle, see Irenaeus, *Adversus Haereses* 4.16.3, applying 1 Tim 1:9 to the patriarchs of Israel (cf. his *Demonstration of the Apostolic Preaching* #35).

general. In a previous generation Paul, in an intramural Christian controversy, had taught, "now it is evident that no man is justified before God by the law; for he who through faith is righteous (*ho dikaios*) shall live" (Gal 3:11, cf. 2:16; Rom 1:17, 3:20, 28). The PE set out to rearticulate that Pauline teaching. The Pauline gospel is retained and reaffirmed with the emphatically positioned *dikaiō*, of 1 Tim 1:9. For the upright person (and that means for the believer whom only God has justified), the law as such—whether Jewish or Roman—has no power to make upright and to sanctify. Thus the PE deliberately initiate a dialogue between the Pauline gospel and certain views circulating among those who had not yet believed. The principle adduced in 1 Tim 1:9*a* is another example of the methods used by the believers of the second Christian generation to penetrate and to speak to the ambient cultures and to invite them to the faith.[34]

435   The upright believer is, on the other hand, not antinomian, any more than he is a liar or a murderer (cf. 1 Tim 1:9*b*). He does not reject all laws, divine and human.[35] The point of the contrast here is that the law is "superfluous"[36] for the believer who in virtue of the Spirit and faith in Christ (cf. Gal 5:22–23) already does and more than does what the law can only command.[37] Again the PE presuppose that an observably good Christian life is the only setting within which one can profitably discuss the relation of all law to that life.

436   The Pauline synthesis submitted by the PE draws to a close with the Apostle's last will and testament in 2 Timothy. The great opening thanksgiving prayer, placed on his lips in 2 Tim 1:3–14, has as its doctrinal mainspring a confessional description of God's saving intervention (2 Tim 1:9–10). As Reumann has noted (above, §182) a Pauline teaching about righteousness lies just below the surface of 2 Tim 1:9, which has many links with the confession of Titus 3:4–7, particularly in its references to grace and mercy. The hendiadys in 2 Tim 1:9 of God's grace with his purpose (*prothesis*) ought not to be overlooked. The term and concept are rooted in Rom 8:28 and 9:11 with their specifically Pauline teaching about the altogether and in every sense antecedent plan of God that originated and stood behind all that happened in the life, death, and rising of Jesus.[38] For proclaiming this gospel Paul certainly has suffered.[39] The one who

---

34. See Quinn, E, pp. 232–35; G, pp. 249–50, 259–60.

35. Cf. LXX Esther 3:13*d* (*RSV* 13:4), of the Jews, and Tacitus, *Annales,* 15.44, of the Christians.

36. Theodore of Mopsuestia in loc., repeating *superflua* three times; text in *Theodori Episcopi Mopsuesteni in Epistolas B. Pauli Commentarii,* ed. H. B. Swete (Cambridge, 1880–82), pp. 76–78.

37. See the *Epistle to Diognetus,* 5, 10, and Augustine, *In Iohannem* 3:2 (*Corpus Christianorum, series Latina* 36, p. 21). *Qui enim legem implet, non est sub lege, sed cum lege.*

38. See Käsemann, *Romans,* p. 264, on the relation of the Pauline doctrine on justification to the divine *prothesis.*

39. Cf. 2 Tim 1:8, 12 with 3:10–12, noting that as God's *prothesis* brought sufferings to the Christ, so Paul's *prothesis* brings him persecutions.

shares his apostolic ministry can expect to suffer with him (2 Tim 1:8; 2:3) for the treasure of the gospel that Christ has entrusted to Paul and Paul in turn to Timothy (2 Tim 1:12–14). No mechanical transfer of goods and records is envisioned here, since the Holy Spirit presides over the personal transmission of this deposit.[40]

437   Paul's last captivity is the setting that PE propose for Paul's last testament in 2 Tim 2:1–4:8,[41] and that testament has Paul finally looking over the horizon of his death to "the crown of righteousness (*dikaiosynēs*)" with which "the righteous (*dikaios*) judge," Jesus Christ, "will recompense (*apodōsei*) me on the last day—and of course not only me but all who have their hearts set on his revelation" (2 Tim 4:8). As Reumann has noted (above, §183), one cannot altogether decide between an objective or a subjective sense for the righteousness here. Since the Greek is patient of either interpretation, it is conceivable that the author of the PE did not regard the subjective/objective options as mutually exclusive. The mystery of the inner link between *dikaiosynē* as an upright life and *dikaiosynē* as God's gracious gift on this reading crosses the threshold of human history, to become an integral part of the final *mysterium tremendum,* the appearance of all human beings "before the judgment seat of Christ, so that each one may receive good or evil, according to what he has done in the body" (2 Cor 5:10). Just as Alexander the coppersmith, in the personal note appended to the Pauline testament of 2 Timothy (4:14), is to receive compensation from the Lord (*apodōsei autō*) that accords with the many bad things (*kata ta erga autou*) with which he charged the apostle (*polla . . . kaka enedeixato*),[42] so Paul himself in 4:8 is to receive from the same Lord the victor's crown, which is understood to be *kata ta erga kala k'agatha* of the Apostle. The ecclesial aspect of that reward appears in the closing words of 4:8 with their reference to all those who have set their hearts[43] on the final glorious appearance of Jesus the Lord (cf. 1 Tim 6:14 with 2 Tim 1:10).

---

40. See Quinn, D, pp. 362–63; E, 236–37.

41. On the relation of epistolary parenesis to the testamentary form, see Quinn, H, p. 499.

42. See Quinn, F, pp. 295–96.

43. Contrast the *ēgapēkosi* here with *agapēsas* of Demas in 4:10, "his heart set on this present world."

Epilogue

A Closing Comment by the Essayists

438   While our papers show many areas of agreement (and we declined to explore in them, even in these versions for publication, numerous other avenues of potential agreement or disagreement in which we as biblical scholars might have been interested but which were not directly relevant for the dialogue), we may report that there are a number of areas of seeming disagreement that further discussion might, and in many cases did, narrow. The results of our conversations at the dialogue and the questions and reactions of our colleagues we have not attempted to include here. In many cases they will be seen reflected in Volume 7 of Lutherans and Catholics in Dialogue.

439   The paper of Professor Reumann is, save for minor editing, exactly as presented to the dialogue sessions. The responses of Professor Fitzmyer were delivered in writing and sometimes orally on each of the three occasions; that by Msgr. Quinn was offered in oral form at the Gettysburg meeting; both responses were written for publication in the spring of 1981, after the dialogue completed its discussion of the biblical materials. In a few cases we have inserted at the proper point references to literature now in print that was in process and not yet published at the time of the meeting.

440   The request for further treatment of certain related aspects of the topic (see above esp. § 427) was met in the dialogue by presentations at the February 1981 meeting by Msgr. Quinn, "The Scriptures on Merit," and by Dr. Joseph A. Burgess, "Rewards, But in a Very Different Sense." The dialogue looks to reflection, and possible publication, of these further essays in its Volume 7 on justification.

J.R., J.A.F., J.D.Q.

Indexes

As in the cross-referencing system in the book, references to the body of each essay are made here by *sections,* not by page numbers. E.g., for Gen 2:7, "270" denotes § 270. Since the footnotes to each author's essay begin anew at 1, for footnotes the *page* and note numbers are given; e.g., for Gen ch. 4 "222 n. 54" denotes p. 222, note 54. Sections are cited first; then footnotes. The abbreviation "bibl." (for "bibliography") indicates where literature on a book or topic will be especially found. The most important section(s) where a passage is discussed is/are indicated in boldface; e.g., for Gen 15:6 the chief discussion is in section **103.**

I. Scripture and Related Sources

A. The Old Testament

Genesis

2:7	270
4	222 n. 54
4:4	290
6:9	34, 292, 359
7:1	311, 359
12:2-3	47, 361
14:18	31
15:6	36, **103**, 139, 140, 270, 280, 292, 298, 359
17:11	140
18:19	36, 359
19:19	362
19:30–38	311
20:13	362
21:23	362
22	139, 270, 298
24:49	362
38:26	45; 20 n. 26

Exodus

9:27	35
25:17–22	71
31:7	71
34:6–7	258
35:12	71
37:7–9	71

Leviticus

6:23	60
14:19	60

16:13	395
17	71
18:5	159
19:15	359

Numbers

16:5	431

Deuteronomy

9:5–6	234 n. 15
10:17	128
11:12	297
16:20	233 n. 9
24:13	34
30:11–14	159
32:4	35, 258, 262, 297
33:21	40, 45, 93, 267; 201 n. 8

Joshua

2	270
10:1	31
24:14	362
38:19	362

Judges

5:11	35, 45, 314, 359; 20 n. 26

1 Samuel

12:4	293
12:7	359

2 Samuel

8:15	293

B.   The New Testament

2:9	126
2:10	390
2:11	126, 127, 159
2:12	124; 236 n. 26
2:12–29	131
2:13	124
2:14–16	155
2:16	197
2:26	124, 152
2:26–27	126
3	78
3:1–7	75 n. 80
3:1–8	131
3:1–20	130, **131**
3:2	132; 75 n. 80
3:3	132
3:3ff.	131, 133
3:4	61, 130, 132
3:5	17, 119, 130, 131, 132, 309, 387, 392; 10 n. 14
3:7	75 n. 80
3:7ff	131
3:8	134, 144, 153, 433
3:9	250
3:10	130
3:10–18	124, 136
3:18	130
3:20	124, 126, 130, 136, 174, 363, 401, 434
3:20ff.	128
3:21	118, 126, 132, 136, 137, 138, 156, 309, 357; 75 n. 80
3:21ff.	118, 128, 131, 157, 158; 78 n. 81
3:21–26	19
3:21–31	115, 119, 135, **136**, 170, **393**; 36 n. 49
3:21–4:25	109, 115, 142
3:22	17, 120, 136, 137, 138, 250, 309
3.23	136, 137, 363
3:24	12, 70, 76, 136, 137, 180, 203, 250; 219 n. 43
3:24ff.	66
3:24–25	70, 93
3:24–26a	**70–72**, 76, 82, 114, 136, **137–38**, 374, 380, 405; bibl. 36 n. 49
3:24–26	81; 36 n. 49, 75 n. 80
3:25	17, 65, 66, 75, 76, 136, 137, 157, 298, 309, 380, 400, 406; 36 n. 49, 38 n. 52, 75 n. 80
3:25ff.	138
3:25–26a	70

3:26	3, 136, 137; 75 n. 80
3:27	137, 140; 75 n. 80
3:27–28	402
3:27–31	136
3:28	12, 126, 136, 137, 272, 377, 414, 434; 75 n. 80
3:29	137; 75 n. 80
3:30	137; 75 n. 80
3:31	137, 357
4	78, 115, 132, 136, **139**, 215, 394; 118 n. 127
4–5	155
4–8	69
4:1ff.	136
4:1–18	139
4:2	140, 377, 394, 401, 413
4:3	140, 270
4:3, 7–8	136
4:4	140
4:5	16, 19, 133, 140, 179, 392
4:6	140, 395, 413
4:8	13
4:9	140
4:9–12	139, 140
4:11	140, 396
4:12	270
4:13	140, 394, 396
4:13–17a	139
4:14	394
4:16	394
4:17	141; 38 n. 52
4:17b–25	139
4:20	394
4:24	73
4:24–25	69, 374, 405
4:25	**73–75**, 76, 114, 141, 142, 198, 200, 366, 432; bibl. 38 n. 52
5	109, **142–43**, **397**; 78 n. 81
5–7	152
5–8	141; 35 n. 48
5:1	12, 140, 141, 142, 180, 202, 220, 308, 397; 78 n. 81
5:1–2	69
5:1–11	407; 79 n. 81
5:1–8:39	115
5:7	142
5:9	142; 213 n. 32
5:9–10	159
5:9–11	201
5:10	75, 142, 201, 202; 213 n. 32

II. Persons Index

References to *sections* are cited first; then footnotes, by *page* and note numbers. The first footnote listed usually gives bibliographical data on works cited in the text by author and/or short title. For Biblical Personages, see Index III.

Abbott, T. K., 168; 92 n. 92
Achtemeier, E., 30; 12 n. 17
Achtemeier, P., 9 n. 11
Althaus, P., 73, 125, 275; 155 n. 146
Ambrose, 3
Ambrosiaster, 236 n. 26
Anderson, H.G., xv
Anderson Scott, C. A., 113 n. 120
Antiphon, 434
Aqiba, R., 408
Aquinas, see Thomas Aquinas
Augustine, 67, 125, 151, 272, 274; 12 n. 17, 75 n. 80

Baird, J. A., 23 n. 30
Barr, J., 24; 10 n. 13
Barrett, C. K., 63, 66, 67, 73, 90, 91, 94, 96, 140, 162, 183, 214; 31 n. 45, 33 n. 47, 39 n. 53, 58 n. 69, 80 n. 82, 97 n. 99, 118 n. 126, 143 n. 139, 208 n. 19
Barth, G., 233; 126 n. 131, 136 n. 135
Barth, K., 151, 195
Barth, M., 167, 169, 170, 171, 173, 174; 16 n. 20, 39 n. 53, 92 n. 92, 95 nn. 95, 96; 96 nn. 97, 98
Bartsch, C., 178 n. 164
Basil, 221 n. 51

Bassler, J. M., 128; 71 n. 79
Baur, F. C., 87, 315; 9 n. 11
Beare, F. W., 302; 60 n. 71, 167 n. 154
Beck, J. T., 123
Bekker, J. C., 106 n. 109, 120–21 n. 129
Bengel, J. A., 306
Benoit, P., 201 n. 9
Bergauer, P., 148 n. 143
Berlin, I., 350
Bernard, 221 n. 51
Bertram, G., 83
Bertram, R., 6 n. 6
Best, E., 73, 83, 84, 378; 43 n. 56, 45 n. 58
Betz, H. D., 80, 85, 86, 99, 100, 101, 102, 105, 106, 203, 280, 376, 382; 53 n. 68
Betz, O., 20 n. 24
Bigg, C., 306; 170 n. 155
Billerbeck, P., 231; 213 n. 31
Binder, H., 44 n. 57
Blackman, E. C., 12 n. 17
Bligh, J., 53 n. 68, 58 n. 69
Boehling, G., xii
Bohlmann, R., 5 n. 4
Bornkamm, G., 10 n. 14, 136 n. 135
Bornkamm, G., G. Barth, H. J. Held, 237; 126 n. 131, 136 n. 135
Borse, U., 85

260

III. Subject Index

For Biblical Books, see Index I; for confessional writings, I, D; for church fathers and reformers, e. g., Luther, specific citations in I, D, general references in Index II. References below cite *sections* first; then footnotes by *page* and note numbers. The abbreviation "cf." means compare the reference(s) cited as related to the topic; after a semicolon, in such an instance, direct references begin again.

Abel, 291, 295, 296; 222 n. 54

Abraham, 103, 115, 136, 139–40, 155, 213, 214, 245, 270, 271, 280, 292, 298, 311, 361, 394, 396, 413; 75 n. 80, 118 n. 127, 233 n. 9

Abram, 36

"account righteous," 249; see also "impute" and "reckon righteous"

Acta Apostolicae Sedes, 196 n. 3

Adam, 16, 132, 143, 155, 214; and Christ, 143

Adamic humanity, 9

adikos, adikia, 258, 262 (antonym to *dikaios*), 369, 431; see also "unrighteousness"

Adonizedek, 31, cf. 359

adoption, 15

aequitas, 308–10; see also "distributive justice"

almsgiving, 96, 234, 332

ancient Near East(ern) background, 31, cf. 33; 35, 37, 44, 334, 335

anthropology, 150, 195, 198, 202, 215, 326, 400, 404

antilegomena, 321; 225 n. 58

apocalyptic, 40, 45, 55, 84, 86, 121, 175, 188, 262, 267, 297, 305, 309, 313; 17 n. 21, 104 n. 107, 106 n. 109, 120 n. 129; see also "eschatological, eschatology"

God's righteousness as, 40, 67, 309, 335

apolytrōsis, 70, 71, 203

apostles and laity, 306–08

apostolic faith, common, 76, 81, 87, cf. 121; 135, cf. 193; 249, cf. 252; 301, 304, 375, 388

apostolic preaching, 56, 306; see also "kerygma"

appearing (of Christ), 181, 185; see also "parousia"

articulus stantis et cadentis ecclesiae, justification as, 1, 19, 20, 22, 190, cf. 200; 354

atonement (formulas, doctrine, theme), 43, 54, 56, 57, 68, 76, 100, 201, 249, 251, 253, 257, 258, 276, 300, 303, 417; 38 n. 52, (in Greco-Roman world), 203 n. 12

atoning death of Jesus (Christ), 65, 69, 224, 252, 299, 417; 203 n. 12; see also "sin offering," "expiation"

Augsburg Confession (CA), see Index I; hermeneutics of, 9–10 n. 12